THE POETICS OF PAUL VALÉRY

JEAN HYTIER was born in Paris in 1899. While still a *lycéen*, he published his first collection of verse in 1916. After eighteen months of military service in the Rhineland and Alsace, he took his *licence ès lettres*, started an avant-garde magazine that advocated a contemporary classicism, published a second volume of poems, his two doctoral theses (1923), a study of the novel (*Les Romans de l'Individu*), an edition of Pascal in five volumes. He taught philosophy until 1928, when he was offered a position as professor of French literature at the University of Teheran. He remained there until 1937, when the French government appointed him to the Faculty of Letters in Algiers. Mobilized twice during World War II, he combined, with his military service, his professorship, several positions with the Service Général de l'Information in Algeria, and the Direction of Fine Arts in the Provisional Government. From 1945 to 1947 he directed the Service des Lettres in the Ministry of National Education in Paris, sat on many committees, and was a member of the French Delegation to the General Assembly of UNESCO. Since 1947 he has taught French literature at the graduate school of Columbia University and since 1962 has been general editor of *The Romanic Review*. He was made Chevalier of the Legion of Honor in 1945, Officer in 1959.

Jean Hytier is known for his works of literary criticism and aesthetics. He has edited the definitive edition of the works of Paul Valéry for the Bibliothèque de la Pléiade. His *The Poetics of Paul Valéry*, for which he was made Laureate of the Académie Française, received the Académie's Le Métais-Larivière Prize in 1953.

The Poetics of Paul Valéry

by
JEAN HYTIER

Translated from the French by
RICHARD HOWARD

Here are our myths, our mistakes
that we labored so to set against
their predecessors.

Paul Valéry, *Projet de préface*

ANCHOR BOOKS
DOUBLEDAY & COMPANY, INC.
GARDEN CITY, NEW YORK

CONTENTS

Chapter I

IN SEARCH OF VALÉRY

It would be interesting to know how Valéry arrived at his ideas about poetry. We shall never entirely succeed in doing so, for it is impossible to know with exactitude the life not of a soul (he didn't like that word) but of a mind. Eventually, however, we may learn something more about the history of this body of thought so deliberately personal. The poet's two hundred and fifty unpublished notebooks, when they are made accessible, will permit us to establish its chronology. His correspondence will also provide precious clues, many of which are already revealed in the published letters to Mallarmé, Louÿs, Gide, Thibaudet. . . . For the time being, we must confine ourselves to generalities.

If Valéry's poetry is imbued with critical consciousness and predicates long reflexions on his art, nonetheless almost all his writings dealing with poetics appeared after his collections of verse. Indeed it is only after 1926 that he advances general views and somewhat extended discussions. These essays often contain confidences that explain why he had abandoned poetry so early and how he belatedly returned to it. They inform us in abundance about what might be called his doctrine, and a little less about the latter's connections with his poetic experience. Yet we realize that each has nourished the other. Valéry has observed himself writing his poems, and from this observation has drawn conclusions which extend beyond the frame of his poetics to general views on the mind's functioning; but he has also systematically applied specific procedural methods to the composition of his poems. We must, further, inquire on occasion whether the doctrine is not merely superadded to the work, by the effect of an independent, more or less theoretical meditation. The aesthetic a writer formulates has links with his work, but the explicit aesthetic and the implicit one do not always coincide. There is an enormous disparity between Hugo's plays and his notions about the drama. The same is true of morality: Rousseau's behavior is quite different from his ideal of virtue. The study of Valéry's poems (which would be a different book from this one) would certainly reveal a partial discrepancy between his doctrine and his practice. Still, we may presume that a classical art reduces the difference between theory and creation to a minimum: in Molière, in Racine, even in Baudelaire and Mallarmé, perhaps in Valéry too, lucidity of intent unites with exactitude of execution.

We shall get some notion of the role played by this lucubration along the margin of Valéry's work if we briefly consider the periods into which his literary life can be divided. I make out four:

1. The Period of the Early Poems

Valéry, who was writing verse as early as his *lycée* days, publishes some for the first time on October 1, 1889 (he will be eighteen on the thirtieth of the month) in the *Courrier libre:* a sonnet, *Élévation de la Lune,* followed in November by *La Marche impériale.* Around the same time, having discovered Poe in Baudelaire's translation and been struck by *The Philosophy of Composition,* he sends to Charles Boès, editor of the *Courrier libre,* an article, *Sur la Technique littéraire,* which the collapse of this periodical keeps from appearing, but which has been rediscovered, half a century later, by M. Henri Mondor.[1] Thus we see how from the very beginning of his career Valéry has accompanied his poetic production with theoretical reflections. This attitude, quite a common one moreover, is further avouched by what has been revealed to date of his correspondence with his young friends Pierre Louis (later Pierre Louÿs) and André Gide during the years 1890–92, when Valéry writes the poems that appear in *La Petite Revue maritime* of Marseilles, *La Revue indépendante, La Plume, L'Ermitage, La Syrinx, La Chimère,* and especially *La Conque* (thirteen poems in the eleven issues published from March to December 1891). This correspondence interests us chiefly because it reveals, notwithstanding some ephemeral concessions to literary fashions of the period, the precocity of certain of Valéry's ideas, the antecedents of several positions he assumes publicly after 1917 and from which he never deviates. Another thing this impassioned exchange of youthful letters reveals is the rapidity of the internal revolution taking place in Valéry's mind as to the value of poetry and of literature in general. How much ground has been covered between June 2, 1890, when he writes to Pierre Louÿs: "But above all, for you as for me, literature, the Magic of the word!"[2] and September 1891, when he confides his disillusionment to André Gide:

> . . . I've read the most wonderful writers—Poe, Rimbaud, Mallarmé—analyzed, alas! their expressive means, and everywhere encountered the loveliest *illusions* concerning their genesis and production . . . the most original of our great men, Wagner, Mallarmé, stoop—and imitate.[3]

We hear the voice of Monsieur Teste already. The crisis that occurs one August night in Geneva, in 1892, will determine Valéry's intellectual orientation, his new scale of values, of which the *Soirée avec Monsieur Teste* (written in 1895, published in 1896) is a kind of manifesto.

2. The Period of "Silence"

A relative silence which, though it cannot be dismissed, has been exaggerated. Valéry's abandonment of all poetic ambition is often dated from this year 1892. This must be understood with certain nuances. Actually Valéry will write several more poems: *Été* and *Vue*, published in 1896 in *Le Centaure; Valvins,* in the album for Mallarmé in 1897; *Anne* in *La Plume* in December 1900; *Profusion du soir, poème abandonné* (around 1899, according to the editor's note in volume C of the *Oeuvres complètes*). It is unlikely that while Valéry worked on these poems or on others, he stopped questioning himself as to their fabrication. The legendary notebooks, which he seems to have begun keeping in 1892, certainly contained remarks on literature. The collections of extracts from these notebooks, which were to appear from 1924 to 1930 (*Cahier B 1910, Rhumbs, Analecta, Autres Rhumbs, Littérature, Choses tues, Moralités, Ébauches de pensées, Suite*[4]), abound in observations on literary and artistic problems, and the one group presented in its original form, the *Cahier B 1910* (published first in facsimile), attests to the fact that Valéry, before returning to poetry, had not lost interest in it. It is true, however, that he preferred to study the functioning of his own mind, which step by step led him to reflect on virtually everything. The few writings he published between 1892 and 1900, without directly formulating a poetic doctrine, are nonetheless rich in suggestions toward one, especially the *Introduction à la méthode de Léonard de Vinci* (1895) and the *Soirée avec Monsieur Teste* (1896), though there is a surprising amount of relevant material in *La Conquête allemande* (1897) and in his work for the *Mercure de France: "Durtal"* in 1898 and the three articles under the rubric *Méthodes* in 1897, 1898, and 1899. After 1900 the silence is virtually complete. Nonetheless, in 1904 Valéry gives G. Walch the curious text in prose *L'Amateur de poèmes* to add to the poems reprinted in *L'Anthologie des poètes français contemporains*, which, despite Valéry's assertion that he had forgotten the existence of his own poems, does not indicate a complete lack of interest. And Valéry contributed to the *Nouvelle Revue Française* during its first year: in the December 1909 issue, several pages on dreams, taken no doubt from the notebooks and entitled *Études*. Examination of Valéry's manuscripts, when it is authorized, and the publication of his complete correspondence will no doubt permit the illumination of this obscure period, the most important of his intellectual biography. Up till now the most interesting documents are the correspondence with Gide, four letters to Henri Albert, from 1901 to 1907, on Nietzsche, the letters to Jules Valéry, and the letters or fragments of letters to Mallarmé, to Pierre Louÿs, to Thibaudet, to Albert Coste and others collected in *Lettres à Quelques-Uns*, 1952.

3. THE PERIOD OF THE RETURN TO POETRY

Beginning about 1912, this is marked by the publication of *La Jeune Parque* in late April 1917, of poems in various magazines, of *Odes* and of *Le Cimetière marin* (1920), of the *Album de vers anciens* (1920), of the collection *Charmes ou poèmes* (late June 1922). Valéry will subsequently add to his *Poésies:* two poems from 1917 and 1918 in the *Oeuvres complètes* volume, twelve *Pièces diverses* "from various periods" in the 1942 edition (including one already published in the *Oeuvres complètes,* four in *Mélange,* and a fable prefacing Alain's commentary on *La Jeune Parque*), to which we may add five other poems in *Mélange*—not counting the verses for friends, which will doubtless be collected, like Mallarmé's versified envelopes and Easter eggs. Nonetheless, verse forms will continue to tempt Valéry (*Cantate du Narcisse,* the lyric plays *Amphion* and *Sémiramis*), even in the *Dialogue de l'arbre,* where the verse is concealed in prose, and in certain scenes of the dramatic fairy tale *Le Solitaire,* from the unfinished cycle "*Mon Faust.*" To complete the list, a few fragments halfway between prose and verse, entitled *Poésie brute* (in *Mélange*) and *L'Ange,* a poem in prose, one of his very last writings. But Valéry's astonishing poetic renewal, or rather the true flowering of his lyricism, ends with the republication of *Charmes* in 1926, which includes the second and third of the *Fragments du Narcisse.* During the active period of composition, from 1913 to 1921, there are concomitant reflections on which Valéry has expatiated at some length in texts it is needless to enumerate here, since they will be quoted during the course of this study. A few letters from the period of *La Jeune Parque* and *Charmes,* particularly to Pierre Louÿs, are rich in information. It is not my purpose to trace the development of Valéry's aesthetic thought, but what we can divine of it seems to suggest that the resumption of verse writing obliged Valéry to raise once more the problems that faced him in 1890–91. A letter of 1917 to André Fontainas, referring to the elaboration of *La Jeune Parque,* is indicative of this stock-taking:

Twenty years without writing verse, without ever trying to, almost without reading any . . . Then, when these problems recur, realizing that one knows nothing of the craft: that the little poems written long ago avoided all the difficulties, passed over in silence what they couldn't say, used a childish language . . .[5]

A letter to Pierre Louÿs, written shortly after *La Jeune Parque* (which nonetheless abounds in tropes), shows Valéry still unacquainted with definitions of figures of speech and asking "which book to consult on the old theory of rhetoric."[a] Valéry subsequently described the help he found in chance encounters, the reading of a piece on Rachel by Adolphe Brisson, who quoted comments of Prince Georges von Hohenzollern on the tragedienne's diction,[6] and above all the discovery of Racine, whom he had scarcely read at all since *lycée* days.[b] The letter to Fontainas provides an amusing confirmation of this recourse to Racine:

Funny thing. The influence of schoolboy studies. Enforced recitation of Athalie's dream has taught me unsuspected things—which enlightened me once and for all about the very difficulties I am struggling with.[7]

4. THE PERIOD OF "COMMISSIONS"

Commissions tended to become commands, for Valéry's services were greatly sought after following the death of Edouard Lebey, whose secretary, reader, adviser, and friend he had been. Valéry, as we know, lived by his pen and his voice. From 1922 to 1945 his inexhaustible resourcefulness satisfied the most diverse requirements. It is superfluous to review the masterpieces which this "constraint" produced, from the 1921 dialogues through so many essays on art, literature, politics, and myth, the most diverse problems of civilization and the life of the mind, to—strangely—that affecting

[a] And he adds in the margin: "Do not leave unanswered" (*Oeuvres complètes*, vol. B, p. 139).

[b] See the *Journal de Charles Du Bos*, January 30, 1923, p. 228: ". . . the elements I could retain from Mallarmé have all been passed through the Racinian screen."

start, at the age of sixty-nine, on a work finally freed—for the first time—from the slavery of the pen: the spontaneous and enthralling enterprise of his Faustian cycle. In this abundant production the writings dealing directly with poetry are numerous and important. But more revealing are the less conventionalized texts, lectures, communications to learned societies, prefaces, personal remarks, etc. A great "moraliste," Valéry accumulated many penetrating reflections on artistic creation in *Mélange, Mauvaises pensées et autres;* the impossibility of dating the remarks of these collections, if it temporarily discourages the rigorous study of the development of his ideas, does not noticeably alter the general image we can form of his poetic aesthetic: we shall see why later on. Lastly, the course in poetics Valéry taught at the Collège de France from 1937 to 1945 directly concerns our subject. Unfortunately, except for the opening lecture, a formal speech and general program which, as is customary, has been published, there are few traces left of this instruction. Occasionally an article reproduces notes taken, in passing, by someone who attended the classes. The only really serious effort to take down a part of Valéry's course—insofar as anyone could follow a train of thought which seems to have proceeded by digressions around favorite themes, with sudden flights of improvisation, and which could not have been more alien to the habitual methodical preparation—has been the publication of the notes taken, for the most part by Georges Le Breton, during the first eighteen lectures of the course (in 1937–38); they have been published by the periodical *Yggdrasill.* In them we often recognize the very tone of Valéry's voice. But we also realize that only the master's revision, with the necessary alterations and above all the necessary additions, could have conferred authenticity upon them. We can therefore use these notes, however precious they are, only with discretion. Each time it is apparent that they confirm remarks Valéry made elsewhere (which happens frequently, moreover, and thereby consoles us somewhat for not having the complete and revised text), we shall refer in the notes to the lecture concerned. What we lack, in any case, is the most personal material—what Valéry, during those eight years, might have added to his earlier considerations that was new. Be

that as it may, it is the whole body of Valéry's ideas on poetry, in the extreme dispersion of a quantity of frequently
brief texts, during this period of about a quarter of a century,
which furnishes by far the most important contribution to the
knowledge of his poetics.

The interpretation of all this literature on one genre of
literature raises preliminary difficulties. First of all the chronology, next the contradictions. As a matter of fact, Valéry's
thought, though it was enriched, varied rather little—save
perhaps during the little-known years of his "silence" (a
period of maturation); further, some of Valéry's confidences
and memoirs indicate that many of the opinions he formulated publicly during the last twenty-five years of his life
(a period of exploitation) had been reached in the earlier
periods. One of the impressions reading Valéry produces is
that of countless repetitions, according perhaps to Monsieur
Teste's habit: "He was careful to repeat certain ideas; he
irrigated them with number." Valéry was not unjustified, in
his own case, but generalizing the maxim, in denying the
importance of chronology in thought:

> The disorder that "reigns" (as is said) in *Mélange* ex-
> tends to chronology. One thing was written nearly fifty
> years ago. Another dates from the day before yesterday.
> . . . This quantity of time signifies nothing in matters of
> the mind's production.[8]

There is in him the sense of a permanence which is readily
associated with the mobility of the self. The "digressions" of
reflection do not prevent it from having an axis. Shortly before his death, he said to Gide: "The chief themes around
which I have organized my thought for fifty years remain
for me UNSHAKABLE!"[9]

As for the contradictions—by which I mean the manifest
ones, those which do not derive from the very constitution
of a temperament which always manages to express within
its framework its dissonances or its basic incoherences—they
can often be reduced by exterior considerations: public, occasion, humor, particular angle from which a problem is approached. . . . In Valéry, they also derive not only from his
well-known sense of *boutade* and his intellectual restlessness,

but from a kind of mental experimentation: to see what an idea that has turned up might lead to when it is followed —driven—in a certain direction purely for its own sake, without attempting to relate it to every aspect of a given body of thought. Such a mind is essentially impulsive, particularized, and unconcerned with connections. If Valéry has always rejected system (despite several impulses), it is not only out of boredom or laziness, it is on account of the sporadic nature of his reflections. His notebooks are a litter of lightning flashes. The relative unity of his thought derives from several fixed points, inveterate themes, circles he tirelessly retraces —from what might be called his *mordicus*. Outside of these persistent themes, we find the greatest freedom and the greatest risk in agility. The splendid "coherent" developments of a few official texts are an oratorical effect, a skillful modulation, not the consequence of an organic growth—in which, moreover, he did not believe with regard to thought. It is not surprising that he accommodated himself so readily to the mind's natural inconsistencies:

WATCH IN HAND—One need only wait long enough to see the sceptic turn into a believer; the believer into a sceptic, the classicist into a *fauve*, and vice versa. A matter of patience.[10]

He has even expounded for his own use an ingenious little theory whose applications it would not be impossible to find in certain of his lines, on the transformation of ideas. He warns the readers of *Analecta*[11] not to forget

. . . that there is an incalculable difference, an indeterminate *interval*, between the embryo of an idea and the intellectual entity which it may ultimately become.
This difference can reach the maximum of contrast, which is contradiction.
If one morning I write that *A is B*, I know perfectly well that the judgment *A is not B*, which cancels out its predecessor, could follow from an extended reflection, from a more precise contemplation, or from a somewhat more powerful *enlargement by duration*. The note I have taken will then signify only this to my eyes: there is a *relation* (A, B).
This is only a fecundating act.

ANTINOUS, or a monster, or the most vulgar creature can emerge from it. . . .

Toward the end of his life, he noted that he did not find "unity in his nature" and that he had "a tendency and a great readiness to regard as accidents (which are, actually, rather alien to me) my tastes, distastes, and opinions." He has confessed to

> . . . the kind of natural contempt which any opinion on any subject inspires in me, as soon as I think about it a little. My own is the first to declare itself as futile, a pure expedient. When the opinion is entertained as a *conviction*, the case seems serious to me, and I actually despair of the intelligence of the man who establishes himself in force on the basis of initial disorder and irregular variety which is (and even, which should be) characteristic of the mind. But this too is an opinion.[12]

We recognize Valéry's generalized scepticism. For him, refusal is the very movement and definition of the mind. Hence it is not easy, unless we reduce it to its instability, to make consistent a body of thought which rejects itself on principle.[c] Happily, there is a compensation for this systematic annihilation; in practice, the return of well-defined and even curiously affirmative, aggressive opinions—resulting, perhaps, from a deliberate arbitrariness which alone can dispel doubt —permits us to establish Valéry's aesthetic adequately enough.

Alongside these flippancies tinged with stubbornness, we often encounter in Valéry's ideas on poetry certain theses violently opposed to those of either the public or of specialists in poetry, psychologists, and aestheticians who have dealt with these questions (though Valéry never argues against a specific person). Such paradoxes are one of the charms of his speculation. They result, no doubt, from a long practice of poetry, and thereby suggest Valéry's aesthetic temperament (more artist than poet, a condition, moreover,

---

[c] He has said: "I allow myself to believe that there is a certain poverty of spirit in always being in agreement with oneself" (*Lettre-Préface* to Émile Rideau, *Introduction à la pensée de Paul Valéry*, p. 3).

he finds reason to praise), but reveal even further his basic nature, which is never so much at ease as in a courteous but radical dissension. The key to this spontaneous attitude is found in an early letter to André Gide, dated November 10, 1894: "Do you remember: I told you I abandoned whatever ideas I had as soon as others seemed to have them. This is still true. I want to be the master *chez moi*."[13] This takes us straight into paradox. Valéry has asserted this self-defensive reflex on several occasions. He regarded it as the exercise of a kind of *raison d'État*, and the only way in which he could ever be directly influenced. "An opinion which strikes me as too much like my own makes me doubt my own."[14] And not only "like," but also "directly contrary to," for he quickly shows the effects of counterimitation. He recognizes himself in this sentence from Père Hardouin: "Do you think that I have taken the trouble to get up at four in the morning every day of my life in order to think like everyone else?"[15] If this passion for difference is a great factor or originality, it no doubt has its dangers in the search for truth. "I like to think I see things no one has seen in the things everyone sees. . . ."[16]

There remains one last obstacle to be surmounted, an obstacle to be found in Valéry's attitude to poetry itself and to literature in general. He has on several occasions described how, at twenty, he had begun to question their value. "I suspected literature, and even the most exact undertakings of poetry. The act of writing always demands a certain 'sacrifice of the intellect.'"[17] "I had stopped writing verse; I almost stopped reading as well. . . . Literature . . . had often scandalized me by its lack of rigor, of continuity, of necessity in ideas."[18] Poe had infected him with the "madness of lucidity." The art of verse had "become impossible for me in 1892." This was the moment when, after sustaining Mallarmé's influence, he made his acquaintance, and when he "inwardly guillotined literature." He was looking for something else: "Why not develop in oneself the only thing which interests me about the genesis of the poem?"[19] For Mallarmé, on the contrary, literature was everything; Valéry never took it with that degree of seriousness; he considered himself not a maker of verses but an *homme d'esprit*, according to Charles Du Bos' *Journal* for January 30, 1923. At the same period, Gide records Valéry's irritation at the reputation *La Jeune Parque* and *Charmes* had given him:

> People expect me to represent French poetry. They take me for a poet! But I couldn't care less about poetry. It only interests me by a fluke! It's an accident that I've written poems. I'd be exactly the same if I hadn't written them. In other words, I'd have the same value in my own eyes. For me it has no importance whatever.[20]

If we turn from declarations in private life to the public expression of feelings, the latter are just as clear-cut. Valéry has always regarded literature "with great doubts as to its real value."[21] It is a kind of charlatanism: "One thing is always shady about literature: the consideration of a public";[22] many remarks in *Littérature* make this picture still blacker. The same note is sounded at the end of his life in *Propos me concernant*: "I have produced *literature* as a man who actually isn't too fond of it for its own sake. . . .";[23] and the old grievance reappears: "the first sacrifice to a viable literature is the *'sacrifizio dell'intelletto.'*"[24] Despite this hostility, Valéry's entire output still attests a deeper affection than he admits. He has at least acknowledged that a man may adore what he presumes he has burnt, and in reality his position has not ceased to be ambivalent, oscillating between theoretical renunciation and impassioned performance. His letter of 1912 to Thibaudet sounds the right note in this regard: "Literature, *ad libitum*, is everything or nothing. Hence it is nothing, or *a* nothing. . . . Myself, between this everything and this nothing, I have . . . oscillated." Such oscillation leads him to imprison poetry in the alternative of the void or the divine: "The existence of poetry is essentially deniable; which leads to the imminent temptations of pride. —On this point, it resembles God Himself,"[25] and to formulate the major requirement: "In every nonessential thing, one must be divine. Or not bother."[26]

What poetry was for Valéry, or at least what he thought it was—for as in love and hate, the object differs enormously in tendency and in representation—above all, what Valéry *wanted* poetry to be when he denied its profound attraction for him and tried to reduce it to a secondary, subordinate, and provisional activity of his mind, he has many times summed up in the word *exercise*. This is what the famous dedication of *La Jeune Parque* to André Gide proclaims to the world, and what more than one remark about this poem confirms.[27] The sincerity of this attitude is quite complete, and it is not a new one for Valéry, for it dates back to 1892: "This art . . . I already regarded as an exercise, or an application of more important research."[28] And, generalizing, he was led "to accord no further value to the act of writing save that of pure exercise."[29] Poetry, in fact, is merely a particular case, quite privileged in certain regards, of the mind's general functioning when it succeeds in taking that "central attitude" Valéry extolls in the *Introduction à la méthode de Léonard de Vinci*. This attitude, we shall see, dominates, in principle, every production whether scientific or artistic. It is therefore not surprising that Valéry could have considered not just poetry but all aesthetic creation from this angle: ". . . I reduce whatever I think about art to the notion of *exercise*, which I find the most beautiful in the world."[30] More than the work of art, it is the "mental labor" producing it which interests him: whereas, "usually, the work itself is the capital object of desire," for Valéry it is "application."[31] Mallarmé, as we know, had dreamed of a great work, an orphic, absolute book for which the world itself seemed only a pretext. Valéry's dream was different: ". . . for me the Alchemists' *Great Work* is the knowledge of the labor in itself—of the most general transmutation, whose works are local applications, particular problems. . . ."[32] The point is not to make gold, except as a by-product, but to find the general law by which all things can be made. After which, it would be futile to make them. Monsieur Teste seeks only the power which dispenses with and disdains desire. This youthful ideal has never been better expressed than in a letter of 1894: "I have always acted in order to make myself a potential individual. In other words, I have preferred a strategic life to a tactical one. To have at my disposal, without disposing."[d] We

[d] Letter to Gide, Nov. 10, 1894, in *Gide-Valéry Correspondance*, pp. 217–18. It is doubtless at this moment that Valéry takes the notes and begins reading the memoirs of Dupin, which will

can understand how the young Valéry, who through the mouth of Monsieur Teste was to scorn "genius," had only pity for the name of "poet."[e] So total an ambition—for which only the image of Leonardo which Valéry created for himself could furnish an image less chimerical than that of an ideal Monsieur Teste—was doomed to failure. No doubt "a man who has never tried to make himself like the gods is less than a man,"[33] but the practice of the mind's powers is impossible if that mind is based on a state of definitive omnipotence which it conceives as a goal, but does not possess as a means. What humbly replaces this intellectual dominion is the perpetual quest, the pursuit of the philosophers' stone or, more simply, research. Valéry had realized this, and in 1924 he congratulates one of his exegetes, Monsieur René Fernandat, for having seen that he had:

> You have perfectly grasped the fact that I am nothing but *Research*. What is a man who doesn't seek? I yield so completely to this involuntary will that I cannot even conceive that one might *find*, that one might stop looking.[34]

Yet the key notion of *exercise*, that is, of *application*, assumes, in these circumstances, an entirely different meaning. Whereas at the beginning it meant the use of a kind of infallible and universal mathematics, it is no longer anything but the use of empirically discovered methods, *formulas* (those formulas to which Valéry reduces the validity of science)—i.e., in poetry, conventions, rules, "trade secrets" which have proved themselves, and the occasionally more personal conditions the poet imposes on himself. We are far from the method which would control any possible system of relations and impose its effects with certainty. "This arrogant

---

serve him, the following summer, in writing *La Soirée avec Monsieur Teste*. A curious shaft of light on this psychology, which may seem arrogant but which is perhaps above all defenseless, is cast by the following sentence: "This had a goal of inner, imaginative equilibrium."

[e] In 1891 he wrote to Gide: "Please don't call me Poet any more. . . . I am not a poet, but the gentleman who is bored" (André Gide, *Paul Valéry*, p. 64; *Gide-Valéry Correspondance*, p. 138).

poet fallen from so high," as the prudent Boileau said, must then, in using the word *exercise* apropos of his poems, understand the word in a much more restricted sense than is suggested by the mythology of his twenty-fifth year, that of the fabulous Teste and Leonardo. The poems are indeed applications, but of a will-to-fabrication which possesses chance means, not of a lightninglike superscience. Yet this deliberation of craft, this artistic rather than scientific conscience, has maintained a certain detachment toward the objects it is elaborating. It watches itself perform, and takes—at least Valéry believes it takes—more interest in what it can derive from them by way of instruction as to its own functioning than in the beauty of the result. In Valéry the critic is the poet's contemporary, his spectator, and his collaborator. "I have always watched myself make my verses, whereby I have never perhaps been only a poet."[f] This double attitude is not so rare as one might think among poets, who necessarily are quite conscious of at least a part of their work. What is exceptional is to treat the poem as a by-product or a pretext of a higher activity. Yet this *execution* of the poem, concerning which Valéry will produce his most original ideas, is not without value in his eyes. He prefers to see it as a work of art in itself, a kind of operative dance. But this too is only another fiction that he rejects, for the work is too discontinuous to assume such perfection of demeanor. More modestly, Valéry in the end represents his *exercise* as a gymnastic, a sport, a drill. Literature is "a sport, sometimes a severe one, which requires the exercise of almost all the qualities of the mind."[g]

I regard poetry as the least idolatrous genre. It is the *sport* of men insensitive to the fiduciary values of ordinary language. . . . The true lover of poems considers them

[f] *Calepin d'un poète* in *Oeuvres complètes,* vol. C, p. 195. In the same direction, Valéry writes in March 1940 to Maurice Bémol, who quotes this fragment of the letter in his thesis on Valéry, p. 289: ". . . the long labor of *La Jeune Parque* has given me many lateral observations."

[g] *Sur la chose littéraire et la chose pratique* in *Oeuvres complètes,* vol. D, p. 188. Valéry, who did not want to be called a philosopher, once called himself a *"Philosophe Sportif"* (letter to Albert Coste in *Lettres à Quelques-Uns,* p. 107).

the way horse fanciers regard horses, the way others regard the maneuvers of ships. . . . The great art for me in matters of poetry is to tame and train the animal *Language,* and to take it where it is not used to going. . . .[35]

In return there is an advantage: the poet is transformed "into someone more independent with regard to words, which means, more the master of his thought."[h] This is how, in a more moderate form, the old dream of intellectual dominion persists in the growth of inner freedom, and how the art of poetry contributes to the seduction of abstract thought.

Despite Valéry's propensity, which he has actually made into a method, to focus on his *self* the study of the questions which interested him, his discussions of poetry have not always managed to deal with their subject by referring exclusively to his personal experience. He has not been able to treat the public's (and his own) interest in the greatest examples of poetic creation in the negative light of scepticism of values and on the reductive level of a lateral activity of the mind. When he mentions La Fontaine, Racine, Hugo's late work, Baudelaire, Mallarmé . . . he passes over in silence or leaves in obscurity the great reservation of principle and the instrumental utilitarianism of production. Quite often he seems to regard poetry itself, apropos of the problems it raises, as its own goal. There is, then, given Valéry's complex attitude, if not a doctrine in the strict sense of the word, at least a body of more or less homogeneous ideas which we may legitimately consider as the expression of Valéry's poetic aesthetic. How are we to grasp, how present, most of all how articulate this unsystematic and widely dispersed corpus of thought? We might put questions to it, as Valéry suggested be done with the works of philosophers. For him, obliging them to answer had the special purpose of revealing their

[h] *Propos me concernant*, p. 49. The following page might interest anyone attempting a portrait of Valéry; here we see his distaste for proselytism countering his fondness for intellectual training: "Think as you like! Still, more than once I have been attracted by the notion of composing a kind of *Traité de l'entraînement de l'esprit.* I called it *Gladiator,* from the name of a race horse. . . . I have a lot of its elements already."

inadequacies. If we proceeded in this fashion, we should soon discover the difficulty of completing certain chapters; there are aspects of the aesthetics of poetry on which Valéry touched very little (particularly, strange as it seems, the problems of expression, of metrics, of verbal music: they would have led him all too soon to illuminate his own manner, if only indirectly, which he did not want to do). Or we could start from whatever our present state of knowledge might be, relying on what is considered as *given* in this kind of studies; but, aside from the fact that we are dealing with extremely arguable matters where conclusions cannot be imposed with incontestable force, there is a cheerless pedantry in this appeal at the bar of a great poet's reflections which in spite of everything have less importance for us than his poetry itself. The point is not to oppose one theory to another. The point is to find out what the poet Valéry, reflecting about poetry, believed he could think about it; the point is to follow him sympathetically, in order to understand him better, and not to stop following except when he stops following himself or fails to take us with him. Hence we have been led to adopt an order which relies as much as possible on the connections Valéry has established among the most important elements of his subject. This interplay of ideas, which are associated in his writing with a reassuring regularity and frequency, permits us to classify more or less coherently what he usually presents in lively disorder. If we are careful not to logicalize, by abusive omissions or specious justifications, the "deviations" of his spontaneity, we may hope to present a faithful image of the poetics he has outlined. The groupings of ideas which it involves are not all equally apparent. Some are self-explanatory—he has emphasized them and chosen to discuss them many times: it is apparent that *inspiration, language, composition,* and *diction* were Valéry's favorite themes. Other areas of aesthetic reflection he merely hinted at, and they never constituted the object of a sustained presentation; but their perhaps greater importance is revealed in the multitude of details which they suggested to him: this is especially the case with regard to what I have felt justified in calling his *theory of effects.* We have therefore examined Valéry's congeries of ideas, one after the other, beginning

with those that concern the nature of poetry and continuing
with those which refer to poetic creation. It is our hope that
this study, by an "active but not unsympathetic reader," as
he would have prescribed, will reveal more exactly his conception of an art in which he has excelled and, perhaps,
indirectly illuminate our admiration for his poems.

Chapter II

THE INTELLIGENCE AND "VAGUE THINGS"

THE POETIC STATE

Valéry is reputed, and not without reason, to have evolved an extremely intellectual theory of poetry. But if, as we shall see, the intelligence plays for him a capital role in the poem's elaboration, it would be a mistake to believe that he regards poetic pleasure as merely intellectual, like the pleasure, for instance, of following an elegant mathematical proof—a pleasure in which, moreover, it is not certain that everything is rational. On various occasions Valéry regarded poetry as "a certain kind of emotion,"[1] "a particular emotive state,"[2] "a singular emotion,"[3] "a psychic and affective state."[4] Starting from this point of view, he distinguished two meanings, even "two orders of notions": the poetic state and the poetic art, this latter consisting of "a strange industry whose object is to reconstitute this emotion."[5]

The essential emotive state "is the one which we experience in certain circumstances" and "which can be provoked by the most various causes,"[6] of which Valéry has given a most interesting list: sunsets, moonlight, forests, seas, great events, critical moments of the emotional life, the turmoil of love, evocations of death.[7] "We say of a landscape, of a situation and sometimes of a person, that they are poetic."[8] "Every man can see the poetry of what he does, feels, etc. . . . And many men feel poetically what they encounter in both their life and their work."[9] Valéry insisted on distinguishing this kind of emotion from all other human sentiments. He regards the separation, however, as rather delicate because in reality "one always finds, mingled with the essential poetic emotion, tenderness or melancholy, rage or fear or hope," and because "the private interests and affections of the individual are in-

volved."[10] Here we sense—as in the Abbé Bremond's mystical theory, but for other reasons—the intention to eliminate
sentiment from poetry. In Bremond it reappeared in the mystical impulse itself. We may wonder if it is not concealed in
Valéry's explanation as well, when he describes the poetic
emotion as "that special upheaval" which "everyone knows"
and which he compares

> . . . to our state when we feel, by the effect of certain
> circumstances, excited, enchanted. This state is utterly
> independent of any specific work, and it results natu-
> rally and spontaneously from a certain accord between
> our inner, physical, and psychic disposition and the (real
> or ideal) circumstances that impress us.[11]

This excitement or enchantment closely resembles the
stimulation and satisfaction of a sentiment; this accord between self and circumstances is indeed analogous to the encounter of an affective disposition with the pretexts that permit its satisfaction.

But Valéry above all sought the characteristic of the poetic
impression in a state of the sensibility as a whole. We know
how equivocal this term sensibility is,[a] for it can exclude as
well as comprehend affective states. Valéry used it a great
deal, which is surprising when we recall his diatribes against
the imprecision of the philosophical vocabulary, and he even
broadened its application still further. He includes within sensibility not only the sensations, pleasure and pain, joy and
melancholy,[12] the entire affective life,[b] but even intellectual elements.[13] It includes everything that is a spontaneous
response to any stimulus, and is distinguished from what is
separate from itself only in order to oppose it.[c] Whatever the

[a] See the word in André Lalande's *Vocabulaire de la philosophie.*
[b] See *Notion générale de l'art* in N.R.F., Nov. 1, 1935, pp.
690–91, or as foreword to vols. XVI and XVII of the *Encyclopédie
française* (*Arts et Littérature dans la société contemporaine*). See
also *Suite* in *Tel quel*, II, p. 334: "*Be moved.* There are, then,
duties for the sensibility. . . ."
[c] Many congruent indications in the *Cours de poétique:* "Our
sensibility is everything, except what we have tried to draw from
it, such as the concepts of the external world or of objectivity"
(lecture 3). "We are in a state . . . of continuous sensibility. And
the difficulty is to know not what it is, but what it is not. It is

case, it is in a particular system of this generalized sensibility that Valéry placed the basis of the poetic emotion. This latter, in his analysis, assumes a double sensuous form: it is a sensation or a specific perception, which Valéry calls a *sensation d'univers*, and an impression, both indefinable and precise, which consists in a double correspondence: that of the various representative elements set in play and that of these elements with our sensibility. Valéry returned at least three times to this capital description of the poetic phenomenon, and virtually in the same terms.[14] Here is its completest expression:

> I have said: *sensation d'univers.* I meant that the poetic emotion or state seems to me to consist of a dawning perception, a tendency to perceive a *world,*[d] or complete system of relations, in which beings, things, events, and acts,[e] if they directly correspond to those which inhabit and compose the world of the senses, the immediate world from which they are borrowed, are, further, in an indefinable but marvelously just relation with the modes and laws of our general sensibility.[f] Then, these known objects and beings change value somehow. They stimulate one another, they associate quite differently from the way they do in ordinary con-

simultaneously event, duration, and environment in which the event occurs. . . . The self is ultimately only a product of sensibility" (lecture 4). "I am trying to organize what is not organizable, to define what is not definable: the realm of sensibility" (lecture 6). ". . . a special availability without expressible goal which I have called sensibility . . . While the name of sensibility is commonly applied only to sense-phenomena, I have decided to annex other areas to this restricted sense . . . everything that occurs in certain conditions of spontaneity and of response to need, to a lacuna, to a stimulus. In the habitual sense, sensibility includes little more than sense-phenomena; I add to it phenomena of an intellectual order. . . . I find sensibility everywhere, the difficulty is to manage to define what is not sensibility" (lecture 15).

[d] In *Poésie pure* he says: "the sentiment of an illusion or the illusion of a world."

[e] The enumeration is somewhat different in *Poésie pure:* "events, images, beings, things," and in *Poésie et pensée abstraite:* "beings, events, sentiments, and acts."

[f] Same formula but without "the laws" in *Poésie et pensée abstraite;* "inexplicable but intimate with the whole of our sensibility" in *Poésie pure.*

ditions. They are—so too speak—harmonized, they have become commensurable, echoing and answering each other.[g]

It would not be difficult to translate this analysis into the language of today's psychology. The *sensation d'univers* would then become a world of representations and their *resonance* the orchestration of the play of images; but Valéry does not bring the imagination into his argument at any point, which is curious, since he will presently compare poetry and dreams. As for the mysterious correspondence to the modes of our sensibility, he refuses to seek an explanation for this (it must be undefinable; this is, we shall see, a condition of its beauty); it is conceivable that extension of the analysis would have led Valéry where he didn't want to go, that is, once again, to find in the self's profound affectivity the tendencies which are satisfied in poetic creation.

Like many psychologists, Valéry related the poetic state to that of dreams—but with hesitations. He said, in *Propos sur la poésie:* "The poetic universe . . . offers great analogies with the universe of the dream,"[15] and in *Poésie pure:*

The poetic world . . . maintains close resemblances with the dream state, at least with the state produced in certain dreams. The dream informs us, when we turn back to it in memory, that our consciousness can be awakened or filled, and satisfied, by a group of productions remarkably different in their laws from the ordinary productions of perception. But although we can sometimes know this emotive world through the dream, it is not within the power of our will to penetrate or leave it as we please. . . . *It is enclosed within us, and we within it,* which means that we have no way of acting on it to modify it. It appears and disappears capriciously, but man has done in this instance what he has done or tried to do for all precious and perishable things: he has sought and he has found the means of reconstituting this state at will. . . . Now, among these means of

[g] *Propos sur la poésie,* p. 466. In *Poésie pure* the sentence is completed by "and as though in agreement with our own sensibility," and in *Poésie et pensée abstraite* by "and as though corresponding harmonically."

producing a poetic world . . . the oldest one . . . is language.[h]

In other words, language permits the reproduction in poetry of the dream state. Let us note that it is less with the dream (of sleep) than with the (waking) reverie that the poetic imagination can be legitimately compared. But Valéry, sometimes in the same texts where he accepts this analogy, protests against the assimilation of poetry to these two modes of the imagination:

. . . there has occurred in modern times, starting with romanticism, a quite explicable but rather regrettable confusion between the notion of dreams and that of poetry. Neither dream nor reverie are necessarily poetic; they may be: but figures formed *by chance* are only *by chance* harmonious figures.[16]

To Valéry, nothing seemed to differ from the poet's state more than the dreamer's; he said so apropos of La Fontaine[17] and in his splendid series of remarks on dreams in *Autres rhumbs:* "If the poet were really a dreamer, as a quite modern legend claims, surely he could never reread himself without groaning."[18] The poetry dreamed and found to be "extraordinarily beautiful" is "recognized after a few hours, or a few moments, as detestable."[19]

One may doubt that the psychologists or the aestheticians who have related poetry to dreams or reverie have merely confused these states as critics or literary men may have done. They have, on the contrary, tried to respect the originality of the poetic phenomenon. And this is, basically, the same attitude which Valéry adopts. Once again, his opposition to opinions which he rejects *en bloc* without detailing or discussing them seems more verbal than real. His temperament seeks to preserve, by an irreducible appearance, a personal conception which, upon close consideration, does not differ essentially from rather widely held notions. Thus, after having admitted the analogy of poetry and dreams, then rejected the "legend" that juxtaposes them, he concedes that

[h] Pp. 204–5. And again in *Poésie et pensée abstraite*, p. 137: "The poetic universe . . . offers close analogies with what we may suppose the dream universe to be."

dream and reverie may be poetic by accident, letting it be
understood that only art is capable of giving necessity and an
inner organization to these chance formations (which no psychologist would dream of denying); were Valéry to insist on
the resemblance afforded by poetry and dreams in their relation to consciousness, we should no longer know how to
distinguish his attitude from the one he attacked:

> All the same, our memories of dreams teach us . . .
> that our consciousness can be invaded, filled, utterly
> saturated by the production of an *existence* whose ob-
> jects and beings seem the same as those which are in
> the waking state. . . . In almost the same way, the *po-
> etic state* is established, develops, and finally disinte-
> grates within us. In other words, this state of poetry is
> perfectly irregular, inconsistent, involuntary, and frag-
> ile: we lose it as we obtain it, by accident.[1]

The poetic state does not suffice to make poets.

> Those who believe so merely suffer from a confusion
> between the effects produced and the effects to be pro-
> duced, between the singular or intense vision and the
> means of provoking or reproducing it. —The engineer is
> not strong in the same way as his machine. He is strong
> in a different—entirely different—way.[20]

Of course, the poet can "experience the poetic state," but
"*this is a private matter.*" His function is "to create it in others": the poet "changes the reader into a man 'inspired.'"
The "effect of poetry" is obtained by an "artificial synthesis,"
which differs from the poetic state as an action differs from
a sensation.[21] The poetic art consists of "restoring the poetic
emotion at will, outside of the natural conditions in which
it is produced spontaneously, and by means of the artifices
of language,"[22] but it can also be created "by means quite
different from those of language, such as architecture, music,
etc. . . . ";[23] "all the fine arts aspire to this *Poetry.*"[24] There
is, then, a poetry in the broad sense, which the arts are capa-

---

[1] *Poésie et pensée abstraite* in *Variété* V, pp. 137–88. This passage somewhat develops the passage, quoted in part above, of
Propos sur la poésie, p. 466.

ble of achieving, and a poetry in the narrow sense, which
depends on a particular treatment of language.

INTELLIGENCE AND SENSIBILITY

Valéry posited the sensibility as the basis of all mental
activity,[j] and made it the principle, guide, and goal of art.
Among our impressions, many do not correspond to a vital
necessity and are useless, but among these "it happens that
some . . . impose themselves upon us and cause us to seek
their extension or renewal." They create "a kind of need,"
which induces us to an act in order to increase in intensity
or duration the impressions of the senses. "This action which
has the sensibility for origin and goal," at the same time as
for guide in the choice of its means, "is clearly distinguished
from actions of a practical order." Here "*satisfaction* re-
vives *desire; response* regenerates *demand; possession* engenders a growing *appetite* for the thing possessed; in a word,
sensation exalts its *expectation* and reproduces it. . . ." Art
consists in "conferring . . . a kind of *utility* upon these "*useless sensations,*" in "organizing a system of sensuous things"
possessing the property of "reciprocal stimulation,"[25] of "infinite regeneration."[26] Experience confirms this analysis:

[j] It should be possible to establish, as Charles Blondel has done
for Proust, a "psychography" for Valéry—that is, his personal conception of psychological functioning. The texts on sensibility are
numerous. We shall merely suggest that Valéry was especially
struck by his natural state of incoherence and dispersion, and by
his regime of variability and instability. "The formula of sensibility," according to the *Cours de poétique,* "would be a formula
of eternal disparity. The mind is the variable function par excellence. What would best represent the sensibility in its variability is
the image of Hades. The mind is Sisyphus, Tantalus, the sieve of
the Danaïdes. . . . The variability of the sensibility is our tran-
scendence in relation to other things" (lecture 6). —"Most men are
and must be indifferent to most of the world's phenomena. . . .
Things, in their greatest number, are more or less the same to us.
. . . Sameness means imperceptibility. . . . Perceptibility means
difference . . . the most important thing we can do is to restore
ourselves to zero-sensibility, to regain a certain maximum of freedom, of availability with regard to the external world" (lecture 5).

The need for seeing again, hearing again, experiencing infinitely is characteristic. The lover of form caresses the bronze or the stone that delights his sense of touch without tiring of it. The music lover repeats or hums the melody that has pleased him. The child insists on the retelling of the story and cries: *Again!*[27]

It is because of this need that "a beautiful line of verse is reborn from its ashes an infinite number of times."[28]

To this point Valéry's aesthetic is a pure sensualism, but aside from the fact that the sensibility includes in his eyes certain affective elements, more than one text permits us to add emotional values to the sensuous ones that constitute for him the origin and goal of this infinite circle of artistic pleasure.

The act of the superior artist is to restore by means of conscious operations the value of sensuality and the emotive power of things—an act which completes in the creation of forms the cycle of the being who has utterly fulfilled himself.[29]

We must further include in the process, still without departing from the Valerian sensibility, certain intellectual elements, which he called "intellectual sensibility."[30] No doubt the intelligence intervenes especially in fabrication, beside the will, but it also has its role in pleasure. Further, Valéry, who as we know would have sacrificed literature out of disgust for its lack of rigor, yielded at least once to the temptation of considering artistic (if not literary) creation as the fulfillment of pure thought and of its activity. It is true that this was apropos of his dear Leonardo. The passage from the *Préface* to Da Vinci's notebooks which I have just quoted is, in fact, preceded by the acknowledgment, among the greatest men, of the return to the sensuous by way of creation:

The intellectual knowledge of this complete man does not suffice to exhaust desire, and the production of ideas, even the most precious ones, does not succeed in satisfying the strange need to create: the very demand of his thought leads him back to the sensuous world, and his meditation has as a result the appeal to the forces that control matter.

The poet, despite the uncertainty of his art, is thus an artist of the sensibility. Or rather, it is the sensibility itself which is a poet in him, and in every man.

> The greatest poet—is the nervous system. The inventor of everything—or rather the only poet.[31]

It is not very easy to make out interplay of the two factors when one is reluctant to separate them. But it is clear that for Valéry the sensibility, indistinct from the intelligence, plays nonetheless, in relation to the latter, a specific role; it is its motor, its stimulus and its aliment. He protested against "the crude distinction . . . we are taught . . . between 'sensibility' and 'intelligence,' two terms which . . . are divided only in school."[32] In reality, the sensibility is a "fundamental faculty mistakenly opposed to intelligence, of which it is, on the contrary, the true motive power."[33] It has properties that are not only "receptive or transitive" but "productive."[34] "Sensibility affords the mind the initial sparks . . . the mind borrows from the sensibility the necessary instability which releases its transforming power."[35] "The fundamental law of the sensibility: to introduce into the living system an element of *imminence*, of ever-impending instability."[36] Yet Valéry does not always refuse, granting certain precautions, to oppose intelligence to sensibility.[k] The individual's activity, when the creative sensibility is his principle and goal,

> is opposed . . . to intellectual activity proper, for it consists in a development of sensations which tend to repeat or to prolong what the intellectual tends to eliminate or exceed—as it tends to abolish the auditive substance and the structure of a speech to arrive at its meaning.[37]

This is the opposition, which we shall find again, of ordinary speech and poetic language, and more generally of the *finite* and the *aesthetic infinite*. Reciprocally,

[k] Cf. *Cours de poétique*: ". . . the distinction between sensibility and intelligence seems illusory to me when presented without precision" (lecture 15); "sensibility is everything, minus what we have been able to subtract from it: then we are in the state of pure intellectualism" (lecture 16).

the intellect and its abstract means . . . are occasionally opposed to the sensibility, since they always proceed, contrary to the latter, toward a limit, pursue a fixed goal —a formula, a definition, a law—and tend to exhaust or replace all sensorial experience by conventional signs.[38]

Let us consider then the role Valéry accords the intelligence in art, and especially in poetry. As early as 1892, he could not tolerate "opposing the state of poetry to the complete and sustained action of the intellect." This distinction seemed to him "as crude" as that of sensibility and intelligence.[39] In one of his earliest texts on poetry, the *Avantpropos à la Connaissance de la déesse*, the admirer of Leonardo protested that "poetry does not demand the *sacrifizio dell'Intelletto*. . . . Minerva, Pallas, Apollo have no taste for incomplete victims."[40] We know of Valéry's devotion to the intellect, than which he had not found, he said, a "better idol."[41] We know he tried to represent, in the character of Monsieur Teste, the pure hero of the rigorous intelligence.[1] This cult is linked to that of effort and work, to a degree of contempt for natural gifts.

> A man is of the most pronounced intellectual type when he can be satisfied with himself only at the price of an "intellectual" effort. —Whatever he can accomplish without effort and attention does not give him the sensation of *value*. Compliments do not touch him, and he privately mocks those who pay them. What has cost him nothing does not count.[42]

He "scorns the gratuitous gift and what has not been elaborated."[43] Valéry alluded to the "intensive study" which the role of the intellect in art "warranted," to its contribution ("logic, methods, classifications, analyses of data and criticism"), to the "more or less happy cooperation of thought reworked and reconstructed, constituted into distinct and conscious operations, rich with notations and forms of admirable generality and power," and to its "intervention"— no doubt less happy—in the "various Aesthetics which, consid-

---

[1] As distinguished from what is commonly called "intellectuals," concerning whom Valéry wrote a number of ferocious pages. See *Lettre d'un ami* in *Monsieur Teste*, pp. 90–92.

ering Art as a problem of knowledge, have tried to reduce it to ideas."[44] He asserted that

> Literature is in no way desirable if it is not a superior exercise of the intellectual animal.
> It must involve the use of all the mental functions of this animal. . . .[45]

That the poem is such an exercise is what *La Jeune Parque* has certainly proved.

But Valéry also considered the poem under the aspect of an elaborate ceremony in honor of the intelligence, and this recalls the hieratic aspect of certain works by Mallarmé, even by Leconte de Lisle.

> A poem must be a festival of the Intellect. It cannot be anything else.
> Festival: a celebration, but solemn, regulated, significant; the image of what one ordinarily is not, of the state in which efforts are rhythmical, redeemed.
> One celebrates something by accomplishing or representing it in its purest and finest states.
> Here the faculty of language, and its inverse phenomenon, comprehension, the identity of things it separates. One dismisses its failures, its weaknesses, its banality. One *organizes* all of language's *potential*.
> The festival over, nothing must remain. Ashes, trampled garlands.[46]

This apparent antinomy of exercise and celebration simply manifests the result of hard, conscious labor in the ceremonial and refined pleasure which the poem should afford. It is the intelligence which "sets to work" (*met en oeuvre*) and it is the intelligence which delights in an intelligent work. The primacy Valéry here accords to the mind's highest faculty must not deceive us as to its role. Valéry, of course, did not fall into the error of advocating the show of ideas for their own sake. Nothing could be further from his intentions than didacticism, pedagogy, or a so-called philosophical poetry. For him, intelligence in poetry has first an auxiliary and supervisory function. "The *idea* inhabits *prose;* but attends, surveys, guides poetry."[47] It has, further, a secretly directing function: "The intelligence must be present; either concealed

or manifest. It does the swimming, holding poetry above wa-
ter."[48] But it cannot provide, at least without elaboration
and without transformation, the actual substance of the
poem. Philosophy has its own form, which makes it, to Valéry's mind, a particular art, an art of ideas.

> It cannot be separated from its own difficulties, which
> constitute its *form;* and it would not take the *form* of
> verse without losing its being, or without corrupting the
> verse. To talk today about philosophical poetry (even
> invoking Alfred de Vigny, Leconte de Lisle, and several
> others) is naïvely to confuse conditions and applications
> of the mind that are incompatible with each other.[49]

If we consider the poets called philosophers (of whom
Lucretius is the type), we are obliged to acknowledge, as
we read their works, an irritating division between the attention we must pay to the thought and that required by the
poetry itself, or a discord between the interest of substance
and that of form. This is what Valéry splendidly clarified in
Poésie et pensée abstraite:

> It has nonetheless frequently been the case, as literary
> history shows, that poetry has been employed to express
> theses or hypotheses, and that the *complete* language
> which is its characteristic, the language whose *form*—
> that is, the action and sensation of the *voice*—is of the
> same power as its *substance*—that is, the final modifica-
> tion of a mind—has been used to communicate "abstract"
> ideas, which are, on the contrary, ideas independent of
> their form—or which we assume to be such. Very great
> poets have on occasion attempted such a thing. But
> whatever the talent expended upon these noble enter-
> prises, it cannot keep the attention which follows the
> song. The *De natura rerum* is here in conflict with the
> nature of things. The state of the reader of poems is
> not the state of the reader of pure thought. The state of
> a man dancing is not that of the man advancing into a
> difficult region of which he is making the topographical
> and geological survey.[50]

The speculative thinker has as his goal, according to Valéry,
"to fix or to create a notion—that is, a *power* and an *instrument of power*," while the poet "tries to produce in us a

'state' and to raise it 'to the point of perfect delight.' "[51] The attempt to combine the two activities merely causes confusion. "To philosophize in verse was once, and is still, to attempt to play chess by the rules of checkers."[52] To speak of "philosopher-poets . . . is to confuse a painter of seascapes with a ship's captain."[53] Moreover, thought counts for little or nothing in poetry; Valéry said as much apropos of *La Jeune Parque:* "The meaning matters little. Commonplaces. True thought is not adaptable to verse."[54]

Valéry saw "a very real *progress*" in the effort of modern poets and in the modern tendency (since this is one of the rare occasions Valéry praises the moderns and speaks of progress in art, it is worth pointing out) to rid works in verse of "philosophy" and "morality," and he noted quite justly that philosophy and morality tended to "take their place in the reflections that precede the works"; "abstract thought . . . exiled from a poetry that attempted to reduce itself to its own essence" is transferred "into the phase of preparation and into the theory of the poem."[55] There was also something here to satisfy his preference for clearly distinct operations, and an advance toward a kind of science of poetry. It is therefore no compliment to Valéry to treat him as a philosopher-poet, at least in this sense. But in another, perhaps he would accept the baptism.

> I have said, however, that the poet has his abstract thought and, if you like, his philosophy; and I have said that it was expressed in his very action as a poet. I have said so because I have observed as much, both in myself and in others. I have, here as elsewhere, no other reference, no other pretension or excuse than recourse to my own experience, or else to the most ordinary observation.[56]

There is then, all the same, a philosophy of the poet, but it is not enclosed in the versified expression of his ideas: "you must not seek his true philosophy in the more or less philosophical things he says";[57] it is to be found in the speculation that dominates his strictly artistic labor, and still less in the theories that dominate this labor or can be extracted from it than in the practical thought infused in the poetic activity. There is at work in the creation of the poem an utterly intellectual vigilance, lucid, critical and deliberate, full of initiative and without which composition would be impossible. For Valéry, it is just as important, perhaps more so, as the necessary poetic emotion, but not sufficient. Inspiration, to use a word Valéry didn't like, is nothing without the severest attention.

> I have noticed, whenever I have worked as a poet, that my work required of me not only that presence of the poetic universe which I have mentioned, but a number of reflections, decisions, choices, and combinations without which all the possible gifts of the Muse or of Chance remained like precious building materials on an empty lot without an architect.[58]

It is in this very particular sense, analogous to the one attached to the word *intelligence* when we speak of the intelligence revealed by an artisan's work, that we must interpret Valéry's formulation:

> Every true poet is much more capable than is generally known of accurate reasoning and of abstract thought.[59]

Valéry tried, in a curious analysis treating examples from his personal life, to grasp the common origin of the two activities of the mind which sometimes result in a poem, sometimes in a thought. In both cases, an "insignificant," "banal incident" has caused, or seemed to cause, developments or, as he says, divagations, excursions quite different from each other and from the normal system. And of the two states, it is the second, the abstract one, which Valéry has described most poetically. Here is the passage, which must be quoted complete:

> I have, then, observed in myself such states, which I can indeed call *poetic,* since some of them have finally resulted in poems. They were produced without apparent cause, starting from a banal incident; they developed according to their nature, and thereby I have found myself diverted for a time from my habitual mental regime. Then I returned to this regime of habitual exchanges between my life and my thoughts, my cycle being completed. But it happened that a poem *had been*

made and that the cycle, in its completion, left something behind it. This closed cycle is the cycle of an act which has somehow stirred up and externally restored a power of poetry. . . .

I have noted at other times that an incident no less insignificant caused—or seemed to cause—a quite different excursion, a divagation quite different in nature and result. For instance, a sudden juxtaposition of ideas, an analogy seized me, as a horn call deep in the woods makes us cock our ears and orient virtually all our muscles which feel coordinated toward some distant point in the foliage. But this time, instead of a poem, it was an analysis of this sudden intellectual sensation which took possession of me. It was not lines of verse which were more or less easily detached from my duration in this phase; but some proposition that was destined to be incorporated into my habits of thought, some formula that was henceforth to serve as an instrument in further researches. . . .[m]

We must relate this passage to the pages in which Valéry compares the artist and the scientist. According to him, upon examination, "the distinction between the scientist and the artist disappears"; there are "great similarities in the essential movements of these two modes of producing"; he does not conceive "a difference in depth between the work of the so-called scientific mind and the work of the mind called poetic or artistic. In each case, it is a question of transformations subjected to certain conditions, that is all." Of course, there are differences in the material results, "but the personal act of the scientist, the effect of stimulus and illumination due to his work are all comparable to the acts of the artist and to the effects of the work of art" and, "in both cases, there is a restitution of spiritual energy." Valéry opportunely recalls that "scientific temperaments . . . have occasionally been found among artists and writers," and that "singularly artistic natures . . . occur among the scientists."[60] We may

---

[m] *Poésie et pensée abstraite* in *Variété* V, p. 135. A more curious type of incident—or rather of inspiration—was also noted by Valéry: the stimulus of walking, instead of producing a rhythm or a useful idea, produced in him a combination of rhythms too complex to be of use to anyone but a musician. Cf. *Mémoires d'un poème*, pp. xx–xxii, and *Poésie et pensée abstraite* in *Variété* V, pp. 139–41.

recall the privileged position occupied by Leonardo, who was characterized by an undifferentiated nature preceding all specialization. Leonardo "had found the central attitude which makes the enterprises of knowledge and the operations of art equally possible."[n] In the mind's actual labor, works of art are not clearly distinguished from the point of view of production.

> I find virtually everywhere, in minds, concentration, experiment, unexpected light, darkness, improvisation, new attempts, or urgent repetitions. There are, in any of the mind's hearths, both fire and ashes; prudence and imprudence; method and its opposite; chance in a thousand forms. Artists and scientists are all identifiable in the detail of this strange life of thought. One might say that at any given moment the functional difference of minds at work is undiscernible.[61]

The basic difference between art and science lies in their degree of complexity:

> There is a *science* of simple things, and an *art* of complicated ones. *Science*, when the variables are capable of being enumerated, their number small, their combinations clear and distinct.
> We tend toward the state of science, we desire it. The artist makes formulas for himself. The interest of science lies in the *art* of making science.[62]

If the poet could grasp all the variable functions of his art, the latter would become a science, and we could be sure of producing a beautiful poem, as we are sure of producing chemical synthesis. But poetry is the most difficult, the most complicated of the arts.

This dream had been shared by Poe,

> the first writer who had conceived of introducing into literary production . . . and even into poetry, the same spirit of analysis and of calculated construction . . .[63]

and, from another point of view, by Mallarmé:

[n] *Introduction à la méthode de Léonard de Vinci*, I, *Note et digression* in *Variété*, p. 165. See too, in the *Préface* to the Notebooks of Leonardo da Vinci, in *Vues*, p. 224: "Leonardo is indifferent . . . to our academic distinctions between scientific work and artistic production."

Mallarmé, an essentially formal genius, gradually arriving at the abstract conception of all the combinations of figures and turns . . . the first writer who dared to envisage the literary problem in all its universality . . . he conceived as an algebra what all the rest thought of only in the particularity of arithmetic. . . .[64]

But in Poe, instead of a mathematics, we find a logic and a mechanics of effects; he reduces the problem of literature to a problem of psychology.[65] Valéry told Jean de Latour what he owed Mallarmé in this research:

Mallarmé had carried to their limit the correct consequences of a profound analysis of poetry. I did not admit all his ideas (I was even, by my nature, quite opposed to his doctrine of the capital importance of poetic expression); but I had seen this limit, and I dreamed of arriving at an explanation of his methods that would permit me to adapt them to my own *fabrication*.[66]

For his part, Valéry tried to preserve both his inclination toward poetry and the bizarre need, as he calls it, to satisfy all the demands of his mind.[67] As a result, he liked to consider his work as a writer or a poet under the aspect closest to scientific work, particularly mathematics:

To *write* (in the literary sense) always assumes for me the image of a kind of *calculation*. In other words, I refer what comes to me, my immediacy, to the notion of a problem and operations; I recognize the domain proper to *literature* in a certain mode of combinatory work that becomes conscious and tends to prevail and to organize itself on this model; I thus distinguish what is given from what it can become by work; such work consists of transformations. . . . I justify myself by the example of the musician who proceeds by calculations of harmony, develops and transforms. —I derive this from the work of writing verse, which necessitates arranging *words* quite differently than in ordinary usage. . . .[68]

Unfortunately, the complete analysis of the means that would make the poet's calculation infallible is admittedly impossible. Therefore one must be content with an approximation of rigor which puts as much intelligence as possible in the service of the operations of art. This is how method allows for the less ambitious procedures of criticism. Valéry insisted on the urgency, for the poet, of criticizing his own activity. He indicated, at the same time, the singularity of the alliance of the "virtue of poetry" and of "critical intelligence," which he praises in Baudelaire,[69] and the necessary identity of the "true poet" and the "critic of the first order."[70]

> To doubt this, one must never have conceived what the mind's work is, that struggle against the inequality of moments, accidental associations, failures of attention, external diversions. The mind is terribly variable, deceptive and self-deceptive, prolific in insoluble problems and illusory solutions. How would a remarkable work emerge from this chaos, if this chaos that contains everything did not also contain some serious opportunities of knowing oneself and of choosing in oneself what deserves to be selected from the moment and deliberately employed?[71]

It is in this faculty of self-criticism that Valéry actually saw the assurance of the work's duration: "Every poet will *finally* be worth what he has been worth as a critic (of himself)."[o] This is the logical conclusion of a lofty conception based on the dignity of the mind. We have seen that this conception, which accords such an important place to the intelligence in creation, eliminated its products from the work's content. It remains for us to show how Valéry managed to reintroduce them. If poetry must not be philosophical, if it destroys itself by presenting ideas, it is not because thought is unable to furnish it an affective substance. We shall confine ourselves here to theory, but we know that Valéry has often been hailed as the poet of knowledge or of the intelligence, and this unheard-of success raises, in my opinion, the problem of the poetization of thought: a properly Valerian paradox, if we admit—and how avoid doing so? —that the idea in itself is the object of prose and an obstacle to poetry. Valéry complained that the *Intellectual Comedy*

[o] *Choses tues* in *Tel quel*, I, p. 28. It is in the same way that he defines the classical writer, "who bears a critic within himself and who associates him intimately with his works" (*Situation de Baudelaire* in *Variété II*, p. 155).

(as we say the *Divine Comedy* and the *Human Comedy*) had not found its poet; Leonardo would have been, he felt, its chief character.[72] This was a highly stimulating view, which did not particularly insist on works in verse and did not necessarily involve the poetic emotion. But Valéry also suggested that knowledge could be the material of a certain lyricism.

Remarking that there were "no poets of knowledge in France" like Lucretius or Dante, he noted that "our poetry is ignorant of, or even avoids, all the *epos* and the *pathos* of the intellect"; "when it has ventured in such realms," it has been "gloomy and boring."

> We do not know how to make what can do without song, sing. But our poetry, for a hundred years, has shown such rich resources, and so rare a power of renewal, that the future may soon give it several works of high style and noble severity which transcend the sensuous and the intelligible.[73]

One might say that this promise had already been magnificently kept by the author of *La Jeune Parque* and *Charmes*. In his lecture on Descartes, Valéry traced the program not only of a poetry but of a whole literature which would be endlessly nourished upon the "combinations and fluctuations of the intellect."

> No poetic substance in the world is richer than this one; the life of the intelligence constitutes an incomparable lyric universe, a complete drama which lacks neither adventure nor passion nor suffering (this latter, in the life of the mind, has an essence all its own), nor comedy, nor anything human . . . there exists a vast domain of intellectual sensibility, beneath appearances on occasion so void of the usual attractions that most men turn from them as from reservoirs of boredom, promises of painful contention . . . ; the world of thought . . . is as varied . . . moving, surprising . . . admirable . . . as the world of the affective life dominated by the instincts alone.[74]

There is, in particular, "a poetry of inexhaustible resources" afforded by "the thirst to understand and to create; the longing to surpass" or to equal; "abnegation" and "the renunciation of glory," the detail . . . of the moments of mental action: the waiting for the gift of a form or an idea; for the simple word that will change the impossible into a *fait accompli;* the desires and the sacrifices, the victories and the disasters; and the surprises, the infinity of patience and the dawn of a "truth"; and such extraordinary moments as, for instance, the sudden formation of a kind of solitude which declares itself without warning, even in the middle of a crowd, and falls upon a man like a veil, beneath which will occur the mystery of an immediate evidence. . . . The creative sensibility, in its highest forms and its rarest productions, seems to me as capable of a certain art as all the pathos and the drama of the life of ordinary experience.[p]

Here Valéry reveals the grandiose prospect not only of a literature and a poetry of the life of the mind, but of a poetry of poetry. And in fact, certain of Valéry's poems have for their precise subject this intoxication that seizes upon itself, always assuming an observer. It tends to the lucid monologue, so characteristic of Valéry's lyricism. If he refuses to be called a philosopher-poet, it is not without reason, but he is nonetheless a poet of thought; only he has understood and made us feel, in his finest poems, that it is not thought's objects, pure notions, that are susceptible to poetic treatment, but thought's life incarnate—in short, that whereby thought again becomes feeling. He would not have liked to say so.

THE REJECTION OF SENTIMENT

We have discussed the place Valéry gives, in his conception of poetry, to the sensibility and to the intelligence. It remains to determine what he accords to sentiment. We know already that the poetic is indeed an emotion, although of a very particular nature, and that feeling can be divined in the creative sensibility and in the pathos of intellectual creation. More than a theoretical effort to delimit the role of feeling, Valéry's attitude is a spontaneous tendency to limit

[p] *Descartes* in *Variété IV*, pp. 216–17. See analogous development on the poetry of sensibility in *La Tentation de (saint) Flaubert* in *Variété V*, pp. 206–7.

its importance. He does not deny its existence in poetry: he belittles it at every opportunity. This is not only an effect of that reserve he praised in Mallarmé, nor of that distaste for the sentimentality displayed by too many facile works, but because Valéry sees sentiment as the intellect's chief enemy, the common term applicable to all the idols which oppose the only idol he admits. Doubtless no one is entirely free of such weaknesses, but a free spirit condemns them. Monsieur Teste said: "I am not stupid, because every time I find myself being stupid, I deny myself—I kill myself."[75] And that Monsieur Teste's stupidities are especially of an affective nature is what is proved, among other things, by the little program Valéry attributes to him in one of the fragments added to the last edition of the volume devoted to his hero:

> To consider one's emotions as nonsense, weakness, futilities, idiocies, imperfection—humiliating, like seasickness and acrophobia.
> . . . Something in us, or in me, revolts against the inventive power of the soul over the mind.[76]

But Valéry himself admitted more than once that he shared the same repugnance: "What is stupider than melancholy"[q]—"I suffer, I fear, I even desire, but with scorn."[77] The origins of this attitude date back to his twentieth year, to the emotional crisis which combined with the intellectual crisis of 1892; whereas Valéry expressed himself quite freely concerning the second, he made only veiled and belated allusions to the first. It was at this time that he was "obliged to undertake a very serious action against "Idols" in general, but, he says:

> It was at first only one of them that obsessed me, that made my life almost unendurable. The power of the absurd is incredible. What is more humiliating for the mind than all the suffering caused by this nothing: an image, a mental element destined to oblivion? . . . This crisis turned me against my "sensibility" insofar as it

[q] *Propos me concernant*, p. 17. Melancholy is not absent from Valéry's poems, and for its poetic value in prose, we need only read the penetrating close of the portrait of *Laure* in *Mauvaises pensées et autres*, p. 232: ". . . and I fall with all my heart into a magical melancholy."

threatened the freedom of my mind. . . . I then became
the theater of a singular drama.[r]

It is not difficult to name the idol which was then overwhelming this tormented young man.[s] Valéry will not
change: he will constantly try to reduce this annexation of
the mind's freedom by vague powers—irrational or unreason-
ing—of being. This attitude is itself an emotional one. Refusal
is quite often a sentiment. Valéry realized this. One does not
escape the affective, but the mind's dignity consists in re-
pulsing it.

In a very important passage of *Suite*, which he reprinted
in *Mélange*, Valéry emphasized the mind's impulse to reject
the stupidity of emotion and, at the same time, by his very
response, the impossibility of avoiding it completely:

> All emotion tends to conceal the always stupid and
> naïve mechanism of its genesis and its development. But
> the more complex the mind, the less it consents that its
> man be moved; the result of this is a number of in-
> teresting conflicts.
>
> How endure seeing oneself the victim of an emotion?
> Seeing oneself seduced, jealous, irritated, enraged or
> ashamed or proud—seeing oneself *doting on something*,
> whether money or a person or a place at the table or
> an image of oneself? How is it possible . . . to endure
> this? To feel oneself blush, to hear oneself roar, to find
> oneself obsessed by an image or carried to extremes of
> agitation, what unendurable scenes for consciousness!
>
> But this very awakening and this withdrawal are part
> of consciousness and will immediately take their place
> among the reflexes, in the category of pride. One does
> not escape them. It is impossible not to *reply*. . . .[78]

Valéry's condemnation is quite general, but it is interesting
to note one form of sensibility that escapes it; this is the sensory sensibility, which despite its affective echoes is not a

[r] *Propos me concernant*, pp. 12–13. For the rapid generalization of this attitude, see further p. 52: "I happened at about eighteen . . . to consider vulgar, too familiar, all the natural sentiments,
or virtually so—or rather their expression. . . ."
[s] On the object of this source of disturbance, see Henri Mondor,
Les premiers temps d'une amitié.

diffuse power, but instead is furnished with precise organs affording it the distinctness of intellectual operations:

> Everything that is affective is obtuse, I thought. And the affective is everything that reaches us by simple means, through organs which have neither the delicacy nor the multiple *coordinates* of the specialized organs of the senses.[79]

Before the affective, the mind lays down its arms, whereas before the sensory, it recognizes itself:

> . . . we try to compare these raw, powerful indistinct *values* with the clear knowledge and the precise correspondences of our organized perceptions. We cannot succeed in doing so, before them we are like the geometrician before irrational or transcendent quantities when he tries to translate the continuous into number.[80]

The intelligence has an enemy in our very being. And when Valéry seeks a name for this enemy, he stops at the word sentiment: ". . . what abases reasoning can only be . . . ? One risks nothing by calling it *sentiment*."[81] He objected violently to Pascal's remark on the reasoning that is reduced to yielding to sentiment; in it he saw "a Pythian notion, the idol of the oracle." He decried the attitude that makes "the spontaneous, the unreflected more precious, more worthy of faith than the 'reflected.'"[82] And he blamed the will for this defeat, in the last *pensée* of Analecta:

> If all reasoning is reduced to yielding to sentiment, it is he who yields whom we must mourn. . . . But it is not the reasoning that yields. It is *me*. Who am I? —The one who acts. For the other is a limitless variation; it will reverse its sentiments; it will resume its reasoning. And so on . . .[83]

For Valéry, the heart has no reasons unknown to reason. The heart of course plays a considerable role, too considerable. If we follow Valéry closely, we shall see that he regards the heart as introducing an unjustified choice into the exact order of things; it is an absurd principle of preference, a selective factor without precision.

The "heart" is what gives instantaneous and omnipotent values to impressions and to things. It is in each man the arbiter of various *importances*. It is a central resonator which chooses the equivalence of things.

Superstitions—presentiments—impulsions, repulsions, sudden organization of the inner inequality of ideas . . .

What does this heart prove, and what are these values worth?[84]

Valéry does not appear to have raised the problem of a rectification of the sentiments. It seems that the role of the intelligence in the affective life must consist in an effort to incline the sentiments in a direction acceptable to the eyes of reason and not in a vain attempt to mutilate or extirpate.

He said in *Rhumbs,* and repeated in *Suite,* that "our most important thoughts are the ones which contradict our feelings."[85] This is one of the principles of the Valerian ethic. This "critique of desires"[86] would result in a state of disabused wisdom which he synopsized by questioning himself as to its ultimate meaning:

> Sentiments driven out of the mind.
> A time may come when what was shame, modesty, regret, remorse, etc., in the man of yesterday and today will be reduced to their reflex rudiments and become incapable of psychological importance—incapable of withstanding scrutiny and consciousness—but functional curiosities, vestiges whose naïve mechanisms are quite familiar.
> The man incredulous as to his feelings, and without illusion as to his SELF; who would watch himself blush as he would watch a reagent color a solution—this sage —will therefore have to endure his life like a strange necessity—love, suffer, endure, desire—as one greets the days and the fluctuations of the weather.
> Cynic?—skeptic?—stoic?[87]

Like many psychologists, Valéry regarded emotion as a defectiveness of our nature, a functional disturbance in its relation with the environment:[t] "Every emotion, every sentiment marks a defect in adaptation."[u] It is "a noncompensated

[t] The theory is set forth in often identical terms in *Analecta,* XLIII and in *Mauvaises pensées et autres,* pp. 147–48.

[u] *Mauvaises pensées,* p. 148; in *Analecta,* XLIII: ". . . in construction or in adaptation."

shock" that expresses a "lack of elasticity, or its alteration."[88] However, an "artificial adaptation"[89] functions by "what is called consciousness and intelligence," which "is implanted and developed in these interstices."[90] The result is a strange one:

> The acme of the human is that man has come to enjoy it: a search for emotion, fabrication of emotion, desire to lose one's head, to make others lose theirs, to disturb and to be disturbed.[91]

These inadequacies of his system—"the difficulties of his accommodation, the obligation to endure what he has called *irrational*"[92]—have been "consecrated by man, who has found profundities in them, and that bizarre product 'melancholy'; sometimes, the token of a vanished golden age, or the presentiment of an indefinable destiny."[v] A concession is made only in favor of "the physiological necessity of losing one's mind, of seeing distortedly, of forming fantastic images, so that love can be fulfilled, otherwise the world would come to an end."[w]

If Valéry did not love the emotions, he detested even more their external manifestations. But his artistic experience led him to make one remarkable exception. In opposition to the vulgar expression of gross sentimentality, he distinguished a purified, "dry" emotion, as he calls it, and on one occasion granted reserve the right to a few tears before the spectacle of what is most sublime. In a splendid page, he established a "critique of the gift of tears":

> To win tears from me, you must weep.
> This is not so much false as stupid.
> I do not see what interest there is in weeping.
> Unless it is the pleasure of weeping itself.

[v] *Mauvaises pensées,* pp. 147–48. In *Analecta,* XLIII, the end of the sentence specified: "the presentiment of divinity and of promise."

[w] *Mauvaises pensées,* p. 148. Cf. *Analecta,* XLIII, and *L'Idée fixe,* p. 42: "We must lose our heads or the race." In a passage of *La Jeune Parque,* Valéry has utilized this surprising renewal of the theme of love; and throughout the entire poem, the notion that "the conscious finite functions" go "against life" (*Analecta,* XLIII).

This pleasure of making certain glands function artificially, of inducing all the accessory and related movements which release them, which justify and complete their functioning.

The old "pure beauty" made it a point of honor to avoid the glandular circuits. To produce a kind of emotion which does not have its gland in either a high or a low place, an emotion without juice, a dry emotion—that was its business.

If it drew tears, it was by its own means; by means which do not exist in the forced experience of life: and which life has not anticipated by special organs. No one in general was forced to *weep*. Where everyone *had* to weep was the region from which it abstained. It overwhelmed only certain individuals. And all the rest *had* to ask, without comprehending, why these wept.[93]

We must therefore distinguish among "tears of various orders":

Tears rise from suffering, impotence, humiliation, always a lack.

But there are tears of a divine species, which are born from the lack of force to sustain a divine object of the soul, to equal it and exhaust its essence.

A narrative, a dumb show, a staged drama can cause tears by the imitation of the lamentable things of life.

But if an architecture which resembles, in relation to the sense of sight, nothing of man (or else some other harmony, so exact that it is almost as painful as a dissonance) brings you to the brink of tears, this dawning effusion that you feel struggling out of your incomprehensible depths is of an infinite value, for it teaches you that you are sensitive to objects entirely indifferent and useless to your person, to your history, your interests, to all the matters and circumstances that circumscribe you as a mortal being.[94]

For Valéry, the only admissible emotion is produced upon contact with something that might just as well be called divine, superhuman, inhuman.

Aside from these rare cases, Valéry, perhaps because one might discern in him a tremulous sensibility, a heightened tenderness, refuses all contagion of the emotions. His reading of *Lucien Leuwen* left a "tender and vibrant" impression; it performed in him "the miracle of a confusion he abhors": no longer clearly to distinguish his own affections from those which the artifice of an author communicates to him.[95] He diagnosed in "all men who have exerted a power of an affective kind over numbers of men" certain nervous or psychic taints, whose power was derived from the "external action" of their taint, in the consciousness of which they saw "an indication of their singularity." "They make a doctrine of their weaknesses and have the eloquence of their inclinations." Hence their ruse of public confession and the exploitation of "sincerity."[96] One might examine, under this aspect of the contagion of sentiment, the action exerted upon readers by poets, novelists, dramatists, and even some philosophers. Valéry, for his part, was not at all disposed to accept this ascendancy.

> All the goals of second-rate sensibility, ballads, Musset, beggars, Hugo's poor people, Jean Valjean, etc., inspire me with disgust, if not with rage. Pascal playing on death, Hugo on misery, virtuosos as they are on these affecting instruments, are essentially antipathetic to me. The calculation of drawing tears, of melting hearts, of arousing by the too-beautiful, the too-sad, makes me pitiless. Emotion seems to me a forbidden means. To make someone weak is an ignoble act.
>
> I have been reproached for not using these gross weapons.[97]

Monsieur Teste said: "I feel no need for other people's sentiments, and I take no pleasure in borrowing them."[98] Neither he nor Valéry granted that function of relief, which they would have judged ignoble, so often invoked as the source of literary creation:

> "To confide one's suffering to paper." Strange notion. Origin of more than one book, and of all the worst ones.[99]

To make someone else participate in the intimacy of consciousness is an indecency, an absurd illusion, and an unforgivable weakness.

> How reluctant I am to write my "feelings," to take notice

of what so many enjoy setting down on paper! First of all, there are no valid words for these things with oneself. —What people say of them, even to themselves, smells of the *third person*. I have never been able to write down words except to work out my thoughts or to influence those of other men—which is quite different, a means of calculation or the preparation of an action. But not to relive—that weakness!

And this in accord with my sensibility, which has and has always had a holy horror of itself. Otherwise I could have made a novelist or a poet.

—But my sensibility is my inferiority, my cruelest and most detestable gift, since *I cannot utilize it.*[100]

Valéry has admitted that masterpieces may have been created by following this tendency, but he has clearly indicated his intention, as a poet, to follow another path:

Since I am not interested in modifying other people's sentiments, I find myself, for my part, quite insensitive to their intention of moving me. I feel no need for my neighbor's passions, and it has never occurred to me to work for those who ask the writer to teach or restore to them what one experiences simply by living. Further, most authors undertake to do this, and the greatest poets have marvelously accomplished the task of representing for us the immediate emotions of life. This task is traditional. Masterpieces in this genre abound. I wondered if there was something else to do.[101]

If Valéry refused to represent or to stimulate in his work the emotions which life suffices to inspire, it is not that their power seemed without function. In studying emotion, one is fatally led to regard it either as a vague form of knowledge, or under its aspect of force or tendency. One relates it to the intelligence or to the will. If emotion is a force, one can derive some advantage from it. One can utilize emotion, or the capacity for emotion. Valéry, who proposed comparing the "psychic system with the world of physics,"[102] has, like other modern psychologists, an energy theory of psychology and, like them also, has borrowed certain analogies from banking operations to explain the investment or the transfer of psychic forces. Thus "all feeling is the balance due of an account whose particulars have been lost," and he adds humorously: "original sin is doubtless an integral."[103] Similarly, "belief is a transfer of funds."[104] The "transfer of nervous credits" is a "common occurrence," and Valéry gives as an example of it the fact that on a certain "March 17, 191 . . ." he made "a small poetic labor profit from the excitement provoked by a public scandal, by the shouts of the newsboys."[105] He thus proposed to tap the exaltation resulting from the emotions: "As for enthusiasm, that stupid thunderbolt, learn to bottle it, make it run on docile wires. Separate it from the absurd objects in which the mob experiences it and to which they attach it."[106] The most fruitful of these reinvestments is that of amorous passion:

The true (that is, usable) value of love is in the increase of general vitality which it may afford.
Any love that does not release this energy is bad.
The procedure is to utilize this sexual ferment for other purposes. What assumed it had only men to make is employed to produce acts, works.[107]

This is "the 'production' derived from 'reproduction,'"[108] a theory of the origins of art that is not new. As we have just shown, the emotion excited by scandal, the accumulation of force in the lover furnishes a potential of creation, of poetic creation in particular. A little unrhymed poem entitled *Sagesses* (Two Wisdoms) sums up this program:

One Wisdom shuns Love
As animals do fire.
It is afraid of being
Devoured, being consumed.

Another Wisdom pursues it,
And like the thinking man
Stands fast and fans the flame,
Makes it his strength, melts iron.

Thus Love lends him its powers.[109]

Emotion thereby loses its quality and is reduced to its quantity of available energy: this is, basically, another means of destroying its true value and its originality. Valéry noted this "prodigy of transformation in the poet or the musician:

the transportation of affections, even depression and distress, into poems, into a means of preserving and spreading their true total sensibility . . ." It is a question of "changing one's pain into works. . . ."[110] But Valéry has further diminished, in poetic labor, the importance of this emotive force. Without utterly denying its necessity, he has reduced its responsibility to the strict minimum, replacing its action by that of the intelligence.

> The exalted or deeply moved man believes that his speech is already verse, and that all that he invests by tone, the warmth and the desire in his words, is found there and communicates itself. But this is the common error in matters of poetry. Bad lines are made of good intentions. It is this illusion which encourages verse without pre-established laws. More good lines are written in cold blood than are taken at the heat; and more bad ones are written in the throes of passion. One might say that the intelligence is better able to compensate for warmth than warmth for intelligence. A machine can work at low pressure, but pressure without a machine can do no work at all.[111]

In his *Calepin d'un poète*, using the same mechanical comparison, Valéry set the artist, the fabricator, above the poet, the man of sentiment:

> "X . . . is more poet than artist." Does this mean that X . . . has more energy at his disposal than operations or machinery to utilize it?[112]

Nevertheless Valéry here reduced, without admitting it, the poetic state to emotion, that indispensable force, that pressure without which the machine, however well constructed, however well controlled, would not work. And, abandoning a metaphor too favorable to his thesis, we may wonder if the warmth and also the quality of the sentiment have not an importance unjustly diminished by Valéry to the advantage of artifice. Further, Valéry, despite his disclaimers, could not avoid the importance of sentiment, as confirmed when we study his conception of the relations of matter and form in poetry; in the content of the verse, thought is sacrificed to affective "resonance": "verse does not abide what merely signifies and does not, instead, attempt to create the value of sentiment."[113]

We may, further, note in Valéry's work occasional indications of the creative role of the emotions in art. Creation of the work itself: it was fear that raised the temples, "marvelous supplications of stone,"[114] as well as creation, if one may say so, of the lover of the work: Eupalinos, by the action of intelligence, certainly, but imbued with affectivity, "elaborated the emotions and the soul vibrations of the future contemplator of his work."[115] " 'My temple,' said this man from Megara, 'must move men as the beloved object moves them' ";[116] and it had certainly required much love, as well as reason, to raise "this delicate temple" that was, without anyone's knowing it, "the mathematical image of a girl from Corinth" whose "individual proportions it faithfully reproduces." Eupalinos had put in them "the memory of a bright day in his life."[117] Now we know that memories, like omens, had for Valéry a "resonance that engages the soul in the poetic universe."[118] This mixture of intellectuality and emotivity had struck Valéry himself when he came across this declaration of Wagner's: "I composed *Tristan* in the grip of a great passion, and after several months of theoretical meditation." This "antinomy" corresponded for Valéry to an "expectation" and a "conviction."

> What is rarer, I thought, and more enviable than this singular coordination of two modes of vital activity, commonly considered as independent and even incompatible;—on the one hand, profound agitation of the "emotions," omnipotence of affective disturbances, sensual exaltation of a psychic *idol;*—on the other, complex *theoretical meditation* . . . in which the problems of harmony were to be found combined with its future innovations. . . .[119]

Here emotion is granted equal status with calculation, in an "enviable" combination presented as exceptional, whereas it is actually the rule among impassioned creators, who always mingled fervor with technical speculation.

If Valéry does not give us in poetry an analogous example of this paradoxical alliance he has found in architecture and in music, it is because he is prevented from doing so by the

very position he has taken. He does not care to show us a
great poet whose agonized sensibility has collaborated with a
refined craftsmanship. But he at least admitted that the
poet's task was to excite the reader's emotivity deliberately:

> . . . language contains emotive resources . . . the poet's
> function, task and duty is to make evident and active
> these powers of movement and enchantment, these
> stimuli of the affective life and of the intellectual sensi-
> bility.[120]

Doubtless Valéry here admits only a manipulation of sentiment, to which nothing can correspond in the author. Of
Horace's *Si vis me flere* . . . he accepts, in the final instance
and as a condition of sublimity, only the first part: Make me
weep, provided it is with admiration; but to do so, there is
no need that you yourself should weep. Move me, if you can,
though I am reluctant to be moved—but you will be more
likely to do so by not trembling yourself. It is not for Valéry
that fear and trembling is the best part of humanity. Like
Verlaine at the time of his submission to the Parnassian
credo, he might have asserted that he produced "impassioned verses quite coldly." Indeed. Yet is it not rather a
question of the poet's communicating to us, without his being
moved *during* his work, an emotion he had nonetheless experienced before beginning to work? We have always known
that poets exploit their affective memory. The kind and degree of feeling that accompany the poem's actual composition are not prejudicial to the initial emotion which has
stirred the imagination. If this is the case, Valéry's opposition to emotion is greatly diminished; it would bear less on
the poem's point of departure, on the original sentiment,
than on a confused and simplistic conception of poetic labor,
which makes the poet into a man enthralled or possessed.
This ignores, moreover, the difficult problem of the action of
this sentiment methodically set aside for the sake of greater
lucidity: to what degree does this reserved affectivity intervene, at what moments, with what effects? In any case,
Valéry once again exaggerated the disparity between his
own theory and certain theories—if not current, at least known
—of the mind's role in poetic creation. Similarly, we shall find

that his theory of inspiration deliberately exaggerated, in order to destroy, a naïve explanation, basically the same one that declares the poet exclusively subject to the dictates of his heart. We shall see that ultimately Valéry admits inspiration as he admits sentiment.

For is there any other name we can apply to what he refuses to state precisely in this capital definition:

> *Poetry.* Is the attempt to represent, or to restore, by means of articulated language, *those things* or *that thing* which cries, tears, caresses, kisses, sighs, etc., obscurely try to express, and which objects, in their appearance of life or of assumed design, *seem to try* to express.
>
> This thing is not definable in other terms. It is of the nature of that energy that expends itself responding to what it is. . . .[121]

If this indefinable thing, which is here expressly related to sensibility ("responding to what is"), which is expressed by all the signs of emotions (cries, tears, caresses, kisses, sighs),[x] and which our anthropomorphism rediscovers in nature, is not the spontaneous affective impulse, it can only be classified among the "vague things" without a name. But is this not, thereby, to designate it once again as sentiment?

STUPIDITY AND BEAUTY

We know Valéry's horror of vague things. He once said, borrowing the tone of La Bruyère: "Those who cannot say or are reluctant to say vague things are often mute and always miserable."[122] Not that on occasion, like everyone else, he did not succumb to their spell. Although "impatient with vague things," his "rather rigorous humor . . . nonetheless

---

[x] These signs and several others are given, in *Mauvaises pensées et autres*, p. 202, as approximations created by man in his ignorance of the "language of the gods." "The highest poetry tries to stammer out these things and to substitute expressions for these *effusions*." Faust, in love, says to Lust: "We would be like the gods, harmonic beings . . . is that not . . . the fulfillment of the promise, the substance of poetry which is after all only an attempt at communion?" (Unpublished fragments of *"Mon Faust,"* published by Jean Ballard, *Celui que j'ai connu* in *Paul Valéry vivant*, p. 242.)

relaxed" sometimes "and let itself be seduced by certain words" in which he found "a charm": *Nature, Philosophy.* . . . The word *Orient* suggested a highly colored evocation, due precisely to his ignorance: ". . . one must never have been there. . . . This imagined Orient of the mind offers an intoxicated mind the most delicious disorder and the richest mixture of names, of conceivable things, of fabulous events and times, etc. . . ."[123] Here we catch Valéry in flagrant reverie, as when he expressed a preference for living in Montesquieu's period[124] or when he stopped on London Bridge to look down at the Thames.[125] It seems that poetry cannot protect or detach itself from such vagueness, which somewhat excuses those whom Valéry reproached for having been unable to define it: "Most men have so vague an idea of poetry that its very vagueness is for them the definition of poetry."[126] The profoundest revolution would replace "the old language and *vague* ideas by a *distinct* language, *distinct* ideas."[127] But would this not be the death of poetry? That is what Valéry appears to believe: "Literature is in the savage state. It will emerge from it, and perish."[128] Vagueness is not only the condition of literature, but of any life of the mind: "But perhaps vagueness is indestructible, its existence necessary to psychic effulgence," "for the mind moves in the vague, from the vague to the precise."[129] Impotent to suppress "vague things," Valéry conceded them a substantial and eternal existence. Poetry figures in the enumeration of these "very vague, very crude notions which, moreover, live on us . . . time, universe, race, form, nature, poetry, etc. . . ."[130] and the poet is one of the figures responsible for perpetuating them:

> In every society appears a man in charge of Vague Things. He distills them, orders them, adorns them with rules, with methods, with initiations, with ceremonies, symbols, measures, "spiritual" exercises, until he gives them the aspect of primordial laws. —This is the priest, the magus, the poet, the master of private ceremonies; —even the demagogue or the hero. They make out of mist structures which are not solid but which, on the other hand, are eternal. Every attack dissipates them, none destroys them.[131]

Ultimately Valéry esteems poetry only as an art, on account of the "rather precise labors" it demands, but scorns it as an emanation of the chaotic power of sentiment. When he amused himself sketching a demonology of the enemies of thought, he did not forget to hurl an anathema at the worst of these evil spirits: "I have left out the pale demon of Vague-Things, master of tender beings, soft melancholies. . . . Soul-Mud is his name."[132] In a sense, poetry is silly, since it has a low tolerance for intelligence, and worse still, it is stupidity, for it reduces us to our lowest human level.

STUPIDITY AND POETRY. There are subtle relations between these two orders. The order of stupidity and that of poetry.[133]

This shocking remark has a profundity of its own, and it loses its injustice if we set it in the general context of a mind that constantly opposes the cause of the mind's subjection. Valéry thought the same of love, which consists "of being able to be stupid together," according to Monsieur Teste.[134] It is not only the imprecision of states of feeling that horrifies Valéry, not only their level of intellectual abasement, it is also their intolerable individuality, their fatal and futile attachment to one person, to his private history, his banal, insignificant, and transitory events, valueless with regard to the universality of true knowledge. Valéry provided a very energetic definition of stupidity: "Stupidity—that is, particularity opposed to generality."[135] We realize that the intrusion of the poet's personality spoiled for Valéry a large share of poetry, particularly romantic poetry. As early as 1891, "the almost inevitable silliness of poetry"[136] appalled him. It was in inverse proportion that Mallarmé "astounded" him.[137] Similarly, Monsieur Teste "could not endure the stupid pretensions of the poets—nor the crude ones of the novelists."[138] Valéry, who foresaw that fashion might one day restore to favor the underrated poets of the eighteenth century,[139] remarked that in this period "poetry itself tried to be clear and without silliness; but this is an impossibility, it succeeded only in impoverishing itself."[140] These instances of silliness, most lacking in the dry and elegant versifiers of the eighteenth century, are poetry.

When, instead of insulting it, Valéry tries to account for this ineluctable vagueness in his poetics, he calls it the indefinable. And he finds it at every stage of creation, initially, in the course of the execution, in the relations of matter and form, in the goal of the work itself, its effect upon the public. It is this mixture of incoercible vagueness and the precision of intellectual operations which characterizes the poet's labor. In the inaugural lecture of the *Cours de poétique,* we find this formula-résumé which may at first appear obscure: ". . . in the production of the work, the action comes in contact with the indefinable.ʸ The text which explains it is understandable only if we follow attentively the opposition Valéry establishes between the state of sensibility from which the artist begins and the complex action which applies to this state in his work. The action in question, Valéry says, is "deliberate," "quite artificial," "may require long labors," but its character is to be "necessarily finite"; it is "the essential determination, since an act is a marvelous escape from the closed world of the possible, and an introduction into the universe of fact." The state of being to which this action "will adapt itself in the operation of art" is, on the contrary, "quite irreducible in itself to finite expression"; it "refers to no localizable object"; it is sometimes constituted by "a single sensation generating value and impulse"; its single characteristic "is not to correspond to any finite term of our experience."[141] More clearly, a passage from *Mémoires d'un poème* distinguishes the two factors of creation, in an analysis which recalls the exegesis of Wagner's remark about *Tristan.* Here we see more clearly the role Valéry attributes to the spontaneous, affective, irrational elements and to the voluntary and reflective ones:

> I gave myself a kind of definition of "great art," which challenged all practice! This ideal imperiously demanded that the action of producing be a complete action which made apprehensible, even in the most futile work, the possession of all the antagonistic powers within us: on the one hand, those we might call "transcendent" or "irrational," which are evaluations "without cause,"

ʸ *Variété* V, p. 320. The formula was in capital letters in the first edition, *Introduction à la poétique,* p. 57.

or unexpected interventions, or transports, or instantaneous illuminations—everything that makes us, for ourselves, sources of surprise, of spontaneous problems, of questions without answers, or of answers without questions; everything that makes our hopes as well as our fears "creators," peoples our sleep with rare combinations that can only occur in us during our absence. . . . On the other hand, our "logical" virtue, our sense of the conservation of conventions and relations, which functions without omitting any stage of its operation, any moment of transformation, which develops from equilibrium to equilibrium; and finally, our desire to coordinate, to foresee, by reasoning, the properties of the system we intend to construct—everything "rational."

But the combination of reflective and "conservative" labor with these spontaneous formations which are born from the sensorial and affective life (like figures formed by sand on a drumhead when the drum is struck) and which enjoy the property of propagating states and emotions, but not that of communicating ideas, is always extremely difficult.[142]

Thus the vague, which is already in the unstable sensibility at the start, collaborates, in its way, with the precise. It reappears finally in the action performed upon the reader. The work must result in an effect that is indefinable, unanalyzable, inexpressible, ineffable. A page from *Mélange,* entitled *The Beautiful is negative,* develops this view, in which the intellectual arrives at the mystic's language:

The Beautiful implies effects of inexpressibility, of indescribability, of ineffability. And this term itself says NOTHING. It has no definition, for there is no true definition except by construction.

Now, if one seeks to produce such an *effect by means of* THAT WHICH SPEAKS—by language—or if one experiences, as a result of language, such an effect, language must be used to produce what renders mute, expresses silence.

"Beauty" signifies "inexpressibility"—(and desire to experience this effect over again). Hence the "definition" of this term could only be the description and the conditions of production of the state of being unable to express, in such special cases and of such a kind.

"Inexpressibility" signifies not that expressions do not exist, but that all expressions are incapable of restoring what stimulates them, and that we experience this incapacity or "irrationality" as actual properties of the object-stimulus.

The cardinal property of this beautiful painting is to excite the sentiment of being unable to deal with it by a system of expressions.[143]

The perfect work of art makes us, like the character in the little poem *La Ceinture*, "mute with surprise." The expression of admiration is necessarily deficient:

To love, to admire, to adore, have as expression of their truth the negative signs of the power to express oneself. Further, everything that is strong in feeling and everything that excites a sudden reaction from a remote source immediately dislocates the complex mechanism of language: silence, the exclamation, or the cliché are the eloquence of the moment.[144]

In the state of ineffability, "words fail." Literature tries by "words" to create "the state of the failure of words."[145]

This is doubtless why there cannot be a science of poetry. Valéry did not, like others, postulate mystery in his method, but he ultimately met with it in phenomena themselves, and he accorded it its place in his aesthetic. In the end, science gains ascendancy over its object and somehow causes it to disappear. With beauty we never reach the end, and it is inherent in its definition that this should be the case.

Chapter III

AN ART OF LANGUAGE

We have seen the role Valéry attributed to sensibility and
to intelligence in poetry; but for him poetry is essentially an
art of language.[a] Without posing as a linguist or a philosopher, he meditated at length upon this subject. His point of
departure was an intense mistrust of language; nevertheless,
he admired its power and remarked its importance in the
various realms of the mind and of action; finally, he reflected
on the possible and methodical utilization of its properties.

The idea of creating a science of language for himself
certainly haunted Valéry. It appears here and there in many
of his reflections, but he expressed it principally in a little-
known article, never reprinted since its publication in the
January 1898 *Mercure de France*.[1] Under the symptomatic
title *Méthodes*, Valéry had begun to write a kind of column
in this periodical, in which he offered, at long intervals, only
three brief studies. The second, which concerns us, took as its
pretext a book that has since become famous, Michel Bréal's
La Sémantique (*Science des significations*). Valéry assumed
that "all the transformations language can undergo must
leave invariable a certain number of properties. . . . This
residue would contain the fundamental relations of language
with what we call, by hypothesis, mind." By this means, he
glimpsed the solution of problems "now unapproachable,"
such as the definition of the substantive, of the verb, of the
sentence, and the construction of a "law of all the syntaxes
which would enclose within a single expression the many

[a] As he often repeated. See, for example, *L'Invention esthétique*
in *L'Invention*, p. 148.

necessities of the order of words, of their agreement, and which would determine the unity—with regard to comprehension—of sentences." But these problems were, to Valéry's mind, neither explored nor even raised; the best laws had only "the value of mnemotechnical means"; one did not distinguish "in their content what is constantly assumed from what is not." This impotence was a result of "the nullity of psychology."[b] This youthful condemnation of linguistics and of the psychology of language, which named no names, at least spared Bréal, who had restored "language to its sole site" and who was praised "for having disregarded . . . the shifting questions of origin . . . the search for which, beyond our experience, is purely verbal." At the end of the article, Valéry envisaged a "generalization" of semantics which would bear "on all symbolic systems, en masse": "algebra, musical notation, certain types of ornament, ciphers, etc. . . ." "All these systems and language itself" would "lead to a capital distinction among the modes by which mental states are connected."

In this article, which aims at precision and definition but is clumsily written, Valéry distinguishes two types of associations: in one, between two elements *a* and *b*, there is a "relation of sequence"; in the other, "*b* could be constructed with the help of *a*, and reciprocally." "Any variation in one of the terms will determine a variation in the other." Language consists of relations of the first type, of simple relations of sequence; in other words, of "symbolic or conventional" associations. One should then seek "what these symbols become, subject as they are to repetition, to usage, mixed with groups" of the other "type and exposed to the whim of the individual who distorts them to the ultimate limit of their value. . . ." Valéry promised "to be clearer and more complete, more copious" in another article which never appeared.

[b] On Valéry's conception of psychology, see his article of the following year, *Méthodes, Le Temps,* in the May 1899 *Mercure de France,* p. 485: ". . . a formal psychology to surround and situate formal logic . . . psychology can become a science only when we know why we do not think of everything at once. Then this new science will be, in a sense, the *Geometry of Time*—that is, the summary of the laws according to which states of consciousness replace and reflect each other."

This promise "to determine the fundamental hypotheses of language" was never kept, but certain elements of these pages served as seeds of later reflections. Perhaps Valéry meanwhile realized that the problems which interested him had not been so neglected as he thought. In any case, his ambitious project seems to have been completely abandoned. This was perhaps the last great dream of his youth.[c]

As a matter of fact, the bulk of the program discouraged Valéry. He was to return several times, but in a cursory and quite negative fashion, to the relations of language with the individual and with society; he was to abandon entirely, at least in his publications, the complicated questions of syntax and its relations with thought; he was to entrench himself almost exclusively in a general criticism of vocabulary and in the sample analysis of several terms. He retained, from an excessive undertaking, only what could be of immediate use to him in defining and recording his personal ideas.

In his preface to the second English translation of the *Soirée avec Monsieur Teste*, Valéry was to speak of "this strange brain . . . in which language is always on trial."[2] Valéry's hero displays the linguistic behavior which corresponds to his author's ideal:

> He talked, and without being able to define the motives or the extent of the proscription, one realized that a great number of words were banished from his discourse. Those he used were so curiously uttered by his voice, or illuminated by his sentence structure, that their weight was altered, their value new. At times, they lost all their meaning, they seemed to occupy only an empty place whose assigned term was as yet dubious or unforeseen by the language. I have heard him designate a physical object by a group of abstract words and proper nouns.[d]

Valéry himself, in his personal notes, forbade himself the use of certain words for a period of several years: "I tried to

[c] I do not think Valéry ever alluded to symbolic logic, but he told Charles Du Bos (*Journal*, January 30, 1923) that one would have to be at least a Leibnitz to dare broach the greatest problems.

[d] *La Soirée avec Monsieur Teste* in *Monsieur Teste*, pp. 21–22. On the way in which Valéry's voice put the word *soul* in quotation marks, "with a mixture of grace, ironic half-playfulness and modesty," see Charles Du Bos, *Journal*, January 30, 1923, p. 223.

substitute for them an expression which said only what I meant. If I did not find it, I marked them with a sign that indicated that their status was precarious."[3] The coefficient of precariousness and periphrasis would therefore be a means of protecting oneself against the inadequacy and imprecision of the terms. As for the words "so curiously uttered" by Monsieur Teste's voice, do we not hear them, in the collections of notes, italicized, detached by dashes, bracketed by quotation marks, altered and emphasized by methods of style which isolate, counterpose, or cast them into a singular position within the discourse?

"I mistrust all words," says Monsieur Teste's correspondent in the *Lettre d'un ami*.[4] Many of these words designate vague and, in some sense, illustrious notions. Valéry indicated them by two very picturesque denigrating images; he sometimes called them *trombones*[5] and sometimes *parrots*,[e] depending on whether he wanted to stigmatize their garish effects or their imprecise meanings. A splendid list could be compiled of the words Valéry particularly incriminated. He blamed many of them for being multivocal. He wrote to Pierre Louÿs:

> To think that even today, in ordinary speech, the word *force* designates simultaneously and indiscriminately ten very different notions, of which only *one* retains this dynamic meaning.
> Thus we call *force* what is, depending on cases: effort, intensity, energy, main force (which is not a force), acceleration, labor, power, even duration, etc. . . . I am forgetting some.[6]
> It is impossible to be sure that single, uniform, and constant meanings correspond to words like *reason, universe, cause, matter,* or *idea*.[7]

Any attempt to "define the meaning of such terms . . . ends by introducing under the same name a new object of thought which opposes the original one to the degree that it is new."[8] Worst of all, it is enough to consider a word for it to become obscure: ". . . a certain word, which is quite clear

---

[e] *L'Idée fixe*, pp. 114–19 and 146–47. He also speaks of *"big words: truth, god, justice . . ."* and of *"false notes: soul . . ."* in *Propos me concernant*, pp. 18, 27.

when you hear it or use it in ordinary speech . . . becomes magically cumbrous . . . as soon as you withdraw it from circulation in order to examine it separately. . . ." Thus a word like *time* or *life* "changes into a riddle, an abyss, an agony of thought. . . . This easily observable phenomenon has assumed for me a great critical value."[9] One might even attempt to break down the mental complex designated by the multivocal term into simple elements: "I have tried," he wrote to Louÿs, "to make an analysis of the notion of *time* which separates it into 'pure' notions that can no longer be confused. I am not saying I have succeeded."[10]

> The language of things of the mind is, by nature, disheartening. Words like *will, memory, idea, intelligence, time,* etc. . . . etc. . . . ! They will do for ordinary usage. But an attempt must be made to find sharper tools.[11]

A number of *Rhumbs* and of *Analecta* are sample analyses of this kind. But such analysis turns out to be endless, as Valéry reveals by the ingenious comparison of the microscope:

> Necessary and even sufficient to the rapid movement of the exchanges of thoughts, nonetheless, there is not a single one of these imperfect and indispensable notions which bears being considered in itself. As soon as our attention lingers over them, we immediately perceive a confusion of heterogeneous examples and uses that can never be reduced. What was clear in passing, and so vitally *understood,* becomes obscure when it is fixed; what was simple decomposes; what was with us is against us. A little turn of a mysterious screw modifies the microscope of consciousness, increases the magnification of our attention by its duration, suffices to show us our inner perplexity.
>
> Insist ever so little, for example, on nouns like *time, universe, race, form, nature, poetry,* etc., and you will see them subdivide indefinitely, becoming impassable.[f]

Valéry has very subtly illuminated the double system of words, depending on whether they are used in ordinary

---

[f] *Propos sur l'intelligence* in *Oeuvres complètes,* vol. D, pp. 86–87. The comparison is employed again in *L'Idée fixe,* pp. 115–16.

speech or whether they are picked out by the searchlight of
consciousness. In a comparison that suggests Montaigne, he
considers the word used without special concern as "one of
those thin planks thrown over a ditch, or across a mountain
crevasse . . ."; man must "cross it without bearing down . . .
without stopping—and above all, must not divert himself by
dancing on the slender plank to test its resistance!"[12] Such
words, as a matter of fact, "suffer movement, not arrest. A
man in rapid motion passes over them, and escapes; but if he
insists at all, this brief interval breaks them, and everything
collapses into the abyss."[13]

> Just a moment ago, they helped us to understand our-
> selves; now they change into occasions to confuse
> ourselves. They were imperceptibly united with our in-
> tentions and our actions, like limbs so docile that we
> forget them, and now reflection sets them against us,
> transforms them into obstacles, into resistances. It is as
> if, indeed, words in movement and in combination were
> quite different from the same words inert and isolated.[14]

It is of course the difference in attention which provokes
this impression; but Valéry relates it to the rapidity of discourse: "We understand others . . . and we understand ourselves only as a result of *the speed of our passage through
words*."[15] "A man in haste has understood; one must not
dwell on meanings: one would soon find that the clearest
language is laced with obscure terms."[16]

Valéry proposed renouncing some of them categorically:
"*Time, space, infinity* are inconvenient words. Every proposition which seeks precision abandons them."[17] But of course
he could not do without them (he has, for instance, a theory
of what he calls the "aesthetic infinite"). "I am obliged by
profession to employ a host of vague words and to go through
the motions of speculating on them, by them. But within myself, they are worthless."[18] These are words "good for talking," like *nature, life,* etc. "Hearing them, I have the feeling
of inadequacy, a sense of the provisional, the incomplete.
Anything one might say is utterly vitiated by them."[19] In a
lecture given at the Société française de Philosophie, he
refused to use the words *beau, agréable, gracieux,* because

they were not objective.[g] At the Centre international de synthèse, he declared he did not know what *subconscious* meant.[h]

Valéry went further than the exclusion of ordinary but ill-defined words. He asserted that for the individual the reduction of his lexicon was always desirable. "A limited vocabulary, but one from which one can form many combinations, is worth more than thirty thousand words which merely encumber the acts of the mind."[20] This notion sheds light on Valéry's poetic vocabulary. He belongs to that family of poets, which includes Racine and Mallarmé, whose choice of words is exquisitely limited, whose poverty of vocabulary is compensated by the magical incandescence of certain "star" words which become representative of and somehow inseparable from their regenerators. This power, moreover, is not forbidden to copious authors who employ all the resources of the language; there are Hugolian, Balzacian terms that we recognize and salute as they pass in the parade of language. Valéry is convinced, in any case, that the interior monologue spontaneously avoids a great number of words:

> Thought never employs certain words for its own ends, words which seem to it suitable for external use only; nor certain others, whose content it does not perceive and which can only deceive thought as to its real power and value.[21]

The language of the self, moreover, is extremely limited:

> The soul alone with itself . . . never uses more than *a small number of* words, and *no unusual ones.*[22]

At the very least, before dealing with a problem, it is wise to analyze the vague notions involved. "I do not understand how one can speculate on such matters before undertaking

[g] *Réflexions sur l'art* in *Bulletin de la Société française de Philosophie,* 1935, p. 88. Also see in *Rhumbs* in *Tel Quel,* II, p. 46: " 'Truth, beauty,' these are very old notions which no longer correspond to the requisite precision," and in *Notes sur un tragique et une tragédie,* p. viii: "four essential terms which cannot be defined: 'God, FATE, Freedom, Chance.' "

[h] *Invention esthétique, Discussion* in *L'Invention,* p. 156. On his reluctance to use the word *subconscious,* see the whole of lecture 18 in the *Cours de poétique.*

this labor, yet such is the custom."²³ On several occasions he discussed this cautionary measure, which he termed "the mopping-up of the verbal situation."²⁴ Confronting a "system of words" to which a group of vague notions corresponds, Valéry was in the habit of clearing "the verbal field."²⁵ He compared himself "to the surgeons who first disinfect their hands and prepare their operating table."ⁱ But it is upon the entire terminology one proposes to employ that this prelimi- nary labor should be undertaken: "If I were to attempt to produce a philosophy for myself (may God forbid), I should begin by completely rewriting my dictionary."²⁶ As a matter of fact, for a long time Valéry pursued an undertaking of this nature: "I have tried to create for myself a 'philosophical language,'"²⁷ that is, essentially definitions: "An enormous part of my work, half wasted, half useful, was to work out definitions for myself. To think by means of my own defini- tions was for me a kind of goal."²⁸ This was the transforma- tion of Monsieur Teste into Sisyphus: "I have spent almost the whole of my conscious life creating a kind of 'philosophi- cal dictionary' for my own use—under perpetual, more or less happy revision. . . ."²⁹

Thus Valéry reached the point of trying to illuminate and stabilize the meaning of some of the very words he was indict- ing. For example, apropos of the word *mind*, he doubtless feared being accused in his turn of "making a parrot speak," for he specified that he did not "at all mean a metaphysical entity," but ". . . a power of transformation . . ." whose characteristics he specified, and he allowed himself a *satis- fecit*: ". . . you see that there is a way of defining mind which involves no metaphysic, but which simply gives this word the irreproachable meaning of an observation; which makes it, in a way, the symbol of a group of quite objective observations."³⁰ This is what should be done for such words as *time, matter;* this is what he did "without publishing any- thing, moreover . . . in the case of the word *point*, for which there exists no adequate definition."ʲ

ⁱ *Poésie et pensée abstraite* in *Variété V*, p. 131. See also the letter to M. Jean de Latour in *Examen de Valéry*, note, pp. 130–31.

ʲ Jean de Latour, *Examen de Valéry*, note, pp. 130–31. See how- ever *Analecta*, CVIII, on the relation of point and space.

Whatever Valéry says, the systematic exclusion of a part of the vocabulary, the criticism of certain terms leading to confusion, and the preliminary establishment of a precise terminology are well-known practices, and even traditional ones in many disciplines. The same is true of another practice to which Valéry occasionally resorted, notably in *L'Idée fixe:* the partial creation of a terminology regarded as useful, either by neologism or by the adoption of a term to which a special acceptation is given. *Implex, mental nebula,* and *omnivalence* are described by him, moreover, as "inconsequential amusements," but "most of the notions employed in Psychology are, in truth, not much more 'convenient' or precise."[k]

There exist, however, for Valéry certain precise definitions, the kind "necessarily lacking [in the] ordinary philosophical vocabulary [which] presents that vice of necessarily assuming the appearances of a technical language. . . . The only precise definitions are instrumental ones (that is, definitions which reduce themselves to actions, such as to designate an object or to perform an operation)."[31] Here again we find the same exigency and the same limitation as in Valéry's theory of knowledge; only results have any value, the actions which succeed. We are curious, at this point, to know some of these terms which for Valéry are reliable tools. In his book on Degas, it is evident that he particularly prizes "nautical language" or "that of venery"; he has great praise for these nomenclatures because in them one finds only the "names of what one can see and do," one "knows what one wants," and nothing involves one "in any metaphysic." Thus Valéry also admires the vocabulary of primitive peoples, "in whom the faculties of observation are to ours what the dog's sense of smell is to man's," and some of whom "possess no less than fourteen verbs to designate the fourteen movements of an alligator's head."[l] A moment ago, the restriction of vocabulary was extolled; now the diversity of that of savages is ad-

---

[k] *L'Idée fixe,* pp. 10–11. Note the doctor's remark, p. 104: "Monsieur is creating his own little terminology."

[l] *Degas. Danse. Dessin,* pp. 148–54. The concrete diversity of the vocabulary of certain tribes is misleading; it is linked to the incapacity to abstract.

mired, and Valéry even complains of the poverty of that of civilized men:

> One must never miss an opportunity to emphasize the great poverty of the "psychological" vocabulary. Although a little less indigent than ours in terms of this order, the English language offers no better occasion for distinguishing what we would like to discriminate—what we try to discern by the words: *psychic, mental, intellectual.* . . .[32]

When he was writing *La Jeune Parque*, Valéry had already deplored the extreme poverty of our psychological language, which he had had "to impoverish still further, since the majority of the words that compose it are incompatible with the poetic tone."[33]

The true model of an exact language Valéry finds, of course, in mathematics. Whence this prophecy: ". . . the future will be able to construct a language for the intellect . . . on the model of algebra and geometry."[34] "No more profound revolution than the one which will replace the old language and the old *vague* ideas by a *clear* language and *clear* ideas."[35] It is to the future that the young man's dream is now entrusted.

THE POWER OF LANGUAGE

Inadequate as it seemed to him, language enjoyed a great prestige in Valéry's opinion. We sense, in his early article on Bréal's *Sémantique,* to what degree the young man of twenty-six was sensitive to the pathos of a simple page. Valéry, who was to say so magnificently of Mallarmé, apropos of the *Coup de dés,* in a formula which combines the resonance of Pascal and that of Kant: "He tried . . . to raise a page to the power of the starry sky";[m] was already, it is clear, in the

---

[m] *Le Coup de dés* in *Variété II,* p. 199. In his diatribe against Pascal, *Variation sur une "pensée"* in *Variété,* p. 141, Valéry recalls Kant's famous formula on the moral law and the starry sky. This opposition between the two philosophers was quite available to Valéry in Brunschvicg's note to *pensée* 206 in his little edition of *Pensées et Opuscules.*

grip of that "infinitely connected system," that "incalculable
network" which any text constitutes. He proposes to imagine
the text's "grammatical differences, that is, its laws of plurality, of existence in duration, its psychological nature," then,
adopting the historical, linguistic, and etymological viewpoint
("even if such knowledge is not very certain, it will stand for
true knowledge") to appraise the topographical alteration
effected when words are "associated at their historical stage."

> One will have the impression produced by a monu-
> ment whose members are ancient, whose orders bar-
> barian; or that evoked by a poor man, dressed in ragged
> newspapers which he has pasted together into an im-
> provised shirt. One smiles then at stirring up all this to
> write the least line. A cruel awareness gives the least
> line the grandeur of Wagram, the difficulty of lunar
> theory; and one writes millions of them without even
> suspecting it.[36]

He must have experienced while still very young, even
before his first verses, the power of the word, its metamorphic
force, to write:

> We never know at what point, and to what knot of his
> nerves, someone is affected by a word—I mean: an insig-
> nificant word.
> *Affected*—that is, changed. A word suddenly matures a
> child.[37]

Language permits us to influence the individual: "Speech
is the government of one man by another." One cannot escape it, for however I react, "I am obeying: it was possible
to anticipate my reaction."[38] By the exactitude of his remarks, "merely human" though they are, Monsieur Teste,
the man of lucidity, will carry very far the capacity of putting
himself "prodigiously" in his wife's place: "There is in his
language some mysterious power of making visible and audi-
ble what is most hidden about oneself. . . ."[39] Valéry praised
the rhetor and the sophist, brothers of the man of action, and
he curiously enough regarded as writers certain illustrious
manipulators of peoples: "Napoleon, Caesar, Frederick the
Great—men of letters, eminently endowed for the control of

men and things—by words."[40] The very defects of language
generate powerful sentiments, and even progress:

> Our enthusiasms, our antagonisms depend directly on
> the vices of our language; its uncertainties favor the di-
> vergences, the objections, and all those gropings of intel-
> lectual combatants. They happily keep minds from ever
> achieving repose. . . . One can be sure, leafing through
> history, that a dispute which is not fruitless is a dispute
> without importance.[41]

If language is powerful, its power can be exploited. Phaedrus, in *Eupalinos,* designates it as creative: "No geometry
without speech."[42] The geometrical figures are those "which
are traces of such movements as we can express in few
words."[43] For without speech, "figures are accidents," but by
speech "we know . . . how to construct or enrich space, by
means of properly connected discourse." "Language is con-
structive." It is also "the source of fables," and Phaedrus is
about to say "the very father of the gods" when Socrates in-
terrupts to keep him from being impious. At the end of the
dialogue, we learn that immortality too consists only of words.
Meanwhile Socrates develops an elegant allegory based on
the three aspects of language: vulgar speech, the expression
of the Muses, and the language of the intelligence.

> An altar one would raise to language should present to
> view three faces, variously decorated; and if I had to
> represent it in the form of human appearances, I should
> give it three countenances: one, almost shapeless, would
> signify common speech, which is no sooner born than it
> dies, and which is lost at once, by its very usage. It is
> immediately transformed into the bread asked for, into
> the road pointed out, into the anger of the man insulted.
> . . . But the second face would release, through its
> rounded mouth, a crystalline flood of eternal water: it
> would have the noblest features, large and enthusiastic
> eyes; a powerful, swollen neck, even as the sculptors
> give to the Muses.

> PHAEDRUS
>
> And the third?
>
> SOCRATES
>
> By Apollo, how represent this one? . . . It would re-

quire some inhuman physiognomy, with features of that rigor and subtlety which it is said the Egyptians were able to figure on the countenance of their gods.

PHAEDRUS

What is said is true. Cunning, riddles, an almost cruel precision, an implacable and quasi-bestial finesse; all the signs of feline attention and a ferocious spirituality are evident on the simulacra of these hard divinities. The skillfully proportioned mixture of acuity and coldness inspires the soul with uneasiness and a particular anxiety. And these monsters of silence and lucidity, infinitely calm, infinitely alert, rigid, and seemingly endowed with imminence, or with a momentary flexibility, look like Intelligence itself, an impenetrable animal which penetrates everything.[44]

Is this not the alarming Monsieur Teste encountered once again in the unexpected form of an Egyptian god? Madame Teste occasionally compared her husband to a sphinx. . . . For the Greeks, finally, to whom "all things are forms," who never get lost in their thoughts, and who retain of those thoughts only their relations, one and the same name designates language, reason, and calculation.

Thus language becomes the father of all things of the mind, and especially of the arts and sciences. This would be no more than an old theme if Valéry did not renew it, in *Eupalinos,* by the glamor of his rhetoric and, elsewhere, by insights of detail. Philosophy, its ambition doomed to failure, is nonetheless "an enterprise whose goal is the fulfillment of knowledge insofar as it can be reduced to the functions and combinations of language."[45] In his article *Autour de Corot,* Valéry emphasized the importance of speech in the arts: ". . . all the arts live on words"; and showed that great artists were apt to be great theoreticians.[46] We know how large a part, in his opinion, the speculation of poets plays in the elaboration of their works. But Valéry insisted above all on the literary exploitation of language. Literature as a whole is merely "a development of certain linguistic properties . . . most active among primitive peoples . . ."[n] and language

[n] *Discours prononcé à la Maison d'Éducation de la Légion d'Honneur de Saint-Denis* in *Variété IV,* p. 151. Cf. *De l'en-*

recovers its beauty only by returning to its sources and ridding itself of contemporary vulgarity. "The more beautiful the form, the more it suggests the origins of consciousness and expression; the more conscious it is, the more it seeks to recover, by a kind of synthesis, the integrity of the still-new language in its creative state."[47] Further, the various genres of literature are all based on a special possibility of language: "Every literary genre being the result of some particular use of discourse, the novel can abuse the immediate and significative power of speech to communicate one or several imaginary 'lives.' "[48]

Poetry utilizes language in a very special way. It is thereby distinguished from philosophy, from any search for truth: "In the magic forest of language, the poets advance specifically to get lost, and to intoxicate themselves in the wilderness, seeking the intersections of meaning, unexpected echoes, strange encounters: they do not fear deviations, or surprises, or darkness . . . but the huntsman who spurs himself on to pursue 'truth,' to follow a single, continuous path . . . risks capturing only his own shadow."[49] Poetry is also distinguished from science: Phaedrus, in *Eupalinos*, tells us that only simple words (among the simplest are numbers) are appropriate for calculations. The others afford too many difficulties:

It is because they were created separately; some at a particular moment, and by a particular need; others in another circumstance. A single aspect of things, a single desire, a single spirit has not instituted them as by a single act. Their entirety is therefore appropriate to no particular use, and it is impossible to lead them to certain remote developments, without getting lost in their infinite ramifications. . . . Hence we must adjust these complex words like irregular blocks of stone, speculating on the possibilities and the surprises which arrangements of this kind reserve for us, and giving the name of "poets" to those whom fortune favors in this labor.[50]

This is already a whole *ars poetica*. Yet a *rapprochement*

_____

seignement de la poétique au Collège de France in *Variété V*, p. 289: "Literature is and can only be a kind of extension and application of certain properties of Language."

can be made between poetry and philosophy or science. There are in philosophy certain "verbal nebulae to resolve," an interior spectacle of the transformations of thought, "an exercise of thought upon itself," which can make it comparable to poetry.[51] But elsewhere Valéry preferred poetry and geometry to philosophy, because both the former, "each according to its nature, use language properly and frankly (each fully exploiting some real property), and can use it *without the slightest illusion* (of which they have no need)."[52]

But if we would understand the role of language in poetry, it is with ordinary language as it is used in speech that we must contrast it:

> Language, however intimate it may be within us, however close the fact of thinking in words may be to our soul, is nonetheless of *statistical origin* and of *purely practical destination*. Now, the problem must be to *derive from this practical instrument the means of executing an essentially nonpractical work*.[53]

"To write, then, seemed to me an undertaking very different from immediate expression," Valéry was to say in *Mémoires d'un Poème*.[54] Language is susceptible of two kinds of effects: in the communication of a thought—in conversation, for example—words are abolished immediately for the sake of comprehension, "they are replaced by a counterpart, by images, by relations, by impulses," themselves susceptible of a retransmission in an altogether different language. To understand is to substitute "for a system of sonorities, durations, and signs . . . a modification or an internal reorganization of the person." Thus "the person who has *not* understood repeats, or asks to have repeated, the words that have been spoken." But it happens that the sound of a sentence arrests us, and returns to us; the sentence "has assumed a value . . . at the expense of its finite signification. . . . It has created the need to be heard again. . . . Here we are on the very brink of poetry." This "sensuous form" which "assumes by its own effect an importance such that it prevails and in a sense commands respect," even "commands desire and hence repetition," disposes us to live "according to a system and under laws which are no longer of the practical order."[55] There is a "universe of language," in which "the poet arranges words quite differently from the way usage and necessity do. . . ." They are "the same words, but not at all the same values."[56] There is, moreover, in the poet, a proportion of the two languages, the one natural, the other purified and luxurious.[57] Yet the partition between the two is not absolutely watertight. Valéry contested M. Lucien Fabre's use of certain words difficult for poetic language to absorb, but "this language changes like the other, and the geometric terms . . . will perhaps dissolve in the long run, as so many other technical words have done, into the abstract and homogeneous metal of the language of the gods."[58]

The writer's language must be personal. This is one of the rare cases when, without using the word, Valéry recommends originality, and the advice applies to prose as to poetry: "Best of all would be to think in a form one has invented."[59] "Every jealously and powerfully personal self creates its own secret language."[60] "The powerful mind . . . mints its own coin."[61] We can guess the language toward which Valéry's taste inclines him. He seeks a style which recreates not only thought but language itself.

> I value, and can only value, the writers who manage to express what I have found difficult to express, if the problem of expressing it has ever been proposed to, or imposed upon, me.
>
> This is the only case in which I can measure a value in absolute units—that is, *my own*.
>
> I can admire in other cases; but it is an admiration of pure impression.
>
> I should also say that I value the writer's act only insofar as it seems to me of the nature and the power of an advance in the order of language.[62]

The limit of this advance is a mathematical rigor:

> My preference for the clear, for the pure, for the complete, for the adequate, leads to a system of substitutions —which functions like a linguistic underpinning—replacing language by a kind of algebra—and for *images* attempts to substitute *figures*—reduced to their useful

properties. —Thereby automatically creating a unification of the physical and the psychic world.[63]

This rigor is not as alien to poetry as one might think. In a curious passage, Valéry shows, in Racine and in La Fontaine, a language imbued with their persons; or at least with the person whom they cause to speak, but he notes, in contrast, in Hugo and in Mallarmé, a language detached from the person and, in a sense, inhuman:

> Racinian discourse comes out of the mouth of a living person, though always a rather pompous one.
> The same is true of La Fontaine; but the person is familiar, sometimes quite careless.
> On the contrary, in Hugo, in Mallarmé and several other authors, there appears a tendency to form non-human and in some sense *absolute* discourse—discourse which suggests some being independent of any person —a divinity of language—which the Omnipotence of the Sum of Words illuminates. It is the faculty of speech which is speaking; and in speaking, becomes intoxicated; and intoxicated, dances.[64]

This passage reveals the Valerian ideal. The point is to achieve a style in which it is not so much the poet who speaks as language itself, and whose rigor is that of inhuman science, while retaining the power of the divine charm or spell. Is this not the eulogy of language at the end of *La Pythie*, when the oracle's voice is depersonalized:

> *Honneur des Hommes, Saint LANGAGE,*
> *Discours prophétique et paré,*
> *Belles chaînes en qui s'engage*
> *Le dieu dans la chair égaré,*
> *Illumination, largesse!*
> *Voici parler une Sagesse*
> *Et sonner cette auguste Voix*
> *Qui se connaît quand elle sonne*
> *N'être plus la voix de personne*
> *Tant que des ondes et des bois!*

[Honor of mankind, sacred LANGUAGE, prophetic and embellished discourse, lovely chains which capture the god loose in the flesh, illumination, bounty! Now Wisdom speaks, now sounds that noble Voice which knows itself, when it is raised, no longer the voice of any man, but of the woods and waves!]

Thus extreme personality of form returns to impersonality. This is, indeed, the impression given by the flash of genius when it formulates itself beyond time and place like an ineluctable judgment. And it is also the distinctive character of inspiration, in which the sudden revelation seems without relation to the man who is its "victim." Rimbaud declared that we should not say "I am thinking" but "I am being thought."

A RANGE OF OPINION: FORM AND CONTENT

Between language and thought complex relations obtain which philosophers, psychologists, and philologists have often studied and which can range from quasi identity to extreme differentiation. In the literary arts, the distinction of these two realms is indispensable to analysis, whatever the relation established between them. It rules a whole series of pairs of ideas: matter and manner, form and content, intention and expression, etc. . . . Valéry employed in particular the general antinomy *form and content* [*forme et fond*], and from a more specialized point of view, the opposition *sound and sense*. We shall see how he understood and applied to poetry these two simple systems of relation.

Valéry praised, in the writers who set themselves in opposition to romanticism, "the desire for a more solid substance, and a form that would be more dextrous and pure."[65] This was to postulate a superiority of both content and form. There is no doubt—and Valéry's work, like that of the poets he admires (Baudelaire and especially Mallarmé), attests to it—that this double requirement seemed essential to him. We must not forget it when he seems to sacrifice one factor for the other. Indeed, depending on the rather numerous viewpoints that can be adopted, the relation between the two notions can change to the advantage of one or the other, their proportion can vary, and their predominance be reversed. Thus we get a whole array of opinions. To show this, we shall follow Valéry's thought in its several variations, pursuing its shifts of emphasis, changing our angle of vision with his, and we shall observe an almost continuous transition which causes the importance of content to diminish, and that of form to increase.

Valéry does not like eloquence. The rhetoric of the politician who inflames a naïve public seems to a lucid and cool-headed observer a mask which betrays the weakness of the thought.

> The form refutes the content. The heat of the manner, the energy of the orator, his outbursts, his images, his talent, his genius . . . so many crushing arguments against the content.
> Powerful arguments are naked.
> But if one must embellish and arm them—crushing argument against the audience.[66]

This form without embellishment, which reveals the idea in all its purity, could be an ideal of prose, or even pure prose. But as a matter of fact, language here merely corresponds perfectly to the normal function Valéry assigns it, which is to transform itself instantaneously into "nonlanguage," to transmit thought. "The essence of prose is to perish—that is, to be 'understood.'"° Which is the triumph, from this point of view, of content over form.

Poetry has quite contrary requirements. The content cannot suffice. This is why, according to Valéry, Boileau was talking nonsense when he said:

Et mon vers, bien ou mal, dit toujours quelque chose.

[And my verse, good or bad, always says something.]

and nonsense "aggravated by that abominable *bien ou mal*."[67] The poet is not the man who may rest content, if it is raining, with saying: It is raining. "There is no need of a

---

° *Au sujet du "Cimetière marin"* in *Variété III*, p. 66. See also *L'Invention esthétique* in *L'Invention*, p. 149: ". . . the practical language is destroyed, reabsorbed, once the goal is attained (comprehension)," and *Poésie et pensée abstraite* in *Variété V*, p. 144: "In the practical or abstract uses of language, the form . . . is not preserved."

persuade us to take our umbrella."[68] In poetry, con-
... mands a luxurious and sensuous form, of a particular
value:

> Poetry is quite pagan: it imperiously requires that
> there be no soul without a body—no *meaning*, no *idea*
> which is not the act of some remarkable figure, con-
> structed of timbres, of durations and intensities.[69]

Yet thought has its importance in poetry, where it must in-
sinuate itself with special precautions which separate it from
prose:

> Thought must be hidden in verse like the nutritive
> virtue in a fruit. A fruit is nourishment, but seems only
> delicacy. One perceives only the pleasure, but one re-
> ceives a substance. The enchantment conceals this im-
> perceptible nourishment which it conveys.[p]

We have here a new relation of form and content: it is the
dissimulation of the content beneath the form which is advocated.

Hitherto the thought has not been modified in its value.
But Valéry often declared that a true poet does not hesitate
to sacrifice it, if this is necessary. Boileau recommends

Que toujours le bon sens s'accorde avec la rime.

[that good sense always fit the rhyme.]

Valéry, on the contrary, asserts that "reason would have
the poet prefer rhyme to reason."[q] This is because poetry

---

[p] *Littérature* in *Tel quel*, I, p. 144. *Calepin d'un poète* in
Oeuvres complètes, vol. C, p. 190, gave a different version: "Enchantment, that is the nourishment it conveys." Was there a copy-
ist's error in this first version, or an application, in the second, of
the procedure which finds a new meaning by modifying the form?

[q] On the difficulty of bringing the two requirements into agreement, see the *Cours de poétique*: "To combine the values of sensibility and signification is possible in poetry only at the cost of
reciprocal sacrifices: one must pay in values of sense for what one
gains in values of sensation. Thus we shall arrive, for example, at
inconsistencies, but inconsistencies which will tally with the requirements of musical or visual sensibility; and on the other hand,
we shall be obliged to write a line that has little sonority in order
to say something. Lines of poetry are not written to say something,

obeys special requirements; it seeks, by every means, to re-unite with music. Ordinary language lends itself awkwardly to this song of speech, and the very nature of thought hampers, in certain respects, the musicalization of the poem. Valéry has given a remarkable exposition of this viewpoint in his article on Père Cyprien:

A poet, in general, can bring his work to its conclusion only if he can command his initial or leading thought, impose upon it all the (often very great) modifications which the desire to satisfy the requirements of execution suggests. Thought is an immediate, provisional activity, mingled with a diverse inner language of precarious glimmerings, of futureless beginnings; but also rich in possibilities often so abundant and seductive that they encumber their man more than they bring him closer to his goal. If he is a true poet, he will almost always sacrifice to form (which, after all, is the end and the act itself, with its organic necessities) that thought which cannot be dissolved into the poem if its expression requires the use of words or phrases alien to the poetic tone. An intimate alliance of sound and sense, which is the essential characteristic of expression in poetry, can be achieved only at the expense of something—and that something is thought. Conversely, all thought which must define and ultimately justify itself turns away and frees itself from rhythm, number, timbre—in a word, from any search for the sensuous qualities of language. A demonstration does not sing. . . .[70]

Valéry asserted that Racine would have changed Phèdre's character rather than write a bad line.[71] And declared of himself: "I subordinate (the closer I am to my *best condition*) 'content' to 'form'—always ready to sacrifice the *former* for the *latter*."[72] He had written to Pierre Louÿs, apropos of his *Poétique:* "It is not certain that it is necessary or advisable to say exactly what one meant,"[73] and one of the notes in *Rhumbs* specifies: "It is not always good to be one-

_____

but after all, it must be done now and then" (lecture 9). An example of these sacrifices is perhaps to be found in Baudelaire's poem *La servante au grand coeur* . . . in which the poet "has buried the cook on the lawn, which goes against custom but agrees with the rhyme." (*Littérature* in *Tel quel,* I, p. 159).

self."[74] This lesson seems contrary to the example of Baudelaire, who wanted to do exactly what he had projected. Without arguing Valéry's thesis, let us note that there are two
families of poets, those who attempt to preserve their
thought intact, and those who inflect it according to the opportunities which the accidents of formulation afford. All,
moreover, at least in details, benefit from unexpected encounters which modify and embellish the original thought.
The same is true in the other arts; the sculptor utilizes a
defect in his substance, the painter a blot or an irregularity
in the drawing . . . but this leads us to a new relation of
form and content.

In effect, if we sacrifice content to form, it is because the
latter has been suggestive. It has given ideas. By a reversal
of roles, it is now form which creates content, and, from a
slightly different viewpoint, it is form which is anterior to
content. Valéry returned very frequently to this productive
role of appearance. He regarded the utilization of unexpected
suggestions offered by the medium the very characteristic of
the poet: "A man is a poet if the difficulties inherent in his
art give him ideas—he is not if they deprive him of ideas."[75]
Whence the fruitfulness of rhyme: "There are many more
chances that a rhyme will afford a (literary) 'idea' than that
an idea will generate a rhyme. All poetry is based on this
likelihood, particularly the poetry written from 1860 to
1880. . . ."[r] It has always been known that rhyme generates
ideas. Malherbe, according to Racan, advocated the search
for "rare and sterile rhymes, claiming that they led him to
produce many new thoughts." More hesitant, Boileau recommended suiting rhyme to good sense. But Fontenelle, to
whom I think Valéry bears a certain resemblance, declared,
in his *Réflexions sur la poétique*, that rhyme is "the more
nearly perfect as the two words which form it are the more
surprised to find themselves together"; he preferred them,

---

[r] *Cahier B* in *Tel quel*, I, p. 203. Valéry said to Charles Du
Bos, *Journal*, January 30, 1923, p. 226: "You know that all Mallarmé's things were made the way you make *bouts-rimés*. I mean,
he had all his rhymes set, and nothing but his rhymes. . . . Mallarmé's system in verse is a closed system. . . . Personally, I cannot
work with set rhymes. . . ."

further, "as relaxed as they are surprised"; and with this felicitous rhyme he contrasted the overexpected rhyme, for example *âme* and *flamme*, in which there is an excessive affinity
of meaning, concerning which he said wittily: "Such rhyme
is legitimate, but it is almost a marriage . . . the words are
not surprised, but bored to be together."

Proceeding to the limit, and generalizing these cases of
fortuitous discovery, Valéry put pure form, empty of thought,
at the origin of the entire work. "One might say I took
thought as the 'unknown quantity.'"[76] He made form the
exclusive genetrix: "Beautiful works are the daughters of their
form, which is born before they are."[77] Consequently, he
strongly advised against beginning a poem with ideas and
developing them logically: "If you want to write verse and
you begin with thoughts, you are beginning with prose. In
prose, you can lay out a plan and *follow it!*"[78] Valéry gave
personal examples of poetic creation controlled by the conception of a pre-existing form. These are from his version of
the famous genesis of *The Raven:*

> A certain poem began inside me by the simple sug-
> gestion of a rhythm, *which gradually assumed a mean-
> ing.* This production, which proceeded, in a sense, from
> "form" to "content" and ended by stimulating the most
> conscious labor starting from an empty structure, was
> doubtless related to the preoccupation which had con-
> cerned me for several years, the determination of the
> general conditions of all thought, whatever its content.[79]

This was how *Le Cimetière marin* was born. *La Pythie* had
its origin in an octosyllabic line which completed itself. Another time, a combination of rhythms reached the wrong destination. It needed a composer; it was a poet who received
it: ". . . the substance of a musical work was liberally given
to me; but I lacked the organization which might have
grasped, fixed, reshaped it."[80]

We find in *Léonard et les philosophes* an exposition of this
curious idealism, which tends to make form into an idea of
which the work would be only an effect. The idea of a form
is equivalent, for the artist, to the idea which demands a
form. "A type of sentence can precede any sentence. The

masses of a painting be established before the subject."[81] In Mallarmé, "the 'content' is no longer *cause* of the 'form'; it is one of its effects."[82] In a somewhat different aspect, Valéry explained to the Société française de Philosophie how the means pre-exist and determine their end.[83] "There are some men in whom the development of means becomes so advanced . . . that they manage to 'think,' to 'invent' in the world of execution, starting from the means themselves."[84] Finally, a larger generalization presents all the arts as a deduction from their elements:

. . . music deduced from the properties of sounds; architecture deduced from matter and forces; literature, from the possession of language and from its singular role and from its modifications—in a word, the real part of the arts stimulating their imaginary part, the possible act creating its object . . . such is the consequence of a virtuosity acquired and transcended.[85]

And Valéry added modern geometry to these examples. Here again we find the scientific ideal of an infallible aesthetic. But we have shifted to a higher level in the hierarchy of powers: the form which creates content has been expressly given to us as the real part of the arts in opposition to their imaginary part. . . . Socrates says in *Eupalinos*: "The reality of a speech is, after all, that song and that color of a voice which we wrongly treat as details and accidents."[86]

Valéry carried this idea to extremes by denying content its value: "What is called the 'content' or the 'subject' of works, and which I prefer to call their 'mythical' part or aspect, seemed to me of secondary interest. As, in a proof, one takes a particular case 'to stabilize ideas,' so according to my speculative tastes one should treat 'subjects.' I was trying to reduce idolatry to a minimum."[87] In everyday life, according to the doctor in *L'Idée fixe*, "the way of speaking says more than what one says. . . . The content has no . . . essential importance. 'Oddly enough,' his easily recognizable interlocutor replies, 'that's a theory of poetry.'"[88] In the work, the subject has no importance, it is a pretext. "The subject of a work is what a bad work is reduced to."[89] "The *subject* of a poem is as alien and as important to it as his *name* is to a man."[90] The idea-content of the work is no longer of any importance; its value is entirely relative to time and to persons. Apropos of Bossuet, Valéry says:

> Three centuries of profound changes, of revolutions in all genres . . . make necessarily naïve, or alien, and sometimes inconceivable to the posterity that we are, the substance of works produced by an age so different from our own. . . . The value of ideas is indeterminate; it varies with persons and periods. What one considers profound is to another an insipidly obvious or an insupportable absurdity.[91]

What truly constitutes the work is its form, and it is form alone which ensures its duration:

> . . . the structure of the expression has a kind of reality while the meaning or the idea is merely a shadow.[92]
> The form is the skeleton of works; there are works which have none. All works die; but those which had a skeleton last much longer by this vestige than the others which were only protoplasm.[93]
> Experience shows that works resist the dreadful test, the urgent and constantly renewed rivalry of later creations by only one of their qualities, which is form.[94]

Bossuet is a "treasury of figures, of coordinated combinations and operations." One can "passionately admire these compositions of the highest style," like "the architecture of temples whose sanctuary is empty and whose inspiring sentiments and causes have long since faded away. The arch remains." But the "thoughts to be found in Bossuet . . . seem today scarcely likely to excite our minds very intensely."[95] What lasts is the form, not the content.

The highest value is thus shifted from content to form. There remains, it appears, little to add to this revolution, except to grant form the ancient prestige which the traditional consciousness attached to thought rather than to its expression. Thus it must be said that form has more content than content has. That is what some believe, against the "pure superstition" of the majority of readers:

> Audaciously they hold that the structure of expression has a kind of reality, while the meaning or the idea is

merely a shadow. . . . For these lovers of form, a form, although always provoked or required by thought, has more value, and even meaning, than any thought. In forms they consider the vigor and elegance of *acts;* and in thoughts they find only the instability of *events.*[8]

The poet is urged to accept the superiority of his morphological faith over the naïveté of the believers in thought:

> POET. Your species of verbal materialism.
> You can consider from *on high* novelists, philosophers, and all those who are subject to the word by credulity; who *must* believe that their discourse is *real* by its content and who *must* signify some reality. But you, you know that the reality of discourse is its words, the words only, and the forms.[96]

We are here close to substituting form for content, and that is what Valéry tends to do when he declares: "What is 'form' for most people is 'content' for me."[97] But this still permits the two notions to subsist. A last step remains to be taken, which consists in reabsorbing content by form. It is sufficient to establish that content is only a form of inferior quality. The opposition of form and meaning "has meaning only in the practical world, where there is an immediate exchange of words for acts and acts for words"; what is called

> . . . content is only an impure form—that is, a *mixed* one. Our *content* consists of incidents and incoherent appearances: sensations, images of all kinds, impulses, isolated words, fragments of sentences. . . . But in order to transmit what demands to be transmitted and *wills* to be disengaged from this chaos, all these heterogeneous elements must be represented in the unified system of language, and out of them some discourse must be formed. This transposition of internal events into formulas consisting of signs of the same species—*equally conventional*—can indeed be regarded as the transition from a *less pure form* or appearance to one that is *purer.*[98]

Already, in *Eupalinos,* Socrates says: ". . . for Greeks like ourselves, all things are forms."[99]

---

[8] *Sur Bossuet* in *Variété II,* p. 46. Valéry will make his Faust say: "Ideas cost nothing. . . . What counts is form" (*Lust* in *"Mon Faust,"* p. 89).

We can perhaps go still further and consider ideas as particular cases or various accidents of language. Mallarmé

> . . . conceived and set *above all works* the conscious possession of the function of language and the sentiment of a higher freedom of expression in regard to which all thought is only an incident, a particular event. . . .[100]

Valéry praised in his master "the verbal power of combining, for some supreme end, *ideas that are born of words,*[101] and recognized in Hugo a power of the same nature:

> In him, form is supreme. The act which creates form dominates in him entirely. This sovereign form is in some way stronger than he is, he is like a man possessed by poetic language. What is called Thought becomes, in him, by a strange and very instructive reversal of function, the means and not the end of expression. Often the development of a poem is visibly the deduction from a marvelous accident of language which has occurred in his mind.[102]

It is the sense of this freedom that leads Valéry to use language in his own way, starting from forms in order to arrive at meaning, searching for the meaning most suitable to a certain beautiful form which has seduced him:

> A man is also a poet if he seeks an intelligible and imaginable system, to whose expression a splendid accident of language might belong—a certain word, a harmony of words, a syntactical movement—a certain inception— which he has encountered, awakened, bumped into by accident, and noticed—by his poet's nature.[103]

It seems that there then develops a new power of language, the power of revealing what thought would have been too feeble to conceive. It is, in a sense, a divinized language which thinks, and which thinks more than thought. It is the poet who says more, and more beautifully, than he knows: "Greatness of poets, to grasp powerfully in their words what they have only faintly glimpsed in their mind."[104]

A MYSTICAL UNION: SOUND AND SENSE

We shall now consider the more limited opposition of *sound* and *sense*. We shall not, this time, have to vary the two terms of the relation to the advantage of one of them. Quite the contrary, we shall have to insist on their equality, on their independence, and on their indissolubility.

And first of all, if content is sacrificed to form, this does not mean that content is eliminated; it simply means that the poet has the right to modify it, since his goal is not discursive thought but a sensuous and beautiful creation. The poem thus has a meaning, though one different from that of a page of prose. It has, further, a music, also very different from the sonority of ordinary language. Not only, like everyday speech or sustained prose, does poetry have *meaning* and *sound*, but it has more of them. There is in verse, obviously, more music, and more thought, which is more remarkable and is worth remembering: "Poetry is the ambition of a discourse that *can be charged with more meaning and mingled with more music* than ordinary language bears and can bear."[105] Valéry insisted on the necessary equality of these two factors:

> . . . the thoughts uttered or suggested by a poem's text are not the sole and capital object of the discourse—but *means* which combine *equally* with the sounds, the cadences, the number, and the ornaments to provoke, to sustain a certain tension or exaltation, to engender in us a *world*—or a *mode of existence*—that is entirely harmonic.[106]

There is an "*equality of value* and of powers" between the form and the content, the sound and the sense, the poem and the state of poetry.[107] Verse "establishes itself in an admirable and very delicate equilibrium between the sensuous force and the intellectual force of language."[108]

Sound and sense, in the poem, should be both independent and indissoluble. This is properly the poetic difficulty. It is a question of

. . . conducting at once two developments independent
of each other by nature, one continually musical, the
other creating a psychic state by images and ideas. . . .
Simple solutions of this problem are exceptional; of
course we find many admirable examples in isolated lines
or strophes, but there are very few poems of greater
length in which we do not discern either lapses or dis-
continuities. . . . The reader immediately perceives that
form and content were not inseparable. But to give them
the continuous *appearance* of being indissoluble is an essential object of the poet's art.[t]

Valéry often insisted on the inseparability of these two developments. He made it the criterion of poetry and of the
antipoetic spirit. He always regarded this exceptional success
as a miracle:

What do we seek—except to produce the powerful and
for a time continuous impression that there exists between the sensuous form of discourse and its *exchange
value in ideas* some mystical union, some harmony by
which we participate in another world altogether than
the world in which words and acts correspond to one
another![109]

There must be, in the poem, an alliance of the sensuous
and the significative, a "symbiosis of sound and sense," as in
architecture an intimate agreement "between the *substance*
and the *figure* of the work," which is "the most delicate and
the solidest principle of all the arts."[110]

This inseparability is found not only in the effect on the
reader but in the production of the poem itself. "Composition is, in some way, continuous and cannot be isolated in another time than that of execution. There is not one time for
'content,' another for 'form.' "[111] Valéry analyzed this state of
joint possession in certain lines by Baudelaire:

[t] Frédéric Lefèvre, *Une heure avec Paul Valéry*. See also *Cours
de poétique*, lecture 6: "The great problem is to control the sensuous art and the significative construction like two independent
horses. The poet must drive both sound and sense, the phonetic
variable and the semantic variable."

But now let us listen to lines like this:

> *Mère des Souvenirs, Maîtresse des maîtresses* . . .

[Mother of memories, Mistress of mistresses . . .]

or:

> *Sois sage, ô ma douleur, et tiens-toi plus tranquille.* . . .

[Submit, O my grief, and be more obedient. . . .]

These words act upon us (at least, on some of us) without teaching us much. They teach us perhaps that they have nothing to teach us; that they exercise, by the very means which, in general, teach us something, an altogether different function. They act on us in the fashion of a musical harmony. The impression produced depends greatly on the resonance, on the rhythm, on the number of these syllables; but it also results from the simple *rapprochement* of meanings. In the second of these lines, the harmony of the vague ideas of *Sagesse* and *douleur* and the tender solemnity of the tone produce the inestimable value of a charm: the momentary being who produced this line could not have done so if he had been in a state where the form and the content had proposed themselves separately to his mind. He was, on the contrary, in a special phase of his psychic existence, a phase during which the sound and the sense of language assume or retain an equal importance—a phenomenon excluded from the habits of practical language as from the needs of abstract language. The state in which the indivisibility of sound and sense, the desire, the expectation, the possibility of their intimate and indissoluble combination are needed and sought for or given and sometimes anxiously awaited, is a relatively rare state. It is rare, first because it has against it all the demands of life; then because it is opposed to the crude simplification and the growing specialization of verbal notations.[112]

The true composition of a poem does not reside, for Valéry, in the logical order of developments, but in the intimate association of sound and sense:

> . . . the value of a poem resides in the indissolubility of the sound and the sense. Now, this is a condition which

seems to demand the impossible. There is no relation between the sound and the meaning of a word. . . . And
yet it is the poet's business to give us the sensation of
the intimate union between the word and the mind.[113]

Or, conversely: "If the sense and the sound (or if the form
and the content) can be readily dissociated, the poem decomposes."[114] A crucial consequence: Ideas in poetry are
not at all "values of the same kind" as in prose. Hence Valéry
harshly condemns scholarly habits of analysis. The criteria of
the antipoetic mind are the following:

To distinguish matter and manner, subject and development, sound and sense, to separate rhythm, metrics, and
prosody from verbal expression (words and syntax)—to
paraphrase the poem in prose, to make a poem into a
subject matter for instruction or examinations.[115]

The poem is often disfigured because the poet is at grips
with a "shifting, too-impure substance." Each word, instead of
being a sound and a meaning,

is simultaneously several *sounds* and several *meanings*—
as many sounds as there are provinces in France and almost as many as there are men in each province, and
the musical effects anticipated by the poet are disfigured—several meanings, because the images suggested
are rather different and the secondary images infinitely
different.[u]

There is a great deal of exaggeration in all this. Even if
there is a synthesis of signification and sonority in verse, it
is hard to see what would keep us from examining them
separately; one might recommend studying further the relation of the two factors, to show a suitable concern for their
"indissolubility," but Valéry would still protest, since for him
they are also "independent." To reject analysis comes down
to saying that we kill the poem by studying it. We do not
kill it any more than we kill a painting or a piece of music
by decomposing it abstractly. As for the provincial or individual phonetic alterations, they are generally not serious

[u] *Propos sur la poésie* in *Conferencia*, 1928, pp. 469–70. On the
role of provincial accents in the massacre of poetry, see also *Le
Bilan de l'intelligence* in *Variété III*, p. 299.

among readers of poetry who have sufficient culture to correct them easily; and if we were to take too seriously the
alterations of *meaning* of the vocabulary, we should have to
conclude that no one understands anyone.

The association of sound and sense is not static. It has an
effect which we have already remarked apropos of sensibility,
an effect which, it will be remembered, in the aesthetic domain, seeks to be re-experienced. That is why "poetic form
is automatically regenerated."[116] This is still the theory of
the aesthetic infinite. Valéry defined the poem as a "prolonged hesitation between sound and sense," and to make
himself more clearly understood, he resorted to one of his
ingenious physicist's comparisons, that of the pendulum. This
metaphorical pendulum oscillates between two extreme positions each of which represents one of the two constituent elements of the poem (by and large, *sound* and *sense*); but
Valéry attaches a whole series of terms associated with each
member of his antinomy; on the one hand: form, sensuous
characteristics of the language, sound, rhythm, accents, timbre, movement—"in a word the Voice in action," or again, all
that is sensation; on the other, "all the significative elements":
images, ideas, excitations of sentiment and memory, virtual
impulses, formations of understanding, "in a word, everything
that constitutes the *matter*, the meaning of a discourse," or
again, the thought. A little later, he will identify "all that is
sensation" with Presence, all that is thought with Absence
(that is, the production of absent things, since thought lives
only on memory). Here is how the apparatus functions:

. . . in each line, the meaning . . . far from destroying
the musical form . . . seeks this form again. The living
pendulum which has swung from *sound* toward *sense*
tends to swing back toward its sensuous point of departure, as if the meaning itself . . . found no other issue, no other expression, no other answer than this very
music which has extended it.

Thus, between form and content, between sound and
sense, between the poem and the state of poetry, appears a symmetry, an equality of importance, of value
and of power, which is not in prose; which opposes the
law of prose—for prose decrees the inequality of the two

constituents of language. The essential principle of the poetic mechanism—that is, of the conditions of production of the poetic state by language—is for me this harmonic exchange between expression and impression. . . . Between Voice and Thought, between Thought and Voice, between Presence and Absence oscillates the poetic pendulum.ᵛ

This relation between the *sound* and the *sense* of a line of true poetry is mysterious, and necessarily so:

> The power of verse abides in an *indefinable* harmony between what it *says* and what it *is*. "Indefinable" enters into the definition. . . . The impossibility of defining this relation, combined with the impossibility of denying it, constitutes the essence of verse.[117]

Hence we find again, in the total effect of poetry, in the fruit of the mystical union of thought and music, that impossibility of explanation which Valéry invoked in the definition of ineffable beauty, supreme goal of every work of art. From this point of view, poetry, though it provokes a special emotion, is not distinguished from other aesthetic creations. It aims at beauty, like all the arts, and the inexpressible character of this beauty makes all the arts capable of poetry.

ᵛ *Poésie et pensée abstraite* in *Variété* V, pp. 152–53. Valéry had already expressed the same ideas and used the comparison of the poetic pendulum in *Propos sur la poésie* in *Conferencia*, 1928, pp. 471–72.

Chapter IV

OBSCURITY AND ABSOLUTE POETRY

THE MEANING OF THE POEM

We have just seen that Valéry wanted the poem to be charged with more meaning and more music than the language of every day, and that he saw it as consisting of an indissoluble, harmonic, and indefinable union of these two independent developments. This *composition*, in which sound and sense continuously seek support from each other, illumines the character so peculiar to Valéry's poems if we keep it in mind while rereading them. It also allows us to arrive at a better understanding of the poet's theoretical position on certain points of doctrine concerning meaning and musical expression in poetry. Since Mallarmé, there has been a continuing debate in France on the obscurity of poets, although the sources of the hermetic tradition are much more remote: in Valéry's own time there was a dispute about "pure poetry" [*la poésie pure*], though the term itself had been employed earlier.

I pointed out above that despite the sacrifices of content to form which Valéry advocated, we must not forget the importance he attached to meaning. Meaning, whatever it may be, or rather whatever it may become, counts for half in his poems, and it might well be difficult to make the same claim for many works whose clarity has never been placed in doubt. In certain poets there is a manifest state of imbalance, if we adopt Valéry's point of view, between the harmony of their form and the indigence of their content. Though there are others, it is true, who re-establish the equilibrium by being equally banal in both.

For Valéry, meaning is the organization of a psychic world, parallel to the organization of a sonorous one, a world which participates on an equal footing with the latter in the composition of the poetic universe into which the poem must take us. Rather than meaning, it would be preferable to invoke here a concept such as imagination, or play of images, or system of representations; but the word *ideas*, which Valéry uses constantly, can serve, if taken in its widest sense, to designate adequately the process of mental creation that excites poetic sentiment. In a sense, one can say that this particular world is understood, so that it is legitimate to speak of the meaning of a poem. Nevertheless, this meaning must be interpreted as differing from what we call the meaning of a sentence, or even the meaning of a line. If we wish to understand the meaning of a sentence, we make a sort of translation of it by substituting definitions for the terms to be defined. If we wish to understand the meaning of a poem, a translation of this sort produces a double distortion, first by destroying the values and colors of the words, secondly by substituting an abstract report for the emotive effects and for the internal play of images and their relations to each other. To understand the meaning of a poem does not mean to impoverish it by producing a factual account that robs it of all its overtones; it means, on the contrary, to amplify the psychological resonances implied in it and condensed into its miraculous density. This is why the analysis of poetry is literally an endless task. Valéry is perfectly correct in maintaining that it is not possible to summarize a poem. He ought perhaps to have added that it is possible to expand it. The reader's poetic sensibility, when present in a high enough degree, responds to the extreme condensation of the poet's intentions with an instantaneous and extreme multiplicity of impressions. The analysis of a poem is simply the sorting out, the arrangement of this treasure.

There can be no question therefore, when we wish to grasp the meaning of a poem, of limiting ourselves to the unilateral comprehension we aim at when we read a report. The complexity of the poem cannot be reduced to a sequence of assertions. The notions it introduces are implied in a play of relations that may be variously appreciated by different minds, and this is true of even the clearest poems. Furthermore, if, as I think, feeling is the psychological factor most closely involved in this perception of the world created by a poem, the possibilities of interpretation become even more flexible. But we must not go so far as to claim that they are infinite. The points of reference a poem establishes to guide our straying thoughts channel them more narrowly than is generally supposed. The reader's mind moves, one might say, in a *zone* rather than along a *line*, but it cannot get lost in unbounded space. There is a certain elasticity of comprehension, but it is contained within the unity of the poem. Perhaps commentaries on poems would be less disappointing, and incur less resistance among readers who do not agree with the authors of these difficult attempts at exegesis, if those readers would take into account this narrow but indubitable margin which is probably necessary for the free play of the poetic sensibility. We should be less concerned with an arbitrary fixing of a poem's meaning than with marking out the boundaries within which the meaning develops. I should like to summarize all this by saying that there is meaning in a poem rather than a meaning.

A poem, in my opinion, is an appeal to the feeling of the reader, or even a series of such appeals. It is inevitable that these solicitations—varied but combining to reinforce one another—should result in an emotional state whose general configuration will bear little resemblance to that produced by an ordered argument or demonstration. To speak of the meaning of a poem is to apply, in the realm of the heart, a language made for the reason. Such a thing is not impossible, and it is perhaps inevitable when we make it our business to study this kind of phenomena. It is a difficulty encountered by all psychologists of the emotions who do not reduce them to the will or the intelligence but recognize them as a specific reality. But this translation into the terms of reason should not mistake its object, and if we are careful to examine the impression a poem may make on us we shall see clearly that what is called, improperly enough, the meaning of a poem— a term Valéry also uses, being very intellectual on this point, as is, I may add, the majority of the French public—is much more a matter of feeling it than of understanding it. Many readers of poetry would be embarrassed at being asked point-blank for the meaning of Verlaine's *Clair de lune,* although they still retain a very lively memory of the emotions that a reading of the poem aroused in them. Experience shows that in poems where the thought expressed can be assimilated without difficulty, scarcely any attention is paid to it; readers are much more concerned by the play of the imagination and the emotions, and by the effects of rhythms and sounds. It is only when the thought expressed presents an obstacle, or rather when the mental universe suggested presents a new aspect that demands deciphering, like a less simple kind of music—it is only at this point, where some find themselves attracted by the mystery and the promise of something unknown, that others become disoriented, forgetting that while they were merely sight-reading the piece they were enjoying the melody without asking themselves what the author meant. In fact, the reader of poetry thinks only of concerning himself with the meaning when it is not easily grasped on a first reading. His mistake, sometimes, is to stiffen into an attitude of suspicion. If he would let himself go with the poem, he would find all its obscurities resolved simply by the play of impressions it provokes. If you do not understand a poem, learn it by heart. And I should add: Good poems are memorized quite effortlessly.

Valéry's poems are full of meaning and imprint themselves on the memory. How could it be otherwise with a poet who has the same respect, and an equal gift, for the musical and for the mental aspect of verse? Furthermore, since the inspiration in his work is constantly controlled and manipulated, we can be sure in advance that the intellectual content of his verse will never be flawed by any sins of omission; the obscurity, if there is any, will not be the simple reflection of a confused mind, or the result of inadequacies of expression, things we may find in other poets who achieve obscurity not because of the complexity of their intentions, of their elaboration and their transpositions, but because they begin with the intention of being obscure and end by making the methods by which they achieve their goal much clearer than they suspected. It is not everyone who can be obscure. Nor do we find in Valéry that blind passion, capable sometimes of beautiful cries, nor the sort of disordered outpourings which deliberately sacrifice the total harmony and elegance of a work's

structure to violent attacks upon our sensibilities. Even less
do we find that self-congratulatory indulgence in unbridled
spontaneity that some assume to be the greatest revelation of
our inner resources or of our spiritual life; nor anything
comparable to the automatic writing advocated by the first
Surrealists in hopes of arriving at strange figures that would
surprise and gain control of unknown powers. Moreover, it is
sufficient to listen to Valéry's own abundant and clear explanations on the subject of poetic obscurity. Though couched
in terms that some may have found disturbing, their common
denominator is always, finally, a commendation of lucidity
and a love of clarity.

Perhaps we had best start by exonerating Valéry from the
accusation that has sometimes been leveled against him of
changing the texts of some of his poems. He wrote in his
Mémoires d'un poème:

> On occasion, I have published variant texts of my poems:
> some even contradicted each other, and my critics have
> not failed to blame me for this. But no one has yet told
> me why I should refrain from introducing these varia-
> tions.[1]

In his preface to the commentary on *Le Cimetière marin,*
in which he already expressed his astonishment at having incurred this criticism, he made it quite clear that, far from
yielding to his critics, he felt tempted to

> . . . encourage poets to follow the example of musicians
> and produce different variations or solutions of the same
> theme. There is nothing that would seem to be more in
> keeping with the image I cherish of the poet and of
> poetry.[2]

Even earlier, he had carried this conception to its limits, according to an intellectual tendency which he readily avowed
and which is evident enough in his reflections:

> For one who is particularly interested in the actual work
> of writing verses, variation of subject matter is not per-
> haps of very great importance. I can easily conceive that
> a poet in love with his art might be quite content to
> spend his life continually rewriting the same poem, giv-

ing us a new variation every four or five years on the
theme he has chosen once for all. . . .[3]

And Valéry compared each successive state of the poem to
the launching of the latest version of an automobile chassis in-
corporating improvements on the original model. Without
following him that far, we do not lack examples of poets who
have returned to the same theme, and it is quite usual for
them, in any case, to introduce corrections into successive editions of the same poem; sometimes they even sacrifice good
sections and lower the quality of others (as was the case with
Ronsard). A study of the variants in the works of poets is
sufficient to demonstrate that the meaning of their poems is
rarely fixed in any definitive manner, and that they do not
hesitate to contradict their original meaning in order to obtain a better effect. This is what happened to Valéry when
in *Palme*, to the great horror of certain critics, he bluntly
substituted the preposition *without* for the preposition *with*.
Although the second version says exactly the contrary of the
first, the total meaning of the poem was scarcely modified by
the change, but one detail of it had moved infinitely nearer
to Valéry's particular way of looking at things: this was the
switch, in fact, from the group "with mystery" to the group
"without mystery." It was an advance toward meaning, if we
grant that a poem's true meaning is the one which comes
closest to the original sensibility of the poet. The formulation
of the poem can be regarded as a series of transformations
which represent the progress of the poet, from the first draft
to the definitive version, toward the best possible expression
of meaning. It is a sequence of increasingly condensed approximations to its hidden demands. But for Valéry, there is
no last stage. He has always published his poems as provisional versions still susceptible of indefinite further revision.
A work is always unfinished.[a]

[a] This conviction was strengthened by a great many factors: desire for perfection, the sense of a higher freedom, the temptation
to modify, and above all a feeling for possibilities. If Valéry found
novels and plays distasteful, it is because "the situations, the relations of the characters, the themes of narratives and plays find no
place [in him] in which to take root and follow a single line of
development," and he "dreamed of creating *just once* a work which

But Valéry made statements that seem to be much more inimical to the intelligibility of a text than his successive alterations. He asserted that a text has no true meaning. We should, of course, take into consideration the fact that he has made this statement only when faced with a commentary on one of his poems. He resorted in such cases to the same tactics he adopted when dealing with studies of his thought. While politely praising his interpreters, he dissociated himself from them. He would have acted in the same way with any of his readers. In the *Préface* to Alain's commentaries on *Charmes*—which he nevertheless valued to the point of suggesting to the author: "If you wanted to, you could do a very fine commentary on *La Parque*"[4]—he said: "To meddle, however trivially, with the publication of this commentary— wasn't that tantamount to lending my authority to its entire contents . . . ?"[5] Writing a preface to Gustave Cohen's commentary on *Le Cimetière marin*, Valéry contrasts the writer's *being* with his *appearance*.[6] He is determined to leave the reader his entire freedom, and the author his entire impotence. Apropos of Alain, he notes: "I have no power over what he writes."[7] The work's power is not in the poet, who once the work is finished has no more right over it than anyone else; the work's power is in the work itself, which remains what it is after any interpretation, and shows itself capable of exciting fresh ones:

A work is an object or an event of the senses—whereas the various values or interpretations it suggests are mere consequences of it (ideas or sentiments), which have no

would present, at each of its *nodal points*, all the diverse possibilities that could be offered to the mind, and among which it would *choose* the single course onward given in the text. This would be to substitute for the illusion of a single, imitative determination, that of the possible-at-every-instant which seems to me closer to the truth" (*Mémoires d'un poème*, p. VII). He also dreamed of writing a biography that would display on different levels the possibilities available at any given moment before life commits itself to a definite course: "To reconstitute the randomness present at each instant instead of hammering out a sequence of events *that can be summarized . . .*" (*Suite* in *Tel quel*, II, p. 349). As we know, Socrates contained several other possible Socrates, one of whom could have become an architect (*Eupalinos*).

power to affect its entirely material property of producing other and quite different ones.[8]

This explains his sally: "My poems all have borrowed meanings,"[9] which simply means that the meanings of the poems vary from reader to reader, and that the author is powerless in the matter. An excellent analysis demonstrates the inevitable reactions the work encounters in

. . . the depths of the reader; they are awakened or are stirred in each reader by differences or similarities, by consonances or dissonances that continually manifest themselves between what is read and what was secretly expected.[10]

On this point, Valéry is in the right: the reader betrays the poet. But it is inevitable and indispensable that he should do so: otherwise the poem would not even be felt.

Any text permits many liberties of interpretation. The nature of language encourages them. In his 1898 article on *La Sémantique,* Valéry already noted that

Every form of language manifests itself as a sort of group or totality, composed of fixed signs and ideas. . . . Since the signs employed remain identical, its ideal portion is susceptible of change, it can be replaced by another which is equally satisfactory to the conditions of existence imposed on the totality. The group is capable, in general, of more than one psychological solution. This diversity means that we are able to contradict ourselves, construct false syllogisms—or even correct but absurd ones. It explains logical imperfections, the inconsistencies or formal errors to be found in books, in the most rigorous works of systematic philosophy and, regularly, in the works of the poet.[11]

The nature of poetry authorizes the reader to go even further in his cavalier treatment of the poet's ideas:

Poetry is not in any way a matter of transmitting to one person the intellectual activity of another. It is a matter of creating in the first person a state whose expression is precisely and peculiarly that which communicates it to him. Whatever the image or the emotion that takes shape in the reader, it has value and is sufficient if it produces in him this reciprocal relation between the word-cause and the word-effect. It follows from this that the reader enjoys a considerable freedom in the realm of ideas, a freedom analogous to that granted to the music lover, though less extensive.[12]

To attempt to restrict this freedom would be to kill poetry:

It is an error inimical to the nature of poetry, and one which might even prove mortal, to claim that there exists for every poem a true, a unique meaning that corresponds to it, and in accord with or identical to some thought of the author's.[13]

It is in the name of this principle that Valéry condemns "that absurd academic error which consists in rewriting verse as prose."[14] This exercise would, in fact, be absurd if it existed; for my part, I have never encountered it. The only exercise I have met with entails, on the contrary, the reconstitution of verse whose elements have been barbarously disunited. It is a means of initiating children into the mechanisms of regular versification. If Valéry had to convert verse into prose, it seems to me that his feeling for poetry was not destroyed by the process, though it inculcates, as he says, "the idea most fatal to poetry," since it implies "a belief that poetry is an *accident* of the prose *substance*." It seems to me that the criticism to be made of certain educators would be more usefully concerned with the choice of poems students are assigned to recite or analyze.

If there is no unique or true meaning to a poem, this is not because the author himself cannot provide one, but,

whether verse or prose, a finished work is offered to the reader, and there is nothing about it which its author can suggest or affirm that will have more bearing on it, that will explain it any more exactly, than anything said about it by anyone else.[15]

The meaning he "gives" to his poem "is valid only in relation to himself . . . and cannot be used to refute anyone else."[16]

When the work has been published, any interpretation

of it by the author has no more value than any other interpretation by anyone else.

If I paint a portrait of Pierre, and if someone else
thinks that the result looks more like Jean, there is no
argument I can use against him—and his opinion is as
good as mine.

My intention is only my intention, and the work is the
work.[17]

The poet is almost prepared to say to us: the meaning I
attach to my poems is no business of yours:

> An author can of course tell us about his intentions;
> but it is not his intentions that matter; what matters is
> what subsists and what he has created independent of
> himself.[18]

Valéry separates the work very clearly from the author,
just as, previously, we saw how he separated it from the
reader.

Which does not keep us from still wanting to know our
author's intentions, or from feeling that they would be of no
more hindrance to us in interpreting his work than are the
indications left by composers of music. At a very late stage,
almost regretfully, but also as though yielding to a temptation, Valéry admitted that this might well be the case. The
admission was occasioned by three Spiritual Canticles by St.
John of the Cross, on which the author's own commentaries
struck Valéry as particularly important:

> Thus poetic expression serves here as a text to be in-
> terpreted, as a program to be developed, as well as be-
> ing an illustration—symbolic as much as musical—to the
> account of a mystic theology. . . . The sacred melody is
> accompanied by a skillful counterpoint that weaves
> around the song itself a whole system of internal disci-
> pline.

The enterprise, new to me, gave me food for thought.
I asked myself what effects might be produced in the
field of profane poetry by this remarkable mode of composition which combines the poem with an analysis of it
by the author—always supposing that the author has
something to say about his work, a state of affairs that
would very rarely fail to be held against him. There
would nevertheless be advantages in the method, and

ones that might result in developments of the art of literature hitherto supposed impossible or extremely perilous. The substance or poetic efficacy of certain themes, or of certain ways of feeling, are not immediately evident to minds insufficiently prepared or informed, and the majority of even learned readers will not allow that true appreciation of a poetic work may demand a genuine labor of the mind or the acquisition of more than superficial knowledge. The poet who presumes these conditions to be fulfilled, and the poet who attempts to supply the lack of them in his poem, expose themselves to the severest censure, the one for his obscurity, the other for his didacticism.[19]

The published fragments of the *Mémoires d'un poème* might have served as a prelude to the poet's commentary on *La Jeune Parque*.

But Valéry's refusal to assign any fixed meaning to his poems is more easily grasped once it has been understood that in his case it is the process of creation that determines the poem's meaning. His answer, in the case of *Le Cimetière marin*, is as follows:

> If I am questioned, then; if people start to worry (as they do, and sometimes quite acutely) about what I "intend to say" in such and such a poem, I answer that I had no "intention to say" but only an "intention to make," and that it was this intention to *make* that *intended* to say what I *said*. . . .[20]

The true intentions of the poem are the creative forms, anterior to the poem itself, which we discussed in the preceding chapter; that figure which sought a meaning for itself and finally found it. Doubtless the final meaning that would match it perfectly would also be perfectly foreign to the author, as inhuman as the impersonal speech of the Pythoness in Valéry's poem. But this is an enterprise Valéry never attempted, or at least attempted only in fragments. Although as "universal" as his powers of construction were able to make it, *Le Cimetière marin* is, on Valéry's own admission, a very "personal" soliloquy.[21] And it is not the only one, whatever he may have said on the subject. We recognize Valéry himself everywhere, in *La Jeune Parque* as well as in *Charmes*.

In Praise of Clarity

Liberties of interpretation can produce various meanings; they cannot suppress meaning, nor even necessarily obscure it. Plurality is not the same as confusion. Obscurity itself is a very relative notion. It depends on numerous factors.

First, on the reader:

> The reading public as a whole can be broken down into groups composed of different sorts of minds—very different in culture, very different in their intellectual needs, very different in their capacity for attention. . . . The time each of these groups can give to the reading of a poem—to a careful reading—is naturally very different. It differs in quantity and in quality. . . .[22]

Second, on the difference in clarity between the mind of the author and the spirit of the language itself (in other words, of those who have created it). This is why Valéry addresses Boileau with such vehemence:

> It is extremely difficult to express clearly one's own conceptions with more distinctness than those who have created the forms and the words of the language—among whom we must count those who have taught us to speak.[23]

Third, on the theme treated and on the form adopted.

> Attention and reflection can *always* complicate a thought; they cannot always simplify it. Simplicity of expression is relative to the object to be expressed and to the conditions of the form.[24]

Fourth, on the penetration of the author:

> Obscurity is the inevitable reward of one who responds to things deeply and who feels himself to be in intimate union with those very things.

For light does not penetrate more than a few cubits below the surface.[25] In poetry, furthermore, when we conceive of it as being subject to Valéry's stern conditions,

. . . "simple solutions" to the problems of writing poetry, with its double psychic and musical development, are necessarily "exceptional," if they are to be successful in any consistent fashion.[26]

There is no "willful obscurity" in poets like Mallarmé and Valéry, only "a great deal of will." They eliminate "whatever seems to them without value," whatever "the reader can without effort produce or reconstruct for himself." "The major cause of an effect of obscurity . . . is accumulated work."[27] This was how Valéry stated it in his interview with Frédéric Lefèvre, but in their *Entretiens* he gave the causes of this obscurity in more detail. They are of three sorts. First, "the difficulty of the themes themselves: the more precise you are, the more difficult and irksome the task you impose on the reader." Second, "the number of independent conditions imposed on himself by the poet," for example: harmony, extension of this harmony, continuity of plastic effects, continuity of thought, elegance and flexibility of syntax, all "contained within the armature of classical prosody"; the complexity of this effort and the independence of the conditions he has set himself expose the poet to the danger "of overloading his style, of making the stuff of his work too dense, of employing shortcuts and ellipses that disconcert the minds of his readers," in whom the required " 'tension' becomes disproportionate to the quality of energy which his literary curiosity and his taste for poetry urge him to expend, [for] it is rare that . . . the person who is reading . . . blames himself." Finally, by a combination of these first two causes, "the accumulation, in a poetic text, of work excessively elaborated" (whereas in prose, on the contrary, such work "should always result in a simplification of the expression, the limit of prose [being] the algebraic formula").[b]

This obscurity is in no way desired by the poet. "Nothing

[b] Frédéric Lefèvre, *Entretiens avec Paul Valéry*, pp. 57–61. As an example of obscurity produced by the accumulation of work, Valéry instanced the second version of *L'Après-Midi d'un faune*, very different from the first, since only one line of the latter had been retained. "It demands a decipherment that decimates readers. Liszt decimates pianists" (Frédéric Lefèvre, *Une heure avec Paul Valéry*).

attracts me but clarity," said Valéry, or at any rate Monsieur Teste's correspondent in the *Lettre d'un ami*, but he made no secret of the fact that he usually found "almost none at all":

> Yes, clarity is for me so rare a thing that in this whole wide world—and particularly in the world of writers and thinkers—I see only as much of it as there are diamonds in proportion to the globe as a whole. The obscurities attributed to me are impalpable and transparent beside those I see around me almost everywhere. Fortunate are they who have agreed among themselves that they understand each other perfectly! They write, they speak without a tremor. You must feel how I envy all those lucid beings whose works make one think of the grateful ease with which the sun shines through a crystal world. . . . My bad conscience sometimes suggests the idea of incriminating them in order to defend myself. It whispers that only those who are not seeking anything never encounter darkness, and that we should never offer people anything but what they already know. But I look into the depths of myself, and I must abide by the opinions of so many distinguished persons. Truly, my friend, I was made with an unfortunate mind that is never really sure it has understood what it has understood unless it has done so consciously. I have great difficulty in distinguishing what is clear without reflection from what is positively obscure. . . . This weakness is doubtless the source of my obscurity.[28]

But "neither simplicity nor clarity are absolutes in poetry";[29] it is not the shortest route that we demand of the dancer.

Valéry did, furthermore, defend himself against the charge of being an obscure poet, and shifted the blame to others. André Maurois tells us that Valéry, during a lecture he gave at the Vieux-Colombier, said something more or less like this:

> Obscure? I am obscure? People tell me so, and I try to convince myself they're right. But I find I am less obscure than Musset, or Hugo, or Vigny. That astonishes you? Consider Musset. I don't know if any of you can explain the meaning of these lines:
>
> *Les plus désespérés sont les chants les plus beaux,*
> *Et j'en sais d'immortels qui sont de purs sanglots.*

[The most despairing songs are the most beautiful,
And I know immortal ones that are pure sobs.]

I myself am incapable of doing so! How can a pure sob
be an immortal song? Such a thing appears unintelligible to me. A song has a rhythm, a pure sob has no
form. However obscure I may be, I have never written
anything so obscure as that.[30]

With an amusing slyness he affected not to understand
certain lines by Vigny or Hugo which, in fact, he admired:

J'aime la majesté des souffrances humaines. . . .

[I love the majesty of human sufferings. . . .]

Human sufferings have no majesty . . . the convul-
sions of a tenesmus, the agony of a toothache, the apathy
of despair have nothing august or great about them.

Un affreux soleil noir d'où rayonne la nuit . . .

[A dreadful black sun from which the night beams . . .]

Unthinkable . . .[31]

There are none so deaf as those who will not hear. Voltaire, and even Boileau before him, had a propensity for
hunting out nonsensical lines in Corneille. It would be possible to quote lines really much more obscure than the ones
Valéry selects from the work of poets generally thought of
as extremely clear. Scholars are familiar with the whole series of articles and notes provoked by these two lines from
Musset:

D'un siècle sans espoir naît un siècle sans crainte.
Les comètes du nôtre ont dépeuplé les cieux.

[From an age without hope is born an age without fear.
The comets of ours have depopulated the heavens.]

But in the examples Valéry gives, the obscurity is not
there at the start; it results from a refusal to adhere to the
meaning being propounded because the poet thinks that this
meaning will not be admissible if he delineates it too clearly.
Thus we argue the merits of a sentence that we have understood perfectly. A false idea can still be clear. But Valéry

had elaborated strange maxims for himself on how to approach other people's thought:

> *Perhaps each of us should force himself to regard as, or to render, false anything that is true for everyone—* for private use at least. . . .
> *If anything seems clear or obvious at first glance, try to find it obscure.*[32]

Here we are dealing with a deliberately entertained obscurity which is confused with the obscurity of language as a whole and which only reflection makes evident. In fact, Valéry, like everyone else, experienced the altogether different impression made by works that are immediately hermetic—an impression that alarms some people while attracting others, as in the case, for example, of Mallarmé's *Prose pour des Esseintes* (although that poem has been elucidated for us today) or certain of his sonnets. In his splendid lecture on his master, recalling the first time he encountered Mallarmé's work, Valéry gives a marvelous account of how his mind was astonished by that experience. He described here the essential nature of an experience shared by many fervent admirers of this poet:

> On the one hand . . . fragments that left me *completely* enchanted . . . On the other, certain sonnets that reduced me to a state of stupor; poems in which the clarity of the writing, the brilliance, the movement and the opulence of the sound seemed to be combined with strange difficulties: insoluble associations, occasional singularities of syntax, breaks in thought interrupting the flow of every stanza; in a word, I was forced to recognize that there was a most amazing contrast between what you might call the *contemplation* of these poems, their *physical presence,* and their resistance to immediate intellection. I did not know what to think of a poet capable of uniting so much beauty, so many sensual delights and so many obstacles, so many seductions and so many shadows. I began to form an idea of the Mallarmé problem.[33]

Valéry then gives an admirable illustration of how the musical quality of Mallarmé's verse leads the reader to grasp its form before he apprehends its content and how, once the

reader is haunted by the power this glamorous combination
of words assumes over his memory, the meaning gradually
emerges with its own form, its form of thought, itself endowed with a singular beauty. At the end of this analysis,
it is no surprise to find the two factors which combine to
form the essence of poetry for Valéry: the two plastic forms,
form as sound and form as idea, both of which stand opposed to prose and to ordinary speech. We note, in passing,
at the beginning of this incisive passage, the felicitous use
of the idea of *clarity* applied to the form of the poem in contrast to the obscurity of its content; the impression of strange
lucidity produced, with utter contempt for meaning, by the
perfect clarity of Mallarmé's music, has never been more
forcefully defined:

> And yet, though the meaning of these poems seemed
> to me very hard to decipher, though I did not always
> succeed in resolving these words into a completed
> thought, I did realize that I never before encountered
> lines of verse so *clear* simply as *verse*, lines of verse so
> self-evidently verse, words possessing a more decided,
> a more luminous musicality. . . . I noticed that these
> same very obscure lines possessed a curious property:
> there was something in them so strangely inevitable
> that they forced themselves into my memory. . . . Fur-
> ther: the involuntary repetition of these difficult lines
> began, I also noticed, to dissolve their enigmas and to
> provide me with glimpses of their meaning. The poet
> was justifying himself. Continued repetition made my
> mind stretch toward a limit, toward a perfectly defined
> meaning. I was finding that these bizarre combinations
> of words could provide a very good account of them-
> selves; that the difficulty of comprehension experienced
> at first came from an extreme contraction of figures,
> from a fusion of metaphors, from the rapid transmuta-
> tion of extremely concise images subjected to a sort of
> discipline by condensation (if you will allow me the
> expression) imposed on himself by the poet in accord-
> ance with his intention *to keep the language of poetry
> almost absolutely distinct from the language of prose.*
> One might almost have said that he wanted poetry,
> which must essentially be differentiated from prose by
> its phonetic form and musical content, to be differenti-

ated from it also by the *form of its meaning*. For him, the content of the poem was to be as different from ordinary thought as ordinary speech is different from versified speech.[34]

But Valéry has also given another name to Mallarmé's obscurity, a name that does justice to the complexity of that unprecedented interlacing of internal relations charged with meaning:

> The brilliance of these crystalline systems, so pure and perfectly finished in every way, fascinated me. Doubtless it would not be at all true to say that they are transparent, like glass; but, breaking up the habitual processes of our minds as they do against their facets and the complexities of their structure, what people call their obscurity is nothing, in reality, but their *refraction*.[35]

Cocteau, too, called Mallarmé "obscure as a diamond," which is a play on words reminding us that diamonds are carbon and must be mined. In a different image, but one also borrowed from the language of optics which has always proved suitable for the illustration of intellectual phenomena, Valéry has stated that "music is made beautiful by *transparency*, poetry by *reflection*."[36] The effect of a poem is therefore different from the effect of music, which is compared to the direct transmission of light waves through a pane of glass. The light of poetry is always broken, but in speaking of refractivity Valéry is thinking more of the poem itself, whose structure produces multiple refractions within it, whereas in speaking of reflection he has in mind the reader who receives the reflected ray of light after it "breaks" on the poem's surface of incidence. But the diamond refracts and reflects. The brilliance of a poem can therefore be expressed metaphorically only by a combination of the two analogies. This is what Valéry's ingenuity accomplished when he noted that

> . . . the diamond cutter grinds the facets of the gem in such a way that a ray of light entering it through one particular facet can only emerge again through the same one. . . . A beautiful image of what I think about

poetry: the return of the spiritual ray to the words by which it entered.[37]

When concerned with the musical effect of a poem, it is from acoustics that Valéry naturally borrows the term *resonance*, a concept which expresses a particular deviation in the world of sounds and their sensuous effects, and which also describes that other kind of affective effect of reciprocal reflection and propagation in the uncharted regions of the reader's being that enables a poem to be simultaneously brilliant and obscure.

THE INDEFINABLE HARMONY

But before considering these effects, we must ask ourselves how Valéry conceives of the link which binds the world of verbal sonorities to that world of comprehension which can present, in the poem, the entire range from apparent clarity to that other—occult—clarity. Obviously the word is what constitutes the link of the chain, since it carries both sound and sense. "Words," Valéry says, "because of their twofold nature, often remind me of those complex quantities mathematicians manipulate so lovingly."[c] But this does not take us any further, since we recall the theory that posits as a first principle the independence of these two elements, mystically united in the composition of the poem. Nevertheless, when the American aesthetician George D. Birkhoff discussed the mathematical elements in Art before the Société française de Philosophie, Valéry also spoke, and seemed to express a polite hope that the link between the two given elements of the problem might be found:

> Poetry, in my opinion, is the most complex art of all, since the poet's craft consists in achieving the simul-

[c] *Poésie et pensée abstraite* in *Variété V*, p. 160. See also *L'Invention esthétique* in *L'Invention*, p. 149: "The poet's method of operation is dependent on the complex value of words, that is to say by composing *sound* and *sense* at the same time (I am simplifying . . .), just as algebra operates with complex numbers. I ask your indulgence for this image."

taneous development of two independent, or rather unrelated, variables.

On the one hand you have that part of poetry concerned with signification, on the other you have the musical part. Neither should be sacrificed to the other, even
though we unfortunately see too frequent examples in
France of musical sacrifice. The fact of having to develop two series, and furthermore two discontinuous
series, of different phenomena, between which there is
absolutely no relation (for if there were we should understand all languages), defines the bounds of an art
which is the most complex of all.

I should very much like M. Birkhoff to provide us one
day with the means of constructing some bridge between
these two independent variables. Though I should add
that I have no idea of how it is to be done. They are
sequences belonging to two mutually exclusive worlds.[38]

The problem is, precisely, to establish whether these two
worlds are mutually exclusive. We may well wonder if Valéry, with his preference for clear-cut notions, has not here
succeeded in widening a gulf that others have been trying to
narrow. It is doubtless true that there is no manifest relation
between the meaning of a word and its phonetic aspect—
even though it is not possible to swear that sound and sense
were originally entirely alien to each other. There seems to
be no truth in the idea that language was created by convention. The difference which the various languages display
by expressing the same concept in vocables of dissimilar sonorities is not a very persuasive argument, since the same
object can present itself to the mind under quite different
aspects. But it is certain, after all, that we feel no substantial
connection between the idea of a thing and the word that
conveys it. And yet, through habitual use, through the play of
associated ideas, through the power of the emotions, the effect of analogies, and above all the need for expression—
which grows ever stronger from the coining of popular
phrases to literary creation—there often does come into being a hidden relation between the form of words and our
ways of feeling which ultimately endow them with affective
or visual values. Rightly or wrongly, their phonic content is
incorporated into their mental physiognomy. It is rare for the

two to coincide completely, even in examples of onomato-
poeia, but some aspect of the idea, generally of a vividly
representative or emotional nature, does achieve a lasting attachment to some accident of the phonetic structure. These
combinations may be stable enough to be grasped by a great
many people, at least if they are sensitive to this kind of association. Not only the single word but a whole group of
them, a sequence, a figure of speech, a sentence, may, on
occasion, though obviously with less stability, present the
mind with a perceptible coloration which links its form with
its meaning and enriches the latter by the addition of an ex-
tra nuance. Linguists and specialists in aesthetics have emphasized this expressive side of language, and it has now
become the common coin of verse analysis, though it is used
with varying degrees of success. The coloration of vowels and
the articulation of consonants appear to be particularly susceptible of systematic study, and there seems little doubt
that poets, more or less consciously according to the age they
lived in but with great effectiveness, have achieved a felicitous use not only of the melodic value of sounds but also of
their expressive value. And it is this latter quality that should
provide, it would seem, the means of linking the two worlds,
the world of music and the world of signification, of which
Valéry speaks.

But at this point we must be careful to note that Valéry
almost never made any reference to expression in poetry, and
this lacuna is a very curious one. The sole precise allusion he
made to it is entirely negative. The harmony between poetry's sound and sense, he says, "should not be definable.
When it is, it is an *imitative* harmony, and that is not
good."[39] Doubtless he is referring to imitative harmony in
the very restricted sense of that phrase current in the eighteenth century; and he condemns it as resembling the childish
imitation of natural sounds in program music—which leads
one to wonder whether he would have disapproved of those
critics who have pointed out imitative effects achieved by alliteration in his own work, for example the abundance of
sibilants which have suggested the comparison of the
Ébauche d'un Serpent to one long hiss, the model for which
may be found much earlier in the famous serpentine line

from Racine's *Andromaque*. If we are to keep to the letter of Valéry's doctrine, there is no doubt that he repudiated all attempts to achieve expression by the affective use of sound. If there is to be a harmony between sound and sense, it can be achieved only by composing two independent sequences, as in the use of counterpoint. In reality there are two ways of employing sounds in verse: on the one hand by using the suggestive powers of vowels and consonants, and on the other by tracing a melodic line by the correspondences and contrasts of the vowel timbres. Valéry's theory would admit only the melodic use and consequently reject all reinforcement of sense by sound.

This independent melody plays a major role, not only in the work of a great many poets, and notably those who are not very concerned with direct expression, but particularly in the work of Valéry. He has quite as often utilized the expressive resources of phonemes, and despite his negative theory, we should study them as much in Valéry's work as in the work of so many other poets who have spontaneously relied on them with varying awareness of their power over the sensibility. What complicates a study of this kind is that the melody, which may exist by itself, unrelated to the signification of the verse, may also, in other cases, contain effects of expression due to the suggestive force of the vowels. The consonants, on the other hand, are generally made to figure only in expressive effects; since they possess no timbre, they can take no part in a melodic line. But it is easy, when reading Valéry, to observe that he often constructs his lines on the repetition of a privileged consonant (or of a group of consonants), without its being possible to relate this structure to any expressive effect. This strong consonantal articulation is a sign of a characteristic tendency in his manner of constructing a foundation for the architecture of his verse. Alliteration, without expressive associations, consonantal repetition for its own sake, appears in his work to be as much a solution as certain associations of vowels in other poets. We should add that it does not, of course, exclude other devices. It is curious that Valéry has given this use of consonants no place in his poetics: it is a trade secret.

Let us return to Valéry's ideas on the independence of the

musical variable and the meaningful variable. In a short passage from *Rhumbs* already quoted, Valéry asserts that the
impossibility of defining the relation between these two variables is combined with "the impossibility of denying its existence."[40] If I understand correctly, this relation should be
felt by the reader without his ever being able to analyze it.
Thus there would be, beneath this mystical link, a hidden
analogy. Something, a *"je ne sais quoi,"* as they would have
called it in the seventeenth century, that should establish a
correspondence between the figure of sound and the figure of
sense. There should be a term, an expression to designate this
mysterious relation, this intimate harmony. Such a term is not
to be found in Valéry, but the idea of such a correspondence
emerges from the brief commentary he has given us of Racine's line:

> *Le jour n'est pas plus pur que le fond de mon coeur.*

> [Daylight is no purer than the depths of my heart.]

"This line, the most beautiful of lines . . . is as transparent
as daylight itself."[41]

I thought once, for a moment, that I had found an approximate denomination of this ineffable harmony. Valéry speaks
at one point of a line by La Fontaine "in which the sound is
an image of the meaning."[42] This formulation would seem
applicable to Racine's line that is "transparent as daylight itself." The idea of purity would be reflected in the purity of
the verbal form as in a mirror. But the example from La
Fontaine

> *Prends ce pic et me romps ce caillou qui me nuit*

> [Take this pick and break that stone which hinders me]

had already been quoted by Valéry to the Société française
de Philosophie with a comment that relegated it to the repre-
hensible category of expressive effects: "a line in which the
harmony is quasi-imitative."[43] Despite the equivocation or
hesitation betrayed by that *quasi*, for Valéry *the sound as an
image of the meaning* is an indication of that all-too-definable
reproduction of content in form which "is not good."[d]

---

[d] Nevertheless, Valéry justified his practice of using the diaeresis

Unless Valéry did not understand his own meaning, we should not, therefore, take that most beautiful of lines

Le jour n'est pas plus pur . . .

as an imitative harmony, and consequently it would be a mistake to seek in its sonorities—the two light vowels of *plus pur*, for example—some sort of musical rendering of the transparency of light. For Valéry there seems to be on the one hand the idea of this transparency, and on the other a miraculous line of verse possessing an intrinsic quality such that the epithet *transparent* must inevitably be applied to it. The idea of transparency is thus given twice, as it were, once in the meaning of the discourse and once in the music of the verse. But between these two, there exists no visible connection, no expressive effect susceptible of detailed analysis, even though a substantial link is sensed between them. This way of uniting two heterogeneous essences without a middle term bears a striking resemblance to the efforts of metaphysicians at grips with the problem of uniting body and soul, spirit and matter, thought and space. From another point of view, it suggests the mystery of the incarnation.

Even in Valéry's writings, however, it might not be impossible to pick out a few passages in which he seems almost prepared to venture out onto that bridge he so courteously hoped Birkhoff might be able to build. The poet who links a transparent line of verse to the idea of transparency cannot help seeking the former by using the latter as his starting point, or vice versa, if Valéry prefers moving from form to content. Though of course the search will be a random one, the poet blind and feeling his way. Valéry has characterized this strange quest with a splendid image: "Many a poet is like a man laboriously, desperately searching the whole face of the world for the rocks that by some chance bear a resemblance to the human form."[44] But, apropos of Racine, he gives us a glimpse of how continual modifications of thought may finally coincide with the modulation of the form: "Racine

on the grounds that it is an expressive effect: "If some people find *ti-è-de* more expressive of tepidity than *tiè-de* then I feel justified in having broken the rules" (*Les droits du poète sur la langue* in *Pièces sur l'art*, p. 57).

proceeds by very delicate *substitutions of the idea* he started
with as his theme. He charms it *until it becomes the music
he is striving for.* He never abandons the line of his discourse."[45] It is this melody that, according to Valéry, is the
goal of all his efforts, but the variation of thought turns it into
another sort of melody, a psychological melody which is fused
with its formal model. Thought that becomes music, music
that "musicalizes" the ideas supporting it—the boundaries of
sound and sense disappear. The *bridge* is no longer needed,
for everything has become form.[e]

THE SEPARATION FROM PROSE

Whether the differing natures of thought and song are
separate or linked, whether or not we are able to discover a
more or less precise relationship between them by analysis,
both hold equal rank in the *poetic universe:*

> . . . a universe of reciprocal relationships, analogous to
> the world of sounds in which musical thought is born
> and moves. In this poetic universe, resonance prevails
> over causality, and "form," far from dissolving into its ef-
> fect, is made doubly necessary by its demands. The
> Idea demands its voice.[46]

[e] Despite his distinction between poetry and prose based on the
indissociability of sound and sense, Valéry nevertheless sometimes
praised the musical correspondence of content and form in some
prose writers. Of Leonardo da Vinci, whom he regarded as one of
the greatest possible writers, he said that "the musical form of his
sentences, which is very individual, is always in exact harmony with
their substance" (*Léonard de Vinci* in *Vues,* p. 231). He also
found "a model of adaptation of thought" and "a certain dis-
creetly poetic grace which rhythm, number, and cadences, the well-
proportioned structure make more evident to the senses" in a
fragment of Descartes' *Méditations,* a work he praises for its admirable style, forgetting that it was originally written in Latin and
that a large part of his compliments are therefore addressed to the
excellent translation by M. de Luynes (*Une Vue de Descartes* in
Variété V, pp. 231–33). Valéry is not wrong to praise the musical
values of prose at the same time as its intellectual content, or the
correspondence of these two variables, but we may wonder if his
distinction between prose and poetry is not weakened thereby.

How does the suggestion of this poetic universe function?
How does the poet introduce the reader into it? By methods
derived from thought, or from sounds? For Valéry, there is
nothing doubtful about the answer to this question; the poet
must use a combination of both methods. If he gives us a list
of some of these methods, we notice that he establishes no
distinctions among them from this point of view. "The poetic
universe . . . comes into being by news of number, or rather,
by the condensation of images, figures, consonances and dissonances, and by the linking of phrases and rhythms. . . ."[47]
Forms are what effect this transference, but ideal forms and
verbal forms. This enterprise is the product of a language reworked in both its intellectual and its musical aspects. Its goal
is to reconstitute, even to construct, the special emotion
proper to poetry by a combination of heterogeneous means
whose common character, on which Valéry has insisted so
frequently, is to oppose, in poetic discourse, any element that
might suggest prose. Valéry very often gives the impression
that it is sufficient in his eyes to escape from prose in order
to gain automatic access to the poetic. "The essential," he
says, is "to avoid constantly anything that might lead back to
prose, either by making the reader regret its absence [by expressing thoughts more suitably conveyed in prose] or by
following only the idea . . . [which is not poetic in itself]."[48]
If to be a poet means not to write prose in verse, then any
method of avoiding prose is valid. We shall consider these
magic recipes for doing so a little further on. What concerns
us for the moment is this indifference to the unity of means,
this instrumental pluralism of technique. Which does not
surprise us from a man who characterized his investigation
with the words "methods rather than method."[49]

This spontaneous pluralism, evident enough in Valéry's activities as a moralist as well, can be discerned in his tendency
to consider poetic quality in a poem's details rather than in
the work as a whole. A poem, for him, is above all a series
of successes. "Voltaire put it marvelously well when he said
that 'Poetry consists of nothing but beautiful details.' I agree
entirely."[50] Valéry was very sensitive to the presence of this
quality and could recognize it in a state of sporadic dispersion, even in works of a low poetic content or works not in-

tended to be poetic by nature. He remarked, justly, that
". . . all written works, all works of language, contain certain
fragments, or recognizable elements, endowed with poetic
properties."[51] Anyone of some sensibility will notice them.
They stand out of their own accord. And in every case it is
the extent to which they depart from prose that brings them
to our attention:

> Every time the words display *a certain divergence*
> from the direct, or in other words from the most *unfelt*
> [*insensible*], expression of the thought, every time these
> divergences suggest that there exists a world of relation-
> ships quite distinct from the purely practical world, we
> apprehend more or less clearly the possibility of enlarg-
> ing this exceptional realm, and we have the sensation
> of having grasped one fragment of a noble and living
> substance which is perhaps susceptible of development
> and cultivation; and which, when developed and uti-
> lized, constitutes poetry as an effect of art.[52]

Poetry would thus consist above all of sensitized units of
language, capable of radiating a magic power; it would be in
the first place a collection of precious stones, a necklace of
pearls, a treasure hoard of talismans. We shall see that Valéry
does not, for all this, neglect the poem's architecture or the
continuity of its development, but these observable characteristics do not, in his eyes, constitute poetic values. It is not
easy to ascertain whether Valéry allows poetic quality to reside in the complete poem, taken as a whole. Indeed, the
closed system controlled by its sound values, and through
which we enter the poetic universe, may consist of the slightest fragment of authentic poetry, and we are given to understand that this charm functions in the poem as we encounter
each of its beauties of detail and that the poetry of the poem
is the sum of these happy accidents; but Valéry does not tell
us if the poem, in its entirety, is capable of producing a total
effect of poetry.

At the least, he shows us, as a desirable goal, an uninterrupted succession of perfect poetic moments. For it is again
his pluralism, his sensitivity to the insularity of poetic beauty,
that forms the basis of his conception of *poésie pure*. The
idea of composing a poem of nothing but absolutely poetic

elements could come only from their isolation, from a sort of aesthetic atomism that corresponds very closely to Valéry's mechanical conception of creation by means of separate operations, a conception as far removed as possible from a dynamism that might have located poetic purity in the unity of a creative expansion remaining faithful to its goal down to the last detail of execution. The idea of the completely poetic poem presents itself to Valéry as a problem of integration, of homogeneous fusion without sutures, whose guarantee lies in the purity of the raw materials:

> Whether it is possible to construct a whole work by means of these easily recognizable elements, so clearly distinct from those of the language I have termed *unfelt* [*insensible*]—whether it is possible, consequently, by means of a work in verse or not, to give the impression of a complete system of *reciprocal* relations between our ideas, our images, on the one hand, and our means of expression on the other—a system that would correspond particularly to the creation of an emotive state of the soul, such is, broadly speaking, the problem of pure poetry.[53]

The greatest difficulty in poetry is, precisely, to construct "a whole work" with nothing but poetic "elements." *Poésie pure* is exactly that, and nothing else. This notion, which has been so obscured, is quite clear and simple in Valéry's work; it designates, plainly, poetry without admixture, poetry which is, continuously, nothing but poetry.

This dream of total purity took root in Valéry's life at a very early stage, and it would be possible to follow its ramifications in all the realms he explored, in his conception of science in his aesthetic. He attributed it to Monsieur Teste: "Old desire (there you are again, periodic prompter) to reconstruct everything out of pure materials . . ."[54] Valéry has expressed his alienation from contrary states: "Impurity is my antipodes. . . ."[55] He took the word *mélange* [mixture] as the title for one of his volumes of reflections and made it the synonym of mind, that confused mind to which the pure self constantly denies itself:

> *Un esprit n'est que ce mélange*
> *Duquel, à chaque instant, se démêle le MOI.*

[A mind is merely that mixture
From which, at every instant, the EGO extricates itself.]

It is admixture, impurity, which spoils the art of oratory
for him:

> I don't like eloquence. But it becomes positively in-
> tolerable to me when written down.
> Why? I am aware of the reason. It is because elo-
> quence is form adapted to numbers and to a mixture.[56]

In his *Réflexions sur l'acier*, Valéry has described this "marvelously polytechnical substance" as "not only 'composed,'
but essentially 'impure' . . . and . . . 'heterogeneous,'" and
pointed out in "material civilization [which] lives by alliances
or combinations, the rarity of pure substances whose preparation sometimes demands the use of costly and complicated
methods."[†] The memory of the diligence required for the
preparation of *poésie pure* is not entirely absent from these
lines. In one of his splendid pieces of art criticism, the article
called *Triomphe de Manet*, when he remarks on "some profound relationship" between Baudelaire and the painter of
Olympia, "a real affinity between the painter's preoccupa-
tions and those of the poet," it is because "purity in painting
as in poetry [consists] in rejecting . . . those effects which
cannot be deduced from a clear consciousness and from the
possession of the means of their nature." In the work of these
two artists, emotion and ideas come only after the subtle and
expert organization of "sensation." They are both intent on enchantment, "the supreme goal of art."[57] By pushing the im-
plications of this passage a little further, we should see that
the idea of purity in art tends to be present, for Valéry, at
every stage of creation: purity of notion, purity of means, purity of effect. Art should be an original synthesis of pure elements obtained by an initial analysis:

> There are only two things that count, that have the true
> ring of gold when thrown on the table where the mind
> is playing against itself.
> The first, which I call *Analysis*, and which has "pu-
> rity" as its goal; and the second, which I call *Music*,

† In *Vues*, pp. 63–69. On purity in religions and in modern medicine, see *Discours aux chirurgiens* in *Variété V*, p. 49.

and which composes this "purity," makes something from it.[58]

With regard to poetry, Valéry considered chiefly the elements that enter into verse; hence it is chiefly in opposition to prose that he talked of pure poetry. He used the expression for the first time in the preface to a collection of verse by Lucien Fabre, *Connaissance de la déesse*, in 1920, and he was astonished, subsequently, "to see an expression coined rather carelessly assume such surprising importance as it passed from mouth to mouth."[59] He explained what he himself meant by the expression:

> I write *pure* in the sense in which the physicist speaks of pure water. By which I mean that we are faced with the question of whether or not it is possible to construct a work of this sort which would be *pure* of nonpoetic elements.[60]
>
> I had intended to allude only to that poetry which would result, by a sort of exhaustion, from the gradual suppression of the prosaic elements from a poem. . . . In short, I used the word *pure* in the very simple sense given to it by chemists when they speak of a pure substance.[g]

This notion is not at all mysterious and is understood by everyone:

> A very beautiful line of verse is a very pure element of poetry. The hackneyed comparison of a beautiful line to a diamond shows that a feeling for this quality of purity is present in everyone's mind.[61]

However, this purity ordinarily exists only in fragments. Attention easily isolates them from the rest. And that painful inequality of the poem makes us regret that the entire work is not of the same composition:

[g] Frédéric Lefèvre, *Entretiens avec Paul Valéry*, pp. 65–68. See also the *Cours de poétique*, lecture 11: "I have never taken this term 'pure' in any sense other than that given to it by the chemists. I wondered if it might not be possible to separate those parts of language endowed with particular characteristics from the poetic elements and then go on to constitute a work out of nothing but the latter; my friend Bremond regarded the word 'pure' as a mystical notion, such was not my intention."

. . . it is very easy to show, in every poet, without exception, the elements of pure poetry. They stand out from the text as a whole and become independent of it. We experience a desire to find nothing but beauties of this nature. An attempt to constitute poems out of nothing but the most precious elements is only natural.[62]

A poem is inevitably impure, mixed with prose:

In short, what we call a *poem* is composed in practice of fragments of *pure poetry* embedded in the matter of a discourse.[63]

The idea of pure poetry applied to an entire poem does not therefore signify a reality, but defines an ideal:

Experience would tell us, even if our reasoning powers did not, that pure poetry . . . must be looked upon as a goal toward which we should strive, but one which it is almost impossible to attain in a poem consisting of more than one line.[64]

I have always considered, and I consider still, that it is a goal impossible to achieve, and that poetry is an attempt to approach as closely as possible to this purely ideal state.[h]

But if "the conception of pure poetry is that of an unattainable type, of an ideal limit of the poet's desires, efforts, and powers . . . ,"[65] it can also serve as a norm by which to judge the value of works; "the notion of such an ideal or imaginary state is very precious as a means of gauging the value of all observable poetry."[66] Hence this criterion: "A poem's value depends on its content of pure poetry. . . ."[67]

In order to approach this ideal, the poet must expel numerous elements from the poem. Valéry's poetry, like his thought, is a system of rejections. Similarly, he has praised writers for their denial of facility, thus expressing his ethical and aesthetic viewpoint. The rejections of the poet aspiring to purity

[h] *Poésie pure* in *Oeuvres complètes*, vol. C., p. 200. Cf. *Cours de poétique*, lecture 11: "I added however that what I desired was impossible since language . . . is not intended for that. Normally, it destroys itself by the very act of being used, which implies its replacement by the signification afforded. Language dies in the effect obtained."

refer to elements of content and also to elements of form.
Valéry apparently wishes to empty the poem of its entire
content. There should be no subject, or, since that is impossible, an inane subject, a pure pretext:

> Poetry is simply literature reduced to the essentials
> of its active principle. It has been purged of idols of
> every kind, and of realistic illusions; of the potential mis-
> understanding between the language of "truth" and the
> language of "creation," etc.
> And this quasi-creative, fictive role of language (de-
> spite its practical and truth-telling origin) is made as
> obvious as possible by the fragility or by the arbitrariness
> of the subject.[68]

There should be no descriptions. Description has corrupted the art of writing, just as landscape has corrupted
painting.[69] Valéry delights in the inventions that render it
superfluous. Photography "and its conquests in the realms of
movement and color, not to mention that of depth . . . dis-
courage us from descriptive writing"; this "brings us back to
the limits of articulate language"[70] and reminds writers to
use their means in ways suited to their specific natures:

> A literature would become pure if, abandoning all
> uses of language that other modes of expression or pro-
> duction serve much more efficiently than it can ever do,
> it dedicated itself to what it also could achieve. It would
> thus maintain itself and develop in its true course, either
> toward the perfection of that discourse which constructs
> or expounds abstract thought, or advancing into the vari-
> ety of poetic combinations and resonances.[71]

Nor should poetry contain historical evocations:

> In a poem, the intervention of historical data . . . (a
> date, sometimes) must appear contrary to the goal
> sought by anyone speaking in verse.[72]

The author of *Narcisse* and the *Air de Sémiramis* is bound
to tolerate the presence of characters, but when it comes to
the heroes of La Fontaine's *Adonis*, "he cannot bring himself
to marvel" at their "great simplicity," since "the principal
characters of a poem are always the suavity and the vigor of

the verse."[73] In any case, though myths may be admitted, there must be no narration, no reflections of any sort, whether moral or philosophic, nothing for which prose would suffice:

> We must understand by *prosaic elements* everything that can, *without loss*, be said in prose; everything—history, legend, anecdote, morality, even philosophy—which exists in its own right without the necessary aid of song.[74]

Hence Valéry praised first those symbolist poets who

> . . . took pains to eliminate descriptions, aphorisms, moral observations, and arbitrary details; they purged their poetry of almost every intellectual element that music cannot express.[i]

The reader, though he may be ready to admit that intellectual elements are not poetic in themselves, is less disposed to agree that their total exclusion is necessary. He recalls too many illustrious poems in which the sections given over to descriptions or narration, the legendary evocations and the plunges into metaphysics in no way detracted from his enjoyment. As always, Valéry went far beyond the banal observation that poetry does not consist of the presentation of facts and events nor of philosophic reflection. He did not question whether, under certain conditions, such data can be poeticized, as experience proves that they can.[j] He preferred to deny the possibility altogether. It would not be difficult to show that his own poetry is often at variance with his doctrine, for it contains no lack of ideas, descriptive or narrative elements, sometimes even of historical allusions. It is true that he submits all these to a special treatment that we might call poeticization, but his predecessors did no less. No true poet has ever described, narrated, or expressed ideas in the way these things are done in novels, in history, or in philoso-

---

[i] *Avant-propos* in *Variété*, p. 96. See also the similar remark about Mallarmé's work: "No eloquence; no narratives; no aphorisms" (*Je disais quelquefois à Stéphane Mallarmé* in *Variété III*, p. 14).

[j] It is a little surprising to read his handsome tribute to Verhaeren's poetry, so alien to Valéry's ideal and full of descriptive elements. Cf. *Discours sur Verhaeren* in *Oeuvres complètes*, vol. E.

phy. Pure poetry is not empty poetry, though Valéry said so. The *Fragments du Narcisse* contain eight lines which "cost him the most work" and which he "considers as the most perfect" of all those he wrote—in other words, the lines that "came closest" to what he wanted them to be, "accommodating every constraint" he had imposed on them. This is the passage that begins:

> *O douceur de survivre à la force du jour . . .*
>
> [Oh delight of outliving the day's strength . . .]

Now these lines "are, moreover absolutely innocent of ideas and thus attain a degree of purity that constitutes exactly what I call pure poetry."[75] These lines, innocent of ideas but not of emotion, do at least disclose a plastic content, representations of nature, an evocation of dusk whose descriptive character it would be very difficult to contest. Valéry does, however, agree that it is unfortunately impossible to suppress absolutely all prosaic elements; in any poem there is a minimum of information of no poetic value which is indispensable. Writing of a dull transition in La Fontaine, he notes that "in verse, everything it is necessary to say is almost impossible to say well."[76]

It is not only in the poem's subjects and intellectual content that the poet should aim at purity by exclusion. It is in language itself. Valéry says apropos of Baudelaire that "purity is the result of infinite operations on the language." "Attention to form" means "the deliberate reorganization of the means of expression."[77] But here the recommendations become more positive: "The poet should multiply everything that separates verse from prose":[78]

> Poetry, an art of language, is . . . forced to struggle against the practical, and against the modern acceleration of the practical. It will emphasize everything that can differentiate it from prose.[79]

The poet will seek support from the conventions, whose laws are intended "to provide a constant safeguard against any falling-off into prose."[80] In opposition to whatever tends to the destruction of form, he will set up "the principal means imaginable in order to oppose them: rhythms, rhyme, rigor, and choice of words, search for the limit-expression, etc.":[81]

> Rhymes, inversion, extended figures, symmetries, and images, all these, whether inventions or conventions, are so many means of opposing the reader's prosaic tendency.[82]

In a graceful article on Pontus de Tyard,[k] Valéry eulogized inversion, resorting to etymology to make his point, since prose is precisely the opposite of inversion: it is that discourse which proceeds in a straight line (*prosa oratio*). The poet must above all make himself the master of words so that he can use them with a superior freedom. As he elsewhere said, a little enigmatically:

> I add (though only for certain readers) that the refusal to allow oneself to be manipulated by *words* is not unconnected with what I have named, or believe I have named: *Pure poetry*.[83]

In what, exactly, does this attitude consist? First of all, no doubt, in not letting oneself be guided by words (others, on the contrary, have recommended yielding to this impulse); secondly, by a reversal of tactics, in dominating words by imposing on them a treatment opposed to ordinary usage, by deflections of meaning, the use of tropes, eccentric placements, new combinations, and original syntactical relations. As early as his 1898 article on Huysmans, Valéry already suggested as a source of "purely poetic combinations," the "methodical juxtaposition of the most remote and different sorts of words."[84] There was a little of this same procedure in the marriage of unlikely ideas by rhyme. The most general advice is to avoid direct expression:

[k] In *Oeuvres complètes*, vol. E, pp. 13–15. See also the letter written in 1917 to André Fontainas in *Réponses*, p. 19: "The line you describe as too . . . *inverted* I don't like at all. It belongs to one of the three passages literally improvised in the weary haste to be finished. But I must insist on the principle of inversions. You will find similar if not *worse* ones in Baudelaire and Hugo. In any case, inversion is the only tatter left to us of Virgil's imperial liberties: "*Des cocotiers absents les fantômes épars* [Of the vanished coconut palms the scattered ghosts] . . .""

Victor Hugo was very much aware, and demonstrates the fact throughout his work, that direct expression can only be an eccentricity in poetry, and that its prevalence in a text is equivalent to the total suppression of poetry,[85]

and to give preference to the figurative form of expression that prose employs only exceptionally. In his last poems Hugo tends to substitute "for direct expression a whole system of symbolist expression of the greatest power and the deepest beauty."[86]

We may doubt that poetry is differentiated from prose by these means, by the use of figures, by turns of phrase and expression which we recognize as poetry's favorite recourse, but to which prose, after all, is no stranger. Valéry is not far from acknowledging as much:

Prose and poetry use the same words, the same syntax, the same forms, and the same sounds or timbres. But coordinated and animated differently. Prose and poetry are thus distinguished from each other by the difference of certain links and associations which are formed and dissolved in our psychic and nervous organization, even though the elements of these modes of activity are identical.[87]

Then what is the source of the difference between these two systems? According to Valéry, "the great and decisive difference" is that "utilitarian language . . . vanishes," whereas "poetry can be recognized by its property of tending to reproduce itself in its form: it incites us to reconstitute it identically."[88] This theory, with which we are already familiar, does not tell us exactly what constitutes the poetic language, strictly speaking; it conveys only its effect, its repercussion. For want of anything better, Valéry fell back on a comparison, which he used several times, and which he meanwhile discovered through one of his students had already been exploited by Malherbe, according to Racan. In Valéry's opinion it is an "analogy as substantial and as fruitful as those that are drawn from the fact that in physics identical formulas can sometimes represent two or more phenomena which are in appearance quite different."[89] This analogy, in its most ex-

act sense, is a four-term ratio which likens the relation between poetry and prose to that between dancing and walking.
It doesn't teach us very much more than what Valéry had
already told us, but it makes us feel it more clearly. "Walking, like prose, aims at a particular object . . . dancing . . .
has no direction . . . it pursues a state. . . ."[90] But in the
first form Valéry had given to this graceful parallel, in *Calepin d'un poète,* the analogy was complicated by a third relation, that of spoken word and song. In this text we find some
precious clues to a possible transition from prose to verse,
though we must not insist on them overmuch, for that would
doubtless betray the thought of the man who declared, we
must remember, that to begin a poem with thought is to begin with prose. He certainly did not mean that by relaxing
prose we will arrive at poetry, but rather that language can
suddenly spring to life.[1] This suggestive passage of the *Calepin* contains two further, very revealing notations: the first on
the subject of metaphors, which Valéry defined as "stationary
movements"; the second on the effect of song, recalling the
comparison that Valéry established between the poetic universe and the musical universe: both song and music communicate inner movements, and we recall that Valéry attributes the same effect to the poem:

> The transition from prose to verse; from spoken word
> to song, from walking to dancing. That moment at once
> act and dream.
> The steps of a dance are not intended to carry me
> from this point to that; nor are pure verse and song.
> They exist to make me more present to myself, more
> entirely given over to myself, expended upon myself with
> no useful purpose, myself succeeding to myself, until
> all things and all sensations have no further value. A
> particular movement makes them free, as it were; and
> infinitely mobile, infinitely present, they rush in to serve
> as fuel for a fire. This is the reason for metaphors, those
> stationary movements.
> Song is more real than spoken words; for the latter
> have no value except as a substitution and a process of

[1] The pages entitled *Poésie brute* in *Mélange,* pp. 117–31, in
which the suggestion of verse occasionally appears, in which song
is *in gestation,* can be considered as prepoetic prose.

decipherment, whereas song moves and makes me imitate, makes me desire, makes me tremble as though its variations and its texture were the law and substance of my being. Song puts itself in my place; but the spoken word is on one surface, it enumerates external things, compartmentalizes, attaches labels.

This difference becomes wonderfully obvious if we observe the efforts and inventions of those who have attempted to make music speak and language sing or dance.[91]

These comparisons with dancing (and with music), this definition of metaphors as stationary movements, this motor effect on the reader's sensibility, this possession of which he is the prey are all strikingly dynamic in character. We shall see that the physiological effects Valéry attributes to poetry may completely overwhelm us. We are ultimately obliged to recall the old "enthusiasm" of the classical writers, despite Valéry's rejection of this term in his theory of creation. But in doing so we should thereby fall back into the region of "vague things" that Valéry attempted to exclude from his analyses, and we should perhaps find ourselves a long way from purity, as is inevitable once we open the doors to emotion, if only by the intervention of the stimulus of dance, song, or music. But we must realize that in his description of these transports Valéry is concerned only with the reader, and that nothing suggests they have their place in the poet. Enthusiasm, which is no fit state for the soul of the writer, would therefore be suitable in his readers, and would be a measure of the writer's powers of action upon them. This is the old principle of moving others without being moved oneself, and it is also the principle of forcing the public to obey: intellectual pride's dream of domination when it has turned artist. But we may wonder whether pure poetry would have any likelihood of shedding much light if it did not first generate some vague heat.

This conclusion, which leads to an affirmation of the primacy of emotion in the poetic reader, against Valéry's express desire, is not modified if we consider the project he outlined, though never pursued, of replacing the notion of *pure poetry* by another, slightly different one. Pure poetry itself he never offered to his readers as anything but "a fiction deduced from observation, which should help us clarify our idea of poems in general, and guide us in the difficult and important study of the diverse and multiform relations of language with the effects it produces on men."[92] We have just had a glimpse of these effects: they consist in a sort of transport of the being. Valéry occasionally thought that a better expression might be used:

> It would be better, instead of *pure poetry,* it would be better, perhaps, to say *absolute poetry,* and to understand this term in the sense of an exploration of the effects resulting from the relations of words, or rather from the relations of the sounds of different words, a notion which suggests, in short, *an exploration of that whole region of sensibility governed by language.* This exploration can be made gropingly. That is generally how it is effected. But it is not impossible that it may one day be carried out systematically.[93]

This infallible technique dreamed of by the young admirer of Poe was abandoned as impossible by the poet of *La Jeune Parque,* who nonetheless retained the rigorous ideal which inspired it:

> . . . when I returned after twenty years of nonliterary investigations, to Poetry, this strange undertaking no longer appeared to me in any but its "absolute" aspect— that is, as an activity deriving whatever value it may possess only from *intrinsic* qualities, independent (as far as possible) of the taste of the period, of forecasts concerning the taste of the next generation, of "modern" sensibility and environment.[94]

The only difference between *pure poetry* and *absolute poetry* is that the second adds to the homogeneity of creation an antirelativism and an antimodernism, an atemporality that afford it a sort of irreducibility or eternity.

In the *Avant-propos à la Connaissance de la Déesse,* in which he coined the expression pure poetry rather carelessly, Valéry already used the expression "absolute poetry."[m] And

---

[m] In *Variété,* p. 101: "*Absolute poetry* can proceed only by means of exceptional marvels."

in his remarkable study *Situation de Baudelaire*, immediately after praising Poe for having "understood that modern poetry must adapt itself to the tendency of an epoch which has seen the modes and realms of human activity become more and more clearly separated, so that poetry can now aspire to achieve its own particular goal, and to produce itself in, as it were, a pure state," Valéry sums up his effort in this way: "analysis of the conditions of poetic pleasure, definition-by-*exhaustion* of *absolute poetry*," in other words by suppression of "the data of discursive or empirical knowledge."[n] Thus *pure poetry* and *absolute poetry* are two expressions which, though they may not be synonymous, nevertheless cover the same aspect of reality, or rather aspire to the same ideal, designate the same tendency to purge poetry of foreign elements, to employ to that end a kind of method and to produce by its means a certain effect upon the reader's sensibility. It therefore remains for us to consider the poem as a kind of machine capable of such an effect.

[n] *Situation de Baudelaire* in *Variété II*, pp. 165–67. See also *Triomphe de Manet* in *Pièces sur l'art*, p. 208, in which Valéry says of Mallarmé: "He believed that the world was created in order to end in a beautiful book, and that an absolute poetry was its fulfillment."

Chapter V

INSPIRATION AND WORK

THE PROBLEMS OF POETIC CREATION

To study the nature of an art is essentially an aesthetic enterprise, but to study artistic creation is above all a psychological one. It is the task of aesthetics, over and above the values it determines, to establish the vital conditions of the art or the genre under examination, conditions which, from the aesthetic point of view, are internal ones; aesthetics is therefore focused on the work or on the idea of the work. Psychology, on the other hand, can have nothing valid to say about the work; it can function fruitfully only in relation to persons, or to a certain type of person, or, at a more abstract level, to a particular kind of mental performance. Current expressions such as Psychology of Art, Psychology of Religion, or Psychology of Language, legitimate though perhaps equivocal, should not lead us to forget that psychology's true domain can only be a reality situated in men's minds, and consequently external to the objects with which these minds are in relation. From this point of view, the artistic object, the work of art, is in a double relation with the mind, according to whether it has created it or receives its effect; every psychology of art is twofold in nature—a psychology of the creator and a psychology of the consumer. The one must not be confused with the other, and still less must either be allowed to enter into an analysis of the work which is the transmitting agent between the artist and the public. Nevertheless the study of the relationships among these three factors is extremely important, though it has been rather neglected: we lack a science of the intermediary objects and interpsychological relations that are involved in art and its human ties; within clearly determined limits of time, this science could be the History of Art, and also, within clearly determined spatial limits, the Geography of Art; but if we are seeking to formulate laws or generalities that transcend a limited experience, it would be a Sociology of Art that should concern itself with the study of this twofold human contact of the creation of art and the subsequent aesthetic current transmitted by the work, a social fact first and foremost, if society is not composed merely of minds and institutions, but also of material or quasi-material things which form complex links in their relationships. In short, there would be four orders of problems which concern art, and, to come back to poetry, there would be grounds for studying the psychology of the poet, the aesthetics of the poem, the psychology of the reader, and, finally, the sociology of poetic transmission. This list, moreover, does not include the history of poetry, which would usefully complete these studies. All of which is a great deal, and yet very little, when we think of the complexity of the questions that confront us.

Poetry is, in fact, the least simple of the problems raised by art, because it affects the whole of our deepest psychic life and because the pleasure it provides is perhaps, at bottom, only to a small degree, or perhaps not at all, an aesthetic one, a fact that radically differentiates poetry from the other literary arts as well as from painting, sculpture, or music (insofar, of course, as these arts are not aiming at the creation of poetry by the means proper to their natures); with the result that poetry combines, paradoxically, a genuine art, that of verbal form, and a suggestion of emotion which is all the more penetrating the less artificially produced it seems. The poet cannot succeed in manipulating this emotion as an artist except by taking infinite precautions to preserve its original purity. In this sense, poetry is the art of avoiding art. The most mysterious effects of poetry are naked ones. We find that technique is either totally absent from them or else has been totally reabsorbed. Poetry is the most difficult domain in which to separate aesthetics from psychology because it is the one in which art relies most on nature, sometimes attempting to be pure nature, and sometimes, if it cannot manage this immediately, attempting to attain such spontaneity by artificial means. But this effusion, whether sincere or simulated, is expressed by a verbal music which only rarely coincides with the psychological melody and which usually demands a complicated labor of adjustment that gives the verse its erudite aspect, so opposed in appearance, sometimes, to its true intentions.

Poetry, as a literary genre, seeks to give two sorts of pleasure: a strictly poetic pleasure and an aesthetic pleasure. The first has, in itself, no connection with the sentiment of the beautiful; it is purely natural, and the paradox of poetic literature consists precisely in creating this natural effect by a subtle use of the psychology of feeling; in a really astute poet, I should be less inclined to admire "a critic of the highest order" than a perspicacious psychologist; since the operations by which the poet succeeds in creating emotional values can be appreciated by the reader in the same way as any success of an affective order, they can be judged from an aesthetic point of view. The poem contains, then, a series of inextricably mingled expressions that are nevertheless susceptible to decomposition by analysis: a special affective impression, which is poetic pleasure in its pure state and can be investigated psychologically and psychologically only; an impression of poeticization, which is the fruit of a very subtle technique, and which returns by this roundabout route to the realm of aesthetic pleasure; and finally the impressions habitual to the other literary genres, which can be appreciated for the beauty of their execution, such as the impression caused by the ordinary play of the imagination when it is not specifically poetic (descriptive, dramatic, etc.), qualities of balance and proportion due to composition, to architecture, the impressions proper to the chosen instrument, generally verse, and which concern the aesthetics of formulation. One might say that in a poem the maximum of art is put at the service of an inspiration whose goal is only secondarily artistic and whose essential aim is the creation of a state of feeling to which art is virtually indifferent. This strange condition may be better conveyed perhaps by saying that in a poetic work it is only the poem which is beautiful, but that the poetry in it is content with being poetic.

This way of looking at things is entirely the contrary of Valéry's, but it was necessary to set it forth briefly, so that we can see the more clearly how the aesthetic predominates over the poetic in Valéry's view. We constantly feel that for him the poetic is not distinct from the beautiful, and this is not an entirely false view of the matter, although a partial one, for the characteristic of poetic emotion is its capacity to deal with anything that affords subsistence to the reverie that satisfies it, and under certain conditions beauty may very well provide that nutrition which poets more often glean from other, less intellectual sources nearer to the human heart. We might find examples of this in Valéry's own poems, and perhaps against his will. But this theoretic conception of poetry is much more aesthetic than poetic. It is not for nothing that he criticized what he took to be a derogatory formula: "So-and-so is more of a poet than an artist," which we might easily assume to be laudatory; it is not for nothing that Valéry so curiously combined the two ideas in this unacceptable statement: ". . . a very beautiful line of verse is a very pure element of poetry," as though there were not very beautiful lines of verse that are not in the slightest poetic and even some very poetic lines to which the epithet *beautiful* has very little application. But let us leave aside this distinction between the beautiful and the poetic, and, having examined Valéry's idea of the nature of poetry, let us go on to his way of considering the creation of the poem, in other words to a purely psychological problem, and one concerned essentially with the psychology of the creative artist. A little earlier we distinguished this from the psychology of the reader. To complete our picture, however, we must take note of the capital fact, on which Valéry very happily insisted, that the creator always envisages inside himself, sometimes in a very vivid manner, the real or the ideal reader for whom the work is intended, and that this image necessarily enters into his calculations. In the same way, though this is less important, the reader, too, recreates an author in his own way. Let us then follow Valéry in his exploration of the creative attitude. He certainly did not lack experience; his qualities as a psychologist and as a critic of his own work, his curiosity about the artist's activity and about mental life as a whole, guarantee us an authentic contact with these realities so difficult to analyze.

The Dispute over Inspiration

Poetic creation starts from a particular form of invention to which we traditionally give the name of inspiration. By reason of certain categorical formulations, Valéry passes as an enemy of this inspiration, and of all the states of feeling connected with it, which constitutes aggressive attitude toward current thought on this subject. On the other hand, Valéry emphasized the work and the intellectual aptitudes poetry requires, which also could not fail to violate the image many people have of the poet's activity. But Valéry's attitude has not seemed so shocking to psychologists and critics. Poetic creation has long been known to be a complex, erudite art requiring an extreme acuity of mind, the role of inspiration being singularly disproportionate to that of craftsmanship, though not, for all that, less important and indispensable. And this, if we examine his ideas closely, is exactly what Valéry says. In the end, Valéry, like everyone else, assigns the leading role to inspiration, and, when he seems to be attacking it, is in reality only attacking an extreme theory according to which all poetic activity is a dictation by some mysterious power, either internal or external, a thesis that has never been upheld to this point by anyone, and that never could be. Valéry is opposing the caricature of a theory without followers, or, at most, a naïve idea he encountered in people who had never given any thought to the composition of a poem. We may doubt, whatever he tells us, that he found it in real poets; even if many of them exaggerated the mysticism of inspiration, they always left a place for technical necessities.

Read Valéry and you will see that the argument is concerned not with the reality of inspiration but with its ability to create a work entirely on its own. The debate turns on the use of the word *all:*

> Supposing that inspiration is what it is believed to be, which is absurd, and which implies that *all* of a poem can be dictated to its author by some deity . . .

Valéry has no difficulty in drawing from such an absurdity

consequences which make its inherent contradictions quite clear:

> . . . it would be reasonable to deduce from this that an inspired poet would be able to write in a language other than his own, even one that he had never learned. . . .
>
> The inspired writer might also be ignorant in the same way of the age he lives in, the state of the tastes of his age, the works of his predecessors and of his rivals—unless we are to make of inspiration a power so subtle, so articulate, so sagacious, so knowledgeable, and so adept at calculation that there would seem no reason not to call it Intelligence and knowledge.[a]

This fantastic hypothesis allows Valéry to compare his imaginary poet to an urn full of marbles, a recording machine, a Ouija board, a medium, a newspaper editor, and a madman endowed with the gift of tongues.[1] Hence the following sallies, mocking the supernatural origin of inspired details as well as the miraculous continuity of inspiration throughout an entire work:

> X . . . would have us believe that a metaphor is a communication from on high. A metaphor is *what happens* when you *look in a certain way*, as a sneeze is what happens when you look at a sun. In what way? You feel it. Someday perhaps we shall be able to *say* it very exactly. Do this, do that—and there you have all the metaphors in the world. . . .[2]
>
> One day someone informed me that lyricism is "enthusiasm," or *afflatus*, and that the great lyric poets wrote their odes without stopping, at the speed of the voice in delirium, of the wind of the spirit blowing up a storm. . . . I replied that he was completely right; but that this was not a privilege of poetry alone, and that everyone knows that in order to build a locomotive it is indispensable that the builder be traveling at eighty miles per hour in order to carry out his task.[3]

We see how Valéry, by attributing untenable assertions

[a] *Rhumbs* in *Tel quel*, II, pp. 63–64. Cf. *Littérature* in *Tel quel*, I, p. 148: "One word crossed out—and the principle of total inspiration is destroyed."

to these consistently unidentified persons, triumphs over them
with a facile irony and then goes on to develop a less mythological viewpoint in opposition to these phantoms:

> The idea of inspiration, if one restricts it to this naïve
> image of an insufflation from outside, or of an omnipotent
> soul suddenly and temporarily substituted for our own,
> may suffice for the ordinary mythology of mental life.
> Almost all poets are content with it. Or rather, they do
> not wish to admit any other. But I simply cannot under-
> stand that a man should not try to explore himself as
> deeply as possible.
> There is a risk, it appears, of losing one's talent by at-
> tempting to explore its Underworld. But what does this
> talent matter? May one not find *something else?*[4]

We see how he rejected *en bloc* every sort of emotional
attachment to such a fantastic conception of inspiration: delirium, afflatus, reverie, primitivism, irrationality. . . . The
declarations are famous:

> . . . I found it unworthy, as I still do, to write by "en-
> thusiasm" alone. "Enthusiasm" is not a writer's state of
> mind.[5]

Note that in this passage "enthusiasm" is not denied, only
limited. On the other hand, it is with complete sincerity that
Valéry rejects everything that seems to him to infringe on
the liberty and the dignity of the mind. He taxes "enthusiasm" with insincerity precisely because it cannot last and
requires, in order to be maintained, its own simulation:

> Every "enthusiast" contains a false "enthusiast";
> every lover contains a dissembling lover; every man of
> genius contains a sham man of genius; and, in general,
> every *departure from the norm* presupposes a simulation
> of itself, since *continuity of character* must be main-
> tained, not only with regard to other people but also with
> regard to oneself.[b]

It is always the preoccupation with the totality of the
poem, in terms of practice with its continuity, that compels

[b] *Suite* in *Tel quel*, II, p. 325. Revised and completed in *Mélange*, pp. 180–81: ". . . in order to understand oneself, to count
on oneself, to think of oneself,—and, in short, to be . . . oneself."

Valéry to deny or to minimize the role of a power evidently incapable of accommodating it. He was to put it very well:

> The Pythoness cannot dictate a poem.
> Only one line—in other words a *unit*—and then another.
> This goddess of the Continuum is incapable of continuing.
> It is the Discontinuum which fills in the gaps.[6]

But it is also his desire for lucidity that leads Valéry to reject a power that is blind: "I would have given many a masterpiece that I believed unpremeditated for one page visibly governed. . . ."[7]; and it was a hatred for the physiological disturbance brought on by certain violent stimuli that made him in his youth go so far as to proclaim:

> . . . if I were to write, I should infinitely prefer to write something weak in complete and lucid awareness than to produce by means of a trance, when I was beside myself, a masterpiece of the first order.[8]

It is not only for himself that he fears the effects of this delirium, he also envisaged with repulsion the traces it would leave in the grating notes of an imperfect poem:

> The Gods preserve us from prophetic frenzy!
> In such transports I see above all the low efficiency of a machine—the imperfect machine.
> A good machine is silent. The cams do not make the axle vibrate. —Speak without shouting.
> No transports—they are a poor form of transportation.[9]

We have already remarked on how little Valéry is disposed to regard the poet as a dreamer.

> The true condition of a poet is that which is most distinct from the state of dreaming. In poetry I see nothing but conscious investigations, acceptance of exquisite shackles, inflection of thought, and the perpetual triumph of sacrifice. . . . The words *exactitude* and *style* conjure up the opposite of a dream; and when they are encountered in any work, the reader must ascribe to its author all the toil and all the time he found necessary to prevent the permanent dissipation of his thoughts . . . this was never an idle game, the task of capturing a lit-

tle grace, a little clarity, a little duration from the mobility of the things of the mind; and to change what passes
into what subsists.[10]

Eupalinos was "sparing of reverie"; he did not indulge
himself in dreaming up "imaginary edifices": "what I think is
feasible."[11] What a poet finds in dreams is mediocre or
detestable,[12] even if he found it beautiful at the moment.
Nor is the poet a simple-minded person: "By necessity, the
poet must be the last person in the world to be taken in by
words."[13] And it is not even important for him to experience
a poetic emotion, which is not, in any case, sufficient to make
a poet:

> . . . the effect of poetry and the artificial synthesis of
> this state by means of a work are two very distinct
> things: as different from each other as a sensation and an
> action.[14]
> It is not a poet's function to experience the poetic
> state: that is a private matter. His function is to create
> it in others. A poet can be recognized—or at least each
> of us recognizes his own—by the simple fact that he
> changes the reader into "a man inspired."[c]

This is the way in which Valéry displaced inspiration, shifting it from the writer to the reader, which was the most
ingenious verbal means of ridding himself of it.

It is not difficult, on the other hand, to unearth the inevitable concessions Valéry did make to inspiration. They can
sometimes be found in the same passages that seem to deny
it or its correlatives. On the same page that contains the famous remark about "enthusiasm" not being a state of mind
for a writer, Valéry notes that "the power of the fire . . . becomes useful and propulsive only when it has been harnessed
by the machines of art . . ." and thanks to "correctly applied
restraints." He describes the author of a speech as being simultaneously "source, engineer, and constraint."[15] He re-

---

[c] *Poésie et pensée abstraite* in *Variété* V, p. 138. Cf. *Propos sur
la poésie* in *Conferencia*, 1928, p. 474: "Inspiration—but it is to
the reader that it belongs and for him that it is intended, as it is
the poet's business to make him think of it, make him believe in
it. . . ." Valéry was later to say: "A genius is the man who makes
me one" (*Mauvaises pensées et autres*, p. 204).

turned quite often to this poet-engineer, poem-machine comparison. He always allows the machine pre-eminence, but is unable to deny the necessity of the energy it uses.

This does not mean that there is not something else necessary to make a poet, some *virtue* that cannot be decomposed, that cannot be analyzed into definable acts, into so many hours of work. The Steam-Pegasus and the Hour-Pegasus are still not official units of poetic power. There is a special quality, a sort of individual energy proper to the poet. It appears in him and reveals him to himself at certain moments that are of infinite worth.[16]

In order to characterize the exceptional nature of inspiration, Valéry borrowed an image from theology that is strikingly different from his engineering analogy. He compared inspiration to Grace, a notion not much less surprising than "the naïve image of an insufflation from outside or of an omnipotent soul, etc. . . ." Of course, all comparisons as such are valid to illustrate what analysis cannot encompass. Valéry's comparison here, which is no more original than Boileau's reference to astrological influence, shows very clearly the hiatus that exists between inspiration and the general conditions that precede it:

The artist lives on intimate terms with *his* absolute and in expectation of *his* necessity. He seeks this necessity at every instant; he achieves it by means of the most unexpected, the most insignificant circumstances, and there is no fixed proportion, no uniformity of relation between the magnitude of the affect and the importance of the cause. He expects an *absolutely precise* answer (since it must engender an act of execution) to an *essentially incomplete* question: he wants the effect that will be produced by whatever may arise within him. Sometimes the gift precedes the search, and takes by surprise a man who finds himself gratified without preparation. Such cases of a sudden Grace perfectly demonstrate the contrast between the two sensations accompanying a single phenomenon: what seems to us *something that might not have happened* imposes itself upon us with the same force as *something that couldn't not happen,* and *which had to be what it is.*[d]

Valéry also employed even more widely used mythological analogies: "The Gods, very graciously, give us such-and-such a first line *gratis.*"[17] These indeterminate gods are again invoked in the dialogue *L'Idée fixe* to characterize the independence that products of composition possess with regard to us: "a certain figure" is formed, "that no longer depends on you." / "On whom then, Good God?" / "On the Gods! . . . By God!"[18] In his letters to Pierre Louÿs, Valéry even speaks of several lines that came "already done to a turn by the Muse."[19] Or else, as we have seen, he invokes the Pythoness, but always as capable of dictating only one line. He might just as well have accepted the intervention of a medium or a Ouija board, limiting their power to a single sentence or a series of knocks, since for him inspiration, when all is said and done, is not something to be denied but simply something *momentary.*[e]

Valéry duly noted all the classic characteristics of inspiration: spontaneity, impersonality, unpredictability, surprise; he recognized that it was fragmentary, undependable, impure, variable, and deceptive. The poetic state (like the dreaming state, to which he relates it) is "perfectly irregular, inconstant, involuntary, fragile . . . we keep it as we obtain it, by accident." These "precious formations . . . are given to us by chance, and chance takes them away from us."[20] A splendid page describes the birth of these inspired fragments, out of which *work* will make the poem if they are judged valid by the critical faculties:

[d] *Discours prononcé au Deuxième Congrès International d'Esthétique et de Science de l'Art* in *Variété* IV, p. 258. For Valéry's clear awareness of the parallelism between certain poetic and theological problems, see a long parenthesis in *Poésie pure* in *Oeuvres complètes,* vol. C, pp. 201–2.

[e] This disbelief in continuous inspiration dates back to his youth: "Never again will my ideal artist abandon himself to the accidents of inspiration—never will he write a whole poem in the course of one feverish night . . . (I don't like Musset!)." Letter to Pierre Louÿs, June 2, 1890, quoted by Henri Mondor, *Le Vase brisé de Paul Valéry.*

. . . happy compound, coming into being of itself in the impure current of mental life. As a specific combination is precipitated from a mixture, so some interesting *figure* will separate itself out from the disorder, or from the vagueness, or from the generality of our inner floundering.

It is pure sound that rings amid all the noises. It is a glimpse of diamond in the great mass of blue clay: an instant infinitely more precious than any other, and than the circumstances which engender it! It excites an incomparable satisfaction—and an immediate temptation: it raises the hope that we may find a whole treasure *in its immediate vicinity* . . . and this hope sometimes leads a man on to engage in a limitless task.

Some people think that a certain heaven opens at that instant. . . . But, as ill luck will have it, it is often enough only a piece of childishness, an error, some nonsense that is revealed to us in this way. We must not count only the times when we were fortunate: this miraculous manner of producing affords us no guarantee at all of the product's value. The spirit bloweth where it listeth; we see it blowing in the ears of fools, and to them it whispers what they can understand.[f]

The great creators are not privileged in this respect: "Genius is most fertile in absurdities, from which emerges the marvel that it brings to light."[21]

Nonetheless, among the raw materials of inspiration, some remain utilizable. These are of two sorts: the first naturally pure, and exceptional; the others contain impurities, and must be refined:

> But these are only isolated instants, and this superior energy (by which is meant an energy such that all man's other energies are unable to compose and replace it) *exists, or can function only by brief and fortuitous manifestations.*

[f] *Mémoires d'un poème*, pp. XLIX–L. Cf. *Lust* in *"Mon Faust,"* p. 31: "The spirit bloweth where it can, and what it can," and *Cours de poétique*, lecture 18: "It is because we do not perceive all the moves in the game that we are so struck by these productions with a value that transcends us. . . . We do not count the tricks we lost, only the tricks we won; our silly mistakes are excluded from the statistics."

. . . The treasures it reveals to our mind's eye, the ideas
or the forms it produces for us are far from having an
equal value in the eyes of others. These moments of
infinite worth, these instants that bestow a sort of universal dignity on the relations and on the intuitions they
engender are no less productive of illusory or incommu-
nicable values. *That which has value for us alone is
valueless.* That is the law of literature.[g] These sublime
states are in reality "absences" in which we encounter
natural marvels that exist nowhere else—but these marvels are impure, I mean they are mingled with things
both vile and vain, insignificant or incapable of resisting
the light of day, or else impossible to retain, to preserve.
In the state of exaltation, all that glitters is not gold.

In short, instants show us depths where the best of
ourselves resides—but in the form of motes buried in
formless matter, in fragments of bizarre or crude configuration. We must therefore separate these elements of
noble metal from the mass, take pains to fuse them together, and then fashion some jewel from the result.
. . . Such expressions, welling up from some emotion,
are only accidentally *pure*—they bring a great deal of
dross with them, they contain many defects whose effect
would be to disturb poetic development and to interrupt the prolonged resonance which it is, after all, our
task to excite in another's soul.[22]

The comparison with minerals does not account adequately
for the mobility inherent in the mind's operations. Valéry
understood the instability present in the unexpected combination supplied by an inspiration, and in order to show how
the poet may preserve it before it disappears, he compared
the poet to the metal founder who "anxiously waits for that
single instant when he must draw the incandescent substance
he has produced out of the fire"; thus,

. . . the poet must promptly wrench this precious accident of his enthusiasm from his mind and immediately
stabilize it, before that same mind, *swept beyond the
frontiers of the beautiful,* takes it back, dissolves it, and
fuses it once more with all its other infinite combinations.[23]

[g] Later he was to say, more expressively: "The brazen law of
literature" (*Poésie et pensée abstraite* in *Variété V*, p. 157).

The difficulty of keeping a record of inspirations, which are as evanescent as they are dazzling, and their propensity to disappear into total oblivion are well known to writers and to psychologists of invention.

We have seen in this passage the concession to enthusiasm, a fatal concession once one allows inspiration its role. At a session of the Société française de Philosophie, Valéry was once pressed by Paul Desjardins to provide some clarification of his "rejection of enthusiasm." Valéry was led to distinguish between two successive psychological states that would, in some sense, abolish inspiration by sharing its activities: in the first phase the poet is a prey to what amounts to a foreknowledge of his discovery; in the second he proceeds methodically to the revelation, which may prove either satisfactory or disappointing.

> What I had in mind is this: there are two states; one in which the person exercising the writer's craft is pierced by a sort of lightning flash; for, after all, this intellectual and nonpassive life is composed of fragments; it is, in a way, made up of elements which are fugitive but evidently very rich, which do not illuminate the mind as a whole, which on the contrary suggest that there are completely new forms accessible by means of a certain amount of work. What I have sometimes observed is the onset of a sensation in the mind, of a glow, not an enlightening glow, but a dazzling one. It is a warning, it reveals much more than it illuminates, and, in short, it is itself an enigma which brings with it the assurance that it may be postponed. One says: "I see, and tomorrow I'll look into it further." A phenomenon occurs, a special sort of sensitivity is created; soon one will go into the darkroom and see the image appear.
>
> I don't guarantee that this is a very good description, since it is something very difficult to describe. I have just said that there is the darkroom period: here there can be no enthusiasm or your plate will be spoiled, you must have your reagents, you must work like your own employee, your own foreman. The boss has given you the spark; it's up to you to get something from it. What's very odd is the disappointment that may follow. There are illusory gleams.[24]

The fact nevertheless remains that inspiration, however confused it may be, is the principal element. It may take extremely varied forms, impose itself as obvious and immediate, or appear in the form of an invitation to take a certain path. It is even probable that between spontaneous inspiration and work there exists, in addition, a sort of inspiration that is stimulated, helped into being by research. Auto-excitation is part of the poet's technical apparatus. But the poet is still more a vibrant and trained attention, a receptivity always prepared, and equipped with exquisite antennae. It is, I think, in this sense that Valéry very accurately spoke of "the phenomenon of sensitization":

> . . . I wonder whether the effect of intellectual labor is not to favor some sort of growth of sensibility? Work itself would not provide the solution (in the aesthetic order, moreover, neither problems nor solutions are, in general, determined), but it would greatly increase the number of opportunities favorable to the artist's general design; it would make the artist, momentarily, into a resonator extremely sensitive to all the incidents of consciousness that might serve his design.[h]

It is not certain whether or not this sensitization is to be attributed to intellectual work; more likely it is a sharpening of the sense of the affective suitability of the imagination's

[h] *La création artistique* in *Bulletin de la Société française de Philosophie*, 1928, p. 17. On the sensitization necessary to grasp the evanescent formations of inspiration as soon as they appear, see the *Cours de poétique:* "Sensibility in its pure state is revealed as a mine of happy discoveries, of virgin combinations. In this state there exists a freedom to obey certain mutual affinities, an interplay permitting the elements to attract one another according to certain laws, the law of the maximum probable effect, for example. It is good to be highly sensitized to these first effects occurring before the transition to the solid state, to the ready-made article that is of no use to the artist. The self of the moment must be sensitized to these first combinations. The majority of individuals do not stop to consider these first terms . . ." (lecture 17). "First prize in the lottery is never won by just anyone. The favorable conditions encountered by one individual never fall from the heavens at random, they fall on men who are supersensitized to a certain atmosphere. . . . There must always be a certain gentleman sensitized to something and a special state of sensitization" (lecture 18).

products to the thematic emotion governing the poem. But Valéry always tried to consider the enterprise of poetic exploration from the rational and deliberate angle. One of his last articles even suggests that he had isolated a supreme state of inspiration, which he calls illumination and which is to be distinguished from ordinary inspiration precisely by this character of total discipline:

> I shall say (aware of the risk involved) that Mallarmé, carrying the problem of will in art to its supreme degree of generality, raised himself above the desire for the inspiration which dictates one moment of a poem and reached that of illumination, which reveals the essence of poetry itself.[25]

What emerges, ultimately, is not the negation of inspiration but a great mistrust of it. Inspiration has value only when it is controlled, criticized, re-examined and worked on:

> . . . the retort we make to our "genius" is sometimes worth more than its attack . . . probability is unfavorable to this demon: our mind shamelessly whispers a million stupidities in our ear for one beautiful idea it lets us have; and even that piece of luck will become something worthwhile only by means of the treatment that accommodates it to our end. In the same way minerals, worthless in deposits, in veins below the earth, assume their value when they reach the light of day and are worked on at the surface.
> Far then from it being the intuitive elements which provide the value of works, take away the works and those gleams of yours will be nothing but spiritual accidents lost in the statistics of the brain's local functions.[26]

Their real value comes only "from the collaboration of the whole man."[27]

EXPECTATION AND CHANCE

Insufficient but necessary, then, is inspiration. Yet if Valéry makes so little of it, this is doubtless because for him mental life is perpetual invention: ". . . man does almost nothing but invent";[28] yet this is "automatic and banal invention, which may, moreover, become "less and less automatic."[29] It is also because the faculty of selection amid this chaos seems to him essential. And even then, something worth selecting must appear. Here we are completely helpless: "We have no means of reaching within ourselves exactly what we hope to find there."[30] All we can do is wait. Will is always reduced in this domain

> . . . to a simple halt, to the maintenance, or else to the renewal of certain conditions. . . . We can act directly only on the freedom of our mental system. We lower the degree of this freedom . . . but as for the modifications and the substitutions which this constraint leaves still possible, we simply wait until what we desire appears, for we can do nothing else but wait for it.[31]

Valéry often insisted on this attitude in the poet: "The poet's function is to wait."[32] And, in *Autres rhumbs*, under the heading *Poésie perdue*, he devoted to it a page so charged with intellectual lyricism that it deserved a counterpart in verse, a poem like those in *Charmes*, for it is a passage that illustrates extremely well the pathos Valéry described in the dramas of intellectual life:

> Spirit, *Pure expectation*. Eternal suspense, threat of all I desire. Sword that may spring from a cloud, how I sense its *imminence!* An unknown idea is still in the furrow and worry of my brow. I am still distinct from all thought; equally remote from all words, from all the forms that are in me. My fixed eye reflects a lifeless object; my ear does not hear what it is hearing. O my faceless presence, what a look is your vacant unpeopled look, what power that indefinable power like the power in the air before a storm! I do not know what is being prepared. I am love, and thirst, and no name. For there is no man in Man, and no *me* in *the self. But* there will be an act without being, an effect without cause, an accident that is my substance. The event which has no form and no duration attacks all form and all duration. It makes visible the invisible and invisible the visible. It consumes what attracts it, and illuminates what it destroys. . . . I am here, I am ready. Strike. I am here, my secret eye fixed on the blind center of my expecta-

tion. . . . It is here that an essential event sometimes explodes and brings me into being.[33]

Along with this dramatic description of the poet's expectation of the lightning flash of inspiration, Valéry offered a gentler image of the poet's waiting for poetic grace in the love poem *Les Pas*:

> *Ne hâte pas cet acte tendre,*
> *Douceur d'être et de n'être pas,*
> *Car j'ai vécu de vous attendre,*
> *Et mon coeur n'était que vos pas.*

> [Do not hasten this tender act,
> Sweetness between being and not being;
> For I have lived by waiting for you,
> And my heart was only your steps.]

Between the vigilant mind and the revelation both expected and unexpected there is a relation difficult to analyze. This expectation of something unforeseeable is not without structure, for it is manifestly oriented, so to speak, by the emotion seeking a response to itself: it is a sort of active void, or better still a schema prepared, in the unfolding of the poet's psychic transformations, for the substance its form will accommodate. Valéry defined two cases of these "mysterious relations between desire and event": the mind

> . . . can always anticipate in its penumbra the truth or the decision being sought, which it knows to be at the mercy of the least trifle, of that same insignificant disturbance which seemed to distract and deflect it indefinitely.
>
> Sometimes what we long to see in our thoughts (even a simple recollection), seems to us a precious object we might hold and handle through an enveloping cloth that hides it from our eyes. . . . Sometimes we invoke what we hope for, having defined it by certain conditions. . . . We present our desire to ourselves as we would a magnet to a mixed heap of powder, from which one iron filing would suddenly leap out. . . .[1]

[1] *Leçon inaugurale du Cours de poétique* in *Variété* V, pp. 313–14. Valéry sometimes reversed the terms of the relation: it is the external world that affords him the necessary elements; the mind,

In the first case, we guess, we predict, we recognize in advance, without yet knowing what we are going to discover; we discern in the general confusion, probably thanks to the special form of our desire, a possibility that is capable of answering to it, but that we shall have to elaborate:

> Inventing must closely resemble recognizing a tune in the monotonous dripping of water, in the regular rhythm of a train or of a rotating machine. . . .
>
> There must be an object, I think, or a vague nucleus or substance—and a pattern.
>
> There is a part of man that does not feel itself alive except in the act of creation: I invent, therefore I am.
>
> The general course of all invention belongs to this general type: a succession of almost continuous distortions of the given substance, and a threshold—a sudden perception of the *future* of one of these states.
>
> Future, in other words usable value, significant value, singularity.[34]

In the second case, instead of a pattern there are conditions established in advance, a convention or group of conventions that define the form of the discovery in advance and are then charged by a transformation of the sensibility. The poet "is a modification in a man—which makes him sensitive to certain *terms* of his own development: those which recompense this expectation in order to conform with the convention."[35]

Happy convergence of the oriented pattern with a state to be elaborated, or fortuitous adjustment of a state to the pre-

---

solicited by the empty frame, provides what is needed to fill it. In *L'Idée fixe* (p. 169) he gave the name of "A-propos" to that "tropism" or that "intelligence" of the "Implex" in which "what is needed" is "attracted, summoned up by the circumstance itself." In *Mauvaises pensées* (p. 48), he described a more ordinary type of this attraction, based on the generating power of representations: he named "the soliciting soul," the "naïve soul of the moment" which man is "tempted to merge with," by virtue of the "authority of nascent states" (on a high, steep place, we think of throwing ourselves off; of drinking when confronted with a brimming glass). This is what Renouvier called "mental vertigo." But Valéry prefers to shift the temptation from the individual to the object: "The locked cupboard invokes Bluebeard's wife; the apple, Eve." He concludes: "There exist in us many independent *expectations*."

viously established conditions—such would be the two essential forms of poetic discovery. It would not be impossible to find traces of these two sorts of discovery in Valéry's poems. Both presuppose a vigilance. Desire lies in wait and then abruptly seizes upon the discovery. Valéry liked to express this kind of ambush by the compelling image of the spider crouching at the center of its web:

> I imagine this poet as a cunning and resourceful mind, pretending to be asleep at the imaginary center of her still uncreated work, the better to await that instant of her particular power which is her prey. In the vague depth of her eyes, all the forces of her desire, all the springs of her instinct are taut. There, attentive to the opportunities from which she must select her nourishment; there, dim amid the webs and the secret harp-strings she has fashioned from language, the meshes interweaving and always vaguely vibrating, a mysterious Arachne, a huntress Muse, lies in wait.[j]

This essentially active state of expectation, this attention, has been described by Valéry, in a needlessly complicated fashion, as an "attention with two entrances." The poet waits for "the unexpected word—which cannot be foreseen, but can be waited for"; he is "the first to hear it." "His ear speaks to him":

> To hear? but that is to speak. We do not understand the thing heard unless we have spoken it ourselves by means of another cause.
> To speak is to hear.[36]

Which means that the word and the hearing of the word imply each other; but this solidarity is very general, it concerns the entire use of language and is in no way peculiar to the poet. Valéry has amplified this set of antitheses, which helps create the effect of mystery:

[j] *Au sujet d' "Adonis"* in *Variété,* pp. 69–70. Valéry was struck by the "psychological" bearing of repulsive animals; see the curious page in *Mélange* on the "mythology of nerves," p. 202. On the comparison of the mind to a hunter, see *Propos me concernant,* pp. 34 and 52. The symbolic spider also occurs in the poem *Aurore* (*Charmes*), but by a permutation of roles not infrequent in Valéry, instead of representing the poet it represents his ideas.

In the poet:
The ear speaks,
The mouth listens;
It is the intelligence, the consciousness, that
    engenders and dreams;
It is sleep that sees clearly;
It is image and hallucination that look,
It is lack and lacuna that create.[k]

Revelation is indicated by a shock, but a shock already
allowed for. "I shall give myself a surprise,"[37] the author
tells himself.

Viendra l'heureuse surprise

[The fortunate surprise will come]

sings the poet of *Palme*. And the delight of this surprise is in
the unexpectedness of its content:

It is the unexpectedness, the discontinuity, the form
of reality and of existence which one would never have
thought of—that constitute the charm and the power of
observation and experiment.
    You believed you were contemplating or anticipating
the possible solutions, and there is another one. . . .[38]

This signature is well known to artists. They themselves are
astonished by it. Valéry went so far as to see in it a guarantee
of truth: "Exact ideas are always unexpected. Every unexpected idea has some moments of exactitude."[39] But, if the
writer admires himself, he also abases himself, for he does
not recognize himself in these sudden illuminations:

There was, and remains, a mystery of *inspiration*,
which is the name given to the spontaneous formulation, in someone, of speech or of ideas which to him
seem marvels of which he feels by nature incapable.[40]

We have seen that for Valéry inspiration was less often a
clear and definitive revelation than a gleam, a state to be

[k] *Littérature* in *Tel quel*, I, pp. 142–43. These formulas, and
others, were corrected to suit their own purposes by Breton and
Éluard, in *La Révolution surréaliste*, no. 12, December 15, 1929,
Notes sur la poésie: ". . . the ear laughs, the mouth swears, it is
the intelligence that kills, etc. . . ."

exploited. But whatever the value of these spontaneous products, their character is always accidental. They are the children of chance. Chance is Valéry's true Muse, and the only god of his psychic universe. "My luck is more than myself. A person is merely answers to a quantity of impersonal incidents."[41] All thought rests on memory; now, memory is fortuitously provoked: "The past lives on accidents. Every incident *draws* a memory."[42] Chance is the very basis of the mind:

> The mind is chance. I mean that the very meaning of the word mind contains, among other things, all the significations of the word *chance. Laws* are acted, mimicked by this chance. But it is more profound, stable, and intimate than any known—conscious—law.
> Any law I conceive is unstable, limited, constrained.[43]

Chance blindly rules all human activity, including the most successful artistic activity. Stupidity must be given its place, Valéry says, for "men do not know what they are doing," and "it is enough to consider the developments of the most premeditated action, even the most successful one, to be able —to be obliged—to classify it among the productions of 'chance.'"[44]

The poet's labor must therefore reckon with this mental chance. Valéry seems at first to prefer struggling against it, positing chance as a kind of more positive equivalent of inspiration:

> The image which represents poets as receiving from imaginary creatures the best of their works is or should be intolerable to them.
> *Agents of transmission* is a humiliating conception.
> Myself, I want no part of it. I invoke only that chance which constitutes the basis of all minds; and then, a stubborn labor which is *against* that very chance.[45]

This struggle against chance must inevitably be based upon it: "I realized, of course, that our mind must, by necessity, count on its accidents. . . ." Valéry said in the *Note à l'Introduction à la Méthode de Léonard de Vinci,* but he did not believe "in the power of delirium, in the necessity of ignorance, in the illuminations of the absurd, in creative incoherence."[46] Valéry's art is a controlled and disciplined art opposed to the optimistic aesthetic of improvisation. Valéry is not one of those writers who

> . . . consider their art not as a thing to be mastered—
> *sine qua non*—but as a game of chance in which one
> can try one's luck. They abandon themselves to luck
> entirely and accept the valuation it is pleased to confer
> upon them. (They will even add something.)[47]

But it would be a mistake to suppose that this struggle against chance seeks to eliminate it altogether. First of all, chance plays a subtle role in the production of certain effects (to which we shall return); we can transpose to the poetic level what Valéry says of painting, apropos of Degas:

> Some room must be left for *chance* in the work, so
> that certain charms may function, exalt, and possess the
> palette and the hand.[48]

Then, a general discipline (to struggle against chance on principle) cannot neglect the practical conditions of work which, here, suggest taking advantage of the precious accidents chance affords. We oppose the natural chaos of the mind, but make use of that providential, and moreover indispensable, chance, since without it "we should be without mind."[49] What the poet exploits is not chance in general, though he obviously counts on its capacity for surprise, but the fortunate accidents, the favorable encounters, the opportunities. His vigilant glance detects them, even at the expense of his initial intentions, which he does not scruple to renounce if they seem less fruitful to him. Valéry belongs to the family of poets who gladly collaborate with chance, despite the other part of his doctrine which bases poetic labor on conscious will and control of style.

> Take advantage of the fortunate accident. The true
> writer abandons his idea for the sake of another which
> appears to him as he is looking for the words of the
> chosen one, appears through these very words. He finds
> himself to be more powerful, even more profound, by
> this unexpected interaction of words—though he instantly
> sees their value—and what a reader will derive from

them is his *merit*. And he passes for profound and creative—having been merely a critic and a swift hunter.

The same is true in war, or at the Bourse.[50]

The least satisfactory accidents are not useless, for they
can be improved:

> A certain confusion in the memory brings up a word
> which is not the right one, but becomes the best one
> without relenting. This word gathers others about it, this
> confusion becomes a system, superstition, etc.[51]
>
> And that is how a poet grasps a combination of words,
> perseveres, insists, and gives it a certain value.
>
> Transformation of the fortuitous, of the inadmissible,
> of the shameful.[52]
>
> There is an imbecile in me, and I must take advantage
> of his mistakes. Externally, I must conceal, excuse them.
> . . . But inside, I do not deny them, I try to use them.
> It is an eternal battle against the gaps, the gusts, the
> scatterings, forgetting and neglect. But who am I, if they
> are not?[53]

Even the mind's inadvertences due to an organic lapse may
afford a profitable occasion. Consider the dialogue of *L'Idée
fixe*:

> "The same mental event which, physiologically, is
> . . . similar to a failure, which is a product of fatigue, of
> local exhaustion, an *accident*, a local response compara-
> ble to a *lapsus linguae*, can, on the other hand, assume
> a value . . . a literary value, for example. . . ."
>
> "Thanks for that!"
>
> "Yes. It can afford a very felicitous, very new little
> effect which consciousness evaluates, accepts, approves,
> records. . . . And in an appropriate milieu, this little
> record . . ."
>
> "Will be called Shakespearean!"
>
> "At the very least! . . ."[54]

Valéry rehabilitated the demon *Lapsus*: "*Lapsus*, admi-
rably enough, occasionally grants some very felicitous error,
felix culpa: the tongue has slipped to good advantage."[55]
And he made Faust benefit by an error of his secretary's.[1] In

---

[1] *Lust* in *"Mon Faust,"* pp. 21–22. *"Eros energumen?* . . . It
can't be. . . . That's not me. But it's not bad. . . . It should be

conclusion, the poet uses any means to attain his end:

> A poet is the most utilitarian of beings. Sloth, despair,
> accidents of language, odd looks—everything the prac-
> tical man loses, rejects, ignores, eliminates, forgets, the
> poet collects and by his art gives some value.[56]

The best products of chance have a higher and more lasting role: they serve as models to the creative will, which will
compete with them. The young Valéry envisaged as a pure
method:

> To attempt to rediscover with conscious intent some
> results analogous to the interesting or usable results
> which mental chance affords us (among a hundred thou-
> sand ordinary effects).[57]

Chance teaches us to do without chance. The rare beauties
it allows us invite the intelligence to produce equivalents
which it will owe to itself alone. We find here the opposition
to involuntary creation in a state of trance:

> A lightning flash gets me nowhere. It affords me only
> the means to admire myself. I am much more inter-
> ested in knowing how to produce at my own discretion
> a tiny spark than in waiting to project here and there
> the flashes of an uncertain lightning.[58]

But since the mind can expect only such results, we may
wonder if there is so great a difference between the flashes
and the sparks; it is reduced, apparently, to that between
spontaneous inspiration and provoked inspiration. It is always
chance which gives the idea, but in the first case it has come
of itself and in the second it has been invited. Consciousness
is limited to determining its range, the conditions to which it
must answer—and these vary with each poet:

> Consciousness is a restriction of chance, a chance to
> which we adjust a *convention*. And what is an accident,
> if not that addition which creates an expectation, gives
> an unequal importance to the various faces of a set of
> dice?

---

me. Whether it's a product of chance, a stammer on my part or
carelessness on yours, I like it, I'll keep it. . . . I see what I can
do with it!"

These faces are equal from a certain point of view, unequal according to another. Where one loses, another wins. A certain idea, a certain expression occurring to Racine and rejected by him as a loss, Hugo would have seized upon as a gain. . . .[m]

Chance—supposing that the calculation of probabilities might offer the same original combinations to several poets, and that the latter, instead of avidly seizing upon them, had the freedom to reject or accept them—would thus afford, ultimately, no more than a possibility of choice.

WHAT MAKES A WORK OF ART

Genius, "considered as judgment," consists precisely in the faculty of choosing among accidents:

One must be *two men* in order to invent. The first forms combinations, the second chooses, recognizes what he wants and what matters to him among the former's products.
What is called "genius" is much less the former's act —the act which combines—than the latter's promptness to understand the value of what has just been produced and to grasp this product.[n]

The author examines the product of inspiration in the manner of a scientist: "Inspiration is the hypothesis which reduces the author to the role of an observer."[59] Which brings us back to regarding the great poet as a critic of the first rank. But it is not only among the spontaneous productions of sensibility that this aesthetic selection can function; it also has at its disposal the enormous resources of the creations of humanity's past, on which it can fruitfully draw. Valéry, who

[m] *Calepin d'un poète* in *Oeuvres complètes,* vol. C, p. 182. There is no need to insist that Valéry's antihistorical bias leads him to propose an example in inadequate terms.
[n] *Analecta,* XXXIII. Cf. *Cours de poétique:* "The creative, idea-discovering self is . . . quite limited, not being the complete self. The self which discovers the idea is not the self which evaluates it. There are successive stages of being . . ." (lecture 16). "Our greatest merit is not to find, but to choose what is found" (lecture 18).

rejected in the name of an absolute poetry, independent of fashion and the anticipation of future taste, the solicitations of the moment and who more than once manifested his anti-modernism and condemned the emphasis on originality, here adopts the classical doctrine of imitation. To select deliberately among the wealth of tradition seems to him as meritorious as to invent, and, on the whole, he does not believe it is possible to distinguish the one action from the other:

> . . . despite recent superstition, I attribute a particular principle of glory to the man who selects, who does not pretend to ignore acquired beauties, or who adopts, in his felicitous knowledge of the treasures time has formed, the means of his perfection. The mystery of choice is no less a mystery than that of invention, granted that it is even distinct from it.[60]

Choice, among inspirations, accidents, memories, concerns only details. It cannot create a work. For that, labor is also required, "intelligent labor."[61] "Arrangement and the final harmony of the independent properties which must be composed are never obtained by recipe or automatism, but by miracle or else by effort; by miracles *and* by deliberate efforts combined."[62] When we are given "the state of inner modification" which produces a beautiful line of verse, "it is not enough to produce this complete object, this composition of beauties, this collection of happy accidents for the mind which a noble poem affords. In that way we obtain only fragments."[63] Genius itself cannot replace work. And moreover, Valéry disparaged genius. We recall Monsieur Teste's scorn: "Take me literally: genius is *easy*. . . . I simply mean —that I know how such a thing is conceived."[64] *Cahier B 1910* reduced its power to a kind of mania: ". . . 'genius' is a habit some men get into."[65] And thirty years later, Valéry has Faust answer his disciple:

> I think my genius is merely my habit of doing what I can. . . . I marvel that this genius has taken the regular form, the routine of habits, and has come to "create" (as you say) within me—or by me—from a certain hour to another, almost every day. . . .[66]

We might establish a perfect parallel between what Valéry

says about genius and what he says about inspiration: it is necessary, but insufficient. It gives only fragmentary and isolated results, because, in its essence, it, too, is momentary: ". . . genius resides in a moment."[67]

> Having "genius" is a profoundly different thing from creating a valid work. All the transports in the world produce only *discreet* elements.[68]

Talent must re-establish the continuity, and its role is more important than that of genius. "Talent without genius isn't much. Genius without talent is nothing."[69] Talent can, if necessary, substitute for genius; it can doubtless go as far as to simulate it. But as we have just seen in the case of inspiration, this despised genius remains essential nonetheless, and alone gives the work and the author their value, because it places them above itself: ". . . we are worth something only for having been, and for being able to be, for a moment, outside ourselves."[70]

One must know how to arrest and utilize genius as one grasps and exploits chance. This is, at bottom, the same thing. Genius is, first of all, sensitivity to chance. Faust says to his amazed secretary: "You see how simple it is. It's a matter of being sensitive to some accident."[71] Genius is also a matter of chance, bizarre in its effect on the author: ". . . it's a strange role to distribute the gifts of chance to a crowd of unknown people,"[72] and incomprehensible:

> Intelligence . . . is to be lucky in the game of associations and of appropriate memories.
> A man of mind (*lato* and *stricto sensu*) is a man who has a winning streak. We do not know why. He does not know why.[73]

And genius is nothing without maturation: "That little moment outside myself is a seed [grain] or projects itself as a seed does. All the rest of duration develops it, or lets it perish."[74] Valéry compares to germination the expansive force of these privileged moments: "There is a curiously powerful spring confined in seeds [grains] and in certain moments."[75] And, as the poet is not sparing of images, and inspiration or the association of ideas also affects the essayist,

his genius for homonymy thoroughly exploits the metaphor
of the seed to add to fruitful accidents both dynamic accidents and sterile ones:

> There are particles of time which differ from the rest
> as a *grain* of dust differs from a *grain* of sand. Their
> appearances are almost the same, their futures not
> comparable.[76]

Valéry has not developed the notion of maturation very
far, doubtless because it would have obliged him to reckon
with unconscious labor,[o] a concept which outraged his intellectualism, and also because it contradicted his theory of
human creation by separate acts, which we shall discuss in
the following chapter. Yet Monsieur Teste often said: *"Matu-
rare!"*[77] And the whole of the poem *Palme* is a hymn to
invisible growth:

> Par la sève solennelle
> Une espérance éternelle
> Monte à la maturité.
>
> .   .   .   .
>
> Patience, patience,
> Patience dans l'azur!
> Chaque atome de silence
> Est la chance d'un fruit mûr!

[Through the solemn sap, an eternal hope rises to ma-
turity. . . . Patience, patience in the blue air! Each
atom of silence is the chance of a ripe fruit!]

He insisted, on the contrary, on the importance of conscious and deliberate work. Intellectual, rational, critical, the
poet's effort even requires a quasi-mathematical exactitude:

> Without very precise calculation, a work is worthless
> —does not function. An excellent poem supposes a host
> of exact reasonings. A matter not so much of *forces* as
> of the application of forces.[78]

Valéry saw clearly the danger of this mechanization. He
knew that the chief difficulty is to keep discipline from doing

[o] See in the *Cours de poétique*, lecture 18, the entire development against "the little man inside man."

away with the poetic effect which it is its very aim to emphasize:

> The most difficult enterprise to conceive, to undertake and above all to sustain in the arts and especially in poetry is that of *submitting to conscious will* the production of a work, without this rigorous, deliberately adopted condition altering the essential qualities, the charms and grace mandatory in every work which claims to initiate minds into the delights of the mind.[79]

But the theoretician's bias won out over the poet's anticipation.

The poet's labor begins with inspiration, or even before it, since inspiration can be induced. But it functions at its highest degree of efficiency in its rivalry with inspiration. Valéry often contrasted the "given lines" (products of inspiration, of genius, of luck, of accident—an inseparable complex), with the "calculated" ones,[80] the lines one "finds" with the lines one "makes."[81] Among the lines bestowed gratuitously, some are doubtless perfect from the start, but others still need to be refined: "One perfects those one has found."[82] As for the fabricated lines, they are the product of an effort to equal their natural models encountered by chance: thus the marvels of accidental statuary on the beaches were, according to Eupalinos, "graciously offered by the gods to the architect."[83] The study of *Adonis* has made this distinction famous:

> The gods graciously give us *for nothing* a certain first line; but it is our responsibility to fashion the second, which must be consonant with the other, and not be unworthy of its supernatural elder. All the resources of experience and intellect are not too much to make this line comparable to the one that was a gift.[84]

These fabricated lines, in order to resemble the given ones, undergo a special treatment, which seeks to give them the same appearance of spontaneity: they are "naturalized."[85] This was to acknowledge the superiority of inspiration to work, since the latter could, at best, do no more than arduously attain the innate perfection of its models. One would not have to be Valéry to admit this supremacy once and for all. It occurred to him to assert the capacity of reflection, of consciousness, not only to equal, but to surpass the perfect products of inspiration:

> The artist moves between what is immediate and what is elaborated. The immediate does not always possess the qualities which common opinion attributes to it *a priori.*
> Moreover, the man who in moments of inattention and in his spontaneous speech is favored with *finds,* invents forms and models of original expression—is generally *the same man* whose labor and prolonged attention will manage to produce *at least* the *same* effects.
> A powerful mind tends to obtain from itself the reproduction, *by conscious concern,* of the fruits analogous to those it may sometimes have been able to produce *precisely because it was not consciously concerned to do so.*[86]

The theory of composition and the theory of execution will show, at two other levels, this role of work in poetic creation, which begins to manifest itself on the level of inspiration. But we can already discern its essential character and the consequences Valéry derives from it. All work has an aspect of artifice, which Valéry emphasizes, exaggerating it somewhat. For him, the artist is a gambler and an actor: "There is gambling and play-acting in his work."[87] His aesthetic nihilism goes still further: artistic work is simulation; the work of art is a "fake"; and, finally, the heterogeneous plurality of the artist's actions is such that his personality as an author is completely dissolved into it. Already "found" lines one "perfects" and the "made" lines one "naturalizes" prove a

> . . . double simulation in opposite directions to achieve this fake: perfection . . . equally remote from the purely spontaneous, which is anything at all, and from the entirely conscious production, which is painful, tenuous, vulnerable to any other will, incapable of dominating others.[88]

But the complete work of art is much more deceptive: ". . . a work is always a *fake*";[89] it is impossible to "make it correspond to an author acting on a single impulse. It is the fruit of a collaboration of very diverse states . . . a kind of combination of points of view independent of each other in origin. . . . The act of writing cannot be prolonged . . . without requiring an almost incessant breakdown of the initial design. . . . The least erasure violates spontaneity."[90] That is why "the development of construction [is rendered] almost indecipherable."[91] Valéry sometimes listed several factors of this complex activity:

> . . . that strange use of time and of man's forces so difficult to define and in which the highest degree of willfulness, the most capricious diversity, the most varied motives, the most widely differing sensations, sentiments, reason, passions and circumstances, temperaments and talents are expended, expressed, and organized in order to produce tales, poems, systems. . . .[92]
>
> The artist plays his hand in a game which includes "chance," will, reflection, mastery, etc. It is difficult to enumerate, and first of all to separate, these elements.[93]

And he sketched, in the same direction, a rhetoric of a new genre:

> The true elements of a style are: mania,[p] will, necessity, forgetting, expedience, chance, recollections.[94]

We understand how, in this inextricable network, even the artist does not recognize himself: ". . . authors do not know what they are doing,"[95] and how Valéry could write: "The

---

[p] It is these manias, of which the psychologists of the creative imagination have given celebrated examples, that Valéry is thinking of in this amusing passage, in which he attributes to them a stabilizing role:

The philosopher bites his nails. The general scratches his head. The geometrician tugs at his hair. Bonaparte takes snuff over and over again.

Where do the *solutions* come from?

But on the other hand, a man who is bored whistles endlessly, makes a row of dots along the edge of his paper, sucks his pipe, walks up and down—and does what the clock's pendulum does.

The chin, the nose, the forehead, the fingers, the legs, the body's hair—organs of meditation. Also the chimney across the street, Kant's tree.

These objects, these nibblings are references, guidelines.

(*Mauvaises pensées et autres*, p. 153)

true workman of a beautiful work . . . is positively no one."[96]
There are too many authors in an author. And, since he can
attribute nothing to himself, strictly speaking, it is absurd to
praise him for both what is given him and for what he adds
to it:

> What is there of my own in what comes to me? What
> is there of me in what is made by me? Here the ridic-
> ulous problem of inspiration converges with the ridic-
> ulous problem of responsibility.[97]

The work is not by the author; it is rigorously anonymous:
"What makes a work is not *the man* who signs his name to
it. What makes a work has no name."[98]
There is no use arguing this juicy paradox. It suffices to
generalize it in order to emphasize its inadequacy; applied to
any behavior, it dissolves the agent by reduction to his many
functions. But no one ever supposed that the personality was
anything other than a synthetic unity. This total awareness,
which Valéry is obliged to call *I*, he shows as more appropri-
ately sensitive to its irreducible individuality when, in a moving passage, he describes the writer's glorious martyrdom, his
infinite labor—difficult, demanding, enthralling, disappointing:

> I work knowingly, deliberately, with endless waits for
> the most precious moments; with choices never com-
> pleted; with my ear, with my sight, with my memory,
> with my ardor, with my languor; I work at my work; I
> pass through the desert, through abundance, through
> Sinai, Canaan, Capua, I suffer the season of excess and
> the season of dearth, in order to make as best I can
> something which I know will be nothing, the subject of
> boredom, of oblivion, of incomprehension, and which
> will displease me, will hurt me tomorrow—for tomorrow
> I shall necessarily be inferior or superior to today's man
> who *does his best*.
> My value is in what I lack, for I have the distinct
> and profound knowledge of what I lack; and since that
> is not a little, it constitutes my great knowledge.
> I have tried to create for myself what I lacked.[99]

The writer's greatest virtue is perhaps perseverance. In a
significant combination of words, Valéry spoke of the artist's

"patient impatience."[100] This formula, which summarizes his psychology of creation, we find again, modified by a parodic allusion to Buffon's phrase which has provoked so many commentaries, in the invocation to *Le Serpent*:

> *Génie! O longue impatience!*
>
> [Genius! O long impatience!]

Chapter VI

COMPOSITION

We have noted the way in which Valéry tried to get rid of inspiration. It seems more difficult to eliminate all invention from literary creation, or at least not to grant a large role to imagination. Normally, invention involves, by definition, a degree of originality which renders it relatively rare. Valéry, on the contrary, understands by invention all that comes to the mind: it is the very course of psychic activity. Thus he can assert, with his preferred mixture of banal obviousness in idea and paradoxical texture in formulation: ". . . man does little but invent."[1] In almost the same way he condemns the imagination; a man who avoided imagining, i.e., digressing, would have genius because he saw things as they were, without distortion:

> It is incredible to what degree man resists experience, and what infinite difficulty he has in permanently substituting what he has seen and touched for what he has created and arranged, according to the forms of his mind. *It would suffice not to imagine in order to have a powerful genius.*[2]

Ideas (in the broadest sense, including images, analogies, motifs, rhythms) "cost nothing." Their generation is characterized by "facility," "fragility," "incoherence." It must be prevented. And it is precisely the obstacles the mind raises against this formless, limitless activity which are the true factors of creation:

> . . . the most powerful "creations," the most august monuments of thought, have been achieved by the deliberate use of conscious means of resistance to our im-

mediate and continuous "creation" of propositions, of relations, of impulses, which replace each other without other conditions.[3]

Invention must be "countered and tempered."[4] Artistic creation is the work of constraint.

Basically, Valéry comes close to believing that it is constraint which induces what is conventionally called inspiration. We find in *L'Idée fixe* a number of revealing passages on this point. From them I extract the relevant issues:

> There is a mental labor which is remote from the mind's ordinary state of freedom or of availability, which is contrary both to digression and to obsession, and which tends to be completed . . . only by the possession of a kind of mental . . . object, which the mind recognizes as what it desired . . . there is a mental labor which tends to form or to construct . . . or rather, to permit the formation of an entire order, an entire system, one part of which, or else certain conditions of which, are given. . . . This labor, this production of order, requires . . . two contrary conditions. . . . One must maintain, sustain beyond the moment. . . . One therefore maintains, in the present state and independently, these distinct factors. . . . And then, as in a calm and favorable, and saturated, liquid medium . . . there forms, there is constructed, a certain figure—*which no longer depends on you*. . . . One must, then, submit oneself to a certain constraint; be able to endure it; persist in an obliged attitude, in order to give to the elements of . . . thought which are present, or in control, the *freedom* to obey their affinities, the *time* to unite and to construct and to impose themselves upon consciousness; or to impose some *certainty* upon it. . . .[5]

This constraint generally takes the form of conditions which the artist imposes on himself, the most important of which come to him from tradition: the various conventions and rules he acknowledges and obeys. The discoveries of poetry seem due to the backwash of thought upon these obstacles:

> Verse. The vague idea, the intention, the figured, rhythmic impulse breaking against the regular forms,

against the invincible defenses of conventional prosody, engenders new things and unexpected figures. There are surprising consequences from this collision of will and feeling against the insensibility of convention.[6]

Even more distinctly, Valéry, who had little use for the raw materials of inspiration, envisaged their exploitation as the adaptation of these productions of chance to the imperatives of rule: "What does thought draw from the subject or the seed? Thought is a restriction of accident, an accident to which one adjusts a *convention*."[7] Not only the discovery of details, but the creation as a whole receives the benefit of the constraint of conventions. It is because of the conventions that "we can make a rational work and construct by order."[8] They are a kind of tool in the artist's possession: "The artist, in general, manipulates his substance by the intermediary of a host of *conventions*: convention intervenes in his work."[9] Their effect is to transform the *given* time after time and to increase the interval between the first intention and the final formulation. Such at least is the superiority of classicism:

> The great interest of classical art is perhaps in the series of transformations which it requires in order to express things while respecting the imposed conditions *sine qua non*.[10]
> As a result of the bizarre rules in classical French poetry, the distance between the initial "thought" and the final "expression" is the greatest possible one. This is important. Work is done between the *emotion* received or the *intention* conceived, and the completion of the *machine* which will restore it, or will restore an analogous affection. Everything is redesigned; thought reworked, etc.[11]

Valéry showed, apropos of La Fontaine's *Fables*, how the difference

> . . . between even the clearest impression or invention becomes the greatest possible—and hence most remarkable, when the writer imposes upon his language the system of regular verse.[12]

The role of convention extends far beyond literature. Valéry was to say in the *Préface* added to *La Soirée avec Mon-*

sieur Teste: "Only arbitrary decisions permit man to establish anything: language, societies, knowledge, works of art."[a] He sought them very early—even in the realm of strategy: "Every battle is . . . full of conventions," he wrote in October 1897, in an article in the *Mercure de France* in which he reviews a military work.[b] Somewhat embarrassed to participate in an *Hommage* to Marcel Proust, by whom he had read no more than a single volume, he praises in this author the expression of the society known as "the World":

> Our greatest writers have almost never treated any subject but the Court. They were inspired by the City only to comedies, and by the Country only to fables. But the greatest art, the art of simplified figures and the purest types, entities which permit the symmetrical, and somehow musical development of consequences of an isolated situation, is linked to the existence of a conventional milieu which employs a language decorated with veils and furnished with limits, in which *seeming* governs *being*, and nobly holds it within a constraint which changes all life into an exercise of presence of mind. . . .[13]

We can see that, for Valéry, classicism is based on a governed language and a discipline of manners, on conventions of politeness which mold a society before legislating the literature suitable to it. But the role of conventions greatly exceeds this destination of the work for a select public; it fulfills the writer and permits him to impose himself:

> Methods, well-defined poetics, canons and proportions, rules of harmony, precepts of composition, fixed forms, are not (as is commonly believed) formulas of limited creation. Their profound object is to oblige the whole man, the organized man, *the being made to act, and whose very action completes him in return,* to impose himself in the production of works of the mind.[14]

[a] In *Monsieur Teste,* p. 9. On the role of conventions in social and political life, see, for example, *Réflexions* in *La Revue des Vivants,* March 1929, pp. 371–80.

[b] *Mercure de France,* October 1897, pp. 258–60: *Méthodes, Éducation et Instruction des Troupes, IIe Partie.* "Paroles" selon *Mikhael Ivanovitch, par Loukhiane Carlovitch,* Berger-Levrault, 1897. Those concerned are, respectively, General Dragomirov and, apparently, General Cardot.

These conventions Valéry defines: "links which could be different"[15] or "any correspondence between acts and perceptions which could be replaced by another."[16] He thus notes that their essential character is to be arbitrary. It is in this that they attract Valéry. The love of extreme liberty is easily reconciled in him with the submission to the arbitrary. Everything seems modifiable to him, and, seeking the source of "this very active sense of the arbitrary," Valéry confesses that he cannot help "modifying or causing to vary by thought" whatever suggests "a possible substitution" in what occurs to him. He sees in this pleasure "a mania or a method, or both at once; there is no contradiction."[17] But on the other hand, he is quite willing to load himself down with fetters: "I am free: therefore I fetter myself."[18] No poet is prompter to obey the most rigorous obligations, even the least well-founded ones, of classical prosody. Valéry, who found in Letters "merely a combination of ascesis and play,"[19] utterly justifies the double character of rules as obligatory and contingent: "Such constraints may be quite arbitrary: it is necessary and sufficient that they hamper the natural course of digression or creation step by step." He compares this regulation of invention to that of the "impulses" leading to action: they undergo "the demands of our motor apparatus, and conflict with the material conditions of the medium"; we acquire by this experience "an increasingly exact awareness of our form and of our forces."[20] The conditions are a principle of order and of organization; they canalize, better still: they inform thought which, without them, would remain amorphous and inconsistent.

More than once Valéry declared that, in the aesthetic realm, the arbitrary produces necessity. "All investigations of Art and Poetry tend to make necessary what is essentially arbitrary."[21] The artist's ideal is to achieve a work in which nothing can be changed, which resists the will of the audience, which imposes upon that audience an impression of necessity. Now, this effect has as its cause the will of the author: "In all the arts, and this is why they are arts, the *necessity* a successfully created work must suggest can be engendered only by what is *arbitrary*."[22] This effect of necessity supposes rigorous work (here we return to the notion of calculation in the work of art, of concerted fabrication), but this rigor too is obtained only by arbitrary methods:

Naturae non imperatur nisi parendo.

Art will proceed to constructions similar to those of engineers. To innovate in nature, by means of its means. What I can experience by an appropriate "machine." The result will be an increment in myself, but a viable one. It is not drawn directly from myself by the circumstances of chance, but rather deduces from my properties in general; and if it is correctly deduced, it will defy any skepticism, and will exist.

Rigor is achieved only by the arbitrary.[23]

This transition from the arbitrary to necessity is associated by Valéry with two other movements. First of all with the utilization of the useless: many of our sensations are, with regard to life, "useless"; many of our acts are in excess of our ordinary needs, hence "arbitrary." "The invention of Art has consisted in trying to confer upon the former a kind of utility; upon the latter, a kind of necessity."[c] Subsequently, with the progression from disorder to order:

. . . whether he likes it or not, the artist cannot separate himself from the sense of the arbitrary. He proceeds from the arbitrary toward a certain necessity, and from a certain disorder toward a certain order; and he cannot avoid the constant sensation of this arbitrariness and this disorder, which oppose what is born under his hands and which appears to him necessary and ordered. It is this contrast which makes him feel that he is creating, since he cannot deduce what comes to him from what he has.[24]

Thus the artist proceeds from the arbitrary, and by means of the arbitrary, to the necessary, from the useless to the useful, from the disordered to the ordered. This parallelism helps us understand Valéry's theory, which is not always expounded with entire clarity. In order to determine where we are, we must distinguish three *kinds* of arbitrariness: the au-

---

[c] *Notion générale de l'art* in *Nouvelle Revue Française*, November 1, 1935, p. 686. See *Cours de poétique*, lecture 2: "Art reworks these useless sensations and these arbitrary acts. There is a reprise of utility in a higher octave."

thor's, the reader's, and that of convention, as well as two
levels of arbitrariness: 1) the initial arbitrariness, a condition
of psychic functioning, in the author as in every individual,
and against which the creator struggles, but which accom-
panies him throughout his work, and which is necessary to
him since from it he derives his discoveries (either by a
gratuitous welling-up, or by the response to conventions); 2)
the final arbitrariness of the aesthetic result, which might have
been different, has been obtained by decisions, and yet
triumphs by its appearance of necessity. This we can discern,
beneath the glittering antitheses Valéry elaborates, when he
thus characterizes the poet's enterprise: "The artist lives on
terms of intimacy with *his* arbitrariness and in the expectation
of *his* necessity,"[25] or sometimes describes him as gratified by
a "sudden grace": "what seems to us as if it *might not have
been* imposes itself upon us with the same power as *what
could not keep from being,* and *what had to be what it is,*"[26]
or claims to imprison the effect produced by the beautiful,
which is to strike us dumb, in the language of *"contradiction,"*
in *"scandalous expressions"*: "the necessity of the arbitrary;
the necessary by the arbitrary";[27] in effect, "we feel, on the
one hand, that the source or object of our will"—this means
that the work obliges us to desire the more in proportion as
we possess it: a theory of the aesthetic infinite—"is so appropriate to us that we cannot conceive it as different":[28] an
impression of necessity; but, on the other hand, "we feel no
less, and no less strongly . . . that the phenomenon which
causes and develops this state within us . . . *might not have
existed,* and even *should not have existed,* and is to be classified as "improbable":[29] an impression of accident, of chance,
of the arbitrary.

The arbitrary frees us from the arbitrary; that is, once we
accept the arbitrary, choose it, *will* it, we are liberated from
the arbitrary as an imposed condition—the spontaneous, unconscious arbitrary. Similarly, there are two kinds of conventions, those of which we are not conscious and which dominate us, and those which we choose as laws and which permit
us to create. The "uneasiness" which the feeling of being
"puppets" can cause men, despite the "pretentions of the Self"
which lead them to believe themselves "sources of them-

selves," derives from this awareness of being influenced by a host of vague conventions:

> Our life insofar as it depends on what comes *to* the mind, on what seems to come *from* the mind, and on what controls that life after having controlled that mind —is it not governed by an enormous and chaotic quantity of *conventions* the majority of which are implicit? We should be hard put to express and explain them.[30]

On the contrary, the explicit conventions deliberately adopted as rules of the game permit us to play it quite lucidly.[d] This is why Valéry could say without contradiction: "To depart from the arbitrary; to bar the accidental . . . that is what I prefer,"[e] but could prescribe the rational use of a higher arbitrariness:

> One must . . . stimulate oneself to some perfection. Each man can define his own, some according to a model, the others by their own reasonings. The essential thing is to oppose thought, to create resistances to it, and to establish conditions in order to release oneself from the chaotic arbitrary by means of the explicit and clearly limited arbitrary.[31]

Without these rigorous conventions, the work of art is destroyed, and the lower arbitrary triumphs over the higher species:

> Where would the artist's special quality be if he did not consider certain details as inviolable? Thus the alternation of masculine and feminine rhymes. There is no transport which must not respect it. It may be irritating, it may be a Chinese puzzle, but without *it* everything comes undone and the poet corrupts the artist, and the arbitrary of the moment triumphs over the arbitrary of an order superior to the moment.[32]

[d] See *Cours de poétique,* lecture 9: "These conventions of the arts are calculated and indispensable, in order to combine the successive sensations: otherwise, sensibility is merely a series of accidents. The conventions are as necessary, fundamental, effective in the arts as in the sciences in order to pursue, among the universes of possibilities, a particular goal among groups of sensations."

[e] *Mélange,* p. 40. See the application he gives of this arbitrariness: politics, events, fashion.

This is a condemnation of spontaneity in creation. The rejection of constraint, the abuses of freedom are dangerous for the arts:

> Among the victims of freedom: forms and, in every sense of the word, style. Everything that requires training, observances at first sight inexplicable, infinite reworking, everything that leads by constraint of a freedom to reject obstacles to the higher freedom of overcoming them, all this is in jeopardy, and facility inundates the world with its works. A true history of the arts would show how many movements, so-called discoveries and innovations are merely disguises of the demon of least action.[33]

Valéry might have said, like his friend Gide: "Art is born of constraint, lives by struggle, and dies of freedom."

The praise of constraint, of conventions and rules is not, in Valéry, merely a theoretical view. His entire poetic output bears the mark of this conviction, and we could support it with many confidences concerning his work. He says, of *La Jeune Parque:*

> Yes, in the case of this poem I imposed upon myself certain laws, observances, constants which constitute its true subject. . . . The reader who knows how to read me will find an autobiography in the form.[34]

He insisted on showing how far, in his practice, he departed from the slack taste of his contemporaries:

> I have been led . . . to set my work very strict conditions, more numerous than "inspiration" generally withstands; and I have attached a singular value to all the arbitrary conventions which, limiting the choice of terms and of forms, have become almost intolerable for modern writers. I have a weakness for the formal.[35]

And he underlined the lesson which this aesthetic ascesis affords, in his eyes, merely astonished that it should be less understood by creative artists than by performers, when he gave the purely moral reasons for his attachment to poetry:

> I confess that I was attached to poetry to the degree that it seemed to me a superior exercise and a search for

freedom by means of constraint. Man is so constituted that he can discover all he possesses only if he is obliged to draw it out of himself, by a severe and prolonged effort. One approaches nearest oneself by opposing oneself. A poet, moreover, can indeed impose on himself what the least singer, the least virtuoso imposes; and what all artists did in the age when we had lost neither the leisure to ripen, nor the intention to last. . . .[36]

This aesthetic Arbitrary is therefore the contrary of the anarchic arbitrariness of sensibility. It is "reasoned," Valéry says. And that is how he defined *composition*. Praising Corot, a landscapist "who still composes," he compares *composed painting* with the painting of pure observation which, according to him, can lead only to "total insubstantiality":

It is clear, moreover, that if composition—that is, a *reasoned arbitrariness*—has been invented and so long required, it was in order to answer to some necessity—that of substituting for the unconscious conventions dictated by the simple imitation of what one sees, a conscious convention which (among other benefits) reminds the artist that it is not the same thing to see or conceive the beautiful, and to make others see or conceive it.[37]

What Valéry said of the disadvantages of description in literature, parallel to those of landscape in painting,[38] permits us to glimpse what he thinks of the dangers incurred by the writer who imposes no constraints on himself, or who lacks the sense of the arbitrary. We know that this is precisely, in his eyes, the novelist's case:

A novelist once told me that no sooner were his characters born and named in his mind than they lived in him at their own discretion; they reduced him to submitting to their intentions and to recording their acts. They borrowed his vital forces, and doubtless his gesticulations and the machinery of his voice (which they would pass from one to the other, while he walked up and down, a victim of the feelings of one or another of these literary beings).

I found it admirable and convenient that one can thus cause the substance of one's books to be made by creatures whom it takes only a moment to summon up, alive and free, to perform before you the role they choose.

I also concluded from this that the sensation of the arbitrary was not a novelist's sensation.[39]

There is in the conventions adopted by the poet a kind of beauty and a particular lesson. This is one of the points on which Valéry the aesthetician constructs a bridge between psychology and ethics:

I merely wanted to make it conceivable that the obligatory number of syllables, the rhymes, the fixed forms— all this arbitrary world, once adopted, and opposed to ourselves, has a kind of beauty of its own, a philosophical beauty. Chains which stiffen at each movement of our genius remind us at the moment of all the contempt deserved, no doubt, by that familiar chaos which ordinary people call thought and whose *natural* conditions are, unknown to them, neither less fortuitous nor less futile than the conditions of a charade.[40]

We come upon the same notion, in similar terms, in *Rhumbs*, where Valéry adds:

The rules teach us *by their arbitrariness* that the thoughts which come to us from our needs, our feelings, our experiences are merely a small part of the thoughts of which we are capable.[t]

Thus it is natural that Valéry should conceive of criticism in an entirely moral way. Criticism is the appreciation of a struggle, of a combat against the difficulties which an author has deliberately created for himself. Aesthetic judgment must be based on the estimation of the constraints the author has imposed upon himself:

Every judgment one seeks to bring to bear on a work of art must account, first of all, for the difficulties its author has set himself. . . . The consideration of these deliberate shackles . . . reveals immediately the intellectual degree of the poet, the quality of his pride, the delicacy and the despotism of his nature.[41]

The conventions in literature are or can be very numerous. Some are extremely general, others very specific. Among the

[t] *Rhumbs* in *Tel quel*, II, p. 77. Instead of the *beauty* of the rules, he speaks of their *nobility*.

"formal and explicit conventions which the mind has opposed to itself . . . the best-known and the most important" is logic.[42] Next we should consider the conventions relating to language. They are indeterminate and of uncertain effect, but the artist can benefit, as he can suffer, from this indeterminacy:

> Language involves a group of conventions which are classified by vocabulary and syntax. *Conventions*, in other words links which might be different. But these conventions are generally imprecise; a great number of them are indefinable, or nearly so. Literary art operates on the possibilities which this lack of rigor allows, but it does so at its risks and perils, suffering or profiting by misunderstandings, by differences in the value or effect of words according to persons.[43]

Finally, poetry has its own conventions. Their essential character consists in a kind of conformity with our organic functions:

> It is remarkable that the conventions of regular poetry, rhymes, fixed caesuras, regular numbers of syllables or rhythmic feet imitate the monotonous *system* of the machinery of the living body, and perhaps this mechanism produces certain fundamental functions which repeat the act of living, add one element of life to another, and construct the tempo of life among things, as a structure of coral is raised in the sea.[44]

This regularity of classical prosody corresponded, according to Baudelaire, to our need for monotony. In his splendid apology for regular verse (apropos of *Adonis*), Valéry shows that by adding to the rules of language other rules whose arbitrary nature "is not, in itself, greater than that of language," the artifice of strict prosody "confers upon the natural language the qualities of a resistant substance" and defines "an absolute world of expression." Our emotions are not thereby diminished; "they are multiplied," as we can see by games—for example, chess:[45]

> One of the advantages of the observance of conventional forms in the construction of verse consists in the extreme attention to detail which this discipline devel-

ops, when it is conceived in relation to continuous musicality and to the spell of constant perfection, which a true poem should (as some feel) cast. The absence of prose results—that is, the absence of a break.[46]

Rhyme is the very type of these well-established beneficent conventions. "Rhyme—constitutes a law independent of the subject and is comparable to an external clock."[47] It is often misunderstood:

> Not the least pleasure of rhyme is the frenzy into which it throws those wretches who believe they know something more important than a *convention*. They naïvely suppose that a thought *can* be more profound, more organic . . . than any convention.[g]

We can classify among the conventions certain materials already elaborated by tradition or certain tested methods. The poet receives them ready-made, utilizes them, and benefits from their assured influence to achieve a higher effect:

> Each literary period and each fabricator counts on certain ready-made ideas or poetic forms whose mere use simplifies the poetic problem, permitting more complex combinations of a higher order, like a language thoroughly known.[48]

Finally the poet speculates on successes; analysis of "finds" permits him to establish the means of obtaining equivalent ones for himself:

> True and good rules.
> The good rules are those which recall and impose the characteristics of the best moments. They are drawn from the analysis of these privileged moments.
> These are rules for the author, much more than for the work.[49]

[g] *Calepin d'un poète* in *Oeuvres complètes,* vol. C, p. 191. See further *Littérature* in *Tel quel,* I, p. 151: "The great success of rhyme is to outrage the simple who naïvely suppose that there is something under the sun more important than a convention. They naïvely believe that some thought *can* be more profound, more lasting . . . than any convention. . . . This is not the least pleasure of rhyme, nor the one by which it caresses the ear least sweetly!"

From the most general conventions to the most specific and the most personal, the poet ceaselessly supports himself by a technique which has proved effective. The aesthetic of conventions is, very classically, an aesthetic of imitation. It is by craftsmanship that one achieves original works, not by surrender to impulse.

THE INTOXICATING IDEA OF COMPOSITION

It will be recalled that for Valéry a poem is in practice composed of fragments of pure poetry inlaid in the substance of a *discourse,* and that the poem is worth precisely what it contains of pure poetry, without its ever managing, however, to be constituted of only such elements; if this were the case, it would no longer be a poem, for it would not be constructed. "Voltaire has said marvelously well that 'Poetry consists of nothing but fine details.' I am saying no more than that"[50]—but, on the other hand, "never has a discovery or even a series of discoveries seemed to constitute a work."[51] We can therefore conclude that, to a certain degree, the poem stands in opposition to poetry. Similarly, in the author of the poem, we must distinguish the poet and the constructor, the detector of pure raw materials and the architect who employs them. The first is sensitive to the "poetic universe," the second abandons himself to that enterprise, so remote from inspiration, which demands "many reflections, decisions, choices, and combinations, without which all the gifts of the Muse and of Chance" remain

. . . like precious substances stacked in a building site without an architect. Now, an architect does not necessarily build with precious materials. A poet, as architect of poems, is therefore quite different from what he is as producer of these precious elements of which all poetry should be composed, but whose composition is a different matter and requires a very different mental labor.[52]

The composition of the poem is thus conceived by Valéry as alien to the poetic nature; it does not differ, apparently, from composition in other literary genres or in other arts, such as painting or architecture. The poetry is entirely in the materials, it is not in the movement which assembles them.

Valéry seems to me, here, the victim of the habitual confusion between what is poetic and what is aesthetic. I grant that, in many poems, the composition has, as a matter of fact, that logical and intellectual quality which may have its own beauty and which gives to an ode by Malherbe or to a certain eloquent passage of Hugo the majesty of a noble façade or the satisfying equilibrium of a fresco. I grant that, in many poets, even the most sensitive, a severe order has been reconciled with a very different poetic content, or has accommodated that content to a governing armature. But I believe, on the other hand, that the poetic spirit often seizes upon the composition itself, and that the movement of certain poems, however illogical in appearance, and in any case quite remote from the distribution of the classical discourse, obeys purely emotional requirements and satisfies something else than a need for symmetry and balance of masses. I am not concerned here with the *"beau désordre"* which, according to Boileau, would still be "an effect of art": this conception testifies to the great critic's impotence to escape from his rational ideal; it is still as a cold reasoner that he conceived of lyricism. I am concerned with a mode of composition adapted to the specifically poetic genius and which cannot be attached to logic except by such convenient expressions as the logic of the heart, the logic of feeling. Least remote from this would be that art of pleasing, of which Pascal has spoken, and which, always indicating the goal, proceeds by perpetual digressions—a great scandal in the eyes of the pure geometrician. This would still be translating poetic composition into terms of the intelligence. In my opinion, poetic composition is the composition whose law is the adaptation of details to the emotional theme which sustains them. The order of these details has only a faint relation to the demands of the intelligence. It is, no doubt, limited, like feeling itself, by a minimum of intelligibility, but it is not upon intelligibility that it is based. The true poetic composition is a figure of desire, which proceeds from pleasure to voluptuous pleasure, with the appearances of caprice and the inevitability of passion.

Whatever the case, it is rather difficult to define how Valéry represents this composition of the poem from the psychological point of view. We know that it has always exalted him: "the idea of composition," he says apropos of *Le Cimetière marin*, "remains for me the most poetic of ideas."[h] But by this he meant "the myth of creation which seduces us into wanting to make something out of nothing"; that is, Valéry dreams of "gradually finding his work by starting from pure conditions of form which are increasingly conscious—or at least, a family of subjects."[53] This is something like Poe's problem before the solution of *The Raven*. But we cannot speak seriously of the composition of a poem at the moment when fixed conditions suggest "a subject" or "a family of subjects." What we have then is a program, that is, at best, a framework or, at most, a plan; true composition is internal; within the same network of conditions, it can vary utterly. One might grant, at the limit, that the plan of a machine was an equivalent of the machine itself. The plan of a poem is not the poem. Valéry, guided by his abusive comparisons with the engineer ("a poem is a kind of machine to produce the poetic state by means of words"),[54] forgets that the composition of a poem is much more organic than mechanical.

On the contrary, he seems to remember this when he notes that "a hundred divine moments do not construct a poem, which is a duration of growth and a kind of figure in time. . . ."[55] Here Valéry, who reflected on duration and its effect in the work of art, seems to be orienting himself toward a biological psychology of invention, but, if his remark is too insistent to be merely a digression, it is not in harmony with what follows it, for here he re-establishes the juxtaposition of operations:

> It requires, then, a great deal of patience, stubbornness and industry, in our art, if we wish to produce a work which ultimately appears to be merely a series of those felicitous touches, felicitously linked together.[56]

It is certainly this last formula which represents Valéry's true thought; it turns the poem into a garland of beauties and

[h] *Au sujet du "Cimetière marin"* in *Variété III*, p. 70. Cf. *Propos me concernant*, p. 14: "With regard to literature, I am concerned only by forms and composition. . . ."

recalls "the elements of pure poetry inlaid in the substance of a discourse."

In *Eupalinos*, Socrates distinguishes in visible things "three modes of generation, or of production . . .": chance, growth, and human creation "by separate principles."[57] This fabrication "by abstraction"[58] is opposed to natural generation ("Nature neither abstracts nor composes");[59] here the whole is less complex than the part.[60] These views were developed by Valéry in a communication to the Société française de Philosophie, *Réflexions sur l'art*, in *L'Homme et la Coquille*, and in his *Discours aux chirurgiens*. In his study on shells, he has an odd comparison of their natural forms with certain artistic forms:

> As one says: a "Sonnet," an "Ode," a "Sonata," or a "Fugue," to designate certain well-defined forms, so one says: a "Conch," a "Helmet," a "Cameo," a "Haliotis," a "Porcelain," which are names of shells; and both series of words suggest an action which aims at grace and which concludes successfully.[61]

To the question "How do we recognize whether or not a given object is *made by a man?*"[62] Valéry answered: ". . . every positively human production, every production reserved to man alone, functions by successive, separated, limited, enumerable gestures," but, since "certain animals, builders of hives or nests, closely resemble us even in this," he added that "the work proper to man is distinguished when its different and independent acts demand his express thinking presence, in order to produce and accommodate their diversity to the goal. Man nourishes in himself the duration of the model and of the will."[63] The painful character of this effort led Valéry to see its artificial side and to contrast it, even in man, to his organic nature:

> We know all too well that this presence is precarious and costly; that this duration is rapidly diminishing; that our attention decomposes quite rapidly, and that what stimulates, assembles, arouses, and revives the efforts of our distinct functions is of an entirely different nature: that is why our *premeditated* intentions and our *willed* constructions or fabrications *seem quite alien to our innermost organic activity.*[64]

The spectacle of shells or flowers or crystals makes us aware of our incapacity to produce such objects by the method which has, nonetheless, produced us ourselves:

> We conceive the *construction* of these objects, and thereby they interest and arrest us; we do not conceive their *formation*, and thereby they intrigue us. Although made or formed ourselves by means of imperceptible growth, we can create nothing by this means.[1]

We must not regard this incapacity as an inferiority of the human mind. Rather it is an indication of the primacy of the intelligence. To create by calculation remains far above automatic creation. The *Discours aux chirurgiens*, which continues the analysis of human action by "distinct acts," notes "the inferiority of natural fabrication," which also has its incapacities: "Nature does not know the wheel," and "has not created an animal that can be taken apart."[65]

Is the composition of a work of art reduced to a production by separate operations, as is the case with the construction of a table? Is artistic creation merely a fabrication? Far from opposing artistic creation to organic formation, should they not be related? Often, intellectual creation is accomplished by growth and sprouting. And in Valéry himself we find many such examples: his abundant theoretical production generally derives its seeds from previous remarks (even the essay on *L'Homme et la Coquille* has its origin in the pages of *Eupalinos* on the modes of production).

The analyst in Valéry sought to decompose creation into simple elements, and was convinced that creation developed from these elements: "The problems of composition are reciprocals of the problems of analysis."[66] Praising the Greek geometrician, Valéry admires in him above all "that mag-

[1] *L'Homme et la Coquille* in *Variété V*, p. 12. It seems, however, that Valéry acknowledged, if not complete creations, at least the spontaneous formation of structures which the work of art will use. See *Cours de poétique:* "There are natural formations in the artist's mind. We may think of the geometric ornaments of primitive peoples. This method recalls that of flowers or those patterns which the sea, ebbing, abandons on the sand. . . . The production of rhythms is one of those direct productions of the human organism which are the seed of organized productions" (lecture 2). "Metaphor is a natural production of the mind" (lecture 4).

nificent division of the moments of the Mind" and "that marvelous order in which each act of the reason is clearly located, distinctly separated from the others: this reminds us of the structure of the temples, a static machine whose elements are all visible, each declaring its function." These "members of pure science: . . . definitions, axioms, lemmas, theorems, corollaries, porisms, problems . . ." seem to him "the machinery of the mind made visible, the very architecture of the intelligence drawn in its entirety—the temple erected in Space by Speech, but a temple that can be raised into infinity."[67] In this new *Cantique des Colonnes*, Valéry exalts the operative distinction he later chooses to find in the writer. In a discussion at the Société française de Philosophie, on January 28, 1928, after distinguishing two states in the writer: the explosion, a phenomenon of sensitization, and the labor in "the darkroom" to make the image appear, he noted: "I believe we must distinguish—myself, I distinguish excessively —the different moments of the work's creation, and I repeat that these moments of very different kinds (perhaps they are even incomparable) are necessary to all production."[68] In *Mémoires d'un poème*, he admits having been struck in his youth by the refinements of the poets after 1850, that is, by "the obligation to separate, more than ever before, the initial stimulus and intention from the execution."[69] In the work itself, Valéry finds traces of the adjustment "of the widely different moments of the creative mind":

> . . . almost all literary works require a quantity of prolegomena: expositions, descriptions, preparations, whose function is, on the one hand, to define the pieces and rules of the game, on the other to initiate the unknown reader into the author's sensibility. These are the postulates, the conventions, the *données* from which the work, strictly speaking, can be understood. . . . In sum, any speculation about artistic creation must reckon with the "heterogeneous" diversity of the conditions which impose themselves upon the worker and are necessarily implicated in the work.[70]

The height of separation would be that which Valéry describes in his book on Degas: "A great geometrician once told me that we need two lives; one to acquire the possession of the mathematical instrument, the other to make use of it."[71]

However, the examples of poetic development Valéry cited, drawn from his own experience, actually point in the opposite direction. He even confessed to having been seduced by their resemblance to a phenomenon of continuous growth:

> . . . a line of verse has occurred to me, evidently engendered by its sonority, by its timbre. The meaning this unexpected element of a poem suggested, the image it evoked, its syntactic figure (an apposition), acting as a tiny crystal acts in a supersaturated solution, have led me as though by symmetry to expect, and to construct according to this expectation on either side of this line, a beginning which might prepare and justify its existence, and a continuation which might give it its full effect. Thus from this single line have proceeded, step by step, all the elements of a poem—the subject, the tone, the prosodic type . . . etc.
>
> I could not help comparing this proliferation to that observed in nature where we see, apparently, a fragment of the stem or leaf of certain plants reproduce a complete individual, providing the environment is favorable. The fragment, though differentiated, gradually becomes a complete individual, produces leaves, a stem, roots, all it requires in order to live.[j]

But straightaway, the theoretician refutes the poet and rejects the temptation of organicism:

> But this seductive analogy must not be adopted, because of the radical independence which I just emphasized between the constituents of language, sound, and sense.[72]

It is not only the fact of the two independent developments (as Valéry sees it) which contradict the image of the growth of a living fragment, but also, as will have been noticed, the physicochemical comparison of crystallization in a supersaturated solution. Ten years later, in 1939, Valéry re-

[j] *La Création artistique* in *Bulletin de la Société française de Philosophie*, 1928, pp. 12–13. He is speaking of *La Pythie*, which developed from the line *"Pâle, profondément mordue"* (cf. André Gide's *Journal*, January 2, 1923).

turned to the natural comparison of a biological development. He pursued, but by authenticating it, the example to which he had alluded:

> La Pythie began with an eight-syllable line whose sonority was given. But this line supposed a sentence, of which it was a part, and this sentence supposed, if it had existed, many other sentences. A problem of this kind admits of an infinity of solutions. But in poetry the metrical and musical conditions greatly limit the indeterminacy. This is what happened: my fragment behaved like a living fragment, since, plunged into the (doubtless nutritive) environment which the desires and expectation of my thought afforded it, it proliferated and engendered whatever it lacked: several lines of verse preceding it, and many more following.[73]

Here again, we discover that the image of proliferation is undermined, internally, by a divergent comparison, that of a mathematical problem this time. In all, the growth of La Pythie suggested to Valéry four analogies: two biological, one physicochemical, and one mathematical. Let us add that Valéry's metaphorical genius suggested to him, apropos of another poem, La Jeune Parque, a mixed image which reconciles, in an entirely verbal fashion, the theory of organic development and the theory of fabrication:

> It is from language that I began—first in order to make a fragment a page long; then from passage to passage, this work swelled to its final dimensions. Natural growth of an artificial flower.[74]

How does it happen that between the two explanations, Valéry opted for the least plausible one? Precisely because he insisted on clearly separating the moments of creation. Now, this is possible only in exceptional circumstances, in the phase of preparation of the work (and not always then, for the work is not always methodically conceived), in certain operations which necessitate incompatible activities (correction, or revision, for example, is always posterior, even if only by a second, to expression); but in execution, or even in the inspiration which is often identified with it, everything functions simultaneously: sentiment, images, movement, tone, sentence are manifested at the same time. The poet is an animal that can do many things at once. His labor can doubtless be analyzed, but rather into factors than into moments and into acts corresponding to them. When the psychologist discerns several functions, he is not necessarily obliged to make each of them operate in a determined period, for he comes up against the indivisibility of spiritual continuity, if he claims to impose a too-precise chronology upon his shifting reality. Would one not be tempted, then, to suppose that the poem gets made as best it can ("authors do not know what they are doing," Valéry properly said, and he would have spoken even more properly had he said "only half-know what they are doing"). The series of comparisons Valéry proposes emphasizes the mystery of elaboration more than it elucidates it. Bergson recommended, in order to direct intuition, varying one's images. Those of Valéry are rarely in agreement and not reducible, unless by means of a logical artifice which would gradually contract into each other the mathematical conditions, the physicochemical conditions, and the biological conditions—a problem which constitutes the despair of epistemology. It would still remain to adjust to them the psychological conditions, which curiously enough, in these two passages, Valéry virtually leaves out of account (he merely invokes *desires* and *expectations*), for finally, if a poem is made, it is certainly made in a way which is identifiable neither with the solution of an algebra problem nor with a crystallization nor with a cancer.

Composition by principles and distinct acts, applicable to poetry and to all the arts, was carried by Valéry, in his youth, to an extraordinary degree of generalization. He assumed that all creation—scientific, artistic, and even political —could be, without differentiation, at the disposal of a great mind which had discovered its most general law and would then merely have to make specific applications of it, at will, in the realms of its choice. In 1894, the young Valéry, in the *Introduction à la Méthode de Léonard de Vinci*, seeking to penetrate the mystery of the "generation" of works, insisted on the maturation of the genius, which distinguishes him from other men:

Once again, we suppose that something has been created, for we adore the mysterious and the marvelous insofar as we are ignorant of the happenings in the wings; we call logic a miracle, but the inspired thinker has been ready for over a year. He was ripe. He had thought of it all this time—perhaps without suspecting it—and where the others were still unable to see, he had considered, combined, and merely read his own mind.[k]

In these sometimes abstruse pages in which, addressing himself to artists and art lovers, he believed he had "touched on the, for them, capital problem of composition,"[75] there is a revealing passage on the simplification effected by the man of genius:

> The secret—that of Leonardo like that of Bonaparte, like that which the highest intelligence possesses once and for all—is and can be only in the relations they found —that they were forced to find—*between things whose law of continuity escapes us.* It is certain that at the crucial moment, they had merely to perform certain specific acts. The supreme affair, that which the world considers, was no more than a simple thing—like that of comparing two lengths.[1]

The genius achieves, "after long experiment,"[76] "the unity of method, a "property," an "instrument" whose "implicit resources" permit him to declare: "It is easy to make oneself universal."[77] Leonardo's *facil cosa e farsi universale* corresponds to Monsieur Teste's "Genius is easy."

This view was reinforced, some pages farther on, by an analysis of construction which ultimately emphasized "a common measure of the terms involved" and revealed the psychic

---

[k] Pp. 210–11. See *La Conquête allemande* (1897): "All great inventors of ideas or forms seem to me to have utilized particular methods. I mean that their power and their mastery is based on the use of certain *habits* and of certain conceptions which discipline all their thoughts" (*Mercure de France,* August 1915, p. 65).

[1] Ibid., p. 211. See, in *Oeuvres complètes,* vol. I, pp. 70–71, a marginal note written in 1930: "The word continuity is not entirely appropriate. I recall having written it instead of another word which I have not found. I meant: between things which we cannot transpose or translate into a system of the entirety of our acts. That is, the system of our powers."

continuity beneath the modifications manifested in the work. But the passage is too allusive to be merely summarized:

> To construct, once this effort leads to some comprehensible result, should suggest a common measure of the terms involved, an element or a principle already supposed by the simple fact of becoming conscious, and which can have no other existence than an abstract or imaginary one. We cannot represent a whole consisting of changes, a picture, a structure of many qualities, except as a site of the modalities of a single *substance* or *law,* whose hidden *continuity* is affirmed by us at the same moment that we recognize this structure as a whole, as a limited domain of our investigation. Here again is that psychic postulate of continuity which resembles, in our knowledge, the principle of inertia in mechanics.[78]

Valéry renounced choosing from painting "the striking example" he required "of the communication between the various activities of thought";[79] he took it from architecture:

> The monument (which composes the City, that is almost the whole of civilization) is a being so complex that our knowledge spells out in it, successively, a setting belonging to the sky and changing with it, an extremely rich texture of motives depending on height, width, and depth, infinitely varied by perspective; then a solid, resistant, bold thing, with animal characteristics; a subordination, a framework, and finally, a machine whose weight is the agent, which leads from geometric notions to dynamic considerations and even to the most tenuous speculations of molecular physics, of which it suggests the theories and the representative models of its structures. It is by means of the monument, or rather among its imaginary scaffoldings created to bring its conditions into mutual agreement—its adaptation with its stability, its proportions with its location, its form with its substance—and in order to harmonize each of these conditions with itself, its millions of aspects among themselves, its balances among themselves, its three dimensions among themselves, that we may best recompose the clarity of a Vincian intelligence.[80]

The interest of architecture is to attract our attention to

structure; thereby we can return to construction on the human scale and microscopic construction; we can also shift from the interpretation of space to the constitution of substance:

> The being of stone exists in space: what is called space is relative to the conception of whatever structures one chooses; the architectural structure interprets space and leads to hypotheses as to its nature in a very special fashion, for it is both an equilibrium of materials in relation to gravitation, a visible static whole, and, in each of these materials, another equilibrium, molecular and little known. The man who composes a monument first conceives of weight and immediately afterward penetrates into the obscure atomic realm. He faces the problem of structure: that is, what combinations must be imagined in order to satisfy the conditions of resistance, elasticity, etc., functioning within a given space. The logical extension of the question is evident: how from the architectural domain, so often abandoned to practitioners, we pass to the profoundest theories of general and mechanical physics.
>
> Thanks to the docility of the imagination, the properties of an edifice and the inner properties of any substance illuminate each other.[81] If we note around us in what different ways space is occupied, that is, formed, conceivable, and if we make an effort toward the conditions the various things involve in order to be perceived with their various individual qualities—a fabric, a mineral, a liquid, a gas—we shall reach a clear and distinct idea of all this only by enlarging a particle of these textures and by intercalating into it a structure such that its simple multiplication reproduces a structure having the same properties as the one considered. . . .[82]

Valéry then seeks in architecture a type of thought which allows him to pass in a continuous fashion to all the domains in which the notion of composition is essential, and seems to hope that the analytic decomposition of structures will permit every kind of synthesis, artistic or scientific. This, at least, is how I read him when he says:

> With the help of these conceptions, we may circulate without discontinuity through the apparently discrete

domains of the artist and the scientist, from the most
poetic, and even most fantastic construction to that
which is tangible, weighable. The problems of composition are reciprocals of the problems of analysis; and the
abandonment of oversimple concepts with regard to the
subject of the constitution of matter, no less than of the
formation of ideas, is a *psychological* conquest of our
time.[83]

What we may admire in Leonardo is an "imaginative
logic,"[84] the awareness of a kind of psychic experimentation
"consisting in the establishment of a concrete mental relation
among phenomena—let us say, to be exact, among the images
of phenomena,"[85] whose method has been rediscovered by
scientists such as Faraday, Maxwell, Lord Kelvin . . . ;
thanks to "such men," we can "extend these methods beyond
the physical sciences; it would be neither absurd nor altogether impossible to attempt to create a model of the continuity of the intellectual operations of a Leonardo da Vinci
or of any other mind determined by the analysis of the conditions to be fulfilled. . . ."[86]

These texts are made no clearer by the *Note et digression*
which Valéry appended to them a quarter of a century later:
"In my obscurities, I loved the inner law of this great Leonardo."[87] "I had found no better solution than to attribute
to the unfortunate Leonardo my own agitations, transferring
the disorder of my mind to the complexity of his."[88] But the
Note affords us, at least, the formula which summarizes the
mental situation of the universal mind:

> I felt that this master of his means, this possessor of
> drawing, images, calculation, had found the central atti-
> tude from which the undertakings of knowledge and the
> operations of art are equally possible; the happy inter-
> changes between analysis and actions, singularly proba-
> ble. . . .[89]

Thus the "myth" of Leonardo allowed Valéry to dream of
a universal method, but it goes without saying that it did not
reveal that method to him. On a more limited level, Eupalinos
was to dream, meditating on the relations of architecture and
music, of reaching that central point from which a thousand
possibilities might be deduced:

Just imagine, then, the existence of a mortal being pure enough, reasonable enough, subtle and stubborn enough, powerfully enough armed by Minerva to meditate to the very extremity of his being, and hence to the extremity of reality, on that strange comparison of visible forms and ephemeral assemblages without consequences; think what intimate and universal point of origin he would reach; at what precious point he would arrive; what god he would find in his own flesh! And ultimately possessing himself in this state of divine ambiguity, if he then determined to construct monuments, whose venerable and gracious figure would participate directly in the purity of musical sound, or would communicate to the soul the emotion of an inexhaustible harmony—just think, Phaedrus, what a man that would be! Imagine what edifices! . . . And for us, what delights!

—And do you, I asked, conceive such a thing?

—Yes and no. Yes, as a dream. No, as science.

—And do you find some comfort in these thoughts?

—Yes, as a compass needle. Yes, as a judgment.

—Yes, as struggles . . . But I am not in a position to connect, as I would have to, an analysis to an ecstasy. I sometimes approach that precious power. . . .[90]

This *central attitude*, which consists in the possession of a *common measure*, Valéry apparently pursued in his years of silence. We shall return to it apropos of the role of ornament in composition. A fragment of a letter to Mallarmé, in 1894, shows that he was looking for a formula governing all the fundamental procedures of every possible technique:

I simply dreamed of including in a single *figure* all that, in everything, is the Means—or, from the spade, the pen, the word, the flute to the fugue, to integral calculus—a theory of the instrument. . . .[91]

Valéry did not write a prolegomenon to any possible technique, but his dream of a universal operative science was based on the conviction that every individual contains in himself a plurality of virtual persons, whose life reveals some of them unless it prevents them from being manifested, as in Socrates, a philosopher who might have been an architect, and who said: "I was born *several* . . . died *one*."[92] Without this potentiality, the artist or the scientist could not even be what he is; and in the very activity he practices, we note diverse specializations: the poet is and should be in turn poet and abstractor, just as Einstein is necessarily a mathematician and an artist "of the first order."[93]

I shall even add on this point a paradoxical notion: that if the logician could never be anything but a logician, he would not and could not be a logician; and if the poet were never anything but a poet, without the least hope of abstracting and of reasoning, he would leave no poetic trace behind him. I believe quite sincerely that if each man could not live a quantity of other lives besides his own, he could not live his own.

My experience has therefore shown me that the same *self* represents itself quite differently, that it becomes an abstractor or a poet by successive specializations, each of which is a departure from the purely available state superficially in harmony with the external environment, which is the average state of our being, the state which is indifferent to exchanges.[94]

No doubt few individuals are absolutely limited to a single trade. No doubt, some have managed to succeed in various careers. No doubt every activity requires different qualities. But how can we know whether Socrates could have built the Parthenon, whether Einstein contains an architect of genius? If the logician requires imagination and the poet ratiocination, it is not in the same fashion, or to the same degree, nor in the same sense, as Victor Hugo or Spinoza. The universality of genius is a splendid myth of power and pride, which a theory comparable to that of the universal characteristic may seek to justify, but which is frustrated on the grounds of experience, by the inequality of talents. Even Leonardo was not a great musician. The universal *composer* has not yet appeared.

THE ARCHITECTURE OF THE POEM

To descend from these peaks: there is no need, in order to compose a poem, to have made oneself the master of the most general metatechnical formula. However, the difficulties of poetic composition are sufficiently arduous. Valéry declares them "almost discouraging":

> This is because the detail is at each moment of essential importance and because the finest and most skillful foresight must come to terms with the uncertainty of discoveries.[95]

To compose in this sense means to take into account, to accommodate, and finally to make concessions. "To write is to foresee,"[96] but in poetry the detail, the discovery, is unforeseeable, and it can be of such a nature that it overwhelms all or part of the projected development. We already know that Valéry's Racine would not have hesitated to modify a character in order not to renounce a beautiful formal accident. Such variations of composition engendered by the hazards of execution lead, as we shall see in the next chapter, to *not separating* these two functions from each other. The fact nonetheless remains that foresight, the design, the project, or, more simply still, the intention to compose is a capital factor for Valéry. But this schema, of a variable flexibility, needs to be embodied, as we realize in the case of translations, which offer us merely a kind of diagram:

> The translations of great foreign poets are architectural plans which may be admirable; but they cause the structures themselves, palaces and temples, to disappear. . . . They lack the *third dimension*, which would make them palpable instead of conceivable.[97]

It is this concern to preserve the delectable sensibility of the poem which often made Valéry take the term composition in the sense of combination (as in chemistry). Poetic combination must unite particular ingredients, and above all prove to be indecomposable. The poetic mixture must not come apart in the reader's presence. Valéry gave several related though not entirely equivalent formulas for the poetic synthesis. Composition, in this sense, is above all the inseparability of sound and sense, of which we have spoken at length: "If the sense and the sound (or if the matter and the form) can be readily dissociated, the poem *decomposes*."[98]

We can compare this formula with the definition of poetry as "a *compromise* or a certain proportion" of two functions of language: "to transmit a fact—to produce an emotion."[99] But already the idea, or rather the image of the component elements, gives way to that of two combined activities. It is sometimes three factors that Valéry treats: "the simultaneous conduct of syntax, of harmony, and of ideas" presents "the problem of the purest poetry."[100] This time, the representation of the static synthesis yields altogether to the notion of a combination in movement, of a triple parallel development which suggests comparisons with composition in the musical sense of the word. It is rare, when we speak of composition in poetry, to think of the meaning which this term assumes in chemistry. We think rather of the arrangement of the whole and the relation of the parts. This is also what we do when we speak of painting. But it is difficult to keep within spatial considerations, and, if we take into account the movement of the poem, we arrive at comparisons with music. Valéry noted, as a rather general tendency, the dislike of modern artists for balanced construction. "Today's artists," he says apropos of Veronese's frescoes, "are not comfortable with the problems of composition. . . . If they invent, they succumb too often in matters of detail; if they do not invent, they are incapable of dealing with wholes. The fragment absorbs them: the contrary should be the case."[101] The same remark is made on the poverty of composition in poets, but without restriction of period:

> Composition is what is rarest in certain arts. For example, in poetry. I know infinitely few poems which are really composed.[102]
> Nothing has startled me more in poets and given me more regrets than the slight attention paid to composition.[103]

If Valéry is disappointed by the rarity of composed poems, it is because he eliminates on principle certain schemata of organization. He rejects two in particular: the chronological plan (that of the narrative or the history) and the logical plan (that of the oration or the essay):

I know very few *composed* poems, on condition: 1)

that we do not mean by composition a chronological enumeration. Events succeed each other, they are recounted in the order of time. They begin on a certain day, at a certain moment, they finish a certain other day. This is a succession of events, but there is no composition, for the series of things in someone's life, or in the street, from H hour to H hour is not composition. The work of art which reproduces these events is not a composed work. It is a recording. 2) Nor is a composition in the artistic sense, the procedure which consists in following a *plan* (in the logical sense of the word—categories, kinds, and genera, etc.); in effect, such a plan involves only in a very incomplete way the solidarity of the various parts of the work, which is the crucial point.[104]

On another occasion, Valéry distinguishes two types of so-called composition which do not satisfy him; the second is again chronological, but the first, which he calls "linear," is chiefly characterized by association:

> In the most celebrated lyrics, I find little more than purely linear—or . . . disordered—developments, in other words, those which proceed step by step without any more successive organization than is shown by a train of powder followed by a flame. (I am not speaking of the poems in which a narrative prevails, and the chronology of events intervenes: these are mixed works; operas, and not sonatas or symphonies.)[105]

Valéry did not question whether the development he describes as "disordered" might not be secretly organized by passion, that is, might constitute the very type of true poetic composition. Nor did he consider whether the narrative might not, by complicating the chronological order by another order, lead to complex effects which do not exclude the poetic. As for the logical plan, it is generally conceded that it is not poetic in itself, and that if it is too apparent, it may destroy the poetic content it contains, but it is very difficult to condemn it altogether, for once the analysis of a poem reveals any order (even one of which its author is unconscious), if this order appears to conform with its goal, nothing keeps us from declaring it logical: once the intelligence intervenes, even in the affective realm, it *logifies* everything it touches.

But Valéry, in his views on composition, thinks a great deal more about art than about poetry; what interests him is the harmony of a multiplicity; that is why he insists on the "solidarity of the various parts of the work." It is here that the two meanings of the word *composition*, so remote in current usage, are united in his mind: that of combination and that of architecture. Every true composition is the indissolubility of its internal relations. And every time this unity can be decomposed, the work loses its life. This is the case of the philosophical poem, in which one can set aside the thought. This is the case of the historical or narrative poem, which can be reduced to a series of anecdotes. Everything that can be summarized or recounted is antipoetic. "One cannot summarize a poem. . . ."[106] This is where the epic sins: "An epic poem is a poem that can be recounted. If we *tell* it, we have a bilingual text,"[107] that is, prose alongside the verse. "Nothing beautiful can be summarized," as "barbarous pedagogues" do in the case of the *Aeneid* and the *Odyssey*.[108] Further, epic poems are beautiful *although* they are long, and are so in fragments. Demonstration: A poem of long duration is a poem that can be *summarized*. Yet it is what cannot be summarized that is a *poem*. One does not summarize a melody."[109] The reader has noted, in passing, the condemnation, quite in Poe's sense, of the long poem. But where does this excess of dimension begin? It is obviously to avoid our being able to summarize or recount *La Jeune Parque* that Valéry has blurred its chronology and system of ideas. Dramatic poems share with epic poems "this defect, this antipoetic property, that they can be summarized, recounted . . . while that poetry which is only poetry . . . cannot, without perishing altogether, be put into prose."[110] At the limit, Valéry generalizes his criticism: "To summarize (or replace by a schema) a work of art is to lose its essential quality. We see how illusory this circumstance (if we understand its true effect) renders the aesthetician's analysis."[111] There is no need to argue this childish thesis, which is based on the confusion of pleasure with the psychology of pleasure. Let us merely note that the rejection of the chronological link and of the logical link explains in part Valéry's theory and practice in the conduct of the poem.

By what are these principles of unity to be replaced? By what is the "solidarity" of the work's parts to be insured? Introducing the notion of the substance of the work of art (he defines it: what is "kept" upon hearing a poem), and returning to his conception of the "precious indissolubility of form and content," Valéry notes that composition "requires that each element be in a special solidarity with another element." Having rejected the "logical or chronological link," he is led to "seek composition in and by the substance of the work: that is, the substance of the poem must oppose the immediate transformation of speech into signification. There must be similarities of sonority, of rhythm, of form, etc. . . . which should correspond to each other and return the attention to the form."[112] Thus it is for song or chant, for the musical part of the poem, that the leading role is reserved. This is the element which prevents "decomposition" by attracting attention to the form, keeping it from transforming language into an immediately consumed thought. It will be noted that form itself receives a composition of its own, by an internal play of relations (similarities, correspondences, symmetries . . .). Valéry immediately suggested a solution, one of the least arduous, but not the highest in his opinion, to this problem of internal organization: "This is done quite easily, in a poem, by the strophes. We may thus obtain a kind of unity of the work which derives from its *body*."[m] Only a *kind* of unity, for if the strophe is self-sufficient and if the strophes resemble each other in their structure, the poem is still only a series of similar units.

If, in the total composition of the poem, Valéry seems to distinguish, at the same time that he grants it a directing and regulating function, a composition particular to form, it is not that he thereby neglects the distribution of meanings. We might speak of a composition of meaning. If Valéry rejects logical or chronological composition, he envisages an organi-

---

[m] *Réflexions sur l'art* in *Bulletin de la Société française de Philosophie,* 1935, p. 75. Cf. *Fontaines de mémoire* in *Pièces sur l'art,* pp. 307–8: "There exists one way of solving this problem of composition without infinite difficulty . . . the use of strophes, but of strophes that connect . . . this enterprise is clearly contrary to free development. . . ."

zation of the values of words which exceeds syntax. It seems
to bear both on the multiplicity of meanings suggested by
any figure of style and on the relations which the poet introduces into the series of terms he is employing. We recall nonsyntactical agreements which Valéry pointed out between
two important words of a beautiful line of verse. But the
main thing is to distract the reader from a unilateral simplicity of interpretation as we find it in an account of ideas
whose current must be clear and without ambiguity. Poly-
valence is doubtless the law of poetic language, both in the
terms and in their relations: ". . . between the successive
meanings there should exist *superabundant* relations—more
than are needed for a distinct and *linear* comprehension. It
is this which leads poets to the use of figures, metaphors,
tropes, etc. . . ."[113] These correspondences generally function in a specific passage of the poem, but it is not impossible
that echoes or symmetries or contrasts relate them at greater
distance; there are examples of this in *La Jeune Parque* (and
elsewhere; the procedure is not unknown to prose writers,
nor to novelists). But harmonies of ideas, if they link fragments of a work, cannot suffice to assure its unity of thought.
They are, in relation to the composition of meaning, what
alliterations are in relation to phonic composition: the melody
is more complex than these *reprises*. What the poem composes, from the point of view of meaning (I should prefer to
say of the imagination), is the totality of its mental values.
An initial analysis of *Le Cimetière marin,* made by Valéry
himself, casts some light on the way in which he understood
the distribution, the contrast, the relation, and the equilibrium
of the psychological parts. He begins by recalling the formal
bias at the origin of the poem ("strophes of six lines of ten
syllables"), by means of which he has been able "to distribute quite easily" in his work "what it must contain of the
sensuous, of the effective and of the abstract in order to suggest, to transport into the poetic universe, the meditation of a
certain self." We then see the poet concerned with the "requirement of the contrasts to be produced and with a kind
of equilibrium to be observed among the moments of this
self." This leads him to invoke the philosophy of Eleatic Zeno;
the lines in which his arguments appear ("but animated, con-

fused, extrapolated . . .") are intended to "compensate, by
a metaphysical tonality, for the sensual and the 'all too human' character of the preceding strophes," and to determine
more precisely *"the person speaking—*a lover of abstractions."
But, he says, "I meant to take from the philosophy only a
little of its color."[114] Contrast and equilibrium of the moments of a self—that is, of different emotive states—compensation of the sensual and of the overly human by a subsequent
metaphysical tonality, borrowing of philosophical color by
allusion to famous images, general suggestion of a particular
person—all this gives the idea of a composition which I should
prefer to call *tonal:* it is a matter of reconciling with the general tone of the "lover of abstractions" the various tones of
his successive feelings. It is by these tones, which govern the
choice of language and images, that the poet expresses the
affective color of his thought. If *Le Cimetière marin* is one of
Valéry's finest poems, it is certainly because of this composition in depth. It will perhaps be found that, on the faith of
certain words used here by Valéry (tonality, color), I am
drawing the poem a little too close to an explanation which
his theories reject; it is evident that we are somewhat surprised—but this is apropos of the most personal of his poems,
the only one in which he has admittedly put something of his
own life—to see him appear to concede something to the
values of sentiment in the elaboration of a poem. But beyond
the fact that the nature of things sometimes leads Valéry,
even in his theories, to the brink of concessions to the life of
the heart, it is not forbidden to suppose that in returning in
memory to the composition of *Le Cimetière marin,* he was
led to acknowledge the part of the very real feelings which
inspired him, we may assume, a little more than the deca-
syllabic sextain. My conclusion would be that the composition
of meanings, in order to be poetic, can only be affective play-
ing on themes of sentiment which it is the function of the
tone or the tones of the poem to bring into the language.

Harmonic and superabundant solidarity, in form and in
content, contrary to the method of prose—such then is the
general law of the composition of the poem. It would not be
difficult to attach to it certain prescriptions which Valéry
offered from time to time, and to which we might justifiably

give the name of laws. *The Law of correlation:* "The parts of a work must be linked to each other by more than one thread."[115] *The Law of the relation of details to the whole:* apropos of music and architecture, Valéry very briefly defines composition as "the linking of the whole with the detail."[116] *The Law of economy:* "All the parts of a work must function."[117] This effective arrangement of the composition aims at making the poem a machine of the greatest output by the smallest number of procedures. In his *Petit discours aux peintres graveurs,* Valéry, lightly comparing their art with the writer's, who communicates with them "in *Black* and *White,*" asserted that "the art closest to the mind . . . is that which restores the *maximum* of our impressions or of our inventions by the *minimum* of sensuous means."[118] Valéry also adopted a formula of Racine's to declare that "the myth of 'creation' seduces us into attempting to make something out of nothing."[119]

ORNAMENTAL COMPOSITION

But there is another way of appreciating composition. We can envisage it under its ornamental aspect, and this is doubtless the point of view which Valéry regards as the most important, though it is of a limited application, since Valéry considers this type of construction as an ideal impossible to attain in a long poem. The same is true of musical composition, which as we have already seen obsessed the poet's mind, and which there is no need to discuss separately, since Valéry—rather oddly—does not distinguish it from the other kind and even makes it the very type of ornamental composition in poetry. Speaking, in 1928, at the Société française de Philosophie, of the "almost insurmountable difficulty of composing in poetry," he specified:

> I know nothing rarer—with regard to the works which include more than . . . fourteen lines!—than composition, in what I would call the ornamental sense of this term.[120]

Here he saw "a task almost beyond human powers." Re-

jecting, once again, "the system which consists in following
as a leading thread a succession of dated events, or in adopting an organization of concepts," he acknowledged that he
found "in lyric poetry many examples of developments which
suggest a simple figure, an apparent curve. But these are
never anything but elementary types." When he thinks of
what composition should be, he "thinks of poems in which
one would try to achieve the skillful complexity of music by
introducing among their parts certain 'harmonic' relations,
symmetries, contrasts, correspondences . . . etc."[n] A precious confidence, which would correspond to the concern for
equilibrium which we have just seen governing the composition of *Le Cimetière marin*. But the poet, perhaps in order to
dissuade us, concludes with a fine, discouraged modesty: "I
confess that I have on occasion conceived and even undertaken something in this direction, but my attempts have
never produced a result . . . even a bad one."[121] No doubt
this dream of giving poetic composition the complexity of
musical composition was too vast, too ambitious. We may
also suppose that it mistook the difference between the two
arts. But something of all this went into certain of Valéry's
poems, the most extended ones, moreover, and especially *La
Jeune Parque*, whose symphonic impulses are often apparent.
In fact it was all of literature which Valéry, in his twentieth
year, sought to treat according to musical method, itself related to that of the mathematical sciences:

> Since 1891 I have always considered the art of litera-
> ture by comparing and opposing it to an ideal of labor—
> a labor quite comparable to that of the musical composer
> or of the constructor of a physicomathematical theory.
> We grant the musician the right to turn pale at certain
> combinations of harmony. We refuse the poet the inves-
> tigation of a deliberate and organized development of
> his means. . . .[o]

[n] *La création artistique* in *Bulletin de la Société française de
Philosophie*, 1928, p. 14. Valéry was to say in *L'Idée fixe*, p. 172:
". . . nothing rarer than the faculty to coordinate, to harmonize,
to orchestrate a great number of *parts*."
[o] *Propos me concernant*, p. 55. Cf. *Mémoires d'un poème*, p.
xxvii: "I confess that I sometimes feel a twinge of envy when I
think of the composer at grips with his enormous page of twenty

To grasp the entire application of this ambition, we must again return to the youthful essay *Introduction à la Méthode de Léonard de Vinci*, whose pages on composition I quoted above. I deliberately omitted one extremely curious passage on ornament. We know that while still in the lycée, Valéry, after having eagerly devoured Viollet-le-Duc's *Dictionnaire d'architecture*, had read Owen Jones's *Grammar of Ornament*. It was with a mathematician's perspective that he approached this subject in the *Introduction*. After declaring that "to construct" comes down to "a common measure of the terms involved," he remarks that "only purely abstract combinations," for example, "the numerical ones," are capable of "being constructed by means of determined units," and "that they are in the same relation to the other possible constructions as the regular portions in the world with those which are not." This information seeks to make us realize that there are abstract formulas (whether mathematical or not) which govern all the varieties of ornament, and that they are framed in "irregular" complexes practically impossible to reduce to a law and to numerable factors:

There is in art a word which can name all its fashions, all its fantasies, and which immediately suppresses all the so-called difficulties deriving from its opposition or its connection with that nature which is, and with good reason, never defined: that word is *ornament*. Let us recall in succession the groups of curves, the coincidences of divisions covering the oldest known objects, the outlines of vases and of temples; the diamonds, spirals, ovolos, the striations of the ancients; the crystallizations and the voluptuous walls of the Arabs; the Gothic ossatures and symmetries; the waves, flames, and flowers on Japanese lacquer and bronze, and in each of these periods, the introduction of the likenesses of plants, of animals, and of men, the perfecting of these resemblances: painting, sculpture. Let us invoke language and its primitive melody, the separation of words and music, the arborescence of each, the invention of verbs, of writing, the *figured* complexity of sentences becoming possible, the curious intervention of abstract words; and, on the other

staves . . . able to *compose* in the true sense of the word. . . . His action seems to me sublime."

hand, the system of the sounds growing more flexible, extending from the voice to the resonances of materials, growing more searching by harmony, varying by the use of timbres. Finally, let us note the parallel progress of the formations of thought through the various primitive psychic onomatopoeias, the elementary symmetries and contrasts, then the ideas of substances, the metaphors, the stammerings of logic, the formalisms and the entities, the metaphysical beings. . . .

All this multiform vitality can be appreciated in an ornamental connection. The manifestations enumerated can be considered as the finite portions of space or of time containing diverse variations, which are sometimes characterized and known objects, but whose signification and ordinary use are neglected, until there remain of them only the order and the mutual reactions. On this order depends the effect. The effect is the ornamental goal, and the work thus assumes the character of a mechanism to impress a public, to produce emotions and make images correspond to each other.[122]

Art would thus be a kind of mathematics included in a substance. But the artist and his public would be sensitive only to the organization of the abstract elements which constitute the true meaning of the work. We understand, from this, how a kind of Pythagorean aesthetics might dominate all the arts: "From this point of view, the ornamental conception is to the individual arts what mathematics is to the other sciences." The parallel is explained in its effects:

Just as the psychic notions of time, duration, density, mass, etc., are, in our calculations, merely homogeneous quantities and recover their individuality only in the interpretations of the results, similarly the objects chosen and organized with a view to an effect are as though detached from most of their properties and reassume them only in this effect, in the unprejudiced mind of the spectator.[123]

The work of art is abstract, to variable degrees depending on the complexity of the elements it takes from reality:

It is, then, by an abstraction that the work of art can be constructed, and this abstraction is more or less energetic, more or less easy to define, depending on whether the elements borrowed from reality are more or less complex portions of it.[124]

The appreciation of the work of art is made, inversely, by a kind of induction, by a "production of mental images" that is "more or less energetic, more or less *exhausting*" depending on whether the audience is dealing "with a simple tracery on a vase or a broken sentence by Pascal."[125]

It may seem strange, at first glance, to bring ornament into composition. Ornament seems, indeed, an embellishment which is later added to a whole or to a pre-existing structure. But the reconciliation is easy to make—theoretically—between the two requirements, if we reject *accidental* ornament and demand that ornament be drawn from the content, or rather from the form, of the work. It is no more than a particularly sensitive aspect of a varied continuity. Since ornament can then not be separated from that continuity without destroying it, nothing is an ornament and everything is an ornament. The word can therefore assume two values, pejorative or favorable, and Valéry used it sometimes with one intention, sometimes with the other, depending on whether he made ornament a superfluity or the very law of composition.

Valéry sketched a theory of the origins of ornament. Ornament was born of the void, and of boredom:

A blank space, an empty time are unendurable.

Ornament is born of boredom—as the image of food is born of an empty stomach. —As action is born of inaction, and as the horse champs, and memory is born, as dreams are born, in the interval of actions.

The fatigue of the senses creates. The void creates. Darkness creates. Silence creates.[p] Incident creates.

[p] Silence is a kind of void particularly important for the poet. In his *Calepin d'un poète,* in which Valéry declares the poet to be an *expectation,* he asserts that "silence and attention are incompatible," and assigns himself this program: "To create, then, the kind of silence to which *the beautiful* is an answer. Or the pure line of verse, or the luminous idea . . . Then the line of verse seems born of itself, born of necessity. . . ." (*Oeuvres complètes,* vol. C, p. 184). This is because the line of verse, both expected and unforeseeable, is an answer of the sensibility to the void of silence, a phenomenon of complementarity, comparable to the

Everything creates, except the man who signs and takes responsibility for the work.q

Sensibility needs to fill the void, and creates automatically to this effect; it answers the void by a spontaneous production quite comparable to the apparition of complementary colors on the retina:

> Sensibility . . . has a horror of the vacuum. It reacts spontaneously against the rarefaction of stimuli. Every time a duration without occupation or preoccupation is imposed on man, there occurs in him a change of state marked by a kind of emission, which tends to re-establish the equilibrium of exchanges between the sensibility's *power* and its *act.* The tracing of a décor on a surface that is too bare, the birth of a song in an oppressive silence, these are merely answers, complements, which compensate for the absence of stimuli—as if this *absence,* which we express by a simple negation, *acted* positively on us. . . . We may surprise here the very seed of the production of the work of art.[126]

Ornament is merely a complementary function of the void:

> It seems to me that, for certain very simple and prim-itive forms of the work of art, for example geometric ornament or a combination of colors in braided straw or the weaving of a fabric, one would discover that this ornamentation has a complementary origin. It is proba-ble that at the start the work of art answers only to a need of the author; there is not yet a public, it is the ac-tion itself which interests the person making it; this is a man who is bored. It is the *horror vacui,* whose comple-ment will be ornament: it is the void of time or of space, the blank page which the sensibility cannot endure.r

---

drawing which answers the solicitation of a blank space. It is not easy to grasp, in these rather obscure pages, how the special silence which the poet creates for himself as a stimulus to invention is at the same time expunged of expectation, especially when we recall the expectant attitude which Valéry quite accurately attributes to the poet.

q *Autres rhumbs* in *Tel quel,* II, pp. 150–51. As always, Valéry is led to extend the notion: "Savor *ornaments* the surface of your food; the shape of the mouthful of wine is decorated with aro-mas . . ." (*Instants* in *Mélange,* p. 168).

r *Réflexions sur l'art* in *Bulletin de la Société française de Philos-*

With the progress of techniques, "the *complementary* need to ornament this object, that is, to fill the voids," has become specialized and complicated:

> Then it is no longer only spontaneity, an almost mechanical labor (like that of the man who hums to himself a monotonous melopoeia, or who fills a space with arbitrary doodles) which suffices; we see something else besides pure sensibility functioning; what is called intellect, intelligence, intervenes; and with intelligence, conscious anticipation. In the work of art, we see appearing a kind of calculation. We see appearing, too, a complication of forms, an attempt to make them more interesting.
>
> To abstract ornament is added the representation of *things.* Consequently it is necessary that the intellect, with all its resources, gradually come into play, and with it deliberate observation.[8]

Ornament and calculation—this could be, as much as sensibility and method, a summary of the Valerian aesthetic.

But, if we would understand Valéry's predilection for ornament, we must exclude from it, as much as possible, any decoration having a direct relation to nature, and especially the ornaments suggesting life. We might call it a taste for pure ornament. It is here that the two senses of the word

ophie, 1935, p. 71. *Le Cours de poétique* insists at length on complementarity, and gives interesting examples of it: "The recepto-transmissive character seems to me essential to sensibility. . . . Then, if, captives as we are, there is a bare wall before us, we shall draw upon it. . . . Boredom is a great generator of poetry. As red produces green upon the retina, the void is a creator by complementaries, by need of plenitude. A negation thus functions positively in us" (lecture 3). "I discover the notion of the complementary in all realms of the sensibility and even in the mathematical world. It is also in poetry and at all points: for example, in the very obscure notion of rhythm, and in the very difficult question of "figures," images, etc. . . ." (lecture 4). "We encounter in all the arts phenomena of complementarity and effects of continuity. The sensorial necessity will engender the significative creation. A painter . . . decides: a *green* is needed here, and he puts in a *tree.* In this case, the sensorial phenomenon engenders a significative phenomenon. The reciprocal also occurs" (lecture 6).

[8] Ibid., p. 72. The same ideas, apropos of bookbinding, in *Le Physique du Livre.*

ornament diverge, the ornament of imitation rejected into the impurity of too-human vitality, and abstract ornament joining the severe beauty of mathematical proportions:

> Sometimes I find barbarous and bizarre the practice of ornamenting a structure with statues and representations of living beings.
>
> I understand the Arabs, who refuse to have them. I perceive almost painfully the contrast between form and matter which is emphasized in this ornamental world, where stone shifts from its mechanical role to its theatrical disguise.
>
> I feel that it is not acts of the same attention which have made the wall or the vault, and the saint perched in the niche.
>
> A Parthenon is composed of relations which borrow nothing from the observation of objects. It is subsequently peopled with personages, it is underlined by foliage.
>
> I should prefer that the eye recognize nothing in this heap; but find there only a new object, without reference to external similarities, which is perceived as though created by the EYE for an infinite contemplation of its own laws.[127]

This disgust with the ornamentation of monuments by statues or frescoes, which are too lifelike, is accompanied by the condemnation of program music, of "imitative harmony" in music: "is it not held to be a secondary and clumsy artifice?"

> To imitate, to describe, to represent man or other things, this is not to imitate Nature in her operation; it is to imitate her products, which is quite different. If one wishes to resemble what produces (*Natura:* productress), one must, on the contrary, exploit the entire domain of one's sensibility and one's action, pursue the combinations of their elements, whose objects and given beings are merely singularities, special cases which are opposed to the whole of all that we can see and conceive. . . .[128]

Whence the enthusiastic praise of the Arabs, "who religiously proscribe the investigation of the resemblance of beings," and whose deductive imagination invents the *Ara-*

besque.[129] The confidences of *Mémoires d'un poème* confirm this nostalgia: "Much more than in Letters, I might have put my hopes in the arts which reproduce nothing, which do not feign . . . ,"[130] in which each value of our sensibility is

> . . . detached from all reference and from any function as *sign.* Thus reduced to itself, the sequence of our sensations no longer has a chronological order, but a kind of intrinsic and instantaneous order which gradually declares itself. . . . We need merely think of the productions generally grouped under the name of *Ornament,* or of *pure music* to make ourselves understood. . . . Here there is never any confusion possible between the effect of the work and the appearances of an alien life; but instead a possible communion with the profound springs of all life.
> But I had neither the gifts nor the technical knowledge required to follow this formal instinct for the productions of sensibility developed apart from any representation, which manifest a structure without *resemblance* and which tend to organize themselves into complete constructions by themselves.[131]

As in the search for the central attitude or in the poetic composition on the musical model, Valéry therefore renounced pure ornamental composition. But the sentiment of creation starting from empty forms given by the sensibility never abandoned him. Let us note that these figures are not quite that absolute void which he suggested as the origin of art. It is now a question of a solicitation which is no longer uncharacterized, but which has an orientation and especially a form which is imposed on the response it demands and whose general aspect it predetermines:

> There is a certain void which demands—which summons up; this *void* can be more or less determined. It can be a certain rhythm—a figure or contour; a question, a state—a time ahead of me; a tool, a blank page, a moral surface, a terrain, or a location.[132]

In poetry, sensibility produces rhythms, figures, etc., which seek to gain a content for themselves. "Certain poems I have written have had for their seed no more than these solicitations of 'formal' sensibility anterior to any 'subject,' to any

finite and expressible idea."[133] We have already seen some
examples of this. But Valéry was not content to put ornament
at the source of the poem; he made it the law of the invention of detail and gave it a preponderant role in composition:
"The world of the poem is essentially closed and complete in
itself, being the pure system of the ornaments and opportunities of language," and it is significant that, in this same text
(*Hommage* to Marcel Proust), he sets in opposition to the
poem, detached from reality, the novel which is linked to
reality like all the arts of *trompe-l'oeil*.[134]

These ornaments, opportunities of language, which are essential to poetry, doubtless derive their value from their
originality. But Valéry considered them chiefly in the forms in
which the oldest tradition classified them, that is, as figures of
rhetoric. Not that he was satisfied "with the very imperfect
analysis the ancients made of these 'rhetorical' phenomena."[135] He considered that the question needed to be entirely redefined. Far from doing so, the "criticism of the moderns"[136] and "modern education"[137] neglect it almost
utterly. Valéry himself was interested in the problem only
rather late (when he went back to writing poetry), according
to one of his letters, of 1917, to Pierre Louÿs:

> Where are we to find such definitions of the figures
> of rhetoric, and what book should we consult as to the
> ancient theory of rhetoric?
> I've often wanted to extend this classical analysis, but
> first of all I'd have to be familiar with it, and I don't
> know how to set about it. I have Aristotle's *Rhetoric*,
> and there's nothing in it.[138]

Valéry must have leafed through his Aristotle too fast, for
whatever he says, there is substance in the work, which could
be completed by the *Poetics*. It is difficult to guess what
Valéry's rhetoric would have been—that rhetoric Thibaudet
and Du Bos encouraged him to write,[139] but we can guess
that the former reader of Bréal's *Sémantique* dreamed more
than once of a valid symbolic structure in the entire realm of
the uses of language. He noted, as so many linguists have
done, that figured language is as much a popular creation as
a scientific or literary one:

Figures play a role of the first importance, not only in poetry declared and organized as such, but even in that perpetually functioning poetry which torments the fixed *vocabulary*, dilates or limits the meaning of words, influences them by symmetries or by conversions, constantly alters the values of this fiduciary currency; and sometimes in the mouths of the people, sometimes for the unforeseen requirements of technical expression, sometimes under the writer's hesitant pen, engenders that variation of the language which gradually makes it altogether different.[140]

Valéry sees, very correctly, in the poet's propensity to renew the language by figures the resumption of a spontaneous activity which created that very language. It happens that Literature, he says,

develops the effects which the comparisons of terms, their contrasts, may produce, and creates contractions or employs substitutions which stimulate the mind to produce representations more vivid than those which enable it to understand ordinary language. . . . The formation of figures is indivisible from that of the language itself, all of whose "abstract" words are obtained by some abuse or some shift of meaning, followed by a forgetting of the original meaning. The poet who multiplies the figures thus merely rediscovers in himself the language in its nascent state.[141]

But what interests Valéry most of all is the investigation of the general system of figures, which would comprehend both mathematics and the ornaments of language:

No one seems to have even attempted to extend this analysis. No one is investigating in the enlarged consideration of these substitutions, of these contracted notations, of these meditated mistakes and these expedients hitherto so vaguely defined by the grammarians, the properties which they suppose and which cannot be so different from those sometimes indicated by the geometrical genius and its art of creating increasingly flexible and penetrating instruments of thought. The Poet, without knowing it, moves in an order of *possible* relations and transformations, of which he perceives or pursues only the momentary and particular effects. . . .[t]

It is here that Mallarmé seems to Valéry superior to other poets. When Valéry praises him for having "understood the language as if he had invented it," it is a kind of genius for abstraction that he chooses to see in the older poet. He had

. . . the extraordinary ambition to conceive and to dominate the entire system of verbal expression.

In this he coincided—as I once told him—with the attitude of the men who extended, in algebra, the science of forms and the symbolic part of the mathematical art. This kind of attention makes the structure of expressions more apparent and more interesting than their meanings or their values. The properties of transformations are more worthy of the mind than what it transforms. . . .[142]

Valéry clearly indicates how the figures shift, in a Mallarmé, from the role of accident to that of essence:

In the order of language, the *figures*, which commonly play an accessory part, seem to intervene only to illustrate or reinforce an intention, and thus appear adventitious, like ornaments which the substance of the discourse can do without—become, in Mallarmé's reflections, essential elements: *metaphor*, instead of the decoration it was, or a momentary vehicle, seems here to receive the value of a fundamental symmetrical relation.[143]

Valéry did not undertake to establish this rhetoric whose scope he felt a scientific analysis would renew.[u] The hints we can glean, here and there, in his work are quite rare, and concern little more than metaphor (to which, it is true, we

---

[t] *Questions de poésie* in *Variété III*, p. 49. Cf. *Cours de poétique*, lecture 4: "Metaphor is a natural production of the mind. Its role is crucial in all scientific progress."

[u] As we might expect, Valéry never envisaged this study in the form of a history of figures. All he gives is a few remarks of this sort: "Petrarch invented all the turns of speech that appeared much later in French verse. He had no model, that I can see. But my vision is involved" (Letter of June 6, 1917, to Pierre Louÿs, in *Oeuvres complètes*, vol. B, p. 137).

can reduce most figures; it is between metaphor and comparison that the linguists hesitate in this attempt at unification). Valéry merely utilizes the etymology of this word, when he reminds us that Foch "deliberately used images, which are the promptest if not the surest means of connection between two flashes of the mind."[144] He does not tell us much more when he notes, with a certain secret irony, that

. . . the philosopher makes himself a poet, and often a great poet: he borrows metaphor from us, and by magnificent images which we must envy, he summons all nature to the expression of his profound thought.▼

More interesting is the view which relates the creation of metaphors to the mind's power of modification, parallel to dramatic creation. Valéry notes in Goethe the same "aptitude to accommodate himself and to assume the forms which suit the circumstances" which Goethe, in his biological investigations, had acknowledged in living beings. Now "this genius for transformation is . . . essentially poetic, since it also presides as much over the formation of metaphors and figures, by which the poet controls the multiplicity of expressions, as over the creation of characters and situations in the drama. But in the poet and in the plant, we have the same natural principle. . . ."[145] It is this virtuality of verbal forms at the poet's disposal which characterizes metaphoric expression; if thought were to pursue its effort rigorously to its conclusion, the superabundance of expression would disappear and would yield to an expression without ambiguity, that is, to prose. This is why Valéry instances metaphor as an example of "that part of ideas which cannot be put in prose," those "which are possible only in an excessively intense, or rhythmic, or spontaneous movement of thought" (we can recognize here, alongside the figures, the natural formations of sensibility which are, precisely, spontaneously given rhythms and involuntary discoveries):

▼ *Descartes* in *Variété IV*, p. 216. See the praise of Bergson's style: "He dared borrow from Poetry its magic weapons. . . . The most felicitous images, the freshest metaphors obeyed his desire to reconstruct in men's consciousness the discoveries he was making in his own" (*Discours sur Bergson* in *Vues*, pp. 389–90).

Metaphor, for example, indicates in its naïve principle a *groping*, a hesitation among several expressions of a thought, an explosive impotence exceeding the *necessary* and *sufficient* power. When we have followed and defined thought in its utmost rigor to a single object, then metaphor will be effaced, prose will reappear.[146]

As a result, "the realm strictly proper" to poetry is

. . . the expression of what is inexpressible in terms of the finite functions of words. The true object of poetry is what does not have a single name, what in itself provokes and requires more than one expression; what produces, for the unity to be expressed, a plurality of expressions.[147]

How are metaphors born? Like rhythms, they are natural formations of sensibility. We also know that they can appear as a response to the void, or to boredom, like all ornaments. Unfortunately, this explanation lacks clarity, for if there is anything certain about the creation of a metaphor, or of any figure whose essence is a relation between two terms, it is that it starts not from the void but from one object, in order to express it in a particular aspect by means of another object. Valéry might perhaps have used here his theory of creation by the adjustment of convention to accident. If the poet takes comparison as a condition of his activity, many representations which come to mind will seem to him suitable to receive this treatment. And there is no doubt that the figurative intention is always more or less present in the poetic enterprise. But it does not suffice to provoke that kind of flash which leaps between two images. Valéry saw that this phenomenon was a mysterious one. According to him, metaphor results from a psychological attitude, but one which we are not yet in a position to analyze:

A metaphor is *what happens* when *we look in a certain way,* as a sneeze is what happens when we look at a sun? In what way? You feel it. One day, perhaps, we'll be able to *say* it quite exactly.
Do this and that—and there are all the metaphors in the world. . . .[148]

The comparison with the sneeze (whose purpose is to depreciate inspiration) brings us back, in accord with the theory of sensibility-as-response, to making metaphor a simple reflex. A little more clarity is afforded when Valéry reattaches metaphor to gesture. Language, originally, was purely gesticular; now, the language of gestures is metaphoric:

> The orator's gestures are metaphors. Either he clearly shows between thumb and forefinger the object firmly grasped; or he touches it with his finger, palm to heaven. What he touches, what he grasps, what he slices, what he slaughters, are imaginary things, formerly real acts, when language was gesture; and gesture, an action.[149]

It is perhaps what remains of movement in verbal metaphors—that trajectory which the mind makes from one representation to another—which once led Valéry to designate them in brief by this striking formula: "those stationary movements,"[150] a phrase which suggests, further, that metaphoric expression is manifested on the spot, in a momentary explosion of the poem, and does not participate, as does rhythm, in the poetic current. This would no longer be true of continuous metaphor and developed comparison.

It would seem, from the above, that Valéry grants a large role to the use of figures in style. Yet he often indicated his predilection for a simplified style: "A dry style comes down through time like an incorruptible mummy. . . ."[151] Without absolutely rejecting ornament, he notes the difficulty of its use: "The only man who knows how to ornament a style is the man who is capable of a naked, plain style."[152] Praising Racine for his "amazing economy of the means of art," balanced by "a complete possession of the small number of those means he retains," he admires his art of sacrifices, and manifests, in this regard, a scorn of images that is quite revealing:

> Few realize how much imagination it takes to do without images and to achieve so simple an ideal. In letters as in the sciences, an image no doubt sometimes replaces a certain calculation which would be laborious. But Racine preferred accomplishment.[153]

Racine rejected "all that was so prized after him." Valéry condemned an excess of images:

The abuse, the multiplicity of images produces in the mind's eye a disorder incompatible with *tone*. Everything comes down to nothing in all that dazzle.[154]

But there is a means of saving ornament, which is to legitimize it. Poetry, which cannot do without it, poses the problem in its intensest form. We conceive a naked architecture, a prose without images, not a poetry without figures. The integration of figures can be made in two ways, or better still, in two degrees. We can first show that they constitute not beauties superadded, but the very substance of poetry. Poetry is literally made of figures:

> The old rhetoric regarded as ornaments and artifices those figures and relations which the successive refinements of poetry finally made known as the essential of its object; and which the progress of analysis will some day find as the effects of profound properties, or of what we might call: *formal sensibility*.[155]

Actually, this theory does not rid poetry of parasitical images, but it gives images the most important constitutive role. The second degree of integration of figures internalizes them more deeply and—theoretically—leaves no place for their superfluous manifestations. But in order to grasp this concept, which is the true conclusion of the whole Valerian theory of ornament, we must first of all consider the poem's unity under the aspect of duration, of continuity.

We have already seen that the continuity of a work is obtained only by incessant *reprises*:

> . . . the inequality in a work . . . shocks and even irritates me; perhaps a little more than it should. What is more impure than the frequent mixture of the excellent and the mediocre? It is remarkable that we cannot obtain that continuity and that equality or that plenitude which for me are the conditions of an unmixed pleasure, and which should envelop all the other qualities of a work, except by a necessarily *discontinuous* labor. Art is in opposition to the mind. Our mind . . . admits everything. . . . It literally lives on incoherences, it moves only by leaps. . . . It is only by repetitions, by *reprises* that it can accumulate outside itself, in a constant substance, the elements of its action, chosen in order to

adjust itself step by step and to tend toward the unity of some composition. . . .[156]

Valéry extended this requirement of continuity far beyond art. In all domains, it is the fruit of simulation. We obtain "the Continuous by the Mendacious":

> The continuity of love, of faith, of the virtuous or noble attitude; the permanence of genius, of intelligence, of energy, of purity, and even of vice—is assured by simulation, by the pious imitation of the highest state by the lesser, of the rare state by the frequent.[157]

Simulation is a virtue of the artist, who must seek to equal what was best in himself and in his work:

> It is essential for the artist to be able to imitate himself.
> This is the only means of constructing a work—which is necessarily an enterprise against mobility, inconsistency of mind, of vigor, and of mood.
> The artist takes his best state for a model. What he has done best (in his judgment) serves him as a unit of measurement.[158]

Valéry is close to regarding the obligation of continuity as in itself creative, like the conventions which are shown to be stimuli of invention. The concern for transitions or relations between the parts makes us find the necessary details which will seem natural:

> A charming, touching, "profoundly human" idea (as the fools say) sometimes proceeds from the need to link two strophes, two developments. A bridge had to be built, or threads woven, which would assure the sequence of the poem; and since the always possible sequence is man himself, or a man's life, this *formal* need finds a response—a fortuitous and happy one in the author, who did not expect to discover it—and a *living* response, once it is in place, for the reader.[159]

We know Valéry's predilection for "links," for *enchaînements*.[160] He even went so far as to regret being unable to provide transitions among odors: "One cannot, however, link perfumes. If one only could, what music!"[161] Alas! "odors ignore each other."[162] Continuity can be established among various kinds of elements, and then the complexity of the links coincides with the complexity of that nonlinear composition of which we have spoken and which gives the work its solidity and its absolute independence. It is this kind of link which Valéry admires in Mallarmé:

> These marvelously finished little compositions imposed themselves as types of perfection, so assured were the links of word with word, of line with line, of movement with rhythm, so clearly did they give the idea of an absolute object, in a sense, resulting from an equilibrium of intrinsic forces, freed by a marvel of reciprocal combinations from those vague impulses of revision and change which the mind in its readings unconsciously conceives in the presence of most texts.[163]

This continuity, hopeless in an extended text, is already almost undiscoverable in a brief sequence. Valéry declares "a marvel of eight lines . . . infinitely rarer . . . than eight fine lines."[164] It is in order to preserve the continuity of the melody that the beautiful lines themselves must sometimes yield to his demand. This is what Valéry wrote to Fernand Lot, who had asked the poet to distinguish, in some of his own lines, the results of labor from those of inspiration—which he avoided:

> I should go so far as to suppose that we must not fear sacrificing isolated "fine lines" to what might be called the melodic continuity of a sentence pursued through the rhymes and caesuras.[w]

It is this art of sacrifices—images or fine lines—which Valéry believes he finds in Racine, practiced for the benefit of the melodic design as a whole:

> A certain line of verse which seems flat to us has cost the sacrifice of twenty magnificent ones—magnificent *to us*—but which would have broken a divine outline and

---

[w] In Fernand Lot, *Regard sur la prosodie de Paul Valéry, La Grande Revue*, March 1930, p. 93. Cf. *Existence du Symbolisme* in *Oeuvres complètes*, vol. L, p. 125: "The fine line is often the enemy of the poem."

troubled the august duration of a perfect phase of the soul's movement.[165]

Valéry imagines Racine in his own fashion, and perhaps gratuitously, but with a luminous sympathy:

> I see him first of all drawing, defining, deducing finally, from a thought long reworked and deliberated, those pure periods, in which even violence sings and the most intense and true passion shines like gold, and is never developed except in the nobility of a language which consummates an unequaled alliance of analysis and harmony.[166]

If we consider these texts closely, we see that they treat two kinds of continuity: a psychic continuity ("the august duration of a perfect phase of the soul's movement") and a melodic continuity ("pure period"). The miracle of Racine is to infuse them into each other, to draw the second from the first ("to deduce . . . from a thought long reworked and deliberated . . ."), or, better still, starting from "the idea he has taken as his theme," Racine, by delicate substitutions, "inflects it to the song he wants to achieve."[167] His concern is obviously never to abandon "the contour of his discourse."[168]

> In Racine, the perpetual ornament seems drawn from the discourse, and this is the means and the secret of his prodigious continuity, while in the moderns, the ornament breaks the discourse.[169]

Thus in Racine, ornament ceases to be superfluous by extending itself indefinitely until it is no longer distinguished from the poetic current. Such is the supreme degree of ornament's integration.[x]

[x] It is somewhat surprising that Valéry should have honored the obscure translator of the hymns of Saint John of the Cross with praise analogous to that addressed to his illustrious contemporary. It is true that he confines himself to praising in Père Cyprien the melodic continuity (the other kind being due to his model), but in what privileged terms: "I greatly fear that we can count on our fingers the number of poets in whom the pleasure of continuous melody begins with the poem and ends only with the poem. This is why the amazing success of Père Cyprien in his undertaking has delighted me to the point I have expressed" (*"Cantiques spirituels"*

After having vaunted psychic or melodic continuity, it remained to characterize its quality. This Valéry did splendidly when he defined it as a *modulation*. As we have so often observed, the idea assumed for him a broad extension. He applied it to the most varied realms. In *Mélange*, he described, or rather celebrated, a long caress, "a descent down the shoulders across the breasts," as a "sequence of modulations of forces" in the fingers.[170] Goethe, he tells us, "discerns morphological modulations."[171] Apropos of Frazer's *The Fear of the Dead*, "the almost imperceptible shift . . . from one belief to another, scarcely different but observed to occur thousands of miles from the first" is declared "analogous to a modulation."[172] Marshal Pétain is praised in these terms:

> Monsieur, at Verdun you assumed, organized, embodied that immortal resistance which gradually, in your hands, as though by a skilled and surprising modulation, was reversed into an offensive reaction, and changed . . . into an urgent power, into a retaking of the positions lost, into a victorious counterattack.[173]

Each life has "its timbre of pathos and its modulations of disgust, of pain, of fatigue and of boredom."[174] If we want a pure example of psychological modulation, we need only read the page where Valéry retraces Descartes' spiritual trajectory on the memorable day of November 10, 1619, and on the night of visions which followed it.[175] But it is chiefly architecture which lends itself to these musical analogies. Consider Notre Dame de Paris,

> . . . the profiles of transitional forms, of moldings, of ribs, of strips, of ridges which lead the eye in its movements, you will find in the comprehension of these auxiliaries, so simple in themselves, an impression comparable to that which in music is given by the art of

in *Variété V*, p. 182). We have the impression that many versifiers of the seventeenth and eighteenth centuries shared with Père Cyprien this elegance of diction which is certainly not negligible but whose merit Valéry perhaps overestimates, consisting as it does chiefly of a fluidity without shocks, not of the divine Racinian music which is sustained by timbres.

modulating and of imperceptibly shifting a listener's soul from one state to another.[176]

Eupalinos, according to Phaedrus,

. . . knew . . . the mysterious virtue of imperceptible modulations. No one realized, before a delicately lightened mass of such apparent simplicities, that he was being led to a kind of happiness by gradual curves, by infinitesimal and omnipotent inflections . . .[177]

which are related, for the reader of Valéry, to "that delicate design of inflection, that transparent mode of discourse" which attributes to Racine, though Racine himself probably did not know how he obtained it,[178] and to that "extraordinary flexibility" of form in La Fontaine, which "admits all the tones of speech . . . and adjusts these modulations to every degree required of it. . . ."[179]

In this unfettered art, Eupalinos is specifically compared to the poets and the orators. Thus it is again a universal technique which Valéry seeks, or at least foresees with a kind of affective fervor. As the Pythoness says,

> Toute lyre
> Contient la modulation.

[Every lyre contains modulation.]

This general value of a formula is expressly recalled when Valéry applies it to poetry and confesses that

La Jeune Parque was a research project, a literally endless investigation of what might be attempted in poetry analogous to what is called "modulation" in music. The "transitions" have given me a great deal of trouble. . . . Nothing interests me more in the arts than these transitions in which I find what is most delicate and most difficult, while the moderns ignore or scorn them. I never tire of admiring by what nuances of forms the figure of a living body, or of a plant, is gradually deduced and brought into agreement with itself; and the way in which the helix of a shell ultimately opens, after several convolutions, edged with a layer of its inner nacre.[y] The

[y] Cf. L'Homme et la coquille in Variété V, p. 34: "Nothing . . . allows us to imagine what modulates surfaces so gracefully

architecture of a high period employed the most exquisite[z] and the most calculated cornices in order to harmonize the successive surfaces of its construction. . . .[180]

But modulation is not only, as in several of these examples, a means of felicitously linking heterogeneous parts; when it is *perpetual*, when we can no longer distinguish in it content and form, line and ornament, it is the uninterrupted curve which draws the figure of the work, gives it its style, achieves the very purpose of composition.

. . . and what miraculously harmonizes these curves . . . with a boldness, an ease, a decision whose felicity the most flexible creations of the potter or bronze founder only remotely approximate." The Valerian anthology of modulation also includes smoke; see in *Propos me concernant*, pp. 37–38, the ravishing description of cigarette smoke, in which the word *modulation* does not appear, though everything suggests it.

[z] See in *Pensée et art français* in *Regards sur le monde actuel et autres essais*, p. 184, the praise of stone, taken from the national soil, "which lends itself to elegant connections, to charming outlines . . ."

Chapter VII

THE PROBLEM OF EXECUTION

FROM DISORDER TO ORDER

Explaining the difficulties of lyric composition, Valéry insisted upon two conditions of such work: 1) "foresight" must take into account "the uncertainty of discoveries"; 2) "each moment must consummate an indefinable alliance between the sensuous and the significative."[1] Which means that the idea as a whole in the process of its realization is modified by its detail, and that the treatment of each part involves both form and content at once. Valéry came immediately to the conclusion that it is impossible to dissociate composition from execution:

> The result is that composition is, in a sense, continuous, and cannot be partitioned off from the period of execution. There is not one time for "content" and another for "form"; and composition in this genre is opposed not only to *disorder* or to *disproportion,* but to *decomposition.*[2]

It is not surprising, then, when we examine Valéry's ideas on the theoretically ultimate operation of poetic creation to encounter once again all the problems that the latter posed in its nature or in its preparatory phases. This is evident in Valéry's statements to the Société française de Philosophie in 1935. After having remarked of execution that one might "describe it magnificently as a passage from disorder to order, from the unformed to form or from the impure to the pure, from the arbitrary to the necessary, etc., from confusion to clarity, as a change to which the eye adapts itself . . . ," he attaches to it almost his entire aesthetic:

Execution raises a host of questions and ideas: for ex-

ample, the problem of facility, of impossibilities, of difficulties; the immense problem of various conventions, of
liberties, of the craft itself; chance, which plays an immense role, if one can speak of a role apropos of chance;
the role of reasoning and analogies; of what we may
call the *model*, the type certain artists must have in
mind. . . .

To which he also adds "the artist's ethic and his affective
relationships": "pride," "vanity," "jealousy," "the way in
which the artist conceives his public," and finally the "idols in
art": "myths," "superstitions," "beliefs". . . .[a]

We see that the solution of the problem of execution necessitates the simultaneous intervention of all the factors artificially separated by analysis, and that in short it seems to
contradict the Valerian dogma of creation by separate principles. But this would be to misjudge the vitality of a theoretician whose convictions are well anchored, for the following
passage, one of the most typical we can cite, returns with increased force to the thesis of clearly articulated acts. Valéry
wonders "why the execution of a work of art" might not "itself be a work of art," and borrows from Goncourt a conclusive example:

Goncourt relates that a Japanese painter came to Paris
and gave a demonstration for a few art lovers. After having prepared his tools, he moistened the paper on his
easel with a sponge, then threw a drop of India ink upon
this wet paper. When the drop had spread, he lighted
newspapers crumpled into balls in order to dry the paper. He wet the dry paper a second time in another cor-
ner, made another spot, etc. He's a charlatan, the ob-
servers declared. But when he had finished the dryings
and the applications of India ink, he went over to the
paper on the easel and, with a fine brush, drew two or
three lines, here and there. The work immediately appeared: a bird ruffling its feathers. Not one operation
had been unsuccessful, and it had all been done with a
scrupulous order that proved that he had done it a
hundred times and had arrived at this marvel of execu-

[a] *Réflexions sur l'art* in *Bulletin de la Société française de Philosophie*, 1935, p. 76. I have corrected the obvious error that listed
among the idols *superpositions*, instead of *superstitions*.

tion. This man made of the execution of a work of art another work of art. One can thus conceive of a painter or a sculptor functioning in a sort of dance, performing rhythmically. Execution, after all, is mimicry. If one could reconstitute all its movements, one would define the painting by a sequence of ordered actions; this sequence could then be repeated, be reproduced, and the artist become comparable to the actor who plays the same role a hundred times.

This shows, in the form of a fantasy, how all these acts of art, once they are well acquired, are capable of a certain repetition, and that the true artist attains (though not as precisely as I have said) a knowledge of himself that extends to practice and to the *automatic* use of his personality, of his *originality*.[b]

Here again we find, at least as an ideal, the essential idea of creation through order (and the accessory ideas of self-imitation and the reabsorption of originality into mechanics). But this is only an ideal. The complexity of poetry in fact prohibits the adoption of such a method. We would have difficulty finding examples of almost instantaneous poetic execution analogous to that of the Japanese painter. The closest situation would be the composition of impromptu verse or verses on given rhymes, with the proviso that the versifier continually think aloud. One occasionally sees on the stage poetasters of this kind, who ask the audience to give them rhymes, and it is said that the poet Glatigny, a disciple of Banville's, earned his living in this manner for a time. (Mendés has dramatized this picturesque incident.) Let us note that this execution out of whole cloth accords with Valéry's love of virtuosity, but is opposed to his own experience of poetic activity, full of retouches and hesitations. In fact, the art of literature is the furthest from this operative perfection. It cannot be reduced to a succession of pure and perfectly

[b] Ibid., p. 77. When Mme. R. Vautier sculpted a bust of Valéry, he was again attracted by the idea of considering as a work of art the execution of a work of art. Sculpture seemed to him to be a kind of dance, and continuing to "dream on this theme" he even "conceived a project for notating the music of this dance. For a given sculpture, one could have a corresponding piece of music, based on the rhythms of the sculptor's acts" (*"Mon buste"* in *Pièces sur l'art*, pp. 289–90).

connected movements, for it brings into play the whole of the
mind's activity:

> The art of literature, derived from language and by
> which, in turn, language is influenced, is thus, of all the
> arts, the one in which convention plays the greatest role;
> the one in which memory intervenes at each moment,
> through every word; the one which acts above all by
> *relays* and not by direct sensation, and which engages
> simultaneously, and even in competition, the abstract
> intellectual faculties and the properties of emotion and
> sensibility. It is, of all the arts, the one which engages
> and utilizes the greatest number of independent parts
> (*sound, sense, syntactic forms, concepts, images* . . .).
> Its study . . . is basically . . . an analysis of the mind
> executed with a particular intention. . . .[3]

It is not easy to describe the labor of execution. Its general
movement is a shift from chaos to cosmos, from disorder to
order. The initial disorder is that of the sensibility as a whole.
The problem is to change "disorder to order" and "luck into
power."[c] A risky enterprise whose extremes are "genius" and
"madness": "Both having fallen into the rushing current, one
swims and the other drowns."[4] To effect the transformation,
an agent is necessary: ". . . the *mind* must be introduced,
that is, whatever will cause order to appear once the die is
cast."[5] The mind will oppose disorder; but in a fundamental
way the mind makes no distinction between itself and the in-
coherent sensibility from which it must separate itself in order
to reply, for the mind itself is disorder: "Once the mind is
engaged, everything is engaged; everything is disorder and
every reaction against disorder is of the same nature as it,"[6]
but a disorder which turns against itself in order to conquer
and discipline itself:

> The mind engaged in production seems to seek to im-
> print upon its own work characteristics completely op-

[c] *Je disais quelquefois à Stéphane Mallarmé* in *Variété III*, p. 23.
A note in *Cours de poètique*, unfortunately only slightly developed,
attributes to language the function of saving the mind from its
natural incoherence: "If we were at the mercy of these effects of
sensibility, our thought would be nothing but disorder. . . . But
the presence of language constantly recalls the possibility of a
master plan" (lecture 11).

posed to its own. It seems to avoid, in a work, the instability, incoherence, and inconsistency which it recognizes in itself and which constitute its most frequent regime.[7]

Disorder is necessary to the mind's creation; it is the "condition of its fruitfulness,"[8]—not only as a primordial basis of its labor, since "this fruitfulness depends on the unexpected,"[9] but in its functioning: "Vagueness is indestructible, its existence necessary to psychic functioning," for "the mind moves in vagueness, from the vague to the precise."[10] In creation, disorder is not merely an impediment, it is a source of discoveries:

> . . . this dispersion, always imminent, is important and contributes to the work's production almost as much as concentration itself. The mind at work, struggling against its own mobility, against its constitutional restlessness and its own diversity, against the dissipation or the natural degradation of any specialized attitude, finds, on the other hand, incomparable resources in this very condition. The instability, the incoherence, the inconsistency of which I was speaking, which are hindrances and limits to the mind in its enterprise of construction or of ordered composition, also provide it with precious possibilities whose imminent richness it is aware of from the very moment it considers itself. These are reserves from which it can expect everything, reasons for hoping that the solution, the signal, the image, the missing word are closer than it imagines.[11]

The artist must thus avoid prematurely solidifying his composition; he would sterilize in advance the work's chances of enrichment; he must possess to the end reserves of disorder, of fruitfulness:

> The mind proceeds, in its work, from *its* disorder to *its* order. It is important that it keep until the end resources of *disorder,* and that the order it has begun to impose on itself does not bind it so completely, does not become such a rigid master, that it cannot change it and utilize its initial liberty.[12]

In short, the progress toward order is accompanied by a relative maintenance of disorder, and it is the interplay of these two tendencies that best assures execution. Valéry compared this method of operation with that of an energy-transformation machine. For the mind to perform "its characteristic transformation, it must of course be supplied . . . with disorder. . . . And it takes its disorder where it finds it. Within itself, around itself, everywhere . . . It must have an *Order-Disorder* differential in order to function, as a machine must have a thermal differential. . . . Here, in any case, is a justification for Poetry."[13] But the comparison needs to be adjusted; as a matter of fact, the mind "works in a direction contrary to the transformation effected by machines, which change a more ordered energy into a less ordered energy. . . ."[14] On the other hand, it is quite evident that, if disorder is maintained for its fruitfulness, it yields increasingly to the need for organization. The need for disorder is limited: "Our mind would be nothing without its disorder—but a limited one."[15]

How does the artist proceed from disorder to order? Can this movement, in itself, be methodical? Valéry asked himself this in his *Calepin d'un poète*, in a passage which offers a curious contrast between the precision of the question and the confusion with which he answers it:

> Poetry. Is it impossible, given time, application, ingenuity, desire, to proceed by orderly means and attain poetry?
>
> To end by *meaning* precisely what one desires to mean, by a skillful and patient direction of that desire?
>
> You want to write a certain poem, with a certain effect, more or less, upon a certain subject: these are at first images of various *orders*.
>
> Some are persons, landscapes, aspects, attitudes; others, unformed voices, notes. . . .
>
> Words are still nothing but signboards.
>
> Other words or scraps of sentences are without a function, but seek to function and simply drift.
>
> I see everything and I see nothing.
>
> Other images make me see entirely other conditions. They seem to present the states of an individual *undergoing* the poem, his awakening, his suspense, his patience, his expectations, which must be created, amused, frustrated, or satisfied.

Hence I have several levels of ideas, some about the result and others about the execution; and the idea of uncertainty above all; and finally the idea of my own expectation, ready to seize upon the already conscious elements, the *writable* elements, which present themselves or might present themselves, even when not restricted to the subject.[16]

The poet, then, has an awareness of a goal, of various means, of the uncertainty of his methods, of the attitude of expectation that will permit him to seize favorable opportunities. This analysis reveals only a mixture of precise intentions and the possibilities of luck. What Valéry told us elsewhere about inspiration and work, about conventions and accident, confirms the idea that execution cannot be entirely regular and that the poet's enterprise rests to a large degree upon the unknown. The poet is indeed a calculator, but, on the other hand, he does not know what he is doing.

Insofar as it is possible to distinguish phases in execution, Valéry was particularly interested in its inception. He was struck by the fact, drawn from his personal experience, that the poem can be born of almost any element destined to enter into its synthesis, or even to disappear from it. This kind of equality among the sources of the poem led him to formulate a sort of theory of the equivalence of germinating principles. It is interesting not only because it reminds us of Valéry's love of generalization, but because it also returns to the problem of composition as a gradual growth, of the whole developing from a fragment, contrary to his belief in human creation in clearly separate acts, and finally as an application of the principle of complementarity, which we have studied in connection with his theory of ornament and the void: it would seem, this time, that the poem is completed gradually, starting from a given indication, until it constitutes a totality in response to the solicitation of its initial element. In the text quoted above, where Valéry said that the mind must be introduced for an order to appear, he added: "Or again, a determinate element, if it is granted a usable value, will ultimately generate the whole, by means of complements."[17] This particular element, chosen, utilized, may, in fact, be anything at all:

. . . the conditions of birth for poems can be very different: a certain subject, a group of words, perhaps a simple rhythm, perhaps (even) a prosodic schema, may serve as germinating principle and develop into an organized whole.

It is important to note this equivalence of germinating principles. I was forgetting, among those I listed, to mention the most astonishing. A sheet of blank paper; unoccupied time, a lapsus; a misreading; a congenial pen in the hand.[18]

We can say that each work might have been produced in several ways. Nothing in an objective examination shows us whether a certain poem was born of certain hemistich, of a rhyme, or of an abstractly formulated plan.[19]

However, these origins form two series: the poet begins with a content which is seeking its form, or with a formal procedure seeking its application:

> The poet wakes in the man because of an unexpected event, an interior or exterior incident: a tree, a face, a "subject," an emotion, a word. And often it is a desire for expression that initiates the poem, a need to translate what one feels; but often it is, on the contrary, a formal element, the rudiment of an expression that seeks its cause, that seeks a meaning for itself within my soul. . . . Take note of this duality possible from the first moment: at times something seeks to express itself; at times some means of expression seeks something to serve.[20]

Valéry admits that long poems come under the first category:

> The most general case, when we are concerned with very large works, is naturally that in which the author begins with a subject and comes eventually to versification. This is the case of classical epics, of dramatic poems. . . .[21]

These are precisely the kinds of poems that are the most mixed, the most impure for Valéry, those that can be summarized. This is why they start from a subject. But Valéry also insists that the subject can result from the process of creation: "It may happen . . . that the *germinating prin-*

ciple is only a word or scrap of a phrase, a line of verse seeking and working to create a justification for itself and thus engender a context, a subject, a man, etc. . . ."[22] He said that the subject of *Le Cimetière marin* and that of *La Pythie* had been obtained; the general meaning of *La Jeune Parque* was found only after the fact. This is because for Valéry the subject is really only a favorable context for treating a series of synthetic beauties. "The poet has essentially 'the intuition' of a type of specific combinations." Among these combinations, he distinguishes the "combination of things" (alongside the "combination of sounds"), that is, "figures of a particular order." Now, "a 'subject' for this poet is the arrangement in which the maximum number of things of this order can be placed, or obtained." The "combination of things," which he "must translate," is opposed to the combination of words (enjoying certain properties), which he must "justify":[23] it is the double movement of sense toward sound and of sound toward sense which perfectly covers the transition from thought to expression and inversely.

THE SYSTEM OF EXECUTION

It is more difficult to represent execution after its initial phase, at least to limit ourselves to what we have learned from a study of composition or reflections on the simultaneous behavior of sense and sound. These are general principles rather than an examination of the practice of poetry. Valéry did, however, throw some light on this instrumentation, but in a very general way and rather concerning art as a whole. "What is an artist? Above all, he is an executor of his own thought, when that thought may be realized in several ways," that is, when execution is not reduced to a code, a recipe, "and thus when the personality no longer intervenes at the purely psychic level where the idea is formed and arranged, but in the act itself. The idea is nothing, and in fact costs nothing";[24] in other words, the artist reveals himself not by his subject but by his technique, by what is personal in his technique. This leads to style. "It is in the act of expression that the person is indicated. In it are to be found his unique rhythms, the nervous constants of his character, his more or less original verbal resources, his familiar methods, and his preparation, his reservations . . ."[25] Style "is therefore by no means the mind alone applied to a particular action"; "it is the *entirety* of a living system which expends itself, which imprints itself, which becomes recognizable in expression."[26] And this leads to the body. We are familiar with the strange and admirable prayer addressed to it by Eupalinos. In his work as an architect, it seems to him that his body is "part of the project."[27] The same thing is true in poetic creation, where the collaboration of the entire living being, acting as a sensuous *resonator*, transmits to expression much more than intelligence, in its pure work of abstraction, could give, rediscovers the magic character of primitive language, and bears witness to a complete and particular individual:

> If instead of abstracting, we maintain and invoke, during the labor of expression, a certain presence of the entire being, of its perceptual and motor life, then the participation of this true *resonator* communicates much greater powers to discourse, restores its primitive characteristics. Rhythm, gesture, the collaboration of the voice through the timbre of vowels, accents, introduce in some way the living body, reacting and acting—and adding to the *finite* expression of a "thought" what is needed to suggest what it is in another sense—the response, the act, and the moment of a man.[28]

But what is still more significant for the theory of execution is that there is established between the body and the intelligence (or the mind) a special communication, a system of exchanges favorable to creation:

> But this body and this mind, this invincibly real presence, and this creative absence which dispute being between them, and which must be reconciled; but this finite and this infinite that we contribute, each according to his nature, must now be united in an ordered construction; and if, by the grace of the gods, they work together, if they exchange suitability and grace, beauty and durability, movements for lines, and numbers for

thoughts, they will have discovered their true relation, their act.[29]

These mysterious and salutary exchanges of powers, qualities, or heterogeneous elements that fall into two series (body and mind), but to which we cannot make the duality of content and form correspond, suppose a common means of evaluation, a possibility of putting them into equation. Like the seeds of creativity, these factors of execution, too, have their equivalence. Valéry notes in the artist "the inevitable and indivisible collaboration, a collaboration *at each instant* and in each of his acts, of the arbitrary and the necessary, of the expected and the unexpected, of his body, his materials, his volition, even his absences. . . .",[30] while, on the contrary, according to him, the philosopher refuses "to consider an intimate, perpetual, equalitarian exchange" between volition and power, accident and substance, form and content, consciousness and automatism, circumstance and intention, matter and mind;[31] "the philosopher cannot easily conceive that the artist passes almost indifferently from *form* to *content* and from *content* to *form*."[32] Earlier, Valéry, describing his experience of musical rhythms, which one day imposed themselves upon him and which he did not know what to do with, had remarked: ". . . there was . . . a point in my work at which ideas, rhythms, images, memories, or inventions were only equivalents."[33] This example is doubtless concerned only with a stimulus, that of movement, "which expended itself as it could," but Valéry, noting that "equivalence, the mind's resource, affords it very valuable substitutions,"[34] suggests that throughout the labor of execution this resource is open to the artist. The end of his first lecture in poetics emphasizes precisely this singular atmosphere:

> For the artist, it indeed happens—in the most favorable case—that the same internal movement of production yields simultaneously and indiscriminately the impulse, the immediate exterior goal and the means or the technical apparatus for action. There is generally established a system of execution during which there is a more or less lively exchange between needs, knowledge, intentions, means, the mental and the instrumental in their entirety. . . .[35]

In inspired improvisation, or, as Valéry puts it, improvisation "of superior degree,"

> between intentions and means, between conceptions of *content* and actions which engender *form*, there is no longer any contrast. Between the artist's thought and the material of his art, there is instituted an intimate correspondence, *remarkable for a reciprocity which those who have not experienced it cannot conceive.*[36]

What may astonish us in this equivalence and this exchange of values or methods, as different as are, for example, a rhythm and an image, so different that we cannot readily see how the poet equalizes and substitutes them for each other, is explained by a formula we already encountered at a higher level, when Valéry, praising the central attitude which governs all art, science, and politics, accounted for it by the discovery of a "common measure." On the more limited level of creation in a particular art, Valéry also believes in a kind of common denominator, in "the existence within the artist of a sort of common measure hidden among elements of extremely different natures,"[37] "as if all our faculties became suddenly commensurable among themselves."[38] This inspiring characteristic, which would truly be the key to poetics, remains unfortunately, like the central attitude, in the realm of the unknown. Though we are told that the great poet makes use of it, it remains a secret unveiled. If we readily understand that in the course of execution the poet shifts from content to form, from a rhythm to an idea, from a figure to a play of sonorities, we conceive less easily the ideal formula that would interrelate and reduce to unity the diversity of its operations. Should we not be content to acknowledge, more modestly, that between the intellectual elements and the formal elements, between content and expression, there is an adjustment to be made, adaptations which are already sufficiently obscure without being transcended by a more abstruse entity? But perhaps Valéry meant no more than this reciprocal agreement when he assigned its basis to a quasi-mathematical root, for when he remarks that in the poetic state everything happens as if all our faculties had become commensurable with one another, it is only this adjustment of content and form that he gives as a practical example of his psychological common measure: "This is indicated in a work by a mysteriously exact correspondence between perceptible *causes*, which constitute the *form*, and intelligible *effects*, which are the *content*."[39] A brilliant play of stimulating notions, disguised as intellectual speculation, by means of images borrowed from mathematics, the reverie of a poet in love with the idea of rigor, ends in the most traditional counsels of rhetoric.

If he renounced the discovery of the rather mythical secret which reduces the solution of the problem of execution to the sovereign use of a universal tool, a poet would certainly risk being discouraged by the description of difficulties Valéry presents:

> . . . measure all that is necessary in order for a poem by Keats or Baudelaire to take shape on a blank page, in front of the poet. Remember too that among all the arts, ours is perhaps the one that coordinates the greatest number of independent parts or factors: sound, sense, the real and the imaginary, logic, syntax, and the double invention of content and form . . . and all this by means of that essentially practical, perpetually corrupted, adulterated means pressed into every service, *common speech*, from which our task is to extract a pure, an ideal Voice, capable of communicating—without weaknesses, without apparent effort, without offending the ear and without breaking the instantaneous sphere of the poetic universe—an idea of some *self* marvelously superior to *Myself*.[40]

If one reflected upon it,

> the execution of a poetic work . . . by making explicit the problems to be solved . . . would seem impossible. In no other art is the number of undefined conditions and functions to be coordinated greater.[41]

And yet there are poems. The problems raised are solved, the difficulties surmounted. This is doubtless because poets do not take them into consideration as much as Valéry would wish. They avoid impotence and paralysis by acting instead of analyzing,[d] or else genius cuts the Gordian knot instead of trying vainly to untie it. Valéry does not clearly explain this power of solution, but he envisages it as a simplification. "Happily, a virtue of some kind resides at certain moments in certain beings which simplifies things and reduces the insurmountable difficulties I mentioned to the measure of human powers."[42] And I wonder if this is not the place to recall that mysterious little formula he produced one day: " 'Ingenuity' turns to 'genius' when it manifests itself by a simplification."[43]

These problems solved by poets are solved unconsciously, and that is doubtless why they are not always solved. Whence the inequality of their production. It is especially apropos of poetic language that these problems are raised. Valéry sees them as the natural consequence of the double nature of words: sound and sense must be brought into harmony, and must be extended—whence two types, among others, of questions particular to poetry:

> . . . there is a poetic language in which words are no longer the words of practical usage. They no longer associate according to the same attractions; they are charged with two values simultaneously engaged and of equivalent importance: their sound and their instantaneous psychic effect. We are reminded of the geometrician's complex numbers, and the coupling of the *phonetic variable* with the *semantic variable* engenders problems of extension and convergence which poets solve with eyes blindfolded, but which they do resolve (and that is the essential thing) from time to time. . . . *From Time to Time,* that is the key phrase! Hence uncertainty, hence the inequality of moments and of individuals. That is our capital fact: we must return to it over and over again, for all art, poetic or not, consists in defending ourselves against this inequality of the moment.[44]

[d] Valéry realized this danger: "We can imagine . . . a poet legitimately fearing to corrupt his original virtues, his immediate power to produce, by analyzing them. . . . Achilles cannot defeat the tortoise if he thinks of space and time," but Valéry answers, characteristically, that one can be more passionately interested in *the action of doing than in the thing done* (*Leçon inaugurale du Cours de poétique* in *Variété V*, pp. 300–1).

We may say that the poet is helped in a certain measure by inspiration. He does not have to write the line of verse the gods give him *gratis*, the line which is not always, nor only, the first. But he must still write the "calculated" verses.

Calculated verses are those which necessarily present themselves in the form of *problems to solve*—and whose initial conditions are first the *given* verses, and then the rhyme, the syntax, the sense already engaged by the given verses.
We are always, even in prose, led and constrained to write what we did not choose, but what chooses what we chose.[45]

The line of verse to be written thus depends on the lines that were inspired, and also on the lines written and accepted previously, then on conventions (prosodic, grammatical, logical) and on the direction already imposed upon the idea. It is not straining Valéry's thought to say that the problem raised is, by this very fact, solved, since we know that the mind, or the sensibility, will react of itself to these obstacles which are at the same time stimuli. Will the verse thus not write itself? This, in any case, is what a little story of Alain's seems to suggest. During a lunch at Lapérouse, to which he had been invited with Valéry by Henri Mondor, Alain had delivered this axiom: "What is difficult, is not to do, but to undo." Upon which, Valéry

. . . took out his smoking accessories. You must tell me, he said, if I understand you correctly. Here is a pinch of tobacco out of which I wish to make a cigarette; now this pinch is something; I lay it on this paper and I undo it; as you see, I forbid myself to make the cigarette; yet, there it is; it makes itself, and that is the way you make a line of verse.

Alain adds, exciting our envy: "I would have paid dearly for my place, for the scales fell from my eyes."[e] And, in fact,

[e] Alain, *Le déjeuner chez Lapérouse, Nouvelle Revue Française,* August 1939, pp. 236–37. Alain had already quoted this comparison in his *Propos de Littérature,* p. 62: "Have you ever made cigarettes? Yes? You see, you have to undo, then undo some more, and actually refuse to *do* at all, and your cigarette gets done without your even thinking about it."

verses write themselves. They make themselves in the mold
of conditions, and "with eyes blindfolded." Everyone knows
that you can roll a cigarette without looking at it, but that it
is impossible if you watch yourself do it in a mirror.

One would like to know some examples of problems solved
by Valéry. I think I have recognized this one:

> I need a word (the poet says) a word that is:
>   feminine,
>   of two syllables,
>   containing P or F,
>   ending in a mute e,
>   a synonym for break, separation;
>   and not scholarly, not rare
> Six conditions—at least![t]

Reading this curious statement, I was tempted to try to answer it. "Ending in a mute e" and "of two syllables": a three-
syllable word counted as two at the end of a line; "femi-
nine," "a synonym for break," and "containing P or F"; I
thought of *fracture*, then *rupture*. And immediately there
echoed in my memory the line from *Grenades*:

> ### Cette lumineuse rupture.

Is this the line Valéry was thinking of? It doesn't matter,
but I notice that it was not very difficult for me to solve the
problem: "six conditions—at least!" Even if I tell myself that
I was unconsciously oriented by the recollection of Valéry's
line, I am still under the impression that Valéry sometimes
overemphasizes the difficulty. All poets have sought words or
rhymes answering to determined conditions; when the word
existed, they have almost always found it; when it did not
exist (for this happens), they had to change the form. These
minutiae, which are essential, for the texture of the poem is
made up of them, prove that, as Eupalinos puts it so well:
"There are no details in execution."[46] "Eupalinos was a man
of his word. He neglected nothing."[47] And Socrates, leading

---

[t] *Autres rhumbs* in *Tel quel*, II, pp. 153–54. This text is followed
by this *Note*: "If someone were really writing for himself, it would
suffice for him to invent this word defined by six conditions. We can
prove by the absence of invented words that no one writes for himself alone, nor decides by himself to speak his own language."

Phaedrus from architecture to eloquence, before moving on to medicine, was right to insist, in the same sense, on the importance of "the least little words," of "the least silences," and of "apparently insignificant details."[g]

But the material resists the artisan. The latter must thus adopt an attitude that will adapt himself to it. It is no longer the architect Eupalinos but his analogue, the cunning ship-builder Tridon the Sidonian, who this time furnishes the master formula. He "said bluntly that one had to trick nature; and according to the occasion, imitate in order to govern her, set her against herself, snatch from her secrets that turned against her mystery."[48] This is also what Valéry tells us about the writer. We have seen him compare the poet to an architect, to an engineer, to an economist, to a strategist, but in execution, it is above all a diplomat that he resembles:

A work is made by a multitude of "minds" and of events—(ancestors, moods, accidents, previous writers, etc.)—under the direction of the Author.

The latter must thus be a profound politician devoted to reconciling these ghosts and these rival intellectual actions. He must deceive here; and stand aside there; he must delay, dismiss, invite, awaken interest in the work. Evocations, incantations, seductions—with regard to our interior personnel and materiel we have only resources of a magic and symbolic nature. Direct volition is useless; it has no power over variables of this order, which must be opposed by some power as unforeseen, as alive and as variable as they themselves.[49]

Execution has its joys and its reward: ". . . I could execute endlessly,"[50] Valéry admits. In a *Petit Discours aux peintres graveurs*, he showed that this pleasure is linked to difficulties:

Passive pleasure wearies and disgusts us; we must also have the *pleasure of doing*. A strange pleasure, a complex pleasure, a pleasure shot through with torments, mixed with pain, a pleasure in whose pursuit we find no lack of obstacles, nor bitterness, nor doubts, nor even despair . . . a laborious pleasure. . . .[51]

[g] *Eupalinos*, pp. 87–90. Cf. *Mauvaises pensées et autres*, p. 195: "Whoever would do great things must pay profound attention to details."

Moreover, the domination of methods ultimately affords ease, which for the greatest artists is what constitutes mastery. Then we are struck by the sovereign action of execution, which seems to go straight to its goal and to be unaware of hesitation.

> What appears most clearly in the work of a master, is the "will," the *parti pris*. No hesitation between modes of execution. No uncertainty about the goal.[52]
>
> Manet has a decisive power, a sort of strategic instinct for plastic action.[53]

What Flaubert lacked in *La Tentation de saint Antoine* was the "spirit of decision," as is already shown by "his scruples of exactitude and reference"; "intoxicated by the accessory at the expense of the principal," he forgot to animate his hero, "neglected the very substance of his theme" and "the unity of his composition"; "astray among too many books and myths, he lost sight of his strategic thought. . . ."[54] Valéry confessed his taste for spontaneous success: "I do not hate the virtuoso—the man of means."[55] But he distinguished two quite different degrees of virtuosity, one which is merely the facility of a natural gift, the other which is the recompense of an *askesis*. "I like a man to be hard on his genius. If it cannot turn against itself, 'genius' to me is only a native virtuosity, unequal and unfaithful."[56] Let us once again remember Teste: "Genius is easy." Valéry stigmatized the works of this splendid unconstraint: ". . . curiously constructed of gold and mud: though overloaded with dazzling details, time soon disintegrates and sweeps away the clay: only a few verses of a great many poems."[57] The true virtuosos are those

> . . . in whom the development of means becomes so advanced, and moreover so closely identified with their intelligence, that they manage to "think" and "invent" in the mode of execution, starting from the means themselves.[58]

The consequence of this virtuosity, once it is acquired and mastered, is that when "the real part of art stimulates the imaginary part," one can deduce music from the properties of sounds, architecture from matter and forces, literature from "the possession of language and from its unique role and from its modifications."[59] Mallarmé would be the example of this accomplished and superior virtuosity.

Valéry returned to this distinction apropos of Corot, in a somewhat different form. As there are two sorts of virtuosity, there are two sorts of improvisation:

> I maintain that the artist ends with naturalness; but the naturalness of a new man. The spontaneous is the fruit of a conquest. It belongs only to those who have acquired the certitude of being able to conduct their labor to the extreme of execution, preserving its unity as a whole while realizing the parts and without losing on the way either its spirit or its nature. . . . They can proudly consider their entire career as accomplished between two states of happy facility: A primary facility— the awakening of the naïve instinct to produce which arises from the reveries of a lively and sensitive adolescence (but the young creator is soon aware of the insufficiency of ingenuity and the great duty of never being satisfied). The other facility is the sentiment of a conquered freedom and simplicity, which permit the widest play of the mind between the senses and ideas. The result is *the marvel of an improvisation of superior degree.*[60]

The right to improvisation must be "acquired by immense labor and a continual meditation."[h] Thus the highest point of art is simplicity:

> But simplicity is not at all a method. It is, on the contrary, a goal, an ideal limit, which supposes the complexity of things and the quantity of possible ways of seeing reduced and exhausted—replaced finally by a form or a formula that is essential for someone. Each artist has his point of simplicity, situated rather late in his career.[i]

[h] *Autour de Corot* in *Pièces sur l'art*, p. 191. On what improvisation requires in fresco painting, cf. *Les Fresques de Paul Véronèse* in *Pièces sur l'art*, p. 128.

[i] Ibid., p. 162. Apropos of the rare word *funéral* he had used in *Narcisse parle*, Valéry declares: ". . . if simplicity is among the most desirable of things, it is not with simplicity that we must begin; it is toward simplicity that we must strive. We must learn by experience that the apparent nullity of language costs much more

The most difficult part of dancing is walking. The dancer Athikté "begins with the high point of her art: she walks. . . ."[61] Perhaps this idea was suggested to Valéry by the very beautiful anecdote he tells in order to illustrate the disputed comparison between the "simple" and the "classical."

> During the Second Empire, one of the world's first horsemen, now old and poor, received a position as a groom at Saumur. His favorite pupil came to visit him there one day, a young squadron leader and a brilliant horseman. Baucher said to him: "I shall ride a little for you." He mounted; he crossed the riding ring *au pas*; returned . . . the other man, astonished, saw a perfect centaur advancing toward him. "There," the master told him. "No showing off. I am at the summit of my art: *To walk without a fault.*"[62]

And when, at the end of his life, Valéry was to take up the old figure of Faust, he granted him, as a supreme accomplishment, mastery of the simplest activities: "I live. And I do nothing but live. . . . I am at the height of my art, at the classical period of the art of life. That is my work. . . ."[63]

COMPLETION

Execution must achieve a goal. According to Valéry, the great artist, "in the state commonly known as *inspiration*," can scarcely manage to produce even "a *fragment*"; inspiration cannot yield "a *whole* work of any length."

> It is here that knowledge, duration, reworking, judgment intervene. One must have a good head in order to exploit good luck, to master discoveries, and to *finish.*[64]

The finishing state of a work is reached only by discontinuous operations. "*Paradox*. Man has only one way to give a work unity: to interrupt it and to come back to it."[65] There is, moreover, something encouraging in these incessant re-

dearly than all these ornaments" (*Sur les "Narcisse,"* fragments of a lecture given September 19, 1941, in *Paul Valéry vivant, Cahiers du Sud*, 1946, p. 286).

visions. The artist acquires the sentiment of an improvement always possible at the moment when he is closest to despair. What is spoiled on one day will succeed the next:

> Something that succeeds is a transformation of something defective. Thus something defective is defective only because it has been abandoned.[66]

But it is absolutely necessary to bring a work to completion, for

> What is not entirely completed does not yet exist. What is not completed is less advanced than what is not begun.[67]

Work is completed when there no longer remains a sign of operations and methods, when technique has been entirely reabsorbed into execution.

> To complete a work consists in making everything that shows or suggests its fabrication disappear. The artist must . . . acknowledge himself by his style alone, and must sustain his effort until work has erased all traces of work.[68]

This is a lesson that might have been transmitted by Mallarmé, who had it from Whistler, and that Valéry applied to *La Jeune Parque*:

> It is indeed an exercise, intended, and renewed, and revised: a work of will alone; and then, of a second will, whose hard task is to mask the first.[69]

Valéry shows here an entirely classical taste, which recalls the formula of Vauvenargues: "Clarity is the varnish of the masters." Thus he condemns in modern artists, especially in painters, the tendency to be content with sketches or unfinished works on the pretext that the artist's originality is more evident in an execution that preserves its spontaneity:

> . . . concern for personality and for the moment gradually prevailing over concern for the work in itself and for durability, the condition of completion has appeared not only useless and bothersome, but even contrary to *truth*, to *sensibility*, and to the manifestation of *genius*. Per-

sonality seemed essential, even to the public. The sketch was worth as much as the painting.[j]

Valéry is at the antipodes from Claudel, for whom a perfect work is a stoppered flask which does not release its perfume, and from Hugo, for whom genius is great because of its defects.

However, despite so clear an exigency, Valéry said, quite as often, that a work could not be completed. It is always external circumstances that establish the last state of a work. It is an author's decision that brings it to a stop. But it could always be taken up again.

> . . . a work is never completed except by some accident, like fatigue, satisfaction, a deadline, or death; for a work, from the viewpoint of whoever or whatever makes it, is only one state in a series of interior transformations. How many times one would like to begin what one has just considered finished! . . . How many times have I looked at what I was going to reveal to the eyes of others, as the necessary preparation for the desired work, which I was only then beginning to *see* in its possible maturity, and as the very probable and very desirable fruit of a new attempt and of an act completely outlined within my powers. The work actually done then seemed to me the mortal body to which the transfigured and glorious body must succeed.[70]

Completion is always "material."

> . . . for there is no incontestable sign of a work's intrinsic completion. It is always external circumstances which impose that completion upon us. No positive character can reveal it to us. We yield to the public a certain state of a certain enterprise, but there is no essential relation between that act or accident which generally detaches us from the book, and the object of attention or the problem of expression which have been the motivating principle of our endeavors.[71]

Valéry presented *Le Cimetière marin* as "the result of the *cutoff* of interior work by a chance event": Jacques Rivière,

[j] *Degas. Danse. Dessin,* p. 36. On the value assigned to the incompleted, see also *Le Musée de Montpellier* in *Vues,* p. 269.

having found Valéry "in a 'state' of this *'Cimetière marin,'* planning to rework, to suppress, to substitute, to transpose here and there . . . ," read and carried off the manuscript.[k]

However, Valéry admitted that he sometimes recognized a true state of completion, satisfying the requirements which he assigned to the great artist and whose very possibility, as we have just seen, he seemed to deny. A work always seemed unfinished to him because it always seemed to him possible to modify it. As an author, his appetite for transformation is insatiable. As a reader, that appetite deprecates most works. But if, all of a sudden, he experienced on reading a text the very particular impression of the definitive, that is of an impossibility of modification, there is no doubt that Valéry felt that it was finished. Now, this impression of intangible perfection is exactly what Valéry understands by beauty:

> The impression of beauty so desperately sought after, so vainly defined, is perhaps this sentiment that variation is impossible.[72]

> What is completed, too complete, gives us a sensation of our powerlessness to modify it.[73]

The ideal definition of a poem, its limit-definition, is the one he once gave to Charles Du Bos: "A poem . . . is a closed

---

[k] *Au sujet du "Cimetière marin"* in *Variété III,* pp. 63–64. Cf. *Aphorismes* in *Hommes et Mondes,* October 1946, p. 189. "A work is for me the possible object of an indefinite labor. Its publication is an incident external to this labor; it is an outside force in a development that is not and cannot be stopped except by external circumstances. My detachment, for example. If a work I am writing bores me, my boredom is alien to the interest I had brought to it." Valéry completed the analysis of the artist's reasons for abandoning a work in his *Cours de poétique.* In his second lecture, he limits himself to recalling that a work is never completed internally and that the artist abandons it out of disgust and boredom; but in lecture thirteen, he invokes two quite different factors, satisfaction and the impossibility of going further: "What completes a work is not an opposition between two elements that should coincide, as in science, but, on the one hand, a well-known phenomenon of sensibility, which is satisfaction (the artist will dance before his painting, which will not prevent him, that very evening, from crying in the same place) and, on the other hand, the work can go no further, sensibility has exhausted all means of reexcitation; then the artist abandons it."

system in all its parts, in which nothing can be modified."[74]
It is this immutability of the work that is the guarantee of
its solidity and durability. "A work is solid when it resists
the substitutions which the mind of an *active* and refractory
reader always tries to inflict upon its parts."[75]

God knows Valéry was an active and refractory reader
(when he consented to read . . .), always eager to alter the
text before him: "I used to read little, but in that little I
could not help imagining a host of changes, of substitutions,
of equivalences. . . . Whoever stops over a passage tends to
transform it."[76]

I respond spontaneously to what is proposed, by the
changes I attempt to make. And this constitutes the basis
of my feelings about literature, history, philosophy, etc.
. . . everything that involves the *maximum of the
author's discretion exposed to the maximum of the
reader's.*[77]

This is why Valéry did not like the novel, which he contrasted to the poem, as "an open system . . . in which some
elements are replaceable by others and into which new elements can be introduced."[78] He assigned to Monsieur Teste
this vain concession: "As for adventures, they can divert me
as long as I do not perceive that I can modify them without
effort."[79] As a private joke, Valéry turned this mania for
modifying texts into a lively taste for parody (in *"Mon Faust,"*
in *L'Idée fixe,* and elsewhere, even in a poem like the
Ébauche d'un serpent, there is no lack of quotations mali-
ciously altered in their sense and in their form), by witty
turns and even puns based on famous sayings or proverbs
(for example: *"Entre deux mots, il faut choisir le moin-
dre"*).[80] Examples of texts modified with more serious intent are rarer; some can be found in his collections of reflections, but it is almost inevitable that the game of inverting
maxims be accompanied by a smile.[1] *Pensées* rectified, or
sharpened, improved, worthy of the "energetic" reader
vaunted by Valéry, are less frequent in his work than satirical

[1] *"Les vilaines pensées viennent du coeur"* (*Mélange,* p. 65).
"Les grandes flatteries sont muettes" (*Autres rhumbs* in *Tel quel,*
II, p. 174).

deprecations: *"Le vacarme intermittent des petits coins où nous vivons nous rassure."*[81] There is no doubt that Valéry employed his metamorphic capacities on famous verses. I know of only one case where he accompanied this operation by an instructive commentary: this was a line from La Fontaine, which he transferred from the climate of the fable to the system of the cosmogonic poem, and to which I shall return in the next chapter. Moreover, this propensity was at times manifested without Valéry even knowing it; he would often quote verses inexactly (for example, the two lines of Corneille that he used as an epigraph for *La Jeune Parque*). But we can be sure that Valéry was never led to modify the—very few—lines he admired without reservations. To touch Mallarmé would have seemed a sacrilege. It was only by a bizarre accident that he happened, one day, in spite of himself, to try to modify Racine. He recounts that at the time when he was hastily writing the libretto of a cantata (evidently the *Cantate du Narcisse*), "my head still full of the movement of a passage," he had stopped before a shopwindow

> . . . where there was on display a beautiful page of verse, in a large format and splendid letters. . . . I had the impression that I was still working on my draft, and I began unconsciously, for a good minute, trying to change some terms in the text displayed. . . . But the text would not allow itself to be possessed. *Phèdre* resisted me. I found out by direct experience and immediate sensation what is meant by the perfection of a work. It was not a pleasant awakening.[82]

If Valéry was unable to change Racine's verse, it was because that day he was "in good faith" and his admiration excluded any pranks. If perfection can resist attempts at mutation, it is only because it has been approached with respect. This condition is implicit whenever one declares that it is impossible to change anything in a phrase or a strophe that gives the impression of completion. Valéry was not unaware of this, although he hated "seriousness"; but he would doubtless have insisted that it was the responsibility of the work to create this condition in the reader. He was so well aware of it that he tried to find the means of preventing the reader from yielding to the temptation to transform a text. He recommended two: logical coherence and harmony of form.

> It was necessary for me that conditions of logic, or else harmonic conditions of form, be always produced in support of what one wrote. One or the other condition opposes the possibilities of substitution that the reader may be able to inflict upon a text, if he is left free to think of modifying the form, to deny a conclusion, or simply to make the author's assertions one combination among others that are equally conceivable.[83]

The fate of the work is entirely bound up with the quality of the execution. Execution has the power to transform the material it utilizes: ". . . there is, in the order of the arts, no theme or model that *execution* cannot ennoble or vilify, make a source of disgust or a pretext of delight. Boileau said as much!"[84] To provide an example of a serpent or a hideous monster embellished by art, Valéry went straight to the naturalistic writers: I think "their positive merit was to have found poetry (or rather to have brought poetry), and sometimes the greatest poetry, in certain objects or subjects hitherto considered ignoble or insignificant."[85] Valéry here reveals himself "that critic of exquisite justice" he discovered in Mallarmé, appreciating in Zola "what was powerfully poetic, and somehow intoxicating in its insistence."[86] After so many summary condemnations, it is wonderful to see the two purest poets since Baudelaire pay homage to a work so remote from their own, and precisely for its lyric tenor. Indeed, it is the poets who have found the poet in Zola, just as it is the philosophers who have found philosophy in Hugo and ideas in Stendhal; perhaps Renouvier and Taine knew what they were doing as well as Faguet. Yet one cannot suppose that Valéry profoundly admired Zola's qualities of execution.[m] Besides, if execution permits us to transpose, it has other powers as well. Upon it depend all the effects of the work, which we must now consider.

[m] See the same text, pp. 206–8, for what he says about Zola's naïveté of conception, the illusions of his technique, and the contrast he offers to Mallarmé.

Chapter VIII

THE THEORY OF EFFECTS

The Aesthetic Infinite

Though some of Valéry's ideas on poetry have become famous because a striking formula engraved them in the memory, a body of reflections that plays an important role in his poetics, and that constitutes perhaps its most original part, has been neglected, because Valéry disseminated its elements in very diverse writings. To establish these ideas, I shall call this part of his doctrine *the theory of effects*. It logically completes his aesthetic and crowns, in particular, his views on the problem of execution. The poem has as its goal to produce a certain number of effects.

The effects produced by the poem belong, in Valéry's eyes, to the category of aesthetic effects, which he characterizes as being *effects of infinite tendency*, as opposed to *effects of finite tendency*, which refer to the order of practical things. Effects of finite tendency are the responses by which we annul our perceptions: you ask me for a light, I give you one, and everything is over.[a] Effects of infinite tendency are excited by perceptions that tend to preserve and to reproduce themselves: you quote me a beautiful line of verse, I remember it, and I am led to repeat it to myself. "A beautiful line of verse is infinitely reborn from its ashes."[b] This is what Valéry chose to call the *aesthetic infinite*.

[a] See *Poésie et pensée abstraite* in *Variété V*, p. 142. But if the sound and the shape of the little phrase return to the mind of the person who has heard it, and assume some value, "we are then on the very brink of the state of poetry."

[b] *Commentaires de Charmes* in *Variété III*, p. 82. Cf. *Poésie et pensée abstraite* in *Variété V*, p. 151: ". . . the poem . . . is made expressly to be reborn from its ashes."

In a short article that has this expression as its title, Valéry linked it to his general conception of the sensibility. When our perceptions are not indifferent to us, they excite in us the means to annul them. We return to the state we were in before experiencing them:

> It seems that the major business of our life is to restore to zero some index of our sensibility, and to regain, by the shortest route, a certain *maximum* of freedom or availability of our senses.[1]

These effects, by which we suppress our modifications in order to regain a previous equilibrium, constitute the *order of practical things*. They are opposed to those that excite in us the desire, the need, the tendency to preserve, to regain, or to reproduce our initial perceptions. Hunger, love, and all the sensations are susceptible of these *effects of infinite tendency*, which as a body form the *order of aesthetic things*.

> In this order, *satisfaction* brings about the rebirth of *need*, *response* regenerates *demand*, *presence* engenders *absence*, and *possession desire*.[c]

We are then in a "universe of sensibility" (and this reminds us of the "poetic universe," which is moreover a species of it) where "sensation and its expectation" are "reciprocal" (this is a case of the theory of equivalence), "complementary" like colors upon the retina (in the same way that ornaments are born), in a perpetual "oscillation" (and we recall the comparison of the *poetic pendulum*), which can be interrupted only by an external circumstance, like fatigue. It is this latter that causes the search for "*variety*," as a remedy for "*satiety*," and introduces the "*desire for desire*." If this is not satisfied by "an object worthy of an infinite development," the

---

[c] "*L'Infini esthétique*" in *Pièces sur l'art*, p. 249. Cf. *Cours de poétique*, lecture 3: "Art possesses, among its necessary elements, this purpose of organizing a system of sensuous things which have the property of making themselves desired again and again without ever assuaging the need they provoke. The problem of art consists in arousing desire, and arousing desire continually. Creation aims at producing the object that engenders desire for itself. This is what I call the *aesthetic infinite* and what most clearly distinguishes the work of art from the other works of man."

sensibility "is led to produce itself the images of what it desires, as thirst engenders ideas of marvelously cool drinks"
(and we return to the theory of the creative void). The work
of art is for Valéry a combination of the practical order and
the aesthetic order, understandably enough, since it is, on the
one hand, the product of an act, and since, on the other, its
aim is to excite *effects of infinite tendency*. It is

> . . . the result of an action whose *finite* goal is to pro-
> voke in someone *infinite* developments. From which one
> can deduce that the artist is a *double* being, for he com-
> poses the laws and the operations of the world of action
> with the intention of producing the universe of sensuous
> resonance.[d]

Valéry added nothing to this theory when he presented it
to the Société française de Philosophie in 1935, in a lecture
that was quite vigorously debated. Still, remembering perhaps that he had so often invoked this *parrot* [*perroquet*] of
his, he asked his listeners to excuse the word *infinite*, which
he preferred to proscribe in every subject, even mathematics.
"It is a conventional noun that seemed to me exact and diverting to employ."[2] *Diverting* is Valéry being whimsical, but
exact must have caused him some doubt, since he proposed
to substitute an *equivalent* for the notion of the *infinite*, and
reduced it to that of *independence*:

> When one makes a heap of stones, the act of adding
> a stone is independent of the quantity of stones already
> accumulated. We can say that *the infinite* is thus intro-
> duced. . . . It is this notion of the independence of the
> act and the result of the act which is, basically, our idea
> of the infinite taken in this sense.[3]

After which, Valéry made no use at all of this notion, and
began to read his article on *the aesthetic infinite;* he para-
phrased the passage on complementary colors and ended
circuitously:

[d] "*L'Infini esthétique,*" p. 252. Cf. *Cours de poétique,* lecture 5:
"The artist's action develops in the finite order and tends to produce
the aesthetic infinite. The artist borrows means from the domain of
action, uses finite acts, finite instruments, to produce effects which
engage the consumer infinitely."

In short, the major notion I wanted to emphasize as characteristic of research in art is the idea of things that bear within themselves the means to create a need for themselves. The object of the work of art is the intent to produce this effect.[4]

Let us assume no more than that *the aesthetic infinite* is a major part of Valéry's aesthetic, since he links it to numerous problems of creation; that the term *effect* has for him a very wide extension, since he applies it to the entire domain of sensibility; and that the most general effect of the poem, as of any work of art in fact, must be "to make itself desired again and again."

THE POETIC MACHINE

Valéry defined the poem as "a sort of machine for producing the poetic state by means of words."[5] We are thus authorized to question Valéry on the efficacity of this machine. As usual, his answer reveals a great skepticism: ". . . the effect of this machine is uncertain, for nothing is sure in matters of action upon minds";[6] ". . . it is illusory to seek to produce one's own fantasies in another's mind. The project is in fact almost unintelligible."[7] The reader's reactions are "incalculable."[8] Individuals enjoy as they can and what they can; and the malice of sensibility is infinite. It undoes the best-laid plans. . . ."[9] Even if the reader's impressions are favorable, the author (an author like Valéry) feels hurt in his pride and his discipline,[10] since they are not adapted to his intentions.

Has the poet the means of reducing this uncertainty? He can try to estimate the probability of effects. But this is a delicate and hazardous enterprise. He cannot even rely on the discoveries of genius, on those "moments of infinite worth" which reveal him to himself, since experience teaches him that these moments which seem to him "of universal value are often without any future."[11] What is needed is a sanction of the products of his inspiration as of those of his labor, and it can come only from the public. "*What is of value for only*

one person is of no value. That is the iron law of literature."ᵉ
We are thus led to speculate on the public's knowledge, or
more strictly on an "anticipated category of minds."¹² Valéry
certainly cherished the dream of the infallible effect: "Literary ideal, finally to be able to put on a page only what affects
the reader."¹³ To reach this public, one must imagine it to
oneself:

> . . . consideration of *the most probable reader* is the
> most important ingredient of literary composition; the
> author's mind, whether it wants to or not, whether it
> knows it or not, is as it were *attuned* to the idea he
> necessarily forms of his reader. . . .ᶠ

This ineluctable necessity spoils, for him, both art and
artist:

> No matter what the outcome of the enterprise, it thus
> engages us in a dependence upon others, and the mind
> and tastes we attribute to them are thus introduced into
> the intimacy of our own. Even the most disinterested
> and supposedly the most unsocial enterprise gradually
> alienates us from the great project of leading the *ego* to
> the extreme of its desire to possess itself, and substitutes
> the consideration of probable readers for our initial idea
> of an immediate witness or an incorruptible judge of our
> effort. We renounce without knowing it every extreme of
> discipline or perfection. . . .¹⁴

One readily grasps here the antagonism between two of
Valéry's dreams: the dream of purely personal expression and
that of efficacious action on the reader. One cannot explore
one's *ego* to the limit, *à la* Monsieur Teste, and at the same
time be sure of creating beauty, *à la* Poe. It is, in fact, to
Poe that Valéry linked himself expressly, when he abstained

ᵉ *Poésie et pensée abstraite* in *Variété* V, p. 157. To understand
the true meaning of this apparent condemnation, we must counter
it by assertions like the following: "I scorn *whatever-is-worth-
nothing-when-I-am-alone.* . . ." (*Propos me concernant,* p. 30).
   ᶠ *Au sujet d' "Adonis"* in *Variété,* p. 86. See also *Propos me
concernant,* p. 22, where Valéry shows that works are problems
"involving, as more or less determined conditions, the characteristics
of Others—my idea of the external action of works upon hypotheti-
cal Others."

from the splendid isolation of an intellectual Crusoe and consented to envisage a politics or a strategy of effects. Poe, he says, "clearly based the approach to his reader on psychology, on the probability of effects."[15] Valéry is obviously thinking of the *Philosophy of Composition*, which, under the title *Genèse d'un poème*, had been translated by Baudelaire, himself a great speculator on this technique of effects which, in a less elevated domain, has engaged the attention of popular novelists and the authors of melodramas. Their *devices* and *tricks* are ready-made means of producing a precise impression upon a specific public. Crude as they may be, we can perfectly apply to them Valéry's conclusions:

> . . . any shifting of elements made to be noticed and judged depends upon some general laws and a particular adaptation, defined in advance for an anticipated category of minds to which it is specially addressed; and the work of art becomes a machine destined to stimulate and to combine the individual formations of these minds.[16]

The infallibility of these effects, based on a knowledge of the public, was not long a credo of Valéry's. But at eighteen he could believe in it. We have a curious evidence of this, revealed by Henri Mondor: an article *Sur la technique littéraire*, sent on November 10, 1889, to Charles Boès, editor of the *Courrier libre*, and which never appeared, as this little Parisian periodical disappeared at the same period.[17] The article suggests Valéry's confidence in psychological calculation:

> Literature is the art of playing on the souls of others. It is with this scientific brutality that our epoch has seen the problem of the aesthetic of the Word, that is, the problem of Form, raised.
>
> Given an impression, a dream, a thought, it *must* be expressed in such a way so as to produce the maximum effect in the soul of a listener—and an effect entirely calculated by the Artist.[18]

Even this early the rivalry of the poet and the musician is suggested:

> . . . the writer should have different notes on the keyboard of expression, in order to produce many effects—as

the musician has a choice of a certain number of timbres and rhythmic speeds.[19]

And the great Inspirer received his tribute of praise:

> Edgar Allan Poe, mathematician, philosopher, and a great writer, in his curious opusculum *The Philosophy of Composition*, clearly demonstrated the mechanism of poetic gestation, as he practices and understands it.
>
> None of his works contains more acuity of analysis, more rigor in the logical development of principles discovered by observation. It is a technique entirely established *a posteriori* on the *auditor's* psychology, on a knowledge of the diverse notes that must be made to reverberate in another's soul. Poe's penetrating induction insinuates itself into one's intimate reflections, foresees them, utilizes them.[g]

The following year, Valéry put the substance of numerous passages of the stillborn article in his letters to Pierre Louÿs; he still cherished a poetry "written by a refined dreamer who would be at the same time a judicious architect, a wise algebraist, an infallible calculator of the effect to be produced" and declared that "all means will be good in order to produce the maximum of effect."[20] Much later, Valéry was to recognize the precariousness of the poet's image of the reader and his incapacity to predict the yield of the literary machine: "The artist's paradoxical destiny enjoins him to combine definite elements in order to act upon an indeterminate person."[21] "There is in the author a certain presence of the spectator or the listener, but these are ideal personages: the author creates for himself—more or less consciously—an *ideal reader*."[22] Between the author and the real reader there is no common measure: "There will never be a means of comparing exactly what goes on in one and in the other. . . ."[23]

Even if the author succeeds in predicting quite surely the reactions of a reader he knows very well (as in the case of Pierre Louÿs for Valéry), the diversity of the public, or of the

---

g *Sur la technique littéraire* in *Dossiers*, 1, 1946, p. 28. The same optimism in a letter to Gide, September 1891: ". . . writing . . . is the ambition . . . to seize an ideal reader and lead him on without being affected oneself—or even to dazzle him, to stun him, to reduce him. . . ."

various publics, would make the uncertainty of effects inevitable. All one can attempt is to limit the latter, or more modestly still, not to increase it, and this is why Valéry is so strongly attached to the traditions of classical versification. He was astonished that so many poets had, out of sheer wantonness, devised excessively personal poetics which augmented the insecurity of the author's relations with the public:

> Everyone made of his ear and his heart a universal diapason and clock.
> Was this not to risk being misunderstood, misread, mispronounced; or being understood, read, and pronounced in a completely unforeseen way? This risk is always very great. I do not say that an error of interpretation always harms us, or that a strangely shaped mirror may not sometimes embellish us. But those who fear the uncertainty of exchanges between author and reader surely find in the fixed number of syllables, in the more or less factitious symmetries of classical verse, the advantage of limiting this risk in a very simple—even crude—manner.[24]

Effects would therefore find some guarantee in the constraints accepted. And yet Valéry destroyed this assurance by a still more negative theory. According to him, there is an abyss between the poet and the reader that cannot be bridged. The aesthetic or critique in which author, work, and reader intervene in the same proposition is erroneous: "Any proposition that assembles these three entities is imaginary."[25]

> Any proposition in which you include the three terms: an author, a work, a spectator, or listener, is a meaningless proposition—in the sense that you will never find the occasion for an observation that unites these three terms.[26]
> . . . any judgment that announces a three-term relation between the producer, the work, and the consumer —and judgments of this kind are not infrequent in criticism—is an illusory judgment incapable of meaning and, on reflection, immediately invalid.[27]

Only two relations are ever observed, on the one hand between the author and his work, on the other, between the work and the reader:

> . . . never in observation will you find anything but, on one side, the author and his work; on the other, the work and the observer.[28]
> . . . producer and consumer are two essentially separate systems.[29]
> We can consider only the relation between the work and its producer, or the relation between the work and the person it modifies once it is done.[30]

We must therefore

> . . . carefully distinguish our exploration of the work's creation from our study of the production of its value, that is, of the effects it can engender here or there in a certain mind, in a certain period.[31]

The author and the reader are never in rapport. The work separates them, and it does not have the same meaning for them, for

> . . . to one of them the work is the *goal*, for the other, the *origin* of developments that can be as foreign as you like to each other.[32]

Thus there is no rapport between the appreciation of the work by the author and the reader:

> The action of the former and the reaction of the latter can never be identified. The ideas each forms of the work are incompatible.[33]

Not only are the author and the reader without rapport, it is indispensable that they not communicate. It is ordinarily supposed that the work is destined to assure a certain transmission from author to reader. For Valéry, the work is, and must be, an impenetrable intermediary:

> The value *art* . . . depends essentially on this non-identification, upon this necessity of an intermediary between producer and consumer. It is important that there be between them a thing irreducible to the mind, that there *not* be an immediate communication, and that the work, this medium, not afford the person it touches the

means of reducing it to an idea of the author's person and mind.

An understanding of this point is fundamental in the arts. And every time you hear an artist say, with despair, that he could not express himself as he wanted, he is committing an error of expression. It is basically an absurdity: not that this absurdity does not force him to make efforts to express, as he says, his thought in his work, but he will never succeed in doing so. All the artist can do is to elaborate something that will produce in another mind a certain effect.[34]

This extremist thesis raised protests; it was objected that even so something passed from artist to public, a direct and authentic communication by means of the work.[35] But Valéry insisted upon his point of view. Obviously it is not easy to reconcile the paradox of incommunicability with a study of effects. Precarious as the latter may be, it supposes a minimum of action adapted by the author to his public, a certain current of transmission.

We are inclined to believe that it is precisely the communication between the author and the reader that permits effects. Valéry thinks exactly the opposite. Without his having said so, we suppose that, for him, effects are not those of the author but, so to speak, effects of the work. And these effects of the work require a radical break between the fabricator and the interpreter. If, against all probability, contact *was* established, the effects would vanish. Valéry said as much to the Société française de Philosophie, first in an absolute form:

. . . if what happened in the one were directly communicated to the other, all art would be destroyed, all the effects of art would disappear.[36]

then in a more discreet way:

. . . if there were direct communication between the one who creates the expression and the one who receives it, a great part of the *effects* would disappear.[37]

He repeated this in the opening lecture of his course at the Collège de France:

. . . there are many effects—and among the most power-ful—which require the absence of all direct correspond-ence between the two activities concerned.[38]
. . . the independence or the reciprocal ignorance of the producer's thoughts and conditions and the consumer's is almost essential to the effects of a work.[39]

To what, then, are the effects due? To "misunderstand-ings." As far back as 1927, the *Lettre sur Mallarmé* stated that the enchantment which Letters

. . . can produce in others implies, by the very nature of language, a quantity of mistakes and misunderstand-ings so necessary that the direct and perfect transmission of the author's thought, if it were possible, would cease the suppression and as it were the disappearance of the most beautiful effects of art. . . .[40]

Curiously enough, Valéry did not discuss this in his speech to the Société française de Philosophie in 1928, but much later, in the speech of March 2, 1935, he endeavored to dem-onstrate what he called "perhaps rather jokingly, the *crea-tive misunderstanding*."[41] Having shown that "the work of art is an object, a human fabrication, made with a view to a certain action on certain individuals," that "the phenomenon Art can be represented by two perfectly distinct transforma-tions," whose relationship is the same as "that which exists in economy between production and consumption," and that "these two transformations—the one which proceeds from author to *manufactured* object, and the one which expresses the fact that the object or the work modifies the consumer—are entirely independent,"[42] Valéry explained, in terms that we have remarked above, his thesis of the incommunicability which guarantees effects, and defined the role of the work in this action:

The interposition is required of a new and impenetra-ble element which acts upon another's being so that all the effect of art, all the *work* required of the consumer by the author's work can come about. *A creator causes creation.*[43]

The work is thus destined, according to Valéry, to provoke

in the reader interpretations alien to the author. This theory could go as far as the glorification of the misreading:

> "I don't understand this text very well. . . ."
> "Never mind! I find beautiful things in it. It draws them out of me. . . . I'm not interested in knowing what the Author says. My error is the Author!"[44]

He makes no mention of the "creative misunderstanding" in his foreword to volumes XVI and XVII of the *Encyclopédie Française* (1935): *Notion générale de l'art*. The first lecture of the *Cours de poétique* will return to the theory of incommunicability, but only to indicate in passing, and as a result of the incompatibility of the producer's thought and the consumer's *vis-à-vis* the object, that "there are creative misunderstandings."[45] Of these, on the contrary, there will be no mention at all in the discussion at the Centre international de Synthèse of *L'Invention ésthétique* (in 1938), where they might definitely have been expected.

The theory of "misunderstanding" was thus subject to eclipse, and it is difficult to know whether it held a major place in Valéry's thought, analogous to that, for example, of the aesthetic infinite or of equivalence. We can try to reinforce its importance by linking it to some of his other conceptions, such as his attempt to locate inspiration in the reader, or his refusal to determine the meaning of his poems, whose interpretation depends upon the readers, or the declaration that the poet's emotion is a private affair that concerns him alone. . . . This body of attitudes clearly indicates that for Valéry the work's function is not to communicate to the reader the author's states of consciousness. Nevertheless, one has the impression that Valéry suspected the excessiveness of his thesis and that, even if he would have liked to assert it in an absolute form (he did so only once: ". . . all effects would disappear"), he had to content himself by presenting it with implicit restrictions: "the most beautiful effects," "most of the effects," "a quantity of effects," etc. This calls to mind the discussion of inspiration, condemned because it could not dictate an *entire* poem, while Valéry admitted *discoveries* and lines given *gratis* by the gods. In short, without saying so, Valéry seems to believe, like everybody else, that there are many effects which result from an action by the author on the reader. How, if it were otherwise, could he reconcile with their total negation all his theories about the poet as calculator, engineer, politician, and manipulator of souls *à la* Poe? It is one thing to recognize the uncertainty of this exploration of effects, another to deny that they suppose a communication between the one who provokes and the one who experiences them. The role of the work is precisely to relay that excitation.

How is it that Valéry was led to suppress any idea of contact between the poet and the reader or listener? He may have observed that poems, or paintings, provoked reactions that seemed to him quite different from the intentions of the poet or the painter. The history of criticism is full of such false interpretations. They can, however, be explained (by period, orientation of minds, circumstances, training, temperament . . .), and above all it is rare that they are totally aberrant; in the most absurd, there remains something of what the author intended, and the contact has not been entirely broken. Valéry seems to have been particularly struck by the enrichment that works sometimes seem to receive. The author has produced more than he thought or the reader attributes to him more thought than he had given. These would be the true creative misunderstandings. The only grain of truth in this paradox is that everyone responds to a work with his own personality, and that the transmission among the public, thanks to some of its more gifted members, of more sensitive impressions, seems to create a new value for an admired work, but these deeper perceptions do not turn out to be solid and lasting unless the work justifies them and proves that its author had prepared the way for them. One can put what one likes into a work, but one finds in it only what it contains. What conceals this truth from us is the difference in language and ideas between the poet's era and the reader's.

Another factor may have played a part in Valéry's mind. His modesty, his pride, the preservation of his privacy, did not predispose him to regard the reader as the author's confidant. We have already seen that he did not intend to let the reader penetrate the creator's intimacy. This is why his entire theory of incommunicability and independence con-

stantly denies "direct correspondence" and asserts the incompatibility of ideas about the work. But there is an ambiguity about these too categorical expressions. Valéry abuses
the observation that the reader's mind does not reproduce the
author's. Contemplation, even active contemplation, is obviously not creation, although in a certain measure, which
Valéry ignores, it sometimes assumes some of its features. We
shall never, he tells us, be able to compare the two states
exactly. No doubt, but that is not the problem. The problem
is simply to know if something which is in the soul of the
author will be felt by the reader, and if certain impressions
that the artist sought to express will be grasped by his public.
Sentiment and effects, this is about all that art intends to communicate, and if they *are* communicated—with variations,
which must not be abused by theory—it is because they are
comparable at the outset as upon arrival.

To this reservation of the "ego" could be added, when Valéry believed in the possibility of manipulating another's soul
by art, a certain taste for intellectual domination. Whence an
enthusiasm for calculating effects. The poem became a machine for imposing all impressions without the poet having to
experience them himself. This impassability smacks of Par-
nassianism, and a jealousy of the power of music enters into
it. The *Introduction à la méthode de Léonard de Vinci*,
which glorified composition *à la* Poe (but by congealing it),
expressed this desire for a cold method based on a double
analysis, that of technique and that of the reader's psychology, and on the poet's refusal to participate:

> What we call a *realization* is a true problem of *yield*,
> which is not at all affected by the specific meaning, the
> key which each author attributes to his materials, but
> only by the nature of those materials and the mind of
> the public.[46]

When Valéry discovered the uncertainty of these effects
and the fact that the public was not automatically manipu-
lable, he took a dislike to the idea of obtaining, by misunderstandings, unforeseeable reactions:

> . . . the result, for anyone who ponders this reflection, is
> a certain irritation at bothering to speculate on the in-

exact, and at trying to stir others to astonishing thoughts as utterly unforeseen by us as the consequences of some unpremeditated act.[47]

Now, it would remain to ask Valéry, since there are effects that do not require an interruption of the current between author and reader, to distinguish them from the others. He has nowhere done this. But we can quite well see what he meant by these latter—the most important according to him— by some examples that he offered in support of the theory of incommunicability. These examples (there are only two) relate to a case of disproportion between the effect obtained and the author's effort. In the 1935 address to the Société française de Philosophie, Valéry shows that the artist "excites . . . in his public a great number of effects" without needing "to use as much energy as he is able to release." It is as if one spurred an animal or pressed a button governing a transformation of energy:

> It costs a musician very little to write on a score *fortissimo* or even *furioso* in order to release, in the concert hall, a storm of a hundred instruments. . . . It is the same in the arts of language; one can easily write certain powerful words without taking any more trouble than in writing simple ones, or words that mean less.[h]
> As a diversion, I took a line by La Fontaine . . . composed of monosyllables:
> *"Prends ce pic et me romps ce caillou qui me nuit."*
> and replaced two words in this line. In its new form, it could figure in a cosmogonic poem:
> *"Prends ta foudre et me romps l'univers qui me nuit."*
> You have completely changed the atmosphere. It required only a very simple modification to shift from one line to the other.[i]

[h] Cf. *Mauvaises pensées et autres*, p. 199: *"Intensity*, the easiest of means, for it takes no more strength to write a stronger word than any other: to write *tutti* and *fortissimo* instead of *piano*, and *universe* instead of *garden*."

[i] *Réflexions sur l'art* in *Bulletin de la Société française de Philosophie*, p. 65. La Fontaine's line, which is not entirely monosyllabic, was incorrectly quoted by Valéry, who gave it a rather different slant. La Fontaine wrote:
Prends ton pic, et me romps ce caillou qui te nuit.
(*Fables*, book VI, XVIII, *Le Chartier embourbé*)

One has somewhat the impression that Valéry is making fun of us. The poet or musician experiences the reinforcement of an effect exactly as it will be experienced by the hearer. From this point of view, there is no disproportion between them. The second example, in the opening lesson of the *Cours de poétique*, is much more interesting. It belongs to the "powerful" effects that require the absence of direct correspondence between author and reader:

> Every work, for example, is the fruit of long labors, and assembles a quantity of attempts, reworkings, eliminations, and choices. It required months and even years of reflection, and it can also suppose the experience and the acquisitions of a lifetime. Now, the effect of this work will be apparent in a few seconds.[48]

This effect, which we shall study in more detail, also manifests a disproportion, but one singularly different from that which Valéry described to us a moment ago: in the case of the musician writing *fortissimo*, all the labor was on the part of the executants; now, it is the author who has expended an incredible energy whose fruits the amateur will gather in a few instants of pleasure. This time, the accumulation and condensation of impressions, which the author has spent a long time combining and the shock of which the amateur experiences in a brief moment, permits us to speak legitimately of an "action of excess."[49] Only, contrary to what Valéry wanted to show in his first example, this effect depends essentially on the energy expended by the author. This effect, which I shall call total, results from the incorporation into the work of all the author's intentions; it is the sum of all his effects, and it cannot be compared to the local effect of a *fortissimo* or of a strong word. To say here that there is no direct correspondence between the author and reader is to do no more than recognize that the second is not the first. But to assert that the reader experiences in a few moments the mass of these effects, so carefully and so long calculated—does this not refute in its principle the theory of misunderstanding and re-establish contact with the author that was supposedly severed? The basis of Valéry's thought probably comes down to a humbler observation: that the reader cannot guess how the author went about producing an effect of such power. And indeed he must not do so, for the work would then lose its efficacity. The reader must be astonished. Valéry puts this very well, in passing: "The secrecy and surprise that tacticians often recommend in their writings are here naturally ensured."[50]

Valéry's doubts and hesitations often proceed by brutal and, if necessary, by contradictory negations. He has a trenchant skepticism, matched by a dauntless dogmatics which, anchored in its very diverse and very separate pieces of evidence, formulates them with an aggressive clarity. Valéry was never tempted to harmonize his ideas dialectically, but it will not be completely impossible to reduce certain oppositions of his thought artificially. Thus Valéry alternately sought and avoided communication between author and reader. Now, it happens that he imagined a solution that miraculously transcended this antinomy. He envisaged the case in which the work of art creates its own public. This supposes a distinction between two classes of works: those which correspond to ordinary requirements, and those which arouse new tastes. The first please because they satisfy known needs, to which their author has yielded; the others, because they satisfy needs that their author has imposed. Valéry explained this ingenious classification several times. In *Choses tues:*

> Certain works are created by their public. Certain others create their public.
> The first correspond to the needs of average natural sensibility. The second create artificial needs that they satisfy at the same time.[51]

In *Réflexions sur l'art:*

> A certain division of works of art could be based on the observation that a share of these productions is created by the public, and another creates its own public. There are therefore in this regard two categories of intentions: 1) to make a work to order for the public, a work that suits it; 2) or else, to create a public that suits the work.[52]

In his program *De l'enseignement de la poétique au Collège de France,* where he returns to this

. . . important distinction: between works *that are somehow created by their public* (whose expectations they fulfill and are thus practically determined by the knowledge of these latter) and works that, on the contrary, *tend to create their public*. All the questions and disputes born of conflicts between "cliques" and "audiences," the variations of criticism, the fate of works in the long run and their changes in value, etc., can be discussed in light of this distinction.[53]

The "clique," contrary to supposition, is more difficult to reach than the "audience":

Think of what is necessary in order to please three million readers.
Paradox: it takes *less* than to please only a hundred persons exclusively.[54]

And, similarly, it is more difficult for the "precious" author to satisfy himself than for the popular one:

. . . the man who pleases millions always pleases himself and the man who pleases only a few is generally displeased with himself.[55]

It is scarcely necessary to say that it is to works of the second kind that Valéry's predilections lead him, and if we wish to name an example, it is Mallarmé we turn to. The *Lettre sur Mallarmé* contrasts with the ordinary public, which likes only facility, the public that does not seek effortless pleasure:

. . . there are however several publics: among which it is not impossible to find one which does not conceive of pleasure without difficulty, which does not like to enjoy without paying, and even that is not happy if its happiness is not in part its own work whose cost it wants to experience. Moreover, it happens that a very particular public may form.
   Mallarmé thus created, in France, the notion of a *difficult author*. He expressly introduced into art the obligation of mental effort. In this way he raised the status of the reader, and with an admirable understanding of true glory, he chose among society that small number of particular readers who, having once enjoyed him, could

never again tolerate impure, immediate, and defenseless poems. Everything seemed naïve and cowardly to
them after they had read him.[56]

This public receives here the praise it deserves, but, by a
reaction frequent in Valéry, we can expect to see him scorn
what he has glorified:

To train a public for oneself.
To become "a great man" is only to train people to love
everything that comes from you; to desire it— They can
be accustomed to one's ego as to a fodder, and lick it
out of your hand.
    But there are two kinds of *great men:* the ones who
give people what people want; the ones who teach them
to eat what they don't like.[57]

The tribute of admiration is neglected by the proud creator
who knows that "genius is easy," that his masterpieces are
inferior to himself, and that the public is ignorant of the rigor
and the loftiness of his ambition:

    The most profound may not admire themselves by
    means of others' fervor, for they know that no one but
    themselves could conceive what they require from their
    being nor what they hope from their demon. What they
    give to the world is what they reject: the dust, debris,
    the toys of their hidden hours.[58]

All the same, it is to this difficult reader that, according to
Valéry, one must address oneself:

    To write for the "intelligent" reader. For the one
    who is impressed by neither bombast nor tone. For the
    one who will either adopt your idea or destroy it or
    reject it . . .[59]

As for the others, with polite disdain he requests them to
withdraw:

    Here, perhaps, we should cast doubt on whether a
    poet can legitimately ask of a reader the apparent and
    sustained labor of his mind? Does the art of writing
    come down to entertaining our fellow men and manipu-
    lating their souls, without the participation of their re-
    sistance? The answer is easy, there is no difficulty, each

mind is its own master. It is quite easy for it to reject what repels it. Do not be afraid of shutting the book on us. Let us fall from your hands.[60]

Besides, the modern era, which seeks only the "easy to read," has made the attentive reader rarer than ever:

> To ask the reader to stretch his mind and to achieve complete possession only at the price of a rather painful act; to claim to transform him from the passive creature he prefers to be into a demicreator—this would be to offend custom, laziness, and all insufficient intelligence.
>
> The art of reading at leisure, privately, knowledgeably and distinctly, which formerly answered the writer's difficulty and zeal by a presence and a patience of the same quality, is being lost: it has been lost.[61]

And Valéry claims that the reader who had once been accustomed to fruitful effort by Tacitus or Thucydides has been "exterminated" by newspapers and novels. Yet it is this era that is most interested in difficult authors, and we can imagine that the great prose writers of antiquity have long since been given serious competition by our novelists. The valid work must therefore make the reader active, even if there is a risk that he will "unmake" this work, and creative, for he takes more out of it than the author thought he had put in:

> The living arbitrariness of the reader attacks the dead arbitrariness of the work.
>
> But this energetic reader is the only one who matters —being the only one who can draw out of us what we did not know we possessed.[62]

Valéry was to dedicate "Mon Faust"—and would make Faust dedicate the memoirs he attributes to him—"to the reader of good faith and ill-will."[63] The ideal reader would be the one who would spend as much time getting to know the work as the author in creating it.

> The real readers of a work are those who spend on looking into it and into themselves, at least as much desire and time as it took to make it.[j]

---

[j] Littérature in Tel quel, I, p. 175. Cf., in Vues personnelles sur la

To which Valéry adds this provocative observation: "But even more *interested* are those who fear and flee it."[k]

Whatever the precautions taken, the effect of the work depends on the public. It is subject to all sorts of vicissitudes. But there is something that remains unchanged: the work, the poem itself. It is the same after each interpretation. It keeps the property of indefinitely provoking new interpretations. Valéry locates this kind of eternity, the dream of all artists, or its equivalent, in this generative power:

A work is an object or sense datum, although the diverse values or interpretations it suggests are consequences (ideas or affections), which cannot alter it in its purely material property of producing completely different ones.[64]

Valéry compares "the text of a work" to those "rather mysterious bodies that physics studies and that chemistry utilizes" and whose "presence alone . . . in a certain mixture of other substances causes the latter to unite, although they themselves remain unaltered, identical, neither transformed in their nature nor increased or diminished in their quantity."[65] Thus, for the text of a work:

The action of its presence modifies minds, each according to its nature and its state, provoking the combinations potentially there, but whatever the reaction produced, the text remains unaltered and indefinitely capable of stimulating other phenomena by other circumstances or in another individual.[66]

The ingenious periphrasis that alludes to catalytic action saves both the work's independence and the reader's freedom.

Actually, Valéry is far from sure that the text really preserves its integrity. There is a factor that fatally denatures it.

---

science in *Vues*, p. 54, an analogous demand, not without its dangers, on the part of modern science.

[k] *Ibid.*, p. 175. Compare with: "Mallarmé left concerts full of a sublime jealousy" (*Au Concert Lamoureux en 1893* in *Pièces sur l'art*, p. 84) and with: "Some adored Wagner; others, Schumann. I could write that they hated him. At the temperature of passionate interest, the two states are indiscernible" (*Avant-propos* in *Variété*, pp. 95–96).

This is time. "The change of era, which is a change of reader, is comparable to a change in the text itself, a change that is always unforeseen, and incalculable."[1] The relation of three words, in a certain line by Racine, "finds an unexpected reinforcement and an extraordinary resonance in romantic poetry; in a soul of our era, it mingles marvelously with some of the most beautiful lines by Baudelaire."[67] In the same way, La Fontaine's *Adonis* "lives again . . . by the contrast of such a delicate form and such bright melodies with our system of discords and that tradition of excess we have so docilely accepted."[68] He noted sadly that "the fatal lot of most of our works is to become imperceptible or alien," gradually losing "all their chances of pleasing" as their admirers disappear and the "verbal substance," aging, "loses its relations with man."[69]

The effect of the work is further threatened by the diversity of interpretations. But Valéry sees in these divergences a characteristic of the mind and as it were an equivalent in the public to the creator's liberty:

> . . . divergences may be manifest between the poetic interpretations of a poem, between impressions and significations, or rather between the resonances provoked in one and the other, by the action of the work. But this banal observation assumes, on reflection, an importance of the first order; this possible diversity of the legitimate effects of a work is the very sign of the mind. It corresponds, moreover, to the plurality of ways avoidable to the author during his labor of production. This is because any work of the mind itself is always as it were accompanied by a certain atmosphere of more or less apparent indeterminacy.[70]

Thus diversity of affect corresponds to diversity of creation. Which leads, it would seem, to locating the true value of a work in the totality of impressions it could produce, or, in a fashion easier to control, in the sum of interpretations it is

---

[1] *Au sujet d'* "Adonis" in *Variété*, p. 86. Cf. *Littérature* in *Tel quel*, I, p. 168: "A work lasts to the extent that it is capable of appearing completely different from what its author had made of it. It lasts in order to be transformed and insofar as it is capable of a thousand transformations and interpretations."

capable of suggesting. And, in fact, we do measure the richness of a work by its inexhaustible power of suggestion. It would remain to show that these many and often contradictory effects are in close relation with what was the artist's mental activity, and merely develop the plurality of possibilities contained by his work. But it would then be necessary, once again, to renounce the theory of the "creative misunderstanding."

Chapter IX

THE THEORY OF EFFECTS (*concluded*)

THE TOTAL EFFECT

Let us now consider the categories of effects in which Valéry was interested. We can distinguish three: the general effect produced by the work, which we shall call the *total effect;* the effects produced by the poem insofar as we judge it to be poetic, which we shall call the *specific effects;* lastly, various effects without a common denominator, which we shall call the *particular effects.*

The *total effect* is characterized by surprise, instantaneousness, and the disproportion between brevity of impression and the enormous accumulation of labor incorporated in the work:

> A glance will suffice to judge a considerable monument, to experience the shock of its effect. In two hours, all the calculations of the tragic poet . . . all the combinations of harmony and orchestration which the composer has constructed, all the philosopher's meditations . . . may . . . stun, amaze, dazzle, or disconcert the mind of the Other, abruptly subjected to the stimulus of this enormous load of intellectual work. There is, here, an action of *excess.*[1]

> A structure seen at a glance assails the eye in a moment with all the fruit of thousands of hours, all the longueurs of the architects and the masons. And even the action of centuries, erosion, accumulation, even the contrasts of civilization, of fashions, of tastes amassed from the very beginning of time. And a glance suffices to experience the composite essence of all this, as a spoonful of a mixture.[2]

> . . . The compositional duration of even a very short poem may absorb years, the poem's action on the reader

will be performed in a few minutes. In a few minutes, this reader will receive the impact of discoveries, comparisons, flashes of expression accumulated during months of investigation, expectation, patience, and impatience.[3]

As is often the case, the idea is illustrated by an image; Valéry compares "this effect to that of the fall, in a few seconds, of a mass which had been raised, fragment by fragment, to the top of a tower. . . ."[4]

I have dragged up the side a mountain stone by stone, a mass which I hurled down from it in a single piece upon them. I have taken five years, ten years to accumulate it, detail by detail on the heights, and the impact of it they receive all at once, in a moment.[5]

The difference in duration between elaboration and reception forever prevents the most interested party from experiencing this powerful effect. In a monologue which might have become a poem, Valéry expressed this distress of the patient artist severed from the enjoyment of his work:

Alas, says this great artist, the work which I have created, which people admire, which excites those around me, which is talked about, which is praised to the skies, whose beauties are examined and extolled—I am the only one who does not enjoy it!

I conceived its design, I planned and executed all its parts. But the instantaneous effect of the whole, the impact, the discovery, the final birth of everything, the composed emotion, all this is denied me, all this is for men who do not know this work, who have not lived with it, who know nothing of the delays, the gropings, the disgusts, the accidents . . . but who see only something like a magnificent design, achieved at one stroke.[6]

Of course we do not believe that the artist is so pitiable as all this. If his work satisfies him, he has the means to enjoy it more than anyone else. For the effect of surprise and discovery, it will suffice him to wait, and perhaps he will be able to assure himself, like Swift: "What genius I had when I wrote that!"

The effect of shock also serves to explain, in the reader who experiences it, the genesis of his belief in inspiration: he

. . . will attribute to inspiration much more than it can give. He will imagine a person who can create without halts, without hesitations, without retouches. . . .[7]

"Let us suppose . . . the great effect is produced . . . ," we shall be led to imagine

. . . a being of enormous powers, capable of creating such wonders without any other effort than that required to produce anything at all. . . . Certain elements of the work . . . occurring to the author by some favorable accident, will be attributed to a singular value of his mind. In this way the consumer becomes a producer in his turn: a producer, first of all, of the work's value; and subsequently . . . of the value of the imaginary being who has created what he admires.[8]

This would be a very naïve art lover, whom we have already encountered, but who, if he is foolish enough to believe that the artist creates without effort, without criticism, and without luck, is not so wrong in conceiving genius as endowed with a power superior to his own. We can in any case concede him enough modesty not to be tempted to consider himself the producer of the work's value and of its author's. He acknowledges them; he does not create them. This paradox is close to those which make the reader a man inspired, a creator. They do not accord very well with the theory of excess, for if the discrepancy between the author's activities and the reader's, made apparent by the impact of the total effect, is the cause of the reader's faith in the virtue of inspiration in the author, it also justifies that faith: the reader knows only too well that his own accumulated labor would never achieve a result of this value. It does not occur to him to mistake the half-passive pleasure of contemplation for a form of original creation. If his belief in the author's inspiration is naïve, the illusion of being inspired himself would be still more so. The beauty of paradoxes is that, reversed, they lead back to banality.

Let us leave aside the dubious consequences which Valéry drew from the *total effect* and consider the scope we can suitably attribute to it. We notice first of all that such an effect, in the form in which Valéry presents it, is conceivable only in the case of brief works (in poetry and in music), or of works whose totality is comprehensible in a limited time (in the plastic arts). As a matter of fact, Valéry regarded as practically instantaneous actions of highly variable duration: a glance for a monument, several minutes for a poem, two hours for a tragedy, a symphony, a philosophical treatise. . . . If the disproportion between the time of creation and the time of contemplation is well founded, and even banally obvious, it is a mistake to identify with the same type of effect impressions which vary in degree and in nature if our attention is concentrated or distributed within its duration. The glamorous effect of inspired instantaneousness, a sudden effect which we might call one of *dazzlement*, would be more suitable to certain beauties of detail than to the beauty of totality or perspective, except for static or brief works which we can grasp, or rather which grasp us, in a single glance; this would also be true, at times, of the *terminal effect*, of a whole or of a part. Every time development in duration is essential to the work, to reduce the *total effect* to a momentary one is unwarranted.

There are cases in which the *total effect* is not distinguished from the terminal one—for example, when the brevity of the text which dazzles the reader is extreme.[a] We think of the maxim, the epigram, the witticism, but also of the isolated line of verse (the monostich, as the poet Emmanuel Lochac calls it). Valéry described its mechanism: "Wit—is the use of the word or the act for its instantaneous shock effect. Slight mass, great speed."[9] And with a touch of humor, he added: "There are flashes of stupidity as considerable, as rare, as precious as flashes of wit,"[10] a pertinent remark which might have opened a door to *comic effects*, notably to expression of character.[b] Another case is that in which the terminal effect is prepared by the entire text, or everything in the text is subordinated to it. The sonnet has often been conceived in

[a] Valéry regretted the absence in literary histories of a chapter devoted to the "short genre." "There exists more than one masterpiece of compendious genius" (*Variations sur la céramique illustrée* in *Pièces sur l'art*, pp. 273–74).

[b] Yet Valéry was interested in laughter, of which he spoke in various works.

this fashion. We await the fall, the climax, or the major culminating effect. It seems to me that Valéry did not discuss this matter after his early years. But the projected article *Sur la technique littéraire* of 1889 assigned the lion's share to the conclusive line of verse: ". . . a sonnet . . . will be a veritable quintessence . . . carefully *composed* with a view to a final and overpowering effect. . . ."

> . . . the poem, as we see it, has no goal but to prepare its *dénouement*. We can best compare it to the steps of a magnificent altar, to the porphyry stairs crowned by the Tabernacle. The ornament, the candles, the gold and silver work, the clouds of incense—everything functions, everything is arranged in order to fix the attention upon the monstrance—upon the final verse!c

In the same article, the young Valéry was concerned with a more complex case. He compared the use of repetitions and refrains in *The Raven* with Wagner's technique:

> When the poem has a certain amplitude, say a hundred lines, the artist must take pains to fix the thought at several important points which, compressed and fortified at the end, will contribute powerfully to the final and decisive explosion.[11]

Let us suppose that instead of a single and one-stringed refrain, we introduced several, that each char-

---

c In *Dossiers*, 1, pp. 27–28. On June 2, 1890, he wrote to Pierre Louÿs that the sonnet will be composed "with a view to a final and decisive stroke," and he copied out, almost to the word, the comparison with the altar and the monstrance (letter quoted by Henri Mondor, *Le Vase brisé de Paul Valéry* in *Paul Valéry. Essais et temoignages inédits recueillis par Marc Eigeldinger*, pp. 14–16). If Valéry did not speak of the sonnet's technical effect again, it is because his conception of the sonnet changed: ". . . the finest yet remains to be written: this will be one whose four parts will each fulfill a function different from that of the others, this progression of differences in the strophes nonetheless quite justified by the *line* of the entire discourse" (*Calepin d'un poète* in *Oeuvres complètes*, vol. C, p. 194). "The sonnet is made for the simultaneous. Fourteen *simultaneous* lines, powerfully designated as such by the interrelation and persistence of the rhymes; type and structure of a *stationary* poem" (*Autres rhumbs* in *Tel quel*, II, p. 154). Three very different types: intention is focused on the last line, on the difference and the connection of the four parts, on the equality of the fourteen lines.

acter, each landscape, each mood had its own; that we recognized them in passing; that at the end of the piece of verse or prose, all these known signs flowed together to form what has been called the *melodic stream* and that the terminal effect was the fruit of the opposition, of the encounter, of the confluence of the refrains; thereby we arrive at the conception of the *leitmotiv* or dominant motif which is the basis of Wagnerian musical theory. Is it impossible, then, to apply these principles to literature?[12]

We have here the beginning of the dream of the great symphonic composition in poetry. From the point of view of the theory of effects, this particular case of total and terminal effect is remarkable for the convergence of anterior effects.

Valéry, always sensitive to what can destroy art, did not fail to consider the collapse of the total effect:

> . . . the effect . . . does not always come off; it may happen, in this intellectual mechanics, that the tower is too high, the mass too great, and that we observe a blank or negative result.[13]

It is a particular work that is in question here. But I believe Valéry also thought occasionally of the general effect which an author seeks to make on a vast public by abundance and accumulation. This is no longer an instantaneous effect, but it is still a total effect, insistent and quantitative. Thus Valéry described Zola believing "in all naïveté in things themselves: nothing is too solid, too heavy and powerful for him; and in literature, nothing too expressed," "convinced of the effectiveness of prose in *rendering*—almost in re-creating—the earth and its human inhabitants, cities and organisms, manners and passions, flesh and machines," and ultimately "relying on the *effect of mass*, of the quantity of details, of the number of pages and of volumes. . . ."[14] Finally, a writer may, for a personal reason, seek to avoid that total effect which a work almost always produces. We conceive that the author of a collection of maxims or miscellaneous works may fear to be simplified by his reader. The latter has a tendency to unify what was scattered, and to summarize in an image a man who has nonetheless yielded only fragments of himself. Thus Valéry felt he must warn the reader of *Propos me concernant*

that the work was not a work, but an unorganized collection
of "moments," in order to forearm him "against the '*bloc*' effect."[15] Valéry feared that the reader would create out of
these confidences a character, an *effect of unity*, knowing as
he did how it would be obtained, as he says in the same
collection somewhat further on:

> If I take certain fragments in these notebooks, sepa-
> rate them by asterisks and publish them, the whole will
> constitute something. The reader—and even I myself—
> will form a *unity* out of them.
> And this formation will be, will do *something else*—
> unforeseen by me until then—in other minds, or in my
> own. With a hint of a fable which assembles some ob-
> servations, one gets a sufficiently valid character. That is
> how I wrote *Monsieur Teste* in '94 or '95.[16]

We have just seen, then, the modalities of the total effect
as envisaged by Valéry. Few of them are likely to be produced with that instantaneousness, even when extended, in
which Valéry localized them. We may wonder what led him
to sustain so absolute a thesis. It is because for him *effect* and
instant are almost synonyms. We are at one of the points of
his doctrine where the aesthetic, or the *aesthesic* as he liked
to say, is connected to his general conception of the sensibility: ". . . poetic effects are instantaneous, like all aesthetic
effects, like all effects of sensibility."[d] For Valéry, an effect
is what *does not last*. Strange as this position may be, it is
illuminated when we read a very odd and somewhat abstruse
passage, in which Valéry opposes the reader's brevity of impression to prolonged attention. Now, the reader is never
able to shift from the former state to the latter. If he could,
the poetry would disappear. It is the flash, the explosion,
which embellishes what it suddenly reveals, for it suggests a
world different from the ordinary world. Valéry called this
instantaneous illumination "the photo-poetic phenomenon":

> A great advantage for a poet is the incapacity of most
> people to extend their thought *beyond* the point where
> it dazzles, excites, transports.

[d] *L'Invention esthétique* in *l'Invention*, p. 150. Cf. *La Tentation
de* (*saint*) *Flaubert* in *Variété* V, p. 200: "Literature . . . aims at
immediate and instantaneous effects."

The spark illuminates a site which seems infinite in the brief interval given in which to see it. The expression dazzles.

The marvel of the shock cannot be distinguished from the objects it reveals. The strong shadows which appear at the moment remain in the memory like admirable furnishings.

They are not distinguished from real objects. They are transformed into positive things.

But note that, by a great stroke of luck for poetry, the brief interval I have referred to cannot be expanded; one cannot substitute for the spark a *continuous fixed light*.

Such a light would illuminate something altogether different.

Here the phenomena depend on the illuminating source.

The *brief interval* affords glimmers of another system or "world" which a *lasting clarity cannot illuminate*. This world (to which a metaphysical value must not be attached—such a value being useless and absurd) is essentially *unstable*. Perhaps it is the world of the *free connection* of the mind's virtual resources? The world of attractions, of the shortest paths, of resonances. . . .[17]

We know this world of attractions: it is the world of creation; and this world of resonances: it is the poetic universe.

It is doubtless to this glamorous effect of the inspired instant that Valéry alluded in a brief note in which he opposes two discrepant series of psychological states, and which suggests that it is not only in the reader that disproportion and excess are active:

Masterpiece, marvelous machine to measure the entire distance and degree between a brief interval and a very long elaboration, between a happy stroke and billions of ordinary possibilities; between a Self artificially raised to the highest power and a Self at zero; between what is necessary to create a work and what, in a glance, in a contact, is *given*.

Perfection, purity, profundity, delight, ravishment which reinforces itself.[18]

The artist, in effect, knows the inspiration, or the accident,

or the luck which, in a privileged moment, overwhelms him
with grace and makes him powerful as a god, and, on the
other hand, the persevering and labor and the frequent fail-
ures of execution, the sensibility at dead center, the thousand
constraints of his discipline.

The accumulation, in the work of instantaneous effect, of
so much labor and so much duration recurs, from another
point of view, in the artist considered, somewhat mythically,
as concentrating in himself centuries of thought. He becomes,
in a sense, a moment, an infinitely precious one, and in a
certain manner offers himself as a contrary of time. This at
least is how Socrates describes him in *Eupalinos:*

> It is not entirely impossible, a piece of marble or of
> shapeless stone being entrusted to the permanent agita-
> tion of the waters, that it should be taken from them
> someday, by an accident of another kind, and that it
> should now affect the semblance of Apollo.

PHAEDRUS

> But then, dear Socrates, the labor of an artist, when
> he produces immediately, and by his deliberate desire, a
> certain bust (like that of Apollo)—is it not, in some sense,
> the contrary of indefinite time?

SOCRATES

> Precisely. It is indeed the contrary, as if the actions
> enlightened by thought abridged the course of nature;
> and one might say, quite safely, that an artist is worth a
> thousand centuries, or a hundred thousand, or even
> more! In other words, it would have required this almost
> inconceivable time for ignorance or accident to produce,
> blindly, the same thing which our excellent man has
> achieved in a few days. Thus we have a strange meas-
> urement for works of art!

PHAEDRUS

> Very strange. It is a great misfortune that we have no
> occasion to employ it.[19]

But the point of view of the instantaneous effect cannot
always be maintained. It is all too obvious that complex
works require a lasting attention, and many returns of this
attention, which necessarily subject the interplay of effects to

their extension and persistence (and to their weakening too, it must be admitted). Depending on their ambition, such works will have a long-range action, while others, being lighter, are rapidly consumed:

> Some texts are made, or seem to be made, to act momentarily and energetically.
> A newspaper article is not to be compared with a book. Others are made for slow, lasting, growing action. Made for a third, a fourth reading . . .
> A newspaper article can be regarded as restoring in three minutes an accumulation of two hours.
> A book can restore in four hours a thousand hours of work. But a thousand hours of work are very different from a total of minutes. The breaks, the discontinuities, and the repetitions play a capital role.
> And one text has value as a stimulus or *apéritif* of thought, and another text as a gratifier; an aliment of thought.[20]

It is curious that these reflections, which so clearly mark the differences of regime in works, did not incline Valéry to modify his theory of instantaneous effects. We sometimes have the impression that there were hermetic compartments in his mind.

SPECIFIC EFFECTS

Let us proceed to the specific effects of poetry. Valéry insisted on an effect which is not strictly aesthetic and which psychologists would classify with the organic reverberation of the emotions. The poem, according to Valéry, here much less intellectual than we might expect, addresses life more than the mind. It is a question of *becoming* rather than of *comprehending*:[21]

> Poetry must extend to the whole being; it stimulates its muscular organization by rhythms, releases or liberates its verbal faculties whose total functioning it exalts, organizes in depth.[22]

The living, acting, and reacting body becomes a *reverberator*. It would not be difficult, following Valéry in this direction, to show that having shifted inspiration from the poet to the reader, he performs an analogous transfer in the case of enthusiasm. The effect he describes here is, to a large degree, physiological. It will be noted that this is the effect Valéry finds least vulnerable to uncertainty, apparently willing to reestablish the current between author and reader, doubtless because it is not a current of thought:

> There is virtually nothing but rhythm and the palpable properties of language by which literature can affect the reader's organic being with some confidence in the conformity of intention and result.[23]

Rhythmic and sonorous effects are not the whole of poetry, especially for Valéry who considered *sound* and *sense* as absolutely independent variables. In the separate domain of signification, Valéry isolated a curious phenomenon of reverberation or resonance, not in the purely musical sense of the term, but in a psychic sense; this he calls the *resonance of images*. This means effects "produced by the groupings of words and the physiognomies of words independent of syntactical links, and by the reciprocal (that is, nonsyntactical) influences of their juxtaposition."[24] For example, Racine's line:

> *Dans l'Orient désert quel devint mon ennui!*

contains "a magnificent relation of three words, *Orient, désert,* and *ennui.* The impression of Baudelaire's line:

> *Sois sage, ô ma douleur, et tiens-toi plus tranquille!*

results, beyond the music and the tone, from the simple juxtaposition of the vague ideas of *sagesse* and *douleur.*[26] In Vigny's line:

> *J'aime la majesté des souffrances humaines.*

Valéry sees, first of all, a piece of nonsense, but also "a fine *concurrence* of two *important* words,"[27] *majesté* and *souffrance.* We can imagine a poet systematically trying to invent such relations. Certain words already possess in themselves a poetic potential, and the poet ascertains, in the language, the presence of other words capable of establishing with them that mysterious current of signification which owes nothing to their grammatical relations (in my opinion, we are concerned here with an affective link). We can express this harmony by images taken from electricity or from acoustics (resonance, harmonics); we can also speak of reflections. Valéry mingles the first two when he describes Mallarmé searching for these effects of reciprocal influence:

> Mallarmé had created a kind of science of *his words.* There can be no doubt that he reasoned out their figures, explored the inner space in which they appeared, sometimes as *causes* and sometimes as *effects;* estimated what we might call their *poetic charge;* and that, by this endlessly extended and detailed labor, words were secretly, potentially organized into the *power* of his mind, according to a mysterious law of his profound sensibility.
>
> I imagine his expectations: soul intent on *harmonics,* concentrated on the apparition of one word in the universe of words, determined to grasp the whole order of connections and resonances invoked by a thought eager to be born. . . .
>
> "I say: A FLOWER . . ." he writes.[28]

The notion of resonance or reverberations plays a broader role in Valéry's poetics. It is at the basis of his very conception of the poetic universe. Let us recall that in the poetic state, our inner disposition is harmonized with the circumstances which impress us, in other words, our general sensibility is in a marvelously exact relation to a world in which objects are musicalized, reverberating by means of one another. The resonance is double: we feel it in the relation of the individual to the poetic universe, and in the internal organization of that universe (which, moreover, comes down to the same thing, for this world, or system of relations, is an internal one). We further recall that the reader has been compared to a reverberator. And we have just seen that the poem's physiological effect was to put us in a state of organic harmony. The mutual resonance of images (of the meanings of privileged words) was only a particular case of the system of harmonies constituted by the poem. *L'Amateur de poèmes,* which concludes the *Album de vers anciens,* skillfully conjures up the key word of a paragraph which is an invitation to the voyage in the poetic realm:

> I surrender myself to the adorable progress: to read, to live where words lead. Their appearance is fixed. Their sonorities prepared. Their turmoil is composed according to a previous reflection, and they rush forward, resonant, in magnificent or pure groups.

The notion of resonance extends to all the arts insofar as they manage to create the poetic state, and even to certain aspects of nature or of life. The synonymy of *resonance* and *poetry* in Valéry's lexicon can be attested by many texts:

> We say of a site, of a circumstance, and even of a person, that they are *poetic*.
> This state is one of resonance. I mean—but how to put it?—that the entire system of our sensory and spiritual life is seized by it, there occurs a kind of harmonic and reciprocal liaison between our impressions, our ideas, our impulses, our means of expression—as if all our faculties suddenly became commensurable.[29]
> Many admirable canvases do not necessarily have a relation to poetry. Many masters created masterpieces without resonance. It even happens that the poet is born late in the life of a man who hitherto was merely a great painter. Take Rembrandt . . .[30]
> In his best canvases, [Manet] achieves *poetry*, that is, the supreme degree of art, by what I should like to call . . . *the resonance of execution*.[e]

This metaphor is very often linked, by Valéry, to three more or less equivalent terms (we often find them mixed or substituted for each other) whose substitution for each other was facilitated by the interplay of semantic and etymological relations. This is the series *chant-enchantement-charme*, which leads us to envisage a sequence of related effects. *Chant* [song] is understood here in a broad and symbolic fashion; there are paintings and monuments which sing, and also forms and moments of existence. Eupalinos distinguished, among edifices, those which are *mute*, those which *speak*,

---

[e] *Degas. Danse. Dessin*, p. 54. See further, in *Triomphe de Manet* in *Pièces sur l'art*, pp. 213–14, the means by which Manet, in a portrait of Berthe Morisot, "makes his work reverberate."

and, rarest of all, those which *sing*.[31] Phaedrus compared the "delicate little temple," "mathematical image of a girl from Corinth," to "some wedding song accompanied by flutes,"[32] and he understood how "a façade can sing."[33] Socrates sought "to hear the song of the columns" and to "imagine, in the pure sky, the monument of a melody."[34]

> *Douces colonnes, ô*
> *L'orchestre de fuseaux!*
> *Chacune immole son*
> *Silence à l'unisson.*

[Mild columns, O concert of shafts! Each immolates its silence in their unison.]

Similarly, "the painter's real and particular gift will make the portrait into a work of art and will sing in and of itself, independent of the resemblance."[35] "Thus, in the plastic order: the *man who sees* becomes, suddenly feels he is, the *soul that sings*. . . ."[†]

All painters, however—I mean, all the best ones—are not equally poets.
We find a number of admirable pictures which, masterful by their perfections, nonetheless do not "sing". . . .[36]

Thus, Degas does not achieve "the poetry of painting."[37] "Neither grace nor apparent poetry is his object. His works almost never sing."[38] And, if we seek a transition to the natural spectacles enjoying this property, Valéry tells us that painting "seeks in things seen that by which they sing. . . . Each true painter is a reverberator. . . ."[39] As he distinguished several kinds of monuments, Valéry separates from the "faces of the world . . . [that are] indifferent or else of a specific importance," certain "aspects of the day" which "touch us beyond any determination or classification" and "give us the idea of a certain 'world' of which they are the revelation. . . ." This world is comparable to the universe of music. "Now there are similarly aspects of forms, moments

[†] *Autour de Corot* in *Pièces sur l'art*, p. 185. Valéry also spoke of the "singing state" as a condition preliminary to the poet's labors (*Souvenirs poétiques*, pp. 18–19).

of the visible world that *sing*. Rare are those who first distinguish this song. There are places on earth which we have
seen become admirable. Corot has designated some of
these."[40] Nature, for Corot, is, in her *good sites*, a model or
an example of the singular poetic value of certain arrangements of visible things."[41]

It follows that literature produces analogous effects. We
might distinguish, among poetic monuments, those which are
mute (or muffled), those which speak (Boileau, Molière),
and those which sing. If Valéry took his examples from
painting and architecture, it was to avoid the ambiguity of
the word *chant* applied in this very special sense to the arts
of language. When he sought to evoke this quality of resonance apropos of a writer's work, he resorted to a skillful
transposition:

> Certain prose sentences by Mallarmé are stained-glass
> windows. The subjects are what is least important—are
> caught and drowned in the mystery, the vivacity, the
> profundity, the laughter and the reverie of each frag-
> ment. Each is palpable, each sings. . . .[42]

Thus a sentence can sing in other ways than by its verbal
melody. The transposition turns into "correspondence" (in
the purest manner of Symbolism) when, in front of a drawing,
"an exact memory of themes or of timbres appears. . . .
What a surprise to *recognize* (as I then did), gazing with
delighted eyes at a work by Corot—a delicious passage from
Parsifal."[43]

But what, finally, is this song, which is not music but its
psychic analogue? After having spoken, in the suggestive essay on Corot, "of the aspects, the forms and moments . . .
which sing," Valéry wonders where "the secret of a site's enchantment lies." What sings [*chante*] is therefore what en-
chants. But what is enchantment? Does it reside "in a certain
harmony of figures and light whose empire over us is as
powerful and as unintelligible as that of a perfume, a glance,
a timbre of the voice can be?" Or is it the "echo of emotions of men long ago," who by holding sacred "the most remarkable objects of nature—springs, rocks, peaks, great trees,"
created "the most ancient of arts, which is simply to feel an
expression come to being from an impression, and a singular

moment become a monument of the memory—special favor of a dawn or a wondrous sunset, sacred horror of the woods, exaltation on the heights from which the realms of the earth are revealed"? Magic power or primitive religious emotion? It is a term that Valéry decides on; after having indicated that we are somewhat more skillful at reproducing these emotions "than at reasoning about them," he shows us Corot soliciting Nature as the virtuoso solicits the instrument which "little by little yields him ever more exquisite vibrations, as though closer to the soul of his soul," and drawing "from transparent Space, from the undulant and gently receding or steeply pitched Landscape, from the Tree, the Grove, from Buildings, and from all hours of Light, certain 'charms,' ever more comparable to those of music itself."[44] Thus, from poetry to resonance, from resonance to song, from song to enchantment, the Valerian modulation ends in the *charme*. The equivalence of these expressions would be easy to confirm. "*Charmes* (that is, Poems)," specifies the 1942 edition of Valéry's *Poésies*.[g] The object of Poetry "seemed to me to be to produce *enchantment*."[45] Manet and Baudelaire "pursue . . . and achieve the supreme object of art, *charm*, a term which I take here in its full force."[46]

Valéry sketched a theory of poetry which connects it with magic, in effects as in origins. He expressed the magical value which their loveliest memories of poems assume for poetry lovers, alternately ornaments of their life, privileged references, consolations, and relief:

> . . . by the mysterious operation of a poem, a few moments which might have been, without it, of no value, quite insignificant, are transformed into a marvelously measured and enhanced duration, which becomes a treasure of the soul; and sometimes, a kind of magic formula, a talisman—which our heart preserves in itself and which it offers to our mind in moments of emotion or enchantment in which it fails to find an expression pure or powerful enough for what exalts or overwhelms it.

[g] The famous collection, before being titled simply *Charmes*, had as its title *Charmes ou Poèmes* (1922). The epigraph *Deducere carmen* does not appear in all editions.

I know a man who, subject to a cruel surgical operation whose pain could not be mitigated by anesthesia, found some relief, or rather some restoration of his forces, and of his patience in reciting to himself, between two spasms of pain, a poem he loved.[47]

Valéry traced poetry back to primitive or legendary periods, and his imagination led him to grant the true poets their *lettres de noblesse* by the still visible traces within them of an ancient behavior:

Poetry relates without a doubt to some state of mankind anterior to the written word and to criticism. I find, then, a *very early man* in every true poet: he drinks at the sources of the language; he invents "verses"—more or less the way the most gifted primitives must have created "words" or the ancestors of words.

The more or less desirable gift of poetry seems to me, consequently, to attest a kind of *nobility* accorded not by documents in archives, but by the antiquity now observable in ways of feeling or reacting. Poets worthy of that great name reincarnate Amphion and Orpheus.[48]

In these evocations of a remote past, Valéry always attributed the power of magical incantations rather to their sonority than to their signification:

It was long supposed that certain combinations of words could be charged with more power than apparent meaning; were better understood by things than by men, by the rocks, waters, beasts, and gods, by the hidden treasures, the powers and wellsprings of life, than by the rational soul; were clearer for the Spirits than for the mind. Death itself sometimes yielded to rhythmic spells, and the tomb released a specter. Nothing more ancient nor, moreover, more *natural* than this belief in the force proper to the word, which was believed to act much less by its *exchange value* than by resonances which it stimulated in the substance of beings.

The effectiveness of "charms" was not so much in the resulting signification of their terms as in their sonorities and in the singularities of their form. Indeed, *obscurity* was almost essential to them.[49]

The effect of poetry, today, does not seem to depend on

conditions different from these. When he considers that "it is the poet's business to give us the sensation of the intimate union of language and the mind," Valéry regards this result as

> . . . strictly marvelous . . . in the sense we give this word when we think of the prestige and the prodigies of ancient magic. We must not forget that poetic form has been appropriated to the service of magic for centuries. Those who gave themselves up to these strange operations necessarily believed in the power of the word, and much more in the effectiveness of the sound of these words than in their meaning. Magic formulas are often quite meaningless; but it was not supposed that their power depended on their intellectual content.[50]

And the lines of Baudelaire he then quotes seem to him "to act upon us . . . without having much to tell us." These words "teach us perhaps that they have nothing to teach us . . . they act upon us in the fashion of a musical harmony."[51]

Charme is what Valéry prizes most in poets. It is the quality he recognizes in Baudelaire, at first with certain restrictions:

> B is a curious case. Great art and nonsense mixed together. Discoveries and poverties intimately compounded. Especially (what V.H. might envy him, and does not have), his secret: an "indefinable" charm, something like the momentary transfiguration of an ugly face.[52]

Then more generously:

> . . . he pursues and almost always achieves the production of *continuous charm*, an inestimable and almost transcendent quality of certain poems—but a quality rarely to be met with, and on those rare occasions rarely in a pure state, in the enormous output of Victor Hugo.[53]

When Valéry is delighted by Père Cyprien, it is because he has been ravished, without being able "to analyze the composition of that charm in which the greatest simplicity and the most exquisite 'distinction' unite in an admirable proportion."[54] As for Mallarmé, it is his case that led Valéry to develop his theory of the magical origin of poetry, and he compares the poet himself to a magician:

> It so happened that this poet, the least *primitive* of poets, gave, by the unexpected, strangely singing, and somehow *stupefying* juxtaposition of words—by the musical explosion of his verse and its singular plenitude, the impression of what was most powerful in poetry in its original state: the *magical formula*. An exquisite analysis of his art must have led him to a doctrine and to a kind of synthesis of incantation.[55]

Valéry thus attributes the notions of song, of enchantment, and of charm to the practice of numerous artists and writers; he makes a very seductive use of it, but never offers an analysis: the composition of *charms* remains Valéry's secret, if this secret exists. We occasionally glimpse, however, what constituted in his eyes the supreme effect of poetry. First of all, it separates us from our condition:

> Furthest from what prose performs and pursues, I placed that sensation of ravishment without reference. . . . It was the distance from man which ravished me. I did not know why an author was praised for being human, when everything which fulfills man is inhuman or superhuman. . . .[56]

Then, charm depends on the purity of the means of execution; Baudelaire and Manet

> . . . reject . . . the effects which are not deduced from a clear consciousness and from the possession of the means of their craft: in this consists the *purity* of painting as of poetry. They do not seek to speculate on "sentiment" nor to introduce "ideas" without having skillfully and subtly organized "sensation."[57]

Above all, charm is due to indeterminacy, to uncertainty, and to the incomplete nature of the work. "If a bird could say precisely what it was singing, why it was singing, and *what*, in itself, was singing, it would not sing."[58] And further, if the doctor achieved precision in his diagnoses and therapeutics, "he would lose all the *charm* which derives from the uncertainty of his art and from what individual magic he is indirectly supposed to add."[59] In short, the magician, becoming a scientist, loses his spell or charm. However hostile Valéry may be to "vague things," it is the imprecision of the poet's methods which permits charm: "We must leave some room for *chance* in our work in order that certain charms may function."[60] We do not know precisely how they function, but the theory of the creative misunderstanding here combines with a view which would be the reciprocal of the theory of excess in the total effect: ". . . the magic of literature necessarily derives from a 'certain error,' for the nature of language often permits us to give more than we possess. . . ."[61] Charm is, strictly speaking, a grace.

In a text published by Jean de Latour, Valéry insisted on the negative condition of the charm, which he felt depended on the freedom of the artist who does not force himself to carry the discipline of his labor to the rigor of a science and a complete enumeration of the properties of his substance:

> Work without method—that is, without the awareness that the development of attention invariably leads to properties (possibilities) of a finite number, the initial object of such attention being merely a "system of values"—is incompleted work . . . and OWES ITS CHARMS PRECISELY TO THIS INCOMPLETED STATE.[62]

This decisive formula follows some considerations on monotony, which Valéry regards as the price of method, since method consists in reducing all phenomena to a common measure:

> The acquisition of a "method" is paid for by an appearance of monotony. To record all phenomena in a system of homogeneous notations produces a generally *gray* impression. A "universe" translated into X, Y, Z, T, M, is less alluring than one represented by a painting in particular colors and forms.

Painting is an algebra of acts, but, "if this algebra were made explicit, the most brilliant painting would be defined by colorless expressions."[63] It would be a mistake to let Valéry appear submissive to a definitive defeat of the intelligence. He has just acknowledged that incompleteness produced charm; he will show that, by a method in two stages, one can reconquer—and this time, positively, with the infallibility of the poet-scientist, with the sureness of the man who has found "the central attitude"—all the brilliant and sensual diversity of a personal universe.

> But I also say that, if he desires, the man who employs method can easily, by a second operation, give his formulas an aspect as individual and attractive as is required.[64]

This would certainly be to possess the total science of effects. And charm, being only one effect among others, would then, theoretically, be a part of it. Yet Valéry does not tell us if the completed work can recover the graces of incomplete work, if we can fabricate the indefinable by definition, if to produce charm is equivalent to charming.

Among the specific effects of poetry, what is called the music of verse has an essential place. What Valéry has to say about it is somewhat disappointing and seems much less suggestive than what the analysis of his poems might reveal. He never discussed details of the methods of sonorous execution, which he may have regarded as professional secrets concerning which it is not to the poet's interest to attract attention. Here the implicit aesthetic would be much more interesting than the avowed one. On the other hand, Valéry quite copiously expressed himself on the relations of poetry and music and on the demands of musicality in verse, conceived in a very general fashion.

Valéry's attitude with regard to music is ambivalent. What most attracted him to this art was the mastery of a system of pure forms, without submission to the real objects by which poetry and painting are corrupted, in which composition obeys its own laws and can be developed in the fashion of geometry and analysis, characteristics by which music is related to architecture.[65] Yet Valéry has little sympathy for music; he may love it, but basically scorns and perhaps even fears it. . . . He reproaches it for its extreme hold over the sensibility: "Music is a massage,"[66] "a system of tickles upon a nervous system."[67] "And by it, I see that the profoundest thing . . . the *thing itself* . . . can be manipulated."[68] "I am made to dance, to pant, I am made to weep, to think; I am made to sleep; I am made overwhelming, overwhelmed; I am made light, darkness; diminished to the last thread and to silence."[69] Some entertaining letters to Pierre Louÿs suggest something of this disgust mixed with admiration: "Don't forget . . . that we are *against* music. Apollo *against* Dionysos."[70]

> I love music more than I respect it . . . one is possessed (like the Gadarene swine) and one has the shudder, the pain in the belly, the cold sweat, the nausea in the soul, horripilation—all the symptoms of great art and epilepsy. . . . Symptoms of depth, of the divine intellection, of grace, impossible dances, revolting kindness, the wheedling of a sickly childhood, a woman's despairs; symptoms of forces and fabulous movements, of inimitable melancholies; roars without lions, loves in which the spasm lasts fifty minutes, hysterical forests, marches of the imperial battalion, who knows what!
>
> All the sham of man *in extremis*, all the delirium of greatness, of persecution, everything impossible, irrational, but all this *realized in part!*[71]

Valéry resents music's alienation of his freedom: "It is the type of external control. . . ."[72] "All this is certain rather than *true*, and controlled by pressing a button. . . ."[73] "There is a sense which permits man to manipulate man without mercy."[74] Socrates sees Phaedrus the "slave of Music's general presence," "imprisoned" with "that inexhaustible production of glamor . . . and constrained to be so, like a pythoness in her room of smoke."[h]

Do we not discern in this furious, absurd, and amused vexation an artist's jealousy of an art which possesses means more effective than his own? As a listener, he is disgusted; as an author, he envies it. For "to manipulate man"—is that not the goal of this science of effects which unfortunately appears to wreck the uncertainties of exchanges? When Valéry confessed: "My 'injustice' with regard to Music derives, perhaps, from the sentiment that such a power is capable of sustaining life to the point of the absurd,"[75] is he not giving an idea of the Music's scope quite analogous to that he ex-

[h] *Eupalinos*, p. 126. Cf. *Au Concert Lamoureux en 1893* in *Pièces sur l'art*, p. 80: "Music has its way with us," the beginning of the article of 1889, *Sur la technique littéraire*.

pressed when he exalted the dynamic effects of poetry on the
living being? Further, he concedes that the intellectual pathos
which he reproached poetry for neglecting, and which he
himself established in poetry, can be suggested by Music in
several of its forms:

> Music has in its favor, by its almost direct action on
> the central nervous system, means of producing (and al-
> most in advance) all the illusions of a complete life, all
> the fantasmagoria of the passions, of sensual events, and
> sometimes even goes so far as to insinuate if not intelli-
> gence, at least the acts of intelligence.[1]

In the letter to Pierre Louÿs of June 13, 1917, he acknowledges that music lies in the path of intelligence:

> For me, it always suggests (when I enjoy it) not a
> thing done, but a thing to be done. . . . Music, ac-
> cording to Paul, is a recording method (a very precious
> one) which intercalates itself between the Impression and
> the Intellect. That is why the best music is the most
> *rigorous*.[76]

"Between Being and Knowing, operates Music, powerful
and vain."[77] And when Valéry sought words capable of suggesting the poetry of ideas—or rather of what is stimulating in
ideas, that is, their appearance, for thought is not poetic by
itself—it was words remote from their practical value and
endowed with a power of resurrection close to that of music
that he insisted on:

> What is exciting in ideas is not ideas; it is what is not
> yet thought, what is nascent and not yet born, which
> excites. Hence we must have words with which one can
> never be through—and which are never identically
> canceled out by any representation whatever: *Music
> words*. . . .[78]

[1] *Propos et souvenirs* in *Revue de France*, October 1925. Cf. *Au
Concert Lamoureux en 1893* in *Pièces sur l'art*, p. 80: "It . . .
imitates the combinations of thought," and the letter of February
15, 1944 to Robert Bernard in *Paul Valéry vivant*, p. 494: "Music
intimidates me, and the musician's art confounds me. He possesses
all the powers I envy. He directly influences the system of our emotions. . . . Further, Music is calculation: it offers the intelligence
an enormous realm of pure combination—another subject of envy
for the poet."

Valéry often claimed the poet's disadvantage in relation to the musician. The poet works with an impure instrument, normally intended for practical purposes, the musician possesses means purified by a very long tradition:

> Fortunate the musician! The evolution of his art has granted him, for centuries, a highly privileged situation . . . ancient observations and experiments have permitted the deduction, from the *universe of noises*, of a system or *universe of sounds*, which are particularly simple and recognizable noises, particularly apt to form combinations, associations. . . .[j]

The poet, "pursuing an object which does not differ excessively from the musician's,"[79] is deprived "of the enormous advantages" the latter possesses:

> He does not have in front of him, ready for the goals of beauty, a group of means created expressly for his art. He must borrow *language*—the public voice. . . . Nothing pure; but a mixture of auditory and psychic stimuli which are utterly incoherent.[k]
>
> He must at every moment create or re-create what the musician finds already made and ready to hand . . . *a sound which produces itself is enough to evoke the entire musical universe*.[l]

"Music is granted a universe of choices,"[80] "possesses a domain entirely its own,"[81] while "the poet is constrained to create, with each work, *the universe of poetry*—that is, the psychic and affective state in which language can play a role utterly different from that of signifying what is or was or will be."[82] He must invent "a language within language."[83] "His scale is constructed each time."[m]

[j] *Poésie pure. Notes pour une conférence* in *Oeuvres complètes*, vol. C, p. 206. The idea is developed in *Propos sur la poésie* in *Conferencia*, 1928, p. 468 and pursued in *Poésie et pensée abstraite* in *Variété V*, p. 145.

[k] *Poésie et pensée abstraite* in *Variété V*, p. 146–47. "It is not possible to construct a universe of language similar to that of sounds or colors" (*Cours de poétique*, lecture 8).

[l] *Propos sur la poésie* in *Conferencia*, 1928, p. 468. The same formula occurs in *Poésie et pensée abstraite* in *Variété V*, pp. 145–46.

[m] *Calepin d'un poète* in *Oeuvres complètes*, vol. C, p. 194. Lec-

This privileged music, according to Valéry, exercised a considerable influence on modern poetry. Paying homage to Lamoureux, toward whom, he says, "literature's debt is enormous," he asserts that

> . . . any literary history of the end of the nineteenth century which does not speak of music will be of no use. . . . One can understand nothing of the poetic movement which developed from 1840 or 1850 to our own times if the profound and capital role which music has played . . . is not explained. . . . This kind of re-education of poetry (considered in the period which extends from 1800 to 1900) had Lamoureux and the Concerts Lamoureux, as agents of first importance. As Baudelaire had the Concerts Pasdeloup, Mallarmé and his followers had the Concerts Lamoureux.[84]

Which sounds quite reasonable. Poets may have conceived, at concerts, the desire to compete with music. Let us note, all the same, that this was not the case with Baudelaire, whose *Fleurs du mal* appeared four years before the opening of the *Concerts populaires de musique classique* founded by Pasdeloup. As for Mallarmé, it was only after 1885 that he frequented the *Concerts Lamoureux* (founded in 1880); long before this he had written *Hérodiade* and *L'Après-Midi d'un faune,* at a time when he despised all music.[n] What was the effect of this music cure?

> The musical education . . . of a growing number of French writers contributed more than any theoretical considerations to orienting poetry toward a purer destiny and to eliminating from its productions all that prose can express so exactly.[85]

---

ture 9 of the *Cours de poétique* gives this interesting variant: "The musician has in front of him the possibility of producing an infinite number of effects with a finite number of means."

[n] See Henri Mondor, *Vie de Mallarmé*, p. 458: "On Good Friday, Edouard Dujardin escorted to the Concert Lamoureux, which they had never attended, both Huysmans and Mallarmé," and, in a footnote, these lines by the poet's daughter, Geneviève: "It was around 1886 that my father discovered all the magic of music. As a young man, he had despised it. It used to be said in those days: music is in the verse. He never wanted me to learn to play the piano . . ."

As music separated sounds from noises,

> so Poetry sought . . . to distinguish (insofar as it could)
> in language, expressions in which meaning, rhythm,
> sonorities of the voice and movement harmonize with
> and reinforce one another, while it tried on the other
> hand to proscribe expressions in which meaning is inde-
> pendent of musical form, of any auditive value.[86]

And all this by the major grace of Lamoureux! Valéry evokes
the "young men stacked in the two-franc galleries," and "on a
bench in the Promenoir, sitting in the shadows behind a wall
of standees, a singular listener . . . STÉPHANE MALLARMÉ,"
who

> . . . submitted with delight, but with that angelic sweet-
> ness which is born of superior rivalries, to the enchant-
> ment of Beethoven or of Wagner. . . . He desperately
> searched for the means of recovering for our art the
> marvels, the importance that too-powerful Music had
> stolen from it,[o]

which was an echo of Mallarmé, already repeated by Valéry
in his definition of Symbolism:

> What was baptized *Symbolism* can be summarized
> very simply in the intention common to several families
> of poets (quite hostile to each other, moreover) to "take
> back their own from Music."[p]

Valéry said, in this regard, that he and his colleagues were
"fed on music"; ". . . our literary heads dreamed only of deriving from language almost the same effects as purely sonorous causes produced upon our nervous beings."[87]

The musical effects of poetry have only remote connections
with music proper, and the rhythmic and melodic methods

---

[o] *Au Concert Lamoureux en 1893* in *Pièces sur l'art*, pp. 83–84.
Cf. *Existence du Symbolisme* in *Oeuvres complètes*, vol. L, p. 128:
". . . to restore to Poetry the same empire which great modern
Music had taken from it."

[p] *Avant-propos* in *Variété*, p. 95. Mallarmé had written (*Vers
et musique en France* in *The National Observer*, republished in
Crise de Vers, 1892): ". . . we are now precisely at the point
where we seek . . . an art of completing the transposition, to the
Book, of the symphony, or simply to take back our own. . . ."

the poet employs are scarcely comparable with those of the musician. Verse has its special harmony which has always been required of poets, more or less rigorously. Valéry made it the supreme criterion of poetry:

> I have adopted the system of considering above everything else . . . the language itself, and its harmony. . . .
>
> When it is a question of a poem, the musical condition is absolute; if the author has not taken it into account, pondered on it . . . we must despair of this man who seeks to sing without really feeling the necessity to do so. . . .[88]

Reading the verses of Père Cyprien, Valéry immediately recognized their magical power. "Oh! . . . I thought, this sings all by itself! There is no other way of being sure about poetry."[q] But Valéry never went into the details of this insistence on song. He occasionally employed terms such as rhythm, accent, assonance, and alliteration, he sometimes alluded to a play of timbres,[r] he praised in passing the delicate mute vowels of a line by Mallarmé,[89] he remarked on an effect of symmetry,[s] but we find nowhere an analysis of rhythmic or sonorous effects and of their causes. It is in *Regards sur le monde actuel*, a collection of texts concerning politics, that

[q] *"Cantiques Spirituels"* in *Variété* V, p. 172. He said to Jean Ballard (*Celui que j'ai connu* in *Paul Valéry vivant*, p. 244): ". . . a poem can be judged by three criteria. First of all, I test its music, no more, like a series of notes—then I test its words, its language . . . lastly I turn to the ideas, if there are any left!"

[r] *De la diction des vers* in *Pièces sur l'art*, p. 47. "Take every opportunity to savor the words, listen for the harmonics, the timbres of Racine, the nuances, the reciprocal reflections of his vowels, the distinct and pure acts, the supple links of his consonants and of their arrangement.

[s] See Xavier de Courville, *Un souvenir de Paul Valéry. Le Colloque sur Bajazet* in *Revue de L'Alliance française*, June 1945, p. 6: "In the line *Je voulais qu'il m'aimât: chère Zaïre, il m'aime . . .* Do you hear that correspondence between *il* and *Zaïre*? Do you see that symmetry between *il m'aimât* and *il m'aime*?" In *Les Droits du poète sur la langue* in *Pièces sur l'art*, pp. 56–57, Valéry justifies a curious symmetry between two diaereses of a line in *La Jeune Parque: Délicieux linceuls, mon désordre tiède . . .* ". . . On my own authority and against practice, I employed the 'diaeresis' *ti-è-de*, so as to obtain a certain effect, symmetry: *Deli-ci-eux—ti-è-de*. I found a voluptuous nuance in it. . . ."

we are obliged to seek out what Valéry said at any length on the verbal resources of the French language:

> French poetry differs musically from all others, to the point of sometimes having been regarded as virtually deprived of the charms and resources which are available to the poet in other languages. I believe this is an error; but this error, as often happens, is an illegitimate and subjective deduction from an exact observation.
>
> . . . Three characteristics clearly distinguish French from the other Occidental languages: French, properly spoken, has virtually no *song* in it. It is a discourse of narrow range, a speech flatter than the others. Second: French consonants are remarkably softened: no rough or guttural figures. No French consonant is impossible for a European to pronounce. Lastly, French vowels are numerous and very varied, forming a rare and precious collection of delicate timbres which offer poets worthy of the name certain values by whose interplay they can counterbalance the limited range and general moderation of accents in their language. The variety of *é* and *è*, the rich diphthongs such as *feuille, rouille, paille, pleure, toise, tien*, etc., the mute *e* which sometimes exists, sometimes is virtually imperceptible if not entirely effaced, which affords so many subtle effects of elementary silences, or which terminates or extends so many words by a kind of shadow which an accented syllable seems to cast after it—such are the means whose effectiveness can be shown by an infinity of examples.†

These remarks are judicious (one can find no quarrel with them, except the example of *pleure* as a diphthong: the explosive *e* of *pleure* is as simple as that of the article *le*), but add nothing to our knowledge, even the subtle hints as to the values of the mute *e*. Let us add that Valéry was deeply suspicious of the "phonetic criticism of poems based on the analysis of recorded documents. . . . Aesthetic prescriptions cannot be deduced from these. The machine . . . merely

† *Images de la France* in *Regards sur le monde actuel et autres essais*, pp. 126–27. Some of these sentences are repeated in two articles collected in the same volume: *Pensée et Art français*, p. 182, *Coup d'oeil sur les lettres françaises*, p. 278. Lecture 8 of the *Cours de poétique* declares that the French language is not very musical but it has lovely vowels.

takes down the voice in its own fashion . . . and this diction is worth what it is worth." And there we have scrutinized all of Valéry's ideas as to verbal music. The most interesting thing he has to say concerns the melodic curve of the poem, but of this he speaks, though with exquisite sensitivity, only by metaphor. It is his theory of the *recitative*. We know that he was aiming at an effect of this sort in *La Jeune Parque*:

> My intention was to compose a kind of discourse in which the sequence of lines would be developed or deduced in such a way that the entire piece would produce an impression analogous to that of the *recitatives* of the past. Those which are to be found in Gluck, and especially in *Alcestis*, had been infinitely suggestive. I envied that line.[90]

But beyond Gluck, it was Racine he was thinking of:

> Among all the poets, Racine is the one most directly related to music proper—that Racine whose periods so often suggest recitatives only a little less *singing* than those of lyrical compositions—that Racine whose trage- dies Lully was to attend so studiously; and of whose lines and movements the lovely forms and pure develop- ments of Gluck seem immediate transformations.[u]

Whatever the means by which it is obtained, and whatever the effects it produces, the "phonetic figure" enjoys a remark- able property: it engraves itself on the memory. This is an es- sential merit for Valéry. A beautiful line is one that is re- membered:

---

[u] *De la diction des vers* in *Pièces sur l'art*, p. 45. Cf. Charles Du Bos, *Journal*, January 23, 1923, pp. 227–28: ". . . entire passages of *La Jeune Parque* were composed while I was picking out recita- tives by Gluck on the piano." The metaphoric aspect is emphasized when we find Valéry indicating the great difference between Mal- larmé and himself "with regard to the music of verse": "This is because Mallarmé always seeks the orchestral effect . . . as such, *L'Après-Midi d'un faune* seems to me a masterpiece that will not be surpassed. For me, on the contrary, the musical unity in verse is the sound, the voice, the recitative of Gluck, sometimes of Wag- ner, but especially of Gluck. . . ." See further the letter to Aimé Lafont in *Paul Valéry, l'homme et l'oeuvre*, p. 9: "The notion of the recitatives in lyric drama (for one voice) has haunted me. I confess that Gluck and Wagner were my secret models."

These sensuous properties of the language are in a remarkable relation with the memory. The various formations of syllables, of intensities, and of tempi which can be constituted are unequally favorable to preservation by memory, as they are, moreover, to vocal utterance. It is as if some had more affinity than others with the mysterious support of memory: each seems to have a specific probability of exact restitution which depends on its phonetic figure.

The instinct for this mnemonic value of form seems very strong and very sure in Mallarmé, whose verses are so readily remembered.[v]

Valéry was led to investigate the means which favor the preservation of ideas:

The incessant attack of the mind, objection, transmission from mouth to mouth, phonetic alteration, the impossibility of verification, etc., are the causes of destruction, of corruption, of these mental reservations. Given this list of dangers, the chief imaginable means for combating them appear: rhythms, rhyme, rigor, and choice of words, search for the limit expression, etc. . . . auxiliaries of memory, guarantees of the exactitude of exchanges, and of the mind's return to its landmarks.[91]

Or more poetically:

The wisest and the best-inspired of men seek to give their thoughts a harmony and a cadence which protect them from alterations as from oblivion.[92]

This was to make form the guarantee of a work's duration in accord with Mistral's formula: *"There is only form . . . form alone preserves the works of the mind."*[w] It is therefore with form that the poet must be chiefly concerned:

[v] *Je disais quelquefois à Stéphane Mallarmé* in *Variété III*, p. 19. Valéry, who often complained of his verbal memory, who could never learn a lecture by heart, who could recall, he claimed, no more than two hundred or three hundred lines of poetry, was greatly struck by the fact that Mallarmé's poems came back to him without effort (see *Mallarmé* in *Conferencia*, April 15, 1933, and *Propos me concernant*, pp. 5-6, 51).

[w] *Victor Hugo créateur par la forme* in *Vues*, p. 173. Here he actually defines the *form* of a work: ". . . the totality of sensuous characteristics by which the physical action is imposed and tends to

Even in the lightest pieces, he must think of duration, that is, of *memory*, that is, of form, as the builders of steeples and towers think of structure.[93]

Thus the solid work, "*l'art robuste*," survives the city, as Gautier says, if not the civilizations which now know they are mortal; such at least is the ambition which animates its author, if we understand this somewhat composite formula which unites the example of Mallarmé (opposed to that of Zola) with the memory of Gautier:

A diamond lasts longer than a capital and than a civilization. The desire for perfection seeks to make itself independent of time. . . .[94]

But it is difficult for the poet to distinguish, among the words that occur to him, those which will be unforgettable. According to Valéry:

Memory is the writer's judge. It must decide if its Man conceives and determines *forgettable* forms; and warn him. It must tell him: don't leave what you have made at this point, I feel I will not retain it.[95]

Unfortunately this guide is not very clairvoyant. Furthermore, the means of preservation: rhythm, rhyme, etc., function without aesthetic consideration. If we treasure

Dormeuse, amas doré d'ombres et d'abandons

we remember just as well, despite ourselves,

Car elle avait gardé les pattes pour sa mère . . .

Verse preserves everything, even nonsense.

Valéry, who loved the inventors of forms[96] to the point of hoping to greet the inventor of the sonnet among the shades,[97] sketched a theory of *pure verse*—that is, verse whose content would be borrowed and only the form invented. This would be the ultimate separation of sound and sense, which we know must be both independent and indis-

---

resist all causes of dissolution . . ." In *Autres rhumbs* in *Tel quel*, II, p. 159, a less optimistic formula: "Form is the skeleton of works. . . . All works die; but those with a skeleton last much longer than those composed of nothing but soft parts."

soluble in the poem. It involves no more than the very humble phenomenon of verse translation. Valéry made this his pretext for attributing the superiority of the great French poets of the seventeenth century to their habit of translation:

> The men who carried this poetry to the highest point were all *translators* . . . experienced in transferring the ancients into our language.
> Their poetry is marked by these habits. It is a translation. A *faithless fair*—faithless to what is not in agreement with the requirements of a pure language.[98]

Their verse accepts only what suits its nature. This is why Valéry praises Père Cyprien, the adaptor of the hymns of Saint John of the Cross, but this time, granting him fidelity as well:

> It is not possible to be more faithful. The priest-translator has modified the type of the strophe, no doubt. He has adopted our octosyllable instead of following the variations of the meter proposed. He has understood that prosody must accommodate the language, and he has not tried, as others have done (especially in the sixteenth and the nineteenth centuries), to impose on French what French does not impose or does not propose of itself to the French ear. This is truly to *translate*, which is to reconstitute as closely as possible the *effect* of a certain *cause*—here, a text in Spanish—by means of another cause—a text in French.[x]

But Père Cyprien's great merit is especially to have been

> . . . a consummate artist in the fine art of making verses in the pure state. By making verses in the pure state, I mean that there is nothing of *him* in the work I speak of except, precisely, the making of the form. All the rest—ideas, images, choice of words—belongs to Saint John of the Cross. The translation being of an extreme fidelity, nothing remained for the versifier except the narrowest liberty jealously conceded to him by our

---

[x] "*Cantiques spirituels*" in *Variété* V, p. 173. Valéry declared elsewhere that "a true poet is strictly untranslatable; form and thought are of equal power; the virtue of the poem is one and indivisible" (*Allocution solennelle prononcée le 24 septembre 1939 au Théâtre-Français* in *Vues*, p. 381).

severe language and the rigor of our prosody. This meant having to dance loaded with chains. The more explicit this problem is to the mind, the more we admire the grace and the elegance with which it has been solved: to do so required the most exquisite poetic gifts exercised under the most adverse conditions.[99]

If Père Cyprien could manifest "the most exquisite poetic gifts" by working solely upon the language and by obeying the conventions of regular verse, without having to furnish anything of himself in the poem's content, is poetry not, then a pre-eminently formal thing? The Abbé Delille translated Virgil into elegant and often melodious verse; yet we realize that there is an abyss between Virgil and Delille. It is likely that as wide an abyss separates Père Cyprien from Saint John of the Cross. To translate as a poet is not quite to be a poet, unless the imitation is counterbalanced and exceeded by the marks of an evident originality, and this is the only thing that is true in the paradox which makes the classic writers translators. The content of the lines cannot be treated simply as a supplementary convention, and their musicality, however essential, is not the root of poetic sentiment.

Pure verse is merely an ingenious amusement. Valéry offered more interesting considerations on the elocution of verse. This, for him, is the touchstone of the poem. More generally, there is no work without execution, or, at least, for the arts which do not distinguish public from performer, without interpretation:

> A work of the mind exists only in action. Outside this action, what remains is merely an object which affords no particular relation to the mind. Move the statue you admire to a nation sufficiently different from your own: it is no more than a meaningless stone. A Parthenon is merely a minor marble quarry.[100]
>
> Poetry is . . . essentially "*in actu.*" A poem exists only at the moment of its elocution, and its *true value* is inseparable from *this condition of execution.*[101]
>
> It is the execution of the poem which is the poem. Outside of it, these curiously assembled successions of words are inexplicable fabrications.[102]

There must, then, be an interpreter:

A poem, like a piece of music, offers *in itself* merely a text, which is strictly no more than a kind of recipe; the cook who executes it plays an essential part.[103]

It is the interpreter who makes the poem real:

> Texts or scores are . . . merely systems of conventional signs, each of which, syllable or note, must stimulate an action to which it corresponds. The quality of each of these actions, that of their connection and of their mysterious successive correspondence, depends entirely on the person who *acts* and who performs the transmutation of the *virtual* work into a *real* one.[104]

If Valéry had not elsewhere told us that he acknowledged a kind of interior elocution, which is obviously the most frequent kind, since we read poems much more often than we hear them recited, we might find his theory of the poem's realization somewhat exaggerated. Indeed the poem is often spoiled by the interpreter, and there is no lover of poetry whom a simple reading in silence deprives of the poem's song. Every reader of poetry actually hears the lines he reads, or remembers; further, he articulates them; the inner language and the auditive imagination here come close to hallucinatory power. The mute reader of poetry resembles those musical connoisseurs who hear the entire orchestra merely by reading of a score. And he finds the interpreter *in himself*. I do not believe Valéry offers much objection to the fact.

On the diversity of interpretations, Valéry made various perceptive remarks. There are almost as many dictions as poets, each making "his work according to his singular ear," or as genres, types, or meters, and especially as interpreters.[105] An interpreter "can effect astonishing transmutations of euphony into cacophony, or of cacophony into euphony."[106]

> It can happen . . . that a poem or a melody that we *know* to be very mediocre borrows from a carefully modulated voice of fine timbre a power and a pleasure which at first surprise our judgment. The contrary is, I believe, less rare: there is no masterpiece which has not been murdered a thousand times over . . . these great model works are the favorite victims, sometimes of *too much*, sometimes of *too little* talent.[107]

Nonetheless, Valéry took up the virtuoso's defense: "The virtuoso embodies the work"; he "gives it life and real presence";[108] "it is the interpreter who gives the first impressions of the as yet unpublished work to the public: on him depends whether it is understood or acknowledged"; we therefore cannot deny him "a freedom and a certain initiative whose limits it is impossible to define."[109]

The essential thing, in the poem's execution, is to place

> . . . this text in the final conditions where it will assume the power and shape of action. A poem is a discourse which requires and involves a continuous link between *the voice which is* and the *voice which is to come* and *which must come*. And this voice must be such that it imposes itself and stimulates the affective state of which the text is the unique verbal expression. Take away the voice, the right voice . . . and the poem changes into a series of signs. . . .[110]

After what Valéry said of the incommunicability of author and reader, it is difficult to believe he meant to give the interpreter's voice the mission of transmitting the poet's state of feeling to the hearer. It must simply be a question of waking the sentiment with which the text is charged, and which requires, in order to act upon the hearer, "the right voice" of an intelligent and well-endowed interpreter;[y] this would be, as I have said, an effect of the work, not of the author. Yet Valéry seems to have conceded some appearance of communication between the author and the interpreter, when he wrote:

> This human energy, these intelligently directed forces which the constructor had anticipated, this life, this accent, these sonorities which Racine or Mozart had found in their being—it is up to the executant to rediscover them in himself and to apply them to the mechanism constituted by a score or a text. And all this, this entire essential part of the work, is not written. It cannot be written.[111]

[y] "An intelligent reader places the accents, the tone, the timbre, and the rhythms which impose a soul upon the reading" (*Au sujet de Berthe Morisot* in *Vues*, p. 343).

Let us note, all the same, that what the interpreter must rediscover in himself of the poet or the musician is neither ideas nor feelings, but solely dynamic or formal factors (though we do not quite see why they cannot be established within the work, notably the sonorities). It is quite likely that the difficulties which Valéry saw in the exchanges between author and reader are reproduced between author and interpreter, with this aggravation: that the interpreter's distortions are transmitted to the public, or with this advantage: that the distortions are the source of "creative misunderstandings." Valéry certainly accommodated himself to mistakes of execution as to those of reading. If there is no true meaning of a poem, there cannot be a true interpretation:

> There is no very fine work which is not susceptible of a great variety of equally plausible interpretations. The richness of a work is the number of meanings or values which it can receive while remaining itself.[112]

Valéry tried to produce a satisfactory image of the interpreter of poetry, of the "ideal reader" to whom "every poet necessarily entrusts himself in his work . . . and who, moreover, resembles him a little more than a brother."[113] His notion of the elocution of verse derives from the natural position of poetry, which he situates between discourse and song, but closer to the latter; it is a well-tempered music:

> Poetry is not music; it is still less discourse. It is perhaps this ambiguity which constitutes its delicacy. One can say that it is *about to sing*, more than it sings; and that it is *about to explain itself*, more than it actually does so. It dares not ring out too loud, nor speak too clearly. It haunts neither the peaks nor the abysses of the voice. It is content with its hills and with a very moderate profile. But by rhythm, by accents and consonances, doing what it can, it attempts to communicate a quasi-musical virtue to the expression of certain thoughts. Not of all thoughts.[114]

Valéry thus very justly proposed to relate poetic elocution to song, in a fashion likely to remove it from the usual tone of language, but he advised the executant to take a position on the level of the former, requiring him to do no more than attenuate his system in order to reach the correct tone that suits the poem:

> One must not, in the study of a piece of poetry that one wishes to recite, take for the origin or point of departure of one's investigation, ordinary discourse, and common speech, in order to rise from this flat prose to the desired poetic tone; but on the contrary, I believe that one should make *song* one's basis, put oneself in the state of the singer, accommodate one's voice to the plenitude of the musical sound, and from there descend to the somewhat less vibrant state which suits verse. It seems to me that this is the only means of preserving the musical essence of poems. Above all, *place* the voice quite far from prose, study the text in relation to the attacks, modulations, tones which it involves, and gradually reduce this arrangement, which will be exaggerated at the start, to the proportions of poetry.[115]

Madame Croiza, whom Valéry had urged to recite certain poems by Ronsard according to these principles, offered him the ideal interpreter, since the famous soprano could, better than an actress, perform that slight movement of reducing the song to a musical delivery of verse as desired by the poet:

> The usual elocution starts from prose and raises itself to verse. . . . But I wanted to try a voice which on the contrary would descend from the full melody of musicians to our melody of poets, limited and tempered as it is. I dreamed of employing in this singular mode of making oneself heard a voice possessing a full range, a voice much more extended than the voice which generally suffices for poetry: a trained, vital voice, much more conscious, clearer in its attacks, richer in its sonorities, more attentive to tempi and silences, more marked in changes of tone, than the voice ordinarily employed in reciting versified works.[z]

[z] *Lettre à Madame C.* in *Pièces sur l'art*, pp. 52–53. It is diverting to set beside these praises some words flung at the members of the teaching profession with that not always well-informed scorn which was the illustrious poet's favorite sin. He fulminated against "the detestable practice which consists of . . . treating poems like things, cutting them up . . . allowing if not obliging them to be recited in the traditional way, used as tests of memory or spelling" (*Leçon inaugurale du Cours de poétique* in *Variété V*, p. 310),

Valéry was invited to give advice to future interpreters of *Bajazet*. This was an occasion, for a lover of Racine's verses, to restore their melodic value sometimes sacrificed to the dramatic movement. He had already said elocution might "identify the tone of the drama, or the movement of the eloquence, with the intrinsic music of the language. Thereby the interpreter gains in effects what the poem loses in harmony."[116] He was harsher in addressing the actors. He urged them to renounce "that detestable . . . tradition which consists in sacrificing to the direct effects of the stage all the musical scope of the play." This tradition destroys, in effect, "the continuity, the infinite melody which is so deliciously apparent in Racine." And he recommended that they first master the melody of the lines and not be in any hurry to reach the meaning. The latter must not "spoil the form of the music." It must be introduced only at the end, "as the supreme nuance which will transfigure without altering your piece." In the last place, with this music can be mingled "the necessary accents and accidents to make it appear to well up from the affections and the passions of a human being."[117] It is then that the actor will "distinguish among the verses":

> Some serve the play itself . . . they announce, provoke, release events; they answer logical questions; they

utilizing them "as a collection of grammatical difficulties or examples (ibid., p. 309), "considering [sound and sense] separately," "an offense and an absurdity which are unfortunately a constant and virtually obligatory practice in the teaching of Letters" (*La Poésie de La Fontaine* in *Vues*, p. 161), ". . . the teaching of poetry is absurd, being utterly unconcerned by pronunciation and diction" (*L'Invention esthétique* in *L'Invention*, p. 150). "The custom is literally to drone through, moreover with never the least idea of rhythm, of assonance and alliteration . . ." (*Le Bilan de l'intelligence* in *Variété III*, p. 299). "Teaching has no ears . . ." (*Le Musée de Montpellier* in *Vues*, p. 269). The instructors are not the only ones to blame: a love of poetry "is excessively rare. My experience has shown me that a true predilection for poetry is quite uncommon among us, where this form of the art of language is either tinged with some ridicule or incompatible with serious-mindedness, and generally identified with the oratorical expression of tragedy, with rhymed ingenuity, or with sentimental effusions of indigent form" (*Au temps de Marcel Prévost* in *Vues*, pp. 211–12).

allow the drama to be summarized, and are, in a sense,
on a level with prose. It is a great art to articulate these
necessary verses. . . . But other lines, which are the
whole poetry of the work, sing. . . .[aa]

The idea of song dominates the Valerian conception of the
specific effects of poetry. We recognize it to be of three kinds:
1) the song of *charm* (as of a painting that sings); 2) the
song of the *verse* (the continuous melody of the lines); 3)
the song of the *voice*, which interprets and realizes it. That
these meanings are intimately linked is evident in this passage
in which they secretly change places:

It is essential and sufficient, for the certainty of poetry
to exist . . . that the simple arrangement of words . . .
oblige our voice, even our inner voice, to free itself from
the tone and delivery or ordinary discourse, and place
it in an altogether different *tempo*. This intimate control
of impulse and of rhythmic action profoundly transforms all the values of the text which imposes it upon us.
This text . . . functions to make us live a rather different
life, to breathe according to this second life, and supposes a state or a world in which the objects and the beings to be found there, or rather their images, have other
liberties and other links than those of the practical world.
The names of these images play a role henceforth in
their fate: and our thoughts often follow the fate assigned to them by sonority or the number of the syllables of these names; they are enriched by the similarities
and contrasts they awaken: all of this affords finally the

[aa] *De la diction des vers,* pp. 48–49. We know that Valéry,
though he composed lyrical works for the stage (*Amphion* and
Sémiramis, "melodramas"; *Cantate du Narcisse,* libretto) and pon-
dered a "*liturgical* conception of spectacles" (*Histoire d'Amphion*
in *Variété III; Mes théâtres* in *Vues*), always insisted he had been
misunderstood with regard to the theater (*De la diction des vers*
in *Pièces sur l'art,* p. 35; *Notes sur un tragique et une tragédie,*
p. xii). The much greater interest he showed in poetry led him,
oddly enough, to limit the tragedy of *Phèdre:* "There remains for
me the idea of a certain woman, the impression of the beauty of a
discourse. . . . Everyone except the queen dissolves almost at once
into his absence. . . . The work is reduced in memory to a monologue; and shifts within me from the initial dramatic state to the
pure lyric state—for lyricism is merely the transfiguration of a
monologue" (*Sur Phèdre femme* in *Variété V,* pp. 185–86).

notion of an enchanted nature, subject, as though by a charm or spell, to the caprice, to the glamor, to the powers of language.[118]

There remains lastly the effect, or the effects, which we include under the name of beauty. We may wonder if they belong in the category of the poetic. For Valéry, there is no doubt about the matter. He is the man who wrote: "A very beautiful line of verse is a very pure element of poetry." We have already seen that what characterizes the beautiful is perfection and completion, "the sensation of our powerlessness to modify it." "The impression of beauty . . . is . . . that sentiment of an impossibility of variation." When Valéry declared that a poem was never finished, strictly speaking, he was taking the point of view of the author. When he takes the point of view of the reader, it is the work's immutability which seems to him the guarantee of its solidity and duration. The beautiful poem *resists*. Such is the effect of the beautiful on the reader considered as active. If we regard the reader as passive, contemplative (which is a more frequent state, through which the energetic reader must have passed initially), we note that the beautiful produces "effects of ineffability, indescribability, unutterableness,"[119] that is, in practical terms, a mute surprise, or one incapable of expressing itself adequately.[120]

> Literature tries by "words" to create the "state of being at a loss for words." Beauty is thus: negation, plus thirst caused by what is expressed in such powerlessness, plus "infinity" of this thirst, *plux* X. . . .[121]

The beautiful leaves us speechless, eager to delight in it endlessly (this is the "aesthetic infinite"), conscious of the impossibility of explaining it, of exhausting it.[bb] When this effect is produced, it is comparable to the dazzlement of the total effect; it transfixes us in admiration.

[bb] See in *Mélange*, p. 30, the passage: "Beauty speaks or sings, and we do not know what she says. . . ."

PARTICULAR EFFECTS

The particular effects are as numerous as the nuances of
sensibility. Aesthetics has largely neglected them.[cc] Those
Valéry discussed most often were strongly marked by his
spirit of suspicion. One is even shocked to find Valéry apply-
ing this term *effects* to impressions which ordinarily involve
sentiments of respect and authenticity. This is the case of
profundity:

> I loathe false profundity, but I'm not too fond of the
> real thing. Literary profundity is the fruit of a special
> method. It is an effect like any other—obtained by a
> method like any other. —It is enough to see how a
> book of *pensées* is produced—and I mean profound
> thoughts.[122]

He said one day: "There is something that annoys me
about Goethe. I have the impression he has *a device for
sounding profound.*"[123] Such witticisms did not keep him
from paying a brilliant tribute to Goethe nor from admiring
one form of profundity, the kind which is fruitful and exact:
"A *profound* idea is an idea or a remark which profoundly
transforms a given question or situation. If not, it is a matter

[cc] Traditionally classified among aesthetic categories, in a rather
loose way, are effects such as the comic, the tragic, etc. Valéry
spoke very little of them, though he was interested in laughter and
in tears, as in all emotive reactions. He was surprised that in La
Fontaine's *Contes,* "the things of love should be treated as farce
and employed in the production of comic effects, though in reality
they constitute pathetic and tragic powers" (*La Poésie de La
Fontaine* in *Vues,* p. 166). His *Notes sur un tragique et une
tragédie* speak only incidentally of the "intense effects" (p. xiv) of
tragedy, which he regarded as a game "with horror" (p. xv) whose
pleasure continues to seem strange to him and opposed "to the
highest state which art can create . . . the contemplative state."
Thus he praises the Greeks for having imposed "upon the most
horrible stories in the world . . . all the purity and perfection of a
form which communicates to the spectator of the crimes and the
dreadful things being shown him, some sensation of regarding this
hideous chaos with a divine eye" (p. xv).

of resonance, and we are in literature."dd What he pursued with his sarcasms was the simulation of genius by glamor and eloquence:

> A writer is *profound* when his discourse, *once translated from language into unequivocal thought,* impels me to a reflection of perceptibly useful duration.
> But the underlined condition is essential. A skillful fabricator, and there are many of them, even a man accustomed to sounding profound—can always simulate profundity by an arrangement and an incoherence of words which give the appearance. One supposes one is reflecting on the meaning, while one is merely looking for it. He makes you give back much more than what he has given. He makes you take a certain distraction he communicates for the difficulty of following him.
> The truest profundity is the limpid kind.
> The kind which does not derive from a certain word —like *death, God, life, love,* but which does without these *trombones.*[124]

But, since hypocrisy ends by casting suspicion on virtue, Valéry always suspected the profound mind of being hollow.ee He preferred more seductive qualities:

> What does it matter if this pond is four feet deep or four miles? It is the brilliance of its surface that delights us,[125]

Or more exact and rarer ones:

> Profundity is a hundred times easier to get from oneself than rigor.[126]

An irreverent demon might whisper that there are also *effects of rigor,* which impose themselves on the timid reader, and certain admirable pages of *Monsieur Teste* or of the In-

---

dd *Choses tues* in *Tel quel,* I, p. 54. Cf. *Mauvaises pensées et autres,* which contrast, p. 31, ". . . the quality, attributed to an idea, of modifying a situation" and, p. 28, ". . . an idea of the same power as a stroke on a gong in a vaulted hall."
ee He made this defiance a characteristic of the French mind: "What is called profundity . . . will not be accounted among us a positive virtue" (*Pensée et art français* in *Regards sur le monde actuel,* p. 191).

troduction à la methode de Léonard de Vinci might testify
to them.

Valéry wrote in praise of clarity. And yet he sometimes
considered clarity, too, an effect. "Clarity in nonpractical
things *always* results from an illusion."[127] "The clear mind
makes understood what it does not understand."[128] In "nonpractical things"—that is, in art—clarity spoils effects:
". . . anything about which one can reach a clear idea loses
its force of glamor and its resonance in the mind."[129] The
impression of the divine, of the sublime is destroyed by clarity in most readers, who are too weak to appreciate it:

> What is clear and comprehensible and corresponds to
> a distinct idea does not produce the effect of the divine.
> At least, on the enormous majority of men—(which ex-
> plains many things in the arts).
> There are infinitely few men capable of attaching the
> emotion of the sublime to some thing that is quite clear,
> and insofar as it is clear. And there are also few authors
> who have obtained this effect.[130]

As for its contrary, obscurity, which plays such a great part
in Valéry's views on poetry, it has its place in his theory of
effects: it is the condition of the effects indefinable by definition: beauty and charm, and it is the basis of a whole series
of effects relating as much to ethics as to aesthetics:

> The generous, the "noble," the heroic always rest on
> an obscurity—and even a noble house is one whose ori-
> gins are lost, bordering on *legend*, authentically descend-
> ing from great beings who have not existed. . . .
> Everything beautiful, generous, heroic, is *obscure* in
> essence, *incomprehensible*. All that is great *must* be in-
> commensurable.
> This enters into the very *definition* of these *effects*.
> If the hero was limpid, and limpid to himself, he
> would not exist. He who swears loyalty to clarity there-
> fore renounces being a hero.[131]

Sincerity, a moral virtue *par excellence*, can be exploited as
an effect: "from it is taken, to it is given, a rhetorical
force."[132] Valéry saw sheer comedy in Stendhal's insistence
on sincerity.[133] His own Faust, who is writing his *Mémoires*,
knows perfectly how to give them "the color of truth":

I want to give the strongest, most poignant impression of sincerity a book has ever been able to communicate, and this powerful effect is achieved only by loading oneself with every horror, intimate ignominies or execrable experiences. . . .[ff]

There is no reason to stop, and we might catalogue as effects, in the fashion of this mordant moralist when the mood is upon him, all human virtues. We would have the *Maximes* of a La Rochefoucauld turned aesthetician.[gg]

THE LAW OF EFFECTS

Valéry's turn of mind, that of a poet obsessed by a dream of intellectual rigor, led him in search of that central attitude he discussed apropos of Leonardo, an attitude which would govern both the methods of art and those of science. Hence it is not surprising that in reflecting on artistic effects, he should have attempted to discern their laws. This is, in my opinion, the boldest and the most suggestive part of his poetics. In a letter to Pierre Louÿs, in the period of *La Jeune Parque*, he sketched a classification of effects by antinomic pairs, and offered a law of their transformation:

[ff] *Lust* in "*Mon Faust*," p. 28. The impression of truth is achieved with less difficulty in ordinary life: "*Truth* is often called the immediate effect produced upon us by the form or tone of what is spoken" (*Avis au lecteur* in *Tel quel*, I, p. 7). Valéry also remarked on the "effect of life" which "those who identify disorder with life" can find in the collections of ideas he did not have time to organize (ibid., p. 8). Cf. *Littérature* in *Tel quel*, I, p. 176: "We say of a book that it is 'living' when it is as disorganized, as chaotic as life, seen from outside, seems to be to a casual observer."

[gg] We can speak, in certain cases, of an *hypocrisy of effects*: "Every phrase has several meanings of which the most remarkable is assuredly the very cause which has brought this phrase into existence. Thus: *Quia nominor Leo* does not mean: *Because I call myself Lion*, but: *I am a grammatical example*. To say: *The eternal silence*, etc., is clearly to announce: *I want to overwhelm you with my profundity, and amaze you with my style*" (*Autres rhumbs* in *Tel quel*, II, p. 191). "Death, in literature, is a low note. . . . Those who use it are mountebanks" (*Mauvaises pensées et autres*, p. 159).

I have come to that cynicism which considers simple-complex; old-new; as so many colors on a palette . . . these two oppositions have this in common, that in each the qualification depends merely on the point at which you stop. A little more tension and you have shifted from one value to the other.[134]

Valéry certainly hinted at a general systematics of effects. He shows how the aspirations of the conscious artist are connected:

The desire for "realism" leads to seeking ever more powerful means of *rendering*.
What is rendered leads to technique.
Technique leads to classification, to order.
Order leads to a systematics, to complete exploration, to the widest use of all means, to their general freedom greater than any achieved thing.
And starting from the exact reproduction of some phenomenon, one arrives at a sort of gymnastics which includes the "false" and the "true."[hh]

At the limit, the work would be created starting from effects, or, better, by means of effects. A period like our own may have seemed favorable to this intention:

Literatures of what is called decadence are systematic. They are the results of men more learned, more ingenious, and even profounder, sometimes, than the earlier writers whose enumerable *effects* they have discovered, classified, concentrated—insofar as they can be grasped and isolated.[135]

Valéry did not extend this program to the point of establishing a complete technique of effects,[ii] but he formulated

[hh] *Cahier B* in *Tel quel*, I, p. 206. *Psaume S* in *Mélange*, p. 91, suggests another connection:

> In the beginning was Surprise
> And then came Contrast:
> After this appeared Oscillation;
> With it, Distribution,
> And then Purity
> Which is the End.

[ii] Valéry attributed a program of this kind to Mallarmé, who "dedicated himself without respite or reservation, without repetition or retreat, to the unheard-of enterprise of grasping in all its

some very curious fragments of one. The *conditioning of effects*, for example, more than once engaged his attention:

> The probability of lucky strokes in succession is very slight in poetry, because of independent simultaneous conditions. Language, made up of discrete and complex elements, affords the man who adopts the conventions only accidental solutions. . . .

According to Valéry, certain effects are very easy to achieve, because they depend on only "one or two extrinsic conditions": this is the case of *profound phrases* and *sonorous phrases*. We can even produce them in succession without their seeming to resemble one another, for "the instrument is created once one has created one of them."[136] The favorite words of writers each condition a category of favorite effects:

> The mere timbre of a cello exerts in many persons a veritable visceral dominion. There are words whose frequency in an author reveals that they are, for him, endowed with a very different resonance, and consequently with a positively creative power, from their general status. This is an example of those personal evaluations, of those *great values for one person*, which certainly play a splendid part in a production of the mind, in which singularity is an element of the first importance.[jj]

But we must not forget the "iron law of literature": "what is important for only one man is worth nothing." The "great values for one person" become, however, values for all, or for many, if the work subjugates the public. Then the words

---

generality the nature of his art, and by an enumeration *à la* Descartes of the possibilities of the language, of distinguishing within all its means and classifying all its resources" (*Mallarmé* in *Vues*, p. 187).

[jj] *Leçon inaugurale du Cours de poétique* in *Variété V*, p. 318. Cf. *Au sujet du "Cimetière marin"* in *Variété III*, p. 73: ". . . these returns of terms which reveal the tendencies, the frequencies characteristic of a mind. (Certain words ring out within us among all others, like the harmonics of our deepest nature.)" This did not keep Valéry from assigning to the number of sins of "those men without great appetite for poetry" who have the "responsibility . . . of stimulating and cultivating a taste for it" the waste of time spent in collecting "frequencies" in the vocabulary of poets (*Questions de poésie* in *Variété III*, p. 40).

characteristic of a poet are like a signature. Further, Valéry, who believed in the creative power of the void, asserts that there are *effects of deficiency*, produced by a writer's *lack* of some power or other: "A literary value, hence a positive richness, can be due to certain lacunae in a temperament."

> A piano is noticed by the ear, thanks to the absence of certain strings.
> Because your range is incomplete, because a certain order of thoughts—certain means—certain emotions are forbidden or unknown to you, you have made a work which enriches me. I find in it surprise and wonder.[137]

Originality consists of absences as well as presences.

It is especially the way in which the poet functions which suggested to Valéry his most penetrating remarks. Without forcing the texts too much, it is actually laws which he seems to propose. *The law of localization of effects:* words and ideas are "means, which have only instantaneous values, effects of position"[138] (Boileau had already praised Malherbe, who "Of a word in its proper place revealed the power"); *the law of propagation of effects:* "One must toss stones into minds, which make enlarging spheres around them; and toss them into the centermost point, and at harmonic intervals";[139] *the law of intensification of effects:* effects are enlarged or diminished, as by a lens, according to the writer's capacity:

> Language holds up to thought a magnifying lens which projects it to alien eyes as monstrous and dilated, when to itself it was no more than a slight local agitation. But on the other hand the man who has no literary gift expresses his greatest emotions in miniature and can produce only powerless epithets. This is the reducing lens.[140]

The maximum intensity of poetic effect is illustrated by the image of the diamond:

> Its beauty results . . . from the acuteness of the angle of total reflection . . . The diamond-cutter fashions its facets so that the ray which penetrates the gem by one of them can emerge only by the same one. Whence the brilliance, the luster. A splendid image of what I believe

about poetry: return of the spiritual ray to the words-of-entry.[141]

Should we seek, finally, a more particular law as to the relation of effects of detail and the total effect, a *law of proportion*? It can be considered as the golden rule of the short poem:

> THEOREM. When works are very brief, the effect of the slightest detail is on the same scale as the total effect.[kk]

There is even a corollary to this:

> The proportion of *scruples* and beauties in a sonnet must be enormous.[142]

Valéry carried aesthetic sensibility to the point of scrutinizing the secondary effects to be encountered in works manifesting a duality of intention, or a secret intention beneath an explicit one. Already Poe, in his analysis of *The Raven*, emphasized the role of what he called a *subterranean current of meaning*. What Valéry examined consists of what he called *lateral effects*. Starting with a painting by Rembrandt representing a philosopher in his study, he remarks on "the secret and somehow lateral action of the dark patches and zones of chiaroscuro": ". . . a subtle art of arranging a rather arbitrary element in order to act insidiously upon the viewer, while his attention is attracted and fixed by clear and recognizable objects." He then turns to "lateral effects that can be produced by the divided harmonies of an orchestra," as in Wagner, and he wonders "if analogous effects . . . could reasonably be pursued in literature." "The essential condition" would be that "the artifice escape the unprejudiced reader, and the effect not reveal its cause."[ll]

[kk] *Littérature* in *Tel quel*, I, p. 156. Abridged in *Autres rhumbs* in *Tel quel*, II, p. 162: "When works are very brief, the slightest detail is on the scale of the whole."

[ll] *Le retour de Hollande* in *Variété II*, pp. 37–39. On this condition of suggestion, a note in *Mélange*, p. 90, following a remark on ornament, says: "The proportion must act without being apparent." On the danger of methods which are too easily discovered, we find this criticism of Huysmans: "He systematically used and abused epithets not implied by the object, but suggested by the circum-

THE SACRIFICE OF EFFECTS

After so many ingenious views, what remained to be done with this treasury of *effects?* It remained to abolish it. The sacrifice of effects was consummated by Valéry, notably in his article on Père Cyprien. He confessed there his irritation that scattered beauties should constitute dazzling accidents to the detriment of the whole:

> Even accumulated major effects, images and always-startling epithets marvelously derived from unexpected and remote sources, obliging one to admire, before the work itself, the author and his resources, offend the poem as a *whole*, and the genius of the father is fatal to the child. Too many diverse values, too many contributions of too much rare knowledge, too frequent and systematic surprises and leaps give us the notion of a man intoxicated by his advantages and developing them by every means, not in the style and order of a single design, but in the free space of the mind's inexhaustible incoherence.[mm]

Alluding one day to the elaboration of *La Jeune Parque*, he confessed that the conditions he had set himself led him "to avoid seeking certain effects (for example, isolable 'beautiful lines') and to sacrifice them when they occurred to me. I got into the habit of rejection."[nn] Effects which isolate

---

stance: a very seductive means, a powerful means—but a dangerous and short-lived one, like all the means of art which can be easily defined" (*Souvenir de J. K. Huysmans* in *Variété II*, p. 240).

[mm] *"Cantiques spirituels"* in *Variété V*, p. 175. See, too, the reproaches addressed to the Parnassian poets in *Existence du Symbolisme* in *Oeuvres complètes*, vol. L, p. 124: ". . . their system, which had the merit of having opposed the negligence of form and of language so apparent in so many of the romantics, led them to a factitious rigor, to a striving for effects, for the 'beautiful line,' a use of rare terms, of strange names, of quite specious magnificences which offended poetry beneath such arbitrary and inanimate ornaments."

[nn] *Mélange*, p. 42. Valéry connected his condemnation of the isolable "beautiful line" to his disgust for *events*. "Events, exaggerations in facts or words displease me. Events are exaggerated facts. I despise effects" (*Propos me concernant*, p. 53). "Events

themselves break the sequence of the poem. The purity of line is broken by these disparate flashes. The sequence of effects must therefore yield to the absence of effects, or rather to the continuity of a single effect. The poem must be a perpetual modulation, whose effect is one of a continual charm. We arrive at the same conclusion as in the theory of ornament.

The quite classical simplicity Valéry recommends is both a supreme taste and an exquisite prudence. A work, he says, again apropos of Père Cyprien, "must inspire the desire to pursue it, to repeat its lines, to carry them within oneself for an indefinite interior use"; now, "in this persistence and by these repetitions, its attractions of contrast and of intensity disappear; novelty, strangeness, the power of shock exhaust their quite relative effectiveness. . . ."[143] This might be a *law of dampening or degradation of effects.* Valéry, the antimodern in poetry, the adversary of aesthetic shock, has no confidence in the abuse of surprise, whose effects lose their point and annihilate each other.[oo] It is with the lasting part

---

are 'effects.' They are products of sensibility. . . . Thus the 'very beautiful line of verse' is an event in a poem; but it must be confessed that it tends to destroy this poem; its value makes it isolable. It is a flower which is detached from the plant, and with which the memory decks itself. A very refined taste might thus condemn these beauties too jealous of their singular power, and suggest eliminating them when they occur. This renunciation would require a strange strength of spirit. . . ." (Ibid., p. 8). This text, which dates from 1944, connects with the reproach Valéry made in 1889 to Heredia's sonnets: "Each line has its own life, its special splendor, and distracts the mind from the whole" (*Sur la technique littéraire* in *Dossiers*, 1, p. 28).

[oo] This is his reproach of the moderns: "The artist will use and abuse surprise effects in order to seduce and astound the consumer" (*Cours de poétique*, lecture 17). See further *Degas. Danse. Dessin*, pp. 135–37, *Mémoires d'un poème*, p. xiv. Now, "time . . . necessarily weakens the effects of surprise and of novelty" (*Au sujet de Berthe Morisot* in *Vues*, p. 341). Valéry protected himself against such abuses: "Among other forbidden things, I did not want to play on systematic surprise, nor on wild transports, for it seemed to me that this meant reducing the effects of a poem to the dazzlement of the mind without attaining and satisfying its depths" (*Réponse* in *Commerce*, Summer MCMXXXII, p. 13). We saw however that the *total effect* and the *effect of beauty* cause surprise—but a surprise which does not disappear after the first shock;

of the poem that we must seek a relation, and this lasting part
is extraordinarily simple, as Valéry shows in the rest of this
passage in moving, almost Bergsonian terms quite rare in his
work. Of a poem one repeats to oneself, "there remains . . .
only what survives repetition as our own internal expression
survives it, whatever we can live with, our ideals, our truths,
and our chosen experiences, in other words all that we choose
to find within ourselves, in the most intimate, that is, the most
lasting state. It seems to me that the soul alone with itself,
and speaking to itself from time to time, between two *absolute* silences, never employs more than a *small number of
words* and *none that is extraordinary*. That is how we know
there is a soul at that moment. . . ."pp

---

it is a marvel which lasts and "makes itself sought again." There
are, then, two kinds of surprise: ". . . a very beautiful thing renders
us *mute* with admiration. This is what we must seek to produce,
and what we must not confuse with the mutism of astonishment.
The latter is the objective of the moderns. It does not discern the
varieties of surprise. There is one kind which is renewed upon each
consideration and becomes all the more indefinable and yet apparent the more profoundly we examine and familiarize ourselves
with the work. This is the good kind of surprise. As for the other, it
results only from the shock which violates a convention or a habit,
and is reduced to this shock. To *dissolve* this shock, it suffices to
change a convention or a habit" (*Degas. Danse. Dessin*, p. 153).
See further *Littérature* in *Tel quel*, I, p. 165: ". . . we are often
deceived with regard to the surprise which is worthy of art. We require not finite surprises, but infinite ones in literature. . . ." The
definitive formula occurs in *Mauvaises pensées et autres*, p. 200:
"This adorable poem, this dazzling façade, this suspended marvel
which crystallizes the attention like a prism, is a surprise stabilized,
grasped . . . a surprise—*surprised*."

pp "*Cantiques spirituels*" in *Variété V*, p. 176. We must not
overlook the fact that the tone of this passage is exceptional; in itself, the word *soul* has a quite un-Valerian ring to it; perhaps, just
as he had gravely suggested to Pascal that learned Jesuits accomplished their salvation no less well . . . (which in the mouth of an
unbeliever has a special savor), Valéry believed he had to accommodate his courtesy to the piety of his hero, Père Cyprien. Sainte-
Beuve recommended that the critic dip his pen in his model's ink-
well. Serious mimicry is very rare in Valéry (he somewhat imitates
Bossuet in his parallel between Foch and Pétain). On the contrary, when he wanted to get a sense of some great man, Valéry
made him resemble himself (an attitude concerning which he developed a whole theory).

To this, then, comes the ambitious project of reducing poetry to a scientific manipulation of the sensibility. "The soul alone with itself, and speaking to itself from time to time . . . ," that naked simplicity of consciousness listening to its melody without concern for effect—did Valéry ever come closer than in this rare moment of perfect humility to the secret of poetic creation?

NOTES

CHAPTER I

[1] It has been quoted in part by A. Berne-Joffroy, *Présence de Valéry*, p. 69, and published entire by Henri Mondor with his study *Le premier article de Paul Valéry* in *Dossiers*, 1, pp. 13-30.

[2] Quoted by Henri Mondor, *Le Vase brisé de Paul Valéry* in *Paul Valéry, Essais et témoignages recuillis par Marc Eigeldinger*, p. 14.

[3] *André Gide-Paul Valéry Correspondance 1890-1942*, 1955, p. 126.

[4] They have been published together in the two volumes of *Tel quel*.

[5] *Réponses*, p. 17.

[6] *Le Prince et la Jeune Parque* in *Variété V*, pp. 119-25.

[7] *Réponses*, p. 18.

[8] *Mélange*, "Avis au lecteur," p. 7.

[9] André Gide, *Paul Valéry* in *L'Arche*, October 1945, p. 14.

[10] *Analecta*, LXXXVI.

[11] Ibid. "L'Auteur à ses amis," pp. 17-18.

[12] *Propos me concernant*, pp. 9-10.

[13] *Gide-Valéry Correspondance*, p. 217.

[14] *Propos me concernant*, pp. 10-11.

[15] Ibid., p. 60.

[16] Ibid., pp. 14-15.

[17] *Préface* in *Monsieur Teste*, p. 8.

[18] *Au sujet d' "Eurêka"* in *Variété*, pp. 112-13.

[19] Letter to Albert Thibaudet in *Lettres à Quelques-Uns*, 1952, p. 97.

[20] *Journal*, December 30, 1922, p. 749.

[21] *Lettre sur Mallarmé* in *Variété II*, p. 232.

[22] *Cahier B* in *Tel quel*, I, p. 201.

[23] *Propos me concernant*, p. 32.

[24] Ibid., p. 17.

[25] *Littérature* in *Tel quel*, I, p. 141.

[26] *Choses tues* in *Tel quel*, I, p. 14.

[27] Letter to Fontainas of 1917, in *Réponses*, p. 16: "It is indeed an exercise. . . ."

28 Letter to Albert Thibaudet in *Lettres à Quelques-Uns*, p. 97.
29 *Lettre sur Mallarmé* in *Variété II*, p. 233.
30 *Propos me concernant*, p. 49.
31 Ibid., pp. 20–22.
32 Ibid., p. 22.
33 *Choses tues* in *Tel quel*, I, p. 34.
34 *Réponses*, p. 37.
35 *Propos me concernant*, p. 49.

CHAPTER II

1 *Poésie pure. Notes pour une conférence* in *Oeuvres complètes*, vol. C, p. 202.
2 *Propos sur la poésie* in *Conferencia*, 1928, p. 465.
3 Frédéric Lefèvre, *Une heure avec Paul Valéry* in *Les Nouvelles Littéraires*, February 28, 1931.
4 *L'Invention esthétique* in *L'Invention*, Centre international de synthèse, 1938, p. 149.
5 *Propos sur la poésie*, p. 465.
6 Frédéric Lefèvre, *Une heure avec Paul Valéry.*
7 *Propos sur la poésie*, p. 465.
8 *Poésie pure, Notes pour une conférence* in *Oeuvres complètes*, vol. C, p. 202.
9 *Calepin d'un poète* in *Oeuvres complètes*, vol. C, p. 189.
10 *Propos sur la poésie*, p. 466.
11 *Poésie pure*, pp. 202–3.
12 See *Petites études* in *Mélange*, p. 103, and *Suite* in *Tel quel*, II, pp. 311–15.
13 Cf. infra, p. 26.
14 In *Propos sur la poésie* in *Conferencia*, 1929, p. 466; in *Poésie pure. Notes pour une conférence*, published first in the collection of essays *Poësie*, 1928, reprinted in *Oeuvres complètes*, vol. C, pp. 202–3; in *Poésie et pensée abstraite* (Zaharoff lecture, at Oxford, in 1939), reprinted in *Variété V*, p. 137.
15 *Propos sur la poésie*, p. 466.
16 Ibid.
17 *Au sujet d' "Adonis"* in *Variété*, p. 56.
18 In *Tel quel*, II, p. 113.
19 Ibid.
20 *Calepin d'un poète* in *Oeuvres complètes*, vol. C, pp. 189–90.
21 *Poésie et pensée abstraite* in *Variété V*, p. 138.
22 *Propos sur la poésie*, p. 465. Cf. also *Poésie pure* in *Oeuvres complètes*, vol. C, p. 203.
23 *Poésie pure* in *Oeuvres complètes*, vol. C, pp. 202–3.
24 Frédéric Lefèvre, *Une heure avec Paul Valéry.*
25 *Notion générale de l'art*, pp. 686–87.
26 Ibid., p. 690.
27 Ibid.

28 *Commentaires de Charmes* in *Variété III*, p. 82.

29 *Préface* in *Vues*, p. 211.

30 *La création artistique* in *Bulletin de la Société française de Philosophie*, 1928, p. 4.

31 *Mélange*, p. 87.

32 *Mémoires d'un poème*, p. xxxv. See too *Cours de poétique*, lecture 18.

33 *Le bilan de l'intelligence* in *Variété III*, pp. 218–86.

34 *Notion générale de l'art*, p. 690.

35 *La politique de l'esprit* in *Variété III*, p. 224.

36 Ibid., p. 223.

37 *Notion générale de l'art*, p. 689.

38 Ibid., p. 691.

39 *Mémoires d'un poème*, p. xxv.

40 *Variété*, p. 103.

41 *La crise de l'esprit* in *Variété*, p. 22.

42 *Analecta*, xxxii.

43 Ibid.

44 *Notion générale de l'art*, p. 691.

45 *Rhumbs* in *Tel quel*, II, p. 72.

46 *Littérature* in *Tel quel*, I, p. 142.

47 *Autres rhumbs* in *Tel quel*, II, p. 162.

48 *Rhumbs* in *Tel quel*, II, p. 73.

49 *Avant-propos* in *Variété*, pp. 98–99.

50 *Poésie et pensée abstraite* in *Variété V*, p. 158.

51 *Avant-propos* in *Variété*, p. 99.

52 *Autres rhumbs* in *Tel quel*, II, pp. 154–55.

53 *Rhumbs* in *Tel quel*, II, p. 82.

54 *Lettre à André Fontainas* in *Réponses*, p. 16.

55 *Avant-propos* in *Variété*, pp. 96–98.

56 *Poésie et pensée abstraite* in *Variété V*, p. 159.

57 Ibid., p. 157.

58 Ibid., pp. 158–59.

59 Ibid.

60 Frédéric Lefèvre, *Entretiens avec Paul Valéry*, pp. 129–41.

61 *Leçon inaugurale du cours de poétique* in *Variété V*, p. 317.

62 *Rhumbs* in *Tel quel*, II, p. 52.

63 *Propos sur le progrès* in *Regards sur le monde actuel et autres essais*, p. 168.

64 *Passage de Verlaine* in *Variété II*, p. 182.

65 *Situation de Baudelaire* in *Variété II*, pp. 159–61.

66 *Examen de Valéry*, p. 45, footnote.

67 *Lettre sur Mallarmé* in *Variété II*, p. 233.

68 *Propos me concernant*, pp. 20–21.

69 *Situation de Baudelaire* in *Variété II*, p. 143.

70 *Poésie et pensée abstraite* in *Variété V*, p. 157.

71 Ibid.

72 *Introduction à la méthode de Léonard de Vinci*, I, *Note et digression* in *Variété*, p. 165.

73 *Au sujet d' "Eurêka"* in *Variété*, p. 113.

74 *Descartes* in *Variété IV*, p. 215.

75 *Extraits du Log-Book* in *Monsieur Teste*, p. 74.

76 *Quelques pensées* in *Monsieur Teste*, p. 129.

77 *Propos me concernant*, p. 36.

78 *Suite* in *Tel quel*, II, p. 354, or *Petites études* in *Mélange*, pp. 104–5.

79 *Autres rhumbs*, p. 144.

80 Ibid.

81 *Analecta*, CXXI.

82 Ibid.

83 Ibid.

84 *Moralités* in *Tel quel*, I, pp. 102–3.

85 In *Tel quel*, II, pp. 87, 328.

86 *Suite*, p. 28.

87 Ibid., pp. 323–24.

88 *Analecta*, XLIII.

89 Ibid.

90 *Mauvaises pensées*, p. 148.

91 Ibid.

92 *Analecta*, XLIII.

93 *Analecta*, XL.

94 *Mélange*, p. 94.

95 *Stendhal* in *Variété*, pp. 77–79.

96 *Mélange*, p. 78.

97 *Propos me concernant*, p. 54.

98 *Quelques pensées* in *Monsieur Teste*, p. 132.

99 *Mauvaises pensées et autres*, p. 47.

100 *Propos me concernant*, p. 42.

101 *Mémoires d'un poème*, p. xvi.

102 *Analecta*, XCII.

103 *Rhumbs* in *Tel quel*, II, p. 28.

104 *Analecta*, XCIII, footnote.

105 Ibid., XCIII.

106 *Dialogue* in *Monsieur Teste*, p. 109.

107 *Suite*, p. 309.

108 Ibid., p. 309, footnote.

109 *Mauvaises pensées et autres*, p. 66.

110 *La politique de l'esprit* in *Variété III*, p. 217.

111 *Autres rhumbs* in *Tel quel*, II, p. 156.

112 *Calepin d'un poète* in *Oeuvres complètes*, vol. C, p. 192.

113 *"Cantiques spirituels"* in *Variété V*, p. 169.

114 *La politique de l'esprit*, p. 218.

115 *Eupalinos*, p. 91.

116 Ibid., p. 92.

117 Ibid., p. 104.

118 *"Cantiques spirituels,"* p. 169.

119 *La création artistique*, p. 5.

120 *Situation de Baudelaire*, p. 170.

[121] *Littérature*, p. 144.
[122] *Instants* in *Mélange*, p. 160.
[123] *Orientem versus* in *Oeuvres complètes*, vol. J, pp. 175 ff.
[124] *Préface aux Lettres persanes* in *Variété II*, p. 63.
[125] *Choses tues* in *Tel quel*, I, pp. 78–80.
[126] *Littérature*, p. 143.
[127] *Analecta*, CXX.
[128] Letter of June 6, 1917, to Pierre Louÿs in *Oeuvres complètes*, vol. B, p. 134.
[129] *Analecta*, CXX.
[130] *Propos sur l'intelligence* in *Oeuvres complètes*, vol. D, pp. 86–87.
[131] *Rhumbs*, p. 47.
[132] *Mauvaises pensées et autres*, p. 223.
[133] *Calepin d'un poète*, p. 190.
[134] *Lettre de Madame Émilie Teste* in *Monsieur Teste*, p. 49.
[135] *Pour un portrait* in *Monsieur Teste*, p. 116.
[136] *Propos me concernant*, p. 16.
[137] Ibid.
[138] *Pour un portrait* in *Monsieur Teste*, p. 120.
[139] Frédéric Lefèvre, *Entretiens avec Paul Valéry*, pp. 277–78.
[140] *Préface aux Lettres persanes*, p. 64.
[141] *Variété V*, p. 320.
[142] *Mémoires d'un poème*, pp. xxxix–xl.
[143] *Instants*, p. 161.
[144] *Mauvaises pensées et autres*, p. 83.
[145] *Instants*, p. 162.

CHAPTER III

[1] Pp. 254–60.
[2] *Préface* in *Monsieur Teste*, p. 12.
[3] *Mémoires d'un poème*, p. xxiii.
[4] In *Monsieur Teste*, p. 89.
[5] *Cahier B* in *Tel quel*, I, p. 221.
[6] Letter of January 14, 1916, in *Oeuvres complètes*, vol. B, p. 123.
[7] *Svedenborg* in *Variété V*, p. 272.
[8] Ibid.
[9] *Poésie et pensée abstraite* in *Variété V*, pp. 132–33.
[10] Letter of January 14, 1916, in *Oeuvres complètes*, vol. B, p. 123.
[11] Ibid.
[12] *Poésie et pensée abstraite* in *Variété V*, p. 133.
[13] *Lettre d'un ami* in *Monsieur Teste*, p. 89.
[14] *Propos sur l'intelligence* in *Oeuvres complètes*, vol. D, p. 87.
[15] *Poésie et pensée abstraite* in *Variété V*, p. 133.
[16] *Lettre d'un ami* in *Monsieur Teste*, p. 89.

17 *Analecta,* CX.

18 *Propos me concernant,* p. 41.

19 Ibid., p. 18.

20 *Discours de l'histoire* in *Variété IV,* p. 141.

21 *Poésie et pensée abstraite* in *Variété V,* p. 135.

22 *"Cantiques spirituels"* in *Variété V,* p. 176.

23 Letter to Pierre Louÿs of January 14, 1916, in *Oeuvres complètes,* vol. B, p. 123.

24 *Poésie et pensée abstraite* in *Variété V,* p. 131.

25 *La création artistique* in *Bulletin de la Société française de Philosophie,* 1928, p. 7.

26 Ibid.

27 *Propos me concernant,* p. 27.

28 Letter to André Gide of May 1921 in *Gide-Valéry Correspondance,* p. 485.

29 *Propos me concernant,* p. 28.

30 *La Politique de l'esprit* in *Variété III,* pp. 216–17.

31 *Svedenborg* in *Variété V,* p. 272.

32 *Quelques fragments des Marginalia* in *Commerce,* XIV, Winter MCMXXVII, p. 28.

33 Frédéric Lefèvre, *Entretiens avec Paul Valéry,* p. 61.

34 *Avant-propos* in *Variété,* p. 103.

35 *Analecta,* CXX.

36 *Méthodes. La Sémantique . . .* in *Mercure de France,* January 1898, p. 260.

37 *Choses tues* in *Tel quel,* I, p. 49.

38 *Suite* in *Tel quel,* II, p. 338.

39 *Lettre de Madame Émilie Teste* in *Monsieur Teste,* p. 52.

40 *Rhumbs* in *Tel quel,* II, p. 48.

41 *Propos sur l'intelligence* in *Oeuvres complètes,* vol. D, p. 87.

42 *Eupalinos,* p. 43.

43 Ibid., p. 140.

44 Ibid., pp. 145–47.

45 *Une vue de Descartes* in *Variété V,* pp. 227–28.

46 In *Pièces sur l'art,* pp. 155–60.

47 *Discours prononcé à la Maison d'Éducation de la Légion d'Honneur de Saint-Denis* in *Variété IV,* p. 151.

48 *Hommage* in *Variété,* p. 152.

49 *Discours prononcé au Deuxième Congrès international d'Esthétique et de Science de l'art* in *Variété IV,* pp. 245–46.

50 *Eupalinos,* pp. 149–50.

51 *Descartes* in *Variété IV,* pp. 217–18.

52 Letter to Jean de Latour in *Examen de Valéry.*

53 *Poésie pure. Notes pour une conférence* in *Oeuvres complètes,* vol. C, pp. 205–6.

54 *Mémoires d'un poème,* p. xiii.

55 *Poésie et pensée abstraite* in *Variété V,* pp. 143–44.

56 *Questions de poésie* in *Variété III,* p. 54.

[57] *Je disais quelquefois à Stéphane Mallarmé* . . . in *Variété III*, p. 28.

[58] *Avant-propos* in *Variété*, pp. 107–8.

[59] *Rhumbs* in *Tel quel*, II, p. 101.

[60] *Stendhal* in *Variété II*, p. 107.

[61] *Rhumbs* in *Tel quel*, II, p. 85.

[62] *Autres rhumbs* in *Tel quel*, II, p. 160.

[63] *Analecta*, XX.

[64] *Rhumbs* in *Tel quel*, II, pp. 75–76.

[65] *Situation de Baudelaire* in *Variété II*, p. 148.

[66] *Rhumbs* in *Tel quel*, II, p. 42.

[67] *"Cantiques spirituels"* in *Variété V*, p. 169. Cf. *Littérature* in *Tel quel*, I, p. 158.

[68] *Propos sur la poésie* in *Conferencia*, 1928, p. 471.

[69] *Je disais quelquefois à Stéphane Mallarmé* . . . in *Variété III*, p. 27.

[70] *"Cantiques spirituels"* in *Variété V*, pp. 178–79.

[71] André Gide, *Journal*, p. 891.

[72] *Propos me concernant*, p. 20.

[73] Letter of June 6, 1917, in *Oeuvres complètes*, vol. B, p. 135.

[74] *Rhumbs* in *Tel quel*, II, p. 70.

[75] *Ibid.*, p. 62.

[76] *Mélange*, p. 42.

[77] *Choses tues* in *Tel quel*, I, p. 17.

[78] *Calepin d'un poète* in *Oeuvres complètes*, vol. C, p. 186.

[79] *Mémoires d'un poème*, p. xxv.

[80] *Poésie et pensée abstraite* in *Variété V*, p. 141.

[81] In *Variété III*, p. 159.

[82] *Mallarmé* in *Vues*, p. 188.

[83] *La création artistique* in *Bulletin de la Société française de Philosophie*, 1928, pp. 11–13.

[84] *Je disais quelquefois à Stéphane Mallarmé* . . . in *Variété III*, p. 24.

[85] *Ibid.*, pp. 24–25.

[86] *Eupalinos*, p. 88.

[87] *Mémoires d'un poème*, p. xxxviii.

[88] *L'Idée fixe*, pp. 204–5.

[89] *Autres rhumbs* in *Tel quel*, II, p. 159.

[90] *Littérature* in *Tel quel*, I, p. 145.

[91] *Sur Bossuet* in *Variété II*, pp. 44–45.

[92] *Ibid.*, p. 45.

[93] *Autres Rhumbs* in *Tel quel*, II, pp. 159–60.

[94] *Goethe. "On dit Goethe comme on dit Orphée"* in *Conferencia*, 1933, p. 481.

[95] *Sur Bossuet* in *Variété II*, pp. 45–46.

[96] *Calepin d'un poète* in *Oeuvres complètes*, vol. C, p. 197.

[97] *Ibid.*

[98] *Je disais quelquefois à Stéphane Mallarmé* . . . in *Variété III*, pp. 27–28.

99 *Eupalinos*, pp. 147–48.

100 *Je disais quelquefois à Stéphane Mallarmé* . . . in *Variété III*, p. 32.

101 *Mallarmé* in *Vues*, p. 185.

102 *Victor Hugo créateur par la forme* in *Vues*, p. 180.

103 *Littérature* in *Tel quel*, I, p. 146.

104 *Choses tues* in *Tel quel*, I, p. 28.

105 *Passage de Verlaine* in *Variété II*, pp. 180–81.

106 *Au sujet du "Cimetière marin"* in *Variété III*, p. 68.

107 *Propos sur la poésie* in *Conferencia*, 1928, p. 472.

108 *De la diction des vers* in *Pièces sur l'art*, p. 45.

109 *Je disais quelquefois à Stéphane Mallarmé* . . . in *Variété III*, p. 14.

110 *Images de la France* in *Regards sur le monde actuel et autres essais*, p. 130.

111 *Au sujet du "Cimetière marin"* in *Variété III*, p. 71.

112 *Poésie et pensée abstraite* in *Variété V*, pp. 154–55.

113 Ibid., pp. 153–54.

114 *Au sujet du "Cimetière marin"* in *Variété III*, p. 71.

115 *Questions de poésie* in *Variété III*, pp. 53–54.

116 *Propos sur la poésie* in *Conferencia*, 1928, p. 471.

117 *Rhumbs* in *Tel quel*, II, p. 78.

CHAPTER IV

1 *Mémoires d'un poème*, p. vii.

2 *Au sujet du "Cimetière marin"* in *Variété III*, pp. 65–66.

3 Frédéric Lefèvre, *Entretiens avec Paul Valéry*, p. 68.

4 Alain, *Le déjeuner chez Lapérouse*, *Nouvelle Revue Française*, August 1939, p. 237.

5 *Préface, Commentaires de Charmes* in *Variété III*, p. 78.

6 *Au sujet du "Cimetière marin"*, p. 62.

7 *Préface, Commentaires de Charmes* in *Variété III*, p. 82.

8 Ibid., p. 83.

9 Ibid., p. 80.

10 Ibid., p. 78.

11 *Mercure de France*, January 1898, pp. 258–59.

12 *Préface, Commentaires de Charmes*, p. 82.

13 Ibid., p. 80.

14 Ibid., pp. 80–81. See also *Au sujet du "Cimetière marin,"* p. 68.

15 *Préface, Commentaires de Charmes*, p. 83.

16 Ibid., p. 80.

17 *Littérature* in *Tel quel*, I, p. 161. The portrait argument can also be found in *Préface, Commentaires de Charmes* in *Variété III*, p. 83, and in *Paul Valéry, Cahiers de la quinzaine*, 21st series, 2nd cahier (10th meeting of the Studio Franco-Russe), p. 67.

18 *Préface, Commentaires de Charmes*, p. 83.

[19] *"Cantiques spirituels"* in *Variété V*, pp. 168–69.

[20] *Au sujet du "Cimetière marin"* in *Variété III*, p. 68.

[21] Frédéric Lefèvre, *Une heure avec Paul Valéry.*

[22] Ibid.

[23] *Autres rhumbs* in *Tel quel*, II, pp. 160–61.

[24] Frédéric Lefèvre, *Une heure avec Paul Valéry.*

[25] *Mauvaises pensées et autres*, p. 15.

[26] Frédéric Lefèvre, *Une heure avec Paul Valéry.*

[27] Ibid.

[28] *Lettre d'un ami* in *Monsieur Teste*, pp. 88–89.

[29] *Au sujet du "Cimetière marin"* in *Variété III*, p. 67.

[30] André Maurois, *Sons nouveaux 1900. Eux et nous. V. Paul Valéry. "Monsieur Teste"* in *Conferencia*, March 15, 1933.

[31] *Littérature*, pp. 159–60.

[32] *Propos me concernant*, p. 61.

[33] *Mallarmé* in *Conferencia*, April 15, 1933.

[34] Ibid.

[35] *Lettre sur Mallarmé* in *Variété II*, p. 225.

[36] *Rhumbs* in *Tel quel*, II, p. 83.

[37] *Mélange*, p. 30.

[38] See *Bulletin de la Société française de Philosophie*, session of June 6, 1931, pp. 97–127.

[39] *Rhumbs*, p. 78.

[40] Ibid.

[41] Ibid., pp. 78–79.

[42] *La poésie de La Fontaine* in *Vues*, pp. 165–66.

[43] *Réflexions sur l'art* in *Bulletin de la Société française de Philosophie*, 1935, p. 65.

[44] *Rhumbs*, p. 62.

[45] Ibid., p. 75.

[46] *Au sujet du "Cimetière marin"* in *Variété III*, pp. 66–67.

[47] Ibid., pp. 67–68.

[48] Ibid., p. 68.

[49] Letter to Albert Coste, 1915, in *Lettres à Quelques-uns*, p. 104.

[50] *Au sujet du "Cimetière marin"* in *Variété III*, p. 67.

[51] *Poésie pure* in *Oeuvres complètes*, vol. C, pp. 198–99.

[52] Ibid., p. 199.

[53] Ibid.

[54] *Extraits du log-book* in *Monsieur Teste*, p. 66.

[55] *Propos me concernant*, p. 23.

[56] *Cahier B* in *Tel quel*, I, p. 218.

[57] *Triomphe de Manet* in *Pièces sur l'art*, pp. 202–3.

[58] *Propos me concernant*, p. 34.

[59] Frédéric Lefèvre, *Entretiens avec Paul Valéry*, p. 59. See also *Poésie pure* in *Oeuvres complètes*, vol. C, pp. 199–200.

[60] *Poésie pure* in *Oeuvres complètes*, vol. C, pp. 199–200.

[61] Ibid., p. 200.

[62] Frédéric Lefèvre, *Entretiens avec Paul Valéry*, p. 66.

63 *Poésie pure* in *Oeuvres complètes*, vol. C, p. 200.

64 Frédéric Lefèvre, *Entretiens avec Paul Valéry*, p. 66.

65 *Poésie pure* in *Oeuvres complètes*, vol. C, p. 211.

66 Ibid.

67 *Calepin d'un poète* in *Oeuvres complètes*, vol. C, p. 192.

68 *Littérature* in *Tel quel*, I, pp. 144–45.

69 See *Autour de Corot* in *Pièces sur l'art*, pp. 193–94 and *Degas. Danse. Dessin*, pp. 133–34.

70 *Centenaire de la photographie* in *Vues*, p. 367.

71 Ibid.

72 Frédéric Lefèvre, *Entretiens avec Paul Valéry*, p. 67.

73 *Au sujet d' "Adonis"* in *Variété*, p. 71.

74 Frédéric Lefèvre, *Entretiens avec Paul Valéry*, pp. 65–66.

75 Jean de Latour, *Examen de Valéry*, note on page 159.

76 *Au sujet d' "Adonis"* in *Variété*, p. 73.

77 *Situation de Baudelaire* in *Variété II*, p. 156.

78 *Autres rhumbs* in *Tel quel*, II, p. 156.

79 *L'Invention esthétique* in *L'Invention*, p. 149.

80 *Je disais quelquefois à Stéphane Mallarmé . . .* in *Variété III*, p. 14.

81 *Suite* in *Tel quel*, II, p. 332.

82 *Questions de poésie* in *Variété III*, p. 54.

83 *Léonard et les philosophes* in *Variété III*, pp. 160–61.

84 "Durtal," *Mercure de France*, March 1898, pp. 770–71.

85 *Souvenirs littéraires* in *Oeuvres complètes*, vol. K, p. 15.

86 Ibid., p. 14.

87 *Poésie et pensée abstraite* in *Variété V*, pp. 150–51.

88 Ibid., pp. 151–52.

89 Ibid., p. 149. See also *Propos sur la poésie, Conferencia*, 1928, pp. 470–71, in which he quotes the letter from Racan to Chapelain.

90 *Poésie et pensée abstraite* in *Variété V*, pp. 149–50.

91 *Calepin d'un poète* in *Oeuvres complètes*, vol. C, pp. 185–86.

92 *Poésie pure* in *Oeuvres complètes*, vol. C, p. 200.

93 Ibid., pp. 200–1.

94 *Réponse* in *Commerce*, Summer MCMXXXII, p. 13.

CHAPTER V

1 *Propos sur la poésie* in *Conferencia*, 1928, pp. 473–74.

2 *Calepin d'un poète* in *Oeuvres complètes*, vol. C, p. 192.

3 *Poésie et pensée abstraite* in *Variété V*, p. 159.

4 *Lettre (du temps de Charmes)* in *Oeuvres complètes*, vol. B, p. 108.

5 *Introduction à la méthode de Léonard de Vinci*, I, Note et digression in *Variété*, pp. 169–70.

6 *Rhumbs* in *Tel quel*, II, p. 63.

[7] *Introduction à la méthode de Léonard de Vinci*, I, *Note et digression* in *Variété*, pp. 170–71.

[8] *Lettre sur Mallarmé* in *Variété III*, pp. 226–27.

[9] *Rhumbs* in *Tel quel*, II, p. 63.

[10] *Au sujet d' "Adonis"* in *Variété*, pp. 56–57.

[11] *Eupalinos*, p. 103.

[12] See *Autres rhumbs* in *Tel quel*, II, pp. 113–14.

[13] *Passage de Verlaine* in *Variété III*, p. 183.

[14] *Poésie et pensée abstraite* in *Variété V*, p. 138.

[15] *Introduction à la méthode de Léonard de Vinci*, I, *Note et digression* in *Variété*, pp. 170–71.

[16] *Propos sur la poésie* in *Conferencia*, 1928, p. 474.

[17] *Au sujet d' "Adonis"* in *Variété*, p. 67.

[18] *L'Idée fixe*, p. 173.

[19] Letter to Pierre Louÿs, June 27, 1916, in *Lettres à Quelques-uns*, p. 116.

[20] *Propos sur la poésie* in *Conferencia*, 1928, p. 466.

[21] *Lettre à quelqu'un* in *Vues*, p. 251.

[22] *Propos sur la poésie* in *Conferencia*, 1928, p. 474.

[23] *De l'éminente dignite des arts du feu* in *Pièces sur l'art*, pp. 10–11.

[24] *La création artistique* in *Bulletin de la Société française de Philosophie*, 1928, pp. 14–17.

[25] *Mallarmé* in *Vues*, p. 184.

[26] *Introduction à la méthode de Léonard de Vinci*, I, *Note et digression* in *Variété*, p. 173.

[27] *Ibid.*, p. 174.

[28] *Mémoires d'un poème*, p. xi.

[29] *L'Idée fixe*, p. 205.

[30] *Leçon inaugurale du Cours de poétique* in *Variété V*, p. 315.

[31] *Ibid.*

[32] *Carnet d'un poète* in *Oeuvres complètes*, vol. C, p. 183.

[33] *Autres rhumbs* in *Tel quel*, II, pp. 127–28.

[34] *Cahier B* in *Tel quel*, I, pp. 221–22.

[35] *Calepin d'un poète* in *Oeuvres complètes*, vol. C, p. 183.

[36] *Ibid.*

[37] *Au sujet d' "Adonis"* in *Variété*, p. 68.

[38] *Analecta*, LXXIX.

[39] *Autres rhumbs* in *Tel quel*, II, p. 187.

[40] *Mallarmé* in *Vues*, p. 183.

[41] *Mauvaises pensées et autres*, p. 173.

[42] *Ibid.*, p. 170.

[43] *Cahier B* in *Tel quel*, I, p. 217.

[44] *Mauvaises pensées et autres*, p. 152.

[45] *Autres rhumbs* in *Tel quel*, II, p. 163.

[46] In *Variété*, p. 172.

[47] *Rhumbs* in *Tel quel*, II, p. 59.

[48] *Degas. Danse. Dessin*, p. 87.

[49] *L'oeuvre écrite de Léonard de Vinci* in *Vues*, p. 227.

50 *Cahier B* in *Tel quel*, I, p. 194.

51 *Littérature* in *Tel quel*, I, p. 153.

52 *Analecta*, XIII.

53 *Cahier B* in *Tel quel*, I, pp. 192–93.

54 *L'Idée fixe*, pp. 75–76.

55 *Mauvaises pensées et autres*, p. 222.

56 *Rhumbs* in *Tel quel*, II, p. 61.

57 *Mémoires d'un poème*, p. xxxiii.

58 Ibid.

59 *Choses tues* in *Tel quel*, I, p. 29.

60 *Remerciement à l'Académie Française* in *Variété IV*, p. 34.

61 *Poésie et pensée abstraite* in *Variété V*, p. 156.

62 *Les deux vertues d'un livre* in *Pièces sur l'art*, pp. 23–24.

63 *Poésie et pensée abstraite* in *Variété V*, p. 155.

64 *La Soirée avec Monsieur Teste* in *Monsieur Teste*, p. 28.

65 *Cahier B* in *Tel quel*, I, p. 189.

66 *Lust* in "Mon Faust," p. 74.

67 *Rhumbs* in *Tel quel*, II, p. 36.

68 *Littérature* in *Tel quel*, I, p. 175.

69 *Instants* in *Mélange*, p. 163.

70 *Rhumbs* in *Tel quel*, II, p. 36.

71 *Lust* in "Mon Faust," pp. 21–22.

72 Ibid., p. 74.

73 *Mauvaises pensées et autres*, pp. 153–54.

74 *Rhumbs* in *Tel quel*, II, p. 36.

75 Ibid.

76 Ibid., pp. 36–37.

77 *La Soirée avec Monsieur Teste* in *Monsieur Teste*, p. 20.

78 *Littérature* in *Tel quel*, I, p. 175.

79 *Mallarmé* in *Vues*, p. 183.

80 *Littérature* in *Tel quel*, I, p. 150.

81 *Cahier B* in *Tel quel*, I, p. 218.

82 Ibid.

83 *Eupalinos*, p. 110.

84 *Variété*, p. 66.

85 *Cahier B* in *Tel quel*, I, p. 218.

86 *Quelques fragments des Marginalia* in *Commerce*, XIV, Winter MCMXXVII, p. 16.

87 *Instants* in *Mélange*, p. 162.

88 *Cahier B* in *Tel quel*, I, p. 218.

89 Frédéric Lefèvre, *Entretiens avec Paul Valéry*, p. 107.

90 Ibid., pp. 107–8.

91 Ibid., p. 107.

92 *Comment travaillent les écrivains* in *Vues*, p. 316.

93 *Instants* in *Mélange*, p. 161.

94 *Rhumbs* in *Tel quel*, II, pp. 61–62.

95 *La création artistique* in *Bulletin de la Société française de Philosophie*, 1928, p. 8.

96 *Au sujet d' "Adonis"* in *Variété*, p. 69.

[97] *Mauvaises pensées et autres*, p. 36.
[98] *Propos me concernant*, p. 59.
[99] *Rhumbs* in *Tel quel*, II, pp. 99–100.
[100] *Petit discours aux peintres graveurs* in *Pièces sur l'art*, p. 141.

CHAPTER VI

[1] *Mémoires d'un poème*, p. xi.
[2] *Instants* in *Mélange*, p. 174.
[3] *Mémoires d'un poème*, p. xii.
[4] Ibid., p. xiii.
[5] *L'Idée fixe*, pp. 170–74.
[6] *Littérature* in *Tel quel*, I, p. 51.
[7] *Calepin d'un poète* in *Oeuvres complètes*, vol. C, pp. 181–82.
[8] *Situation de Baudelaire* in *Variété II*, p. 156.
[9] Ibid.
[10] *Réflexions sur l'art* in *Bulletin de la Société française de Philosophie*, 1935, p. 64.
[11] *Rhumbs* in *Tel quel*, II, p. 77.
[12] *Littérature* in *Tel quel*, I, pp. 171–72.
[13] *Hommage* in *Variété*, pp. 157–58.
[14] *Mémoires d'un poème*, p. xii.
[15] *La création artistique* in *Bulletin de la Société française de Philosophie*, 1928, p. 6.
[16] *Réflexions* in *La Revue des Vivants*, March 1929, p. 374.
[17] *Mémoires d'un poème*, pp. vii–viii. Cf. *Histoires brisées*, p. 10.
[18] *Moralités* in *Tel quel*, I, p. 121.
[19] *Mémoires d'un poème*, p. xiii.
[20] Ibid., pp. xii–xiii.
[21] *Mauvaises pensées et autres*, p. 195.
[22] *Les deux vertus d'un livre* in *Pièces sur l'art*, pp. 23–24.
[23] *Cahier B* in *Tel quel*, I, pp. 215–16.
[24] *Science de l'art* in *Variété IV*, pp. 254–55.
[25] *Discours prononcé au Deuxième Congrès d'Esthétique*, op. cit., p. 258.
[26] Ibid.
[27] Ibid., p. 256.
[28] Ibid., p. 257.
[29] Ibid.
[30] *Réflexions* in *La Revue des Vivants*, March 1929, pp. 379–80.
[31] *Mémoires d'un poème*, p. li.
[32] *Calepin d'un poète* in *Oeuvres complètes*, vol. C, p. 194.
[33] *Fluctuations sur la liberté* in *Oeuvres complètes*, vol. J, pp. 88–89.
[34] Letter of 1917 to André Fontainas in *Réponses*, p. 16.
[35] *Réponse* in *Commerce*, Summer MCMXXXII, p. 13.
[36] Ibid., p. 14.
[37] *Autour de Corot* in *Pièces sur l'art*, p. 193.

38 See *Degas. Danse. Dessin*, pp. 129–35.

39 *Autres rhumbs* in *Tel quel*, II, p. 152.

40 *Au sujet d' "Adonis"* in *Variété*, pp. 65–66.

41 *Avant-propos* in *Variété*, p. 108.

42 *Mémoires d'un poème*, p. xii.

43 *La création artistique* in *Bulletin de la Société française de Philosophie*, 1928, p. 6.

44 *Littérature* in *Tel quel*, I, p. 177.

45 *Au sujet d' "Adonis"* in *Variété*, pp. 60–65.

46 *Mélange*, pp. 39–40.

47 *Littérature* in *Tel quel*, I, p. 151.

48 *Calepin d'un poète* in *Oeuvres complètes*, vol. C, p. 190.

49 *Littérature* in *Tel quel*, I, p. 155.

50 *Au sujet du "Cimetière marin"* in *Variété III*, p. 67.

51 *Au sujet d' "Adonis"* in *Variété*, p. 65.

52 *Poésie et pensée abstraite* in *Variété V*, pp. 158–59.

53 *Au sujet du "Cimetière marin"* in *Variété III*, p. 70.

54 *Poésie et pensée abstraite* in *Variété V*, p. 159.

55 *Je disais quelquefois à Stéphane Mallarmé . . .* in *Variété III*, p. 15.

56 Ibid.

57 *Eupalinos*, pp. 179 ff.

58 Ibid., pp. 172 ff.

59 *Petit discours aux peintres graveurs* in *Pièces sur l'art*, p. 139.

60 *Eupalinos*, pp. 172–73.

61 *L'Homme et la coquille* in *Variété V*, p. 19.

62 Ibid., p. 18.

63 Ibid., p. 23.

64 Ibid.

65 *Discours aux chirurgiens* in *Variété V*, pp. 46–47.

66 *Introduction à la méthode de Léonard de Vinci* in *Variété*, p. 245.

67 *Note* (from a lecture given at the University of Zürich on November 15, 1922) in *Variété*, pp. 47–48.

68 *La création artistique* in *Bulletin de la Société française de Philosophie*, 1928, p. 17.

69 *Mémoires d'un poème*, p. xiii.

70 *La création artistique* in *Bulletin de la Société française de Philosophie*, 1928, p. 11.

71 *Degas. Danse. Dessin*, p. 114.

72 *La création artistique* in *Bulletin de la Société française de Philosophie*, 1928, p. 13.

73 *Poésie et pensée abstraite* in *Variété V*, p. 161.

74 Letter of 1917 to André Fontainas in *Réponses*, p. 17.

75 *Introduction à la méthode de Léonard de Vinci* in *Variété*, p. 250.

76 Ibid., p. 211.

77 Ibid.

78 Ibid., pp. 235–36.

[79] Ibid., p. 240.
[80] Ibid., pp. 241–42.
[81] Ibid., pp. 243–44.
[82] Ibid., pp. 244–45.
[83] Ibid., p. 245.
[84] Ibid., p. 247.
[85] Ibid.
[86] Ibid., pp. 249–50.
[87] Ibid., p. 169.
[88] Ibid., p. 200.
[89] Ibid., p. 165.
[90] *Eupalinos*, pp. 111–13.
[91] In *Lettres à Quelques-uns*, p. 48.
[92] *Eupalinos*, p. 151.
[93] *L'Idée fixe*, p. 182.
[94] *Poésie et pensée abstraite* in *Variété V*, p. 136.
[95] *Au sujet du "Cimetière marin"* in *Variété III*, p. 71.
[96] *Rhumbs* in *Tel quel*, II, p. 59.
[97] Ibid., pp. 81–82.
[98] *Au sujet du "Cimetière marin"* in *Variété III*, p. 71.
[99] *Je disais quelquefois à Stéphane Mallarmé . . .* in *Variété III*, p. 18.
[100] *Au sujet du "Cimetière marin"* in *Variété III*, p. 65.
[101] *Les Fresques de Paul Véronèse* in *Pièces sur l'art*, p. 125.
[102] *Réflexions sur l'art* in *Bulletin de la Société française de Philosophie*, 1935, p. 74.
[103] *Au sujet du "Cimetière marin"* in *Variété III*, p. 70.
[104] *Réflexions sur l'art* in *Bulletin de la Société française de Philosophie*, 1935, p. 74.
[105] *Au sujet du "Cimetière marin"* in *Variété III*, pp. 70–71.
[106] *Léonard et les philosophes* in *Variété III*, p. 158.
[107] *Autres rhumbs* in *Tel quel*, II, p. 154.
[108] *Rhumbs* in *Tel quel*, II, p. 81.
[109] Ibid., p. 80.
[110] *La création artistique* in *Bulletin de la Société française de Philosophie*, 1928, p. 13.
[111] *Léonard et les philosophes* in *Variété III*, p. 158.
[112] *Réflexions sur l'art* in *Bulletin de la Société française de Philosophie*, 1935, pp. 74–75.
[113] *La création artistique* in *Bulletin de la Société française de Philosophie*, 1928, p. 13.
[114] *Au sujet du "Cimetière marin"* in *Variété III*, p. 72.
[115] *Littérature* in *Tel quel*, I, p. 156.
[116] *Histoire d'Amphion* in *Variété III*, p. 90.
[117] *Littérature* in *Tel quel*, I, p. 156.
[118] In *Pièces sur l'art*, p. 140.
[119] *Au sujet du "Cimetière marin"* in *Variété III*, p. 70.
[120] *La création artistique* in *Bulletin de la Société française de Philosophie*, 1928, pp. 13–14.

[121] Ibid., p. 14.

[122] *Introduction à la méthode de Léonard de Vinci* in *Variété*, pp. 236–37.

[123] Ibid., p. 238.

[124] Ibid.

[125] Ibid.

[126] *Notion général de l'art* in *Nouvelle Revue Française*, November 1935, p. 689.

[127] *Mélange*, pp. 89–90.

[128] *Orientem versus* in *Oeuvres complètes*, vol. J, p. 181.

[129] Ibid.

[130] *Mémoires d'un poème*, p. xvi.

[131] Ibid., pp. xvii–xviii.

[132] *Aphorismes* (from the unpublished notebooks of Paul Valéry) in *Hommes et Mondes*, No. 3, October 1946, p. 188.

[133] *Mémoires d'un poème*, p. xviii.

[134] *Hommage* in *Variété*, p. 152.

[135] *Questions de poésie* in *Variété III*, p. 48.

[136] Ibid.

[137] *De l'enseignement de la poétique au Collège de France* in *Variété V*, p. 290.

[138] Letter of June 13, 1917 to Pierre Louÿs in *Oeuvres complètes*, vol. B, p. 139.

[139] Charles Du Bos, *Journal*, January 30, 1923.

[140] *Questions de poésie* in *Variété III*, pp. 48–49.

[141] *De l'enseignement de la Poétique au Collège de France* in *Variété V*, p. 290.

[142] *Je disais quelquefois à Stéphane Mallarmé . . .* in *Variété III*, p. 29.

[143] Ibid., p. 30.

[144] *Réponse au Remerciement du Maréchal Pétain à l'Académie française* in *Variété IV*, p. 86.

[145] *Discours en l'honneur de Goethe* in *Variété IV*, pp. 104–5.

[146] *Calepin d'un poète* in *Oeuvres complètes*, vol. C, pp. 186–87.

[147] Ibid., p. 187.

[148] Ibid., p. 192.

[149] *Autres rhumbs* in *Tel quel*, II, pp. 155–56.

[150] *Calepin d'un poète* in *Oeuvres complètes*, vol. C, p. 185.

[151] *Suite* in *Tel quel*, II, p. 334.

[152] *Choses tues* in *Tel quel*, I, p. 32.

[153] *Remerciement à l'Académie Française* in *Variété IV*, p. 42.

[154] *Littérature* in *Tel quel*, I, p. 152.

[155] Ibid., p. 150.

[156] *Mémoires d'un poème*, pp. li–lii.

[157] *Moralités* in *Tel quel*, I, pp. 110–11.

[158] *Rhumbs* in *Tel quel*, II, pp. 69–70.

[159] Ibid., p. 76.

[160] *Au sujet d' "Adonis"* in *Variété*, p. 83.

[161] *Analecta*, XCIX.

[162] Ibid., C.

[163] *Lettre sur Mallarmé* in *Variété II*, p. 224.

[164] *Au sujet d' "Adonis"* in *Variété*, p. 75.

[165] *Remerciement à l'Académie Française* in *Variété IV*, p. 42.

[166] Ibid.

[167] *Rhumbs* in *Tel quel*, II, p. 75.

[168] Ibid.

[169] Ibid.

[170] *Mélange*, p. 87.

[171] *Discours en l'honneur de Goethe* in *Variété IV*, p. 112.

[172] In *Variété III*, p. 200.

[173] *Réponse au Remerciement du Maréchal Pétain à l'Académie française* in *Variété III*, pp. 77–78.

[174] *Lettres à Albert Coste* in *Cahiers du Sud*, May 1932, p. 247.

[175] *Une vue de Descartes* in *Variété V*, pp. 218–19.

[176] *Images de la France* in *Regards sur le monde actuel et autres essais*, p. 133.

[177] *Eupalinos*, pp. 91–92.

[178] *Au sujet d' "Adonis"* in *Variété*, p. 67.

[179] *La poésie de La Fontaine* in *Vues*, p. 163.

[180] *Mémoires d'un poème*, pp. xviii–xix.

CHAPTER VII

[1] *Au sujet du "Cimetière marin"* in *Variété III*, p. 71.

[2] Ibid.

[3] *De l'enseignement de la poétique au Collège de France* in *Variété V*, p. 291.

[4] *Suite* in *Tel quel*, II, p. 356.

[5] *L'Invention esthétique, Discussion* in *L'Invention*, p. 156.

[6] *Leçon inaugurale du Cours de poétique* in *Variété V*, p. 322.

[7] Ibid.

[8] Ibid.

[9] Ibid.

[10] *Analecta*, CXX.

[11] *Leçon inaugurale du Cours de poétique* in *Variété V*, p. 313.

[12] *Analecta*, XXLV.

[13] *L'Idée fixe*, pp. 77–78.

[14] Ibid., p. 77.

[15] *Mauvaises pensées et autres*, p. 204.

[16] *Calepin d'un poète* in *Oeuvres complètes*, vol. C, pp. 181–82.

[17] *L'Invention esthétique, Discussion* in *L'Invention*, p. 156.

[18] Ibid., p. 150.

[19] *La création artistique* in *Bulletin de la Société française de Philosophie*, 1928, p. 13.

[20] *Poésie et pensée abstraite* in *Variété V*, pp. 160–61.

21 *La création artistique* in *Bulletin de la Société française de Philosophie*, 1928, p. 13.

22 *Calepin d'un poète* in *Oeuvres complètes*, vol. C, p. 182.

23 Ibid., p. 193.

24 *Discours aux chirurgiens* in *Variété V*, p. 55.

25 *Style* in *Vues*, pp. 311–12.

26 Ibid., p. 312.

27 *Eupalinos*, p. 117.

28 Frédéric Lefèvre, *Une heure avec Paul Valéry*.

29 *Eupalinos*, p. 120.

30 *Léonard et les philosophes* in *Variété III*, p. 158.

31 Ibid., p. 157.

32 Ibid., p. 159.

33 *Mémoires d'un poème*, p. xxii.

34 Ibid.

35 *Leçon inaugurale du Cours de poétique* in *Variété V*, p. 321.

36 *Autour de Corot* in *Pièces sur l'art*, pp. 175–76.

37 *Léonard et les philosophes* in *Variété III*, pp. 157–58.

38 *Autour de Corot* in *Pièces sur l'art*, p. 178.

39 Ibid.

40 *Poésie et pensée abstraite* in *Variété V*, p. 162.

41 Ibid., p. 160.

42 Ibid.

43 *Choses tues* in *Tel quel*, I, p. 54.

44 *Leçon inaugurale du Cours de poétique* in *Variété V*, p. 319.

45 *Littérature* in *Tel quel*, I, p. 150.

46 *Eupalinos*, p. 86.

47 Ibid., p. 90.

48 Ibid., p. 191.

49 *Littérature* in *Tel quel*, I, pp. 175–76.

50 *Propos me concernant*, p. 57.

51 In *Pièces sur l'art*, p. 137.

52 *Instants* in *Mélange*, p. 163.

53 *Degas. Danse. Dessin*, pp. 44–45.

54 *La Tentation de (saint) Flaubert* in *Variété V*, pp. 203–7.

55 *Je disais quelquefois à Stéphane Mallarmé . . .* in *Variété III*, p. 23.

56 Ibid., p. 24.

57 Ibid.

58 Ibid.

59 Ibid., p. 25.

60 *Autour de Corot* in *Pièces sur l'art*, pp. 174–75.

61 *L'Âme et la danse*, p. 128.

62 *Autour de Corot* in *Pièces sur l'art*, pp. 163–64.

63 *Lust* in "*Mon Faust*," pp. 95–96.

64 *Degas. Danse. Dessin*, pp. 80–81.

65 *Rhumbs* in *Tel quel*, I, p. 62.

66 *Littérature* in *Tel quel*, I, p. 154.

67 *Instants* in *Mélange*, pp. 162–63.

[68] *Degas. Danse. Dessin*, pp. 35–36.

[69] Letter of 1917 to André Fontainas in *Réponses*, p. 16.

[70] *Mélange*, pp. 41–42.

[71] Frédéric Lefèvre, *Entretiens avec Paul Valéry*, p. 109.

[72] *Analecta*, XXV.

[73] *Instants* in *Mélange*, p. 162.

[74] Charles Du Bos, *Journal*, January 30, 1923, p. 222.

[75] *Rhumbs* in *Tel quel*, II, p. 60.

[76] Frédéric Lefèvre, *Entretiens avec Paul Valéry*, p. 112.

[77] *Propos me concernant*, p. 20.

[78] Charles Du Bos, *Journal*, January 30, 1923, p. 222.

[79] *Quelques pensées* in *Monsieur Teste*, p. 132.

[80] *Littérature* in *Tel quel*, I, p. 157.

[81] *Autres rhumbs* in *Tel quel*, II, p. 191.

[82] *Sur Phèdre femme* in *Variété V*, p. 196.

[83] *Propos me concernant*, pp. 55–56. Cf. *Histoires brisées*, pp. 10–11.

[84] *Triomphe de Manet* in *Pièces sur l'art*, p. 205.

[85] Ibid.

[86] Ibid., p. 209.

CHAPTER VIII

[1] *"L'Infini esthétique"* in *Pièces sur l'art*, p. 247.

[2] *Réflexions sur l'art* in *Bulletin de la Société française de Philosophie*, 1935, p. 68.

[3] Ibid.

[4] Ibid., p. 71.

[5] *Poésie et pensée abstraite* in *Variété V*, p. 159.

[6] Ibid.

[7] *Introduction à la méthode de Léonard de Vinci* in *Variété*, p. 251.

[8] *Lettre sur Mallarmé* in *Variété II*, p. 232.

[9] *Discours prononcé au Deuxième Congrès international d'Esthétique et de Science de l'art* in *Variété IV*, p. 248.

[10] *Lettre sur Mallarmé* in *Variété II*, p. 232.

[11] *Poésie et pensée abstraite* in *Variété V*, pp. 156–57.

[12] *Introduction à la méthode de Léonard de Vinci* in *Variété*, p. 251.

[13] *Cahier B* in *Tel quel*, I, p. 210.

[14] *Mémoires d'un poème*, pp. iv–v.

[15] *Introduction à la méthode de Léonard de Vinci* in *Variété*, p. 251.

[16] Ibid.

[17] See Henri Mondor, *Le premier article de Paul Valéry* in *Dossiers*, 1, 1946.

[18] *Sur la technique littéraire* in *Dossiers*, 1, 1946, p. 27.

[19] Ibid.

20 Letter of June 6, 1890, quoted by Henri Mondor, *Le Vase brisé de Paul Valéry* in *Paul Valéry, Essais et témoignages inédits recueillis par Marc Eigeldinger*, pp. 14–16.

21 *La création artistique* in *Bulletin de la Société française de Philosophie*, 1928, p. 11.

22 *Réflexions sur l'art* in *Bulletin de la Société française de Philosophie*, 1935, p. 64.

23 Ibid.

24 *Au sujet d' "Adonis"* in *Variété*, p. 60.

25 *Commentaires de Charmes* in *Variété III*, p. 83.

26 *Réflexions sur l'art* in *Bulletin de la Société française de Philosophie*, 1935, pp. 63–64.

27 *Leçon inaugurale du Cours de poétique* in *Variété V*, p. 305.

28 *Réflexions sur l'art* in *Bulletin de la Société française de Philosophie*, 1935, p. 64.

29 *Leçon inaugurale du Cours de poétique* in *Variété V*, p. 305.

30 Ibid.

31 Ibid., p. 304.

32 Ibid., p. 305.

33 Ibid.

34 *Réflexions sur l'art* in *Bulletin de la Société française de Philosophie*, 1935, p. 64.

35 See the intervention of M. René Bayer, ibid., pp. 89–90.

36 *Réflexions sur l'art* in *Bulletin de la Société française de Philosophie*, 1935, p. 64.

37 Ibid., p. 65.

38 *Leçon inaugurale du Cours de poétique* in *Variété V*, p. 305.

39 Ibid., p. 307.

40 *Lettre sur Mallarmé* in *Variété II*, p. 232.

41 *Réflexions sur l'art* in *Bulletin de la Société française de Philosophie*, 1935, p. 64.

42 Ibid., p. 63.

43 Ibid., p. 64.

44 *Instants* in *Mélange*, p. 160.

45 *Leçon inaugurale du Cours de poétique* in *Variété V*, p. 205.

46 *Introduction à la méthode de Léonard de Vinci* in *Variété*, p. 251.

47 *Lettre sur Mallarmé* in *Variété II*, p. 232.

48 *Leçon inaugurale du Cours de poétique* in *Variété V*, pp. 305–6.

49 Ibid., p. 306.

50 Ibid., p. 307.

51 In *Tel quel*, I, p. 18.

52 *Réflexions sur l'art* in *Bulletin de la Société française de Philosophie*, 1935, p. 76.

53 In *Variété V*, p. 292.

54 *Littérature* in *Tel quel*, I, p. 164.

55 Ibid.

56 In *Variété II*, pp. 223–24.

[57] *Rhumbs* in *Tel quel*, II, p. 71.
[58] *Je disais quelquefois à Stéphane Mallarmé* . . . in *Variété III*, p. 10.
[59] *Rhumbs* in *Tel quel*, II, p. 72.
[60] *Stéphane Mallarmé* in *Variété II*, pp. 187–88.
[61] *Je disais quelquefois à Stéphane Mallarmé* . . . in *Variété III*, p. 11.
[62] *Rhumbs* in *Tel quel*, II, p. 60.
[63] *"Mon Faust,"* pp. 7, 23.
[64] *Commentaires de Charmes* in *Variété III*, p. 83.
[65] Ibid., pp. 83–84.
[66] Ibid., p. 84.
[67] *Au sujet d' "Adonis"* in *Variété II*, p. 87.
[68] Ibid., p. 88.
[69] *Oraison funèbre d'une fable* in *Variété II*, pp. 50–52.
[70] *Leçon inaugurale du Cours de poétique* in *Variété V*, pp. 310–11.

CHAPTER IX

[1] *Leçon inaugurale du Cours de poétique* in *Variété V*, p. 306.
[2] *Autres rhumbs* in *Tel quel*, II, p. 158.
[3] *Poésie et pensée abstraite* in *Variété V*, p. 159.
[4] *Leçon inaugurale du Cours de poétique* in *Variété V*, p. 306.
[5] *Autres rhumbs* in *Tel quel*, II, p. 150.
[6] Ibid., pp. 149–50.
[7] *Poésie et pensée abstraite* in *Variété V*, p. 159.
[8] *Leçon inaugurale du Cours de poétique* in *Variété V*, pp. 306–7.
[9] *Rhumbs* in *Tel quel*, II, p. 85.
[10] Ibid.
[11] *Dossiers*, 1, p. 28.
[12] Ibid., p. 29.
[13] *Leçon inaugurale du Cours de poétique* in *Variété V*, p. 306.
[14] *Triomphe de Manet* in *Pièces sur l'art*, pp. 206–7.
[15] *Propos me concernant*, p. 4.
[16] Ibid., p. 29.
[17] *Instants* in *Mélange*, pp. 192–93.
[18] *Autres rhumbs* in *Tel quel*, II, pp. 151–52.
[19] *Eupalinos*, pp. 161–62.
[20] *Cahier B* in *Tel quel*, I, pp. 219–20.
[21] *Je disais quelquefois à Stéphane Mallarmé* . . . in *Variété III*, p. 17.
[22] *Propos sur la poésie* in *Conferencia*, 1928, p. 472.
[23] *La création artistique* in *Bulletin de la Société française de Philosophie*, 1928, p. 6.
[24] *L'Invention esthétique* in *L'Invention*, p. 149.
[25] *Au sujet d' "Adonis"* in *Variété*, p. 87.

26 *Poésie et pensée abstraite* in *Variété V*, p. 155.

27 *Littérature* in *Tel quel*, II, p. 159.

28 *Je disais quelquefois à Stéphane Mallarmé* . . . in *Variété III*, pp. 25–26.

29 *Autour de Corot* in *Pièces sur l'art*, pp. 177–78.

30 *Triomphe de Manet* in *Pièces sur l'art*, p. 213.

31 *Eupalinos*, pp. 105–6.

32 Ibid., p. 105.

33 Ibid., p. 133.

34 Ibid., p. 123.

35 *Réflexions sur l'art* in *Bulletin de la Société française de Philosophie*, 1935, p. 73.

36 *Autour de Corot* in *Pièces sur l'art*, p. 179.

37 *Degas. Danse. Dessin*, p. 68.

38 Ibid., p. 87.

39 *Au sujet de Berthe Morisot* in *Vues*, p. 341.

40 *Autour de Corot* in *Pièces sur l'art*, pp. 168–71.

41 Ibid., p. 168.

42 *Mélange*, p. 19.

43 *Autour de Corot* in *Pièces sur l'art*, p. 173.

44 Ibid., pp. 170–72.

45 *Mémoires d'un poème*, p. xli.

46 *Triomphe de Manet* in *Pièces sur l'art*, p. 203.

47 *Discours prononcé à la Maison d'Éducation de la Légion d'Honneur de Saint-Denis* in *Variété IV*, pp. 149–50.

48 *Je disais quelquefois à Stéphane Mallarmé* . . . in *Variété III*, pp. 19–20.

49 Ibid., p. 17.

50 *Poésie et pensée abstraite* in *Variété V*, p. 154.

51 Ibid., pp. 154–55.

52 Letter of June 6, 1917 to Pierre Louÿs in *Oeuvres complètes*, vol. B, p. 137.

53 *Situation de Baudelaire* in *Variété II*, p. 151.

54 "*Cantiques spirituels*" in *Variété V*, p. 174.

55 *Je disais quelquefois à Stéphane Mallarmé* . . . in *Variété III*, p. 16.

56 *Mémoires d'un poème*, p. xli.

57 *Triomphe de Manet* in *Pièces sur l'art*, p. 203.

58 *Choses tues* in *Tel quel*, I, p. 30.

59 *Propos sur l'intelligence* in *Oeuvres complètes*, vol. D, p. 102.

60 *Degas. Danse. Dessin*, p. 87.

61 *Mémoires d'un poème*, p. xxiii.

62 *Remarques*, text by Paul Valéry, unpublished elsewhere, in Jean de Latour, *Examen de Valéry*, pp. 229–30.

63 Ibid., p. 229.

64 Ibid., p. 230.

65 See *Eupalinos*, particularly pp. 126, 131, 132, and *Histoire d'Amphion* in *Variété III*, especially p. 90.

66 *Analecta* in *Tel quel*, II, p. 210.

[67] Ibid., p. 212.
[68] Ibid., p. 209.
[69] Ibid.
[70] Letter of June 6, 1917 in *Oeuvres complètes*, vol. B, p. 138.
[71] Letter of June 13, 1917 in *Oeuvres complètes*, vol. B, pp. 139–40.
[72] *Analecta* in *Tel quel*, II, p. 209.
[73] Letter of June 13, 1917 in *Oeuvres complètes*, vol. B, p. 140.
[74] Ibid.
[75] *Rhumbs* in *Tel quel*, II, pp. 88–89.
[76] Letter of June 13, 1917 in *Oeuvres complètes*, vol. B, p. 139.
[77] *Analecta* in *Tel quel*, II, p. 209.
[78] Ibid., p. 212.
[79] *Propos sur la poésie* in *Conferencia*, 1928, p. 405. Cf. *Poésie pure* in *Oeuvres complètes*, vol. C, p. 206.
[80] *L'Invention esthétique* in *L'Invention*, p. 149.
[81] *Propos sur la poésie* in *Conferencia*, 1928, p. 468. Cf. *Poésie pure* in *Oeuvres complètes*, vol. C, p. 206.
[82] *L'Invention esthétique* in *L'Invention*, p. 149.
[83] *Situation de Baudelaire* in *Variété II*, p. 170; also *Poésie et pensée abstraite* in *Variété V*, p. 142.
[84] *Au Concert Lamoureux en 1893* in *Pièces sur l'art*, pp. 76–78.
[85] Ibid., p. 77.
[86] Ibid.
[87] *Avant-propos* in *Variété*, p. 95.
[88] *Poèmes chinois* in *Pièces sur l'art*, pp. 66–67.
[89] *Rhumbs* in *Tel quel*, II, p. 79.
[90] *Le Prince et la Jeune Parque* in *Variété V*, pp. 120–21.
[91] *Suite* in *Tel quel*, II, p. 332.
[92] *Eupalinos*, p. 80.
[93] *Histoire d'Amphion* in *Pièces sur l'art*, p. 91.
[94] *Mauvaises pensées et autres*, p. 38.
[95] *Littérature* in *Tel quel*, I, p. 157.
[96] See *La Poésie de La Fontaine* in *Vues*, p. 162; also *Victor Hugo créateur par la forme* in *Vues*, p. 173.
[97] *De la diction des vers* in *Pièces sur l'art*, pp. 37–38.
[98] *Littérature* in *Tel quel*, I, pp. 171–72.
[99] "*Cantiques spirituels*" in *Variété V*, p. 178.
[100] *Leçon inaugurale du Cours de poétique* in *Variété V*, p. 309.
[101] *L'Invention esthétique* in *L'Invention*, p. 150.
[102] *Leçon inaugurale du Cours de poétique* in *Variété V*, p. 310.
[103] *De la diction des vers* in *Pièces sur l'art*, p. 41.
[104] *Esquisse d'un éloge de la virtuosité* in *Vues*, p. 355.
[105] *De la diction des vers* in *Pièces sur l'art*, p. 40.
[106] Ibid., p. 41.
[107] *Esquisse d'un éloge de la virtuosité* in *Vues*, p. 353.
[108] Ibid., p. 357.
[109] Ibid., p. 356.

[110] *Leçon inaugurale du Cours de poétique* in *Variété V*, p. 310.

[111] *Esquisse d'un éloge de la virtuosité* in *Vues*, p. 355.

[112] Ibid., p. 357.

[113] *De la diction des vers* in *Pièces sur l'art*, pp. 41–42.

[114] *Lettre à Madame C.* in *Pièces sur l'art*, pp. 51–52.

[115] *De la diction des vers* in *Pièces sur l'art*, p. 42.

[116] *Lettre à Madame C.* in *Pièces sur l'art*, p. 52.

[117] *De la diction des vers* in *Pièces sur l'art*, pp. 46–48.

[118] "Cantiques spirituels" in *Variété V*, p. 172.

[119] *Instants* in *Mélange*, p. 161.

[120] See *Mauvaises pensées et autres*, p. 83.

[121] *Instants* in *Mélange*, p. 162.

[122] *Rhumbs* in *Tel quel*, II, p. 84.

[123] Remark quoted by René Berthelot, *Lettres échangées avec Paul Valéry*, in *Revue de Metaphysique et de Morale*, January 1946, p. 2.

[124] *Cahier B* in *Tel quel*, I, pp. 220–21.

[125] *Rhumbs* in *Tel quel*, II, p. 84.

[126] Ibid., p. 66.

[127] *Choses tues* in *Tel quel*, I, p. 51.

[128] Ibid.

[129] *Fonction et mystère de l'Académie* in *Regards sur le monde actuel et autres essais*, p. 292.

[130] *Mauvaises pensées et autres*, pp. 195–96.

[131] *Suite* in *Tel quel*, II, pp. 342–43.

[132] *Mélange*, p. 79.

[133] *Stendhal* in *Variété II*, pp. 111–18.

[134] Letter of June 6, 1917 in *Oeuvres complètes*, vol. B, pp. 135–36.

[135] *Mauvaises pensées et autres*, p. 32.

[136] *Rhumbs* in *Tel quel*, II, p. 66.

[137] *Autres rhumbs* in *Tel quel*, II, pp. 147–48.

[138] *Mémoires d'un poème*, p. xxvii.

[139] *Autres rhumbs* in *Tel quel*, II, p. 159.

[140] *Analecta*, CIV.

[141] *Mélange*, p. 30.

[142] *Autres rhumbs* in *Tel quel*, II, p. 162.

[143] "Cantiques spirituels" in *Variété V*, p. 175.

INDEX

ANCHOR BOOKS

ESSAYS, BELLES LETTRES & LITERARY CRITICISM

AUERBACH, ERICH Mimesis, A107

BARZUN, JACQUES Classic, Romantic and Modern, A255

BERGSON, HENRI Laughter (with Meredith's *Essay on Comedy*) in Comedy, A87

BLACKMUR, R. P. Form and Value in Modern Poetry, A96

BLOOM, HAROLD The Visionary Company, A372

BROOKS, VAN WYCK America's Coming-of-Age, A129

BURKHART, CHARLES, & TRASK, GEORGIANNE, eds. Storytellers and Their Art, A354

CARY, JOYCE Art and Reality, A260

CASTIGLIONE, BALDESAR The Book of the Courtier, trans. Singleton, A186

CHASE, RICHARD The American Novel and Its Tradition, A116

FERGUSSON, FRANCIS The Human Image in Dramatic Literature, A124

—— The Idea of a Theater, A4

FORSTER, E. M. Alexandria: A History and a Guide, A231

FULLER, MARGARET Margaret Fuller: American Romantic—A Selection from Her Writings and Correspondence, ed. Miller, A356

GRANVILLE-BARKER, H., & HARRISON, G. B., eds. A Companion to Shakespeare Studies, A191

HOFFMAN, DANIEL, ed. American Poetry and Poetics, A304

HOWARD, LEON Literature and the American Tradition, A329

KAUFMANN, WALTER From Shakespeare to Existentialism, A213

KAZIN, ALFRED On Native Grounds, A69

KITTO, H. D. F. Greek Tragedy, A38

KRONENBERGER, LOUIS, ed. Novelists on Novelists, A293

MC CORMICK, JOHN, & MAC INNES, MAIRI, eds. Versions of Censorship, A297

MEREDITH, GEORGE Essay on Comedy (with Bergson's *Laughter*) in Comedy, A87

NIETZSCHE, FRIEDRICH The Birth of Tragedy *and* The Genealogy of Morals, A81

ORTEGA Y GASSET, JOSE The Dehumanization of Art and Other Writings on Art and Culture, A72

ORWELL, GEORGE A Collection of Essays, A29

ROURKE, CONSTANCE American Humor, A12

SCOTT, A. C. Literature and the Arts in Twentieth Century China, A343

SHATTUCK, ROGER The Banquet Years, A238

SHAW, GEORGE BERNARD Shaw on Music, ed. Bentley, A53

SYPHER, WYLIE Four Stages of Renaissance Style, A45

TOKLAS, ALICE B. The Alice B. Toklas Cook Book, A196

TRAVERSI, D. A. An Approach to Shakespeare, A74

TRILLING, LIONEL The Liberal Imagination, A13

VAN DOREN, MARK Shakespeare, A11

WILLEY, BASIL The Seventeenth Century Background, A19